The Birth
of the Banjo

Joel Walker Sweeney and Early Minstrelsy

BOB CARLIN

McFarland & Company, Inc., Publishers

Jefferson, North Carolina, and London

LIBRARY OF CONGRESS CATALOGUING-IN-PUBLICATION DATA

Carlin, Bob.
The birth of the banjo : Joel Walker Sweeney and
early minstrelsy / Bob Carlin.
p.   cm.
Includes bibliographical references and index.

ISBN-13: 978-0-7864-2874-8
(softcover : 50# alkaline paper) ∞

1. Sweeny [sic], J. W. (Joel Walker), 1813–1860.   2. Banjoists —
United States — Biography.   3. Minstrel shows — History.
4. Banjo — History.   I. Title.
ML419.S93C37   2007   787.8'8092 — dc22   2006102897
[B]

British Library cataloguing data are available

On the cover: illustration from sheet music cover, "Where Did You
Come From, Nock A Nigger Down," showing Joe Sweeney in 1843
"at the Theatre Royal English Opera House" in
London (D'Almaine, London, 1843, British Library
Reproductions); Joe Sweeney's banjo (Los Angeles County Museum)

Manufactured in the United States of America

*McFarland & Company, Inc., Publishers
Box 611, Jefferson, North Carolina 28640
www.mcfarlandpub.com*

Acknowledgments

Writing a book of this type takes an immense amount of research over a large expanse of time in a great number of geographically isolated collections. This difficult task would be impossible without the work of previous professional and amateur scholars for a guide. Those living "Sweeney-ologists" have generously shared their time, opinions and resources.

For my chapter on the Sweeney family and Joe's childhood, I received a lot of help from genealogists. Nancy Jamerson Weiland, who works at the Lynchburg area's premier historical collection, the Jones Memorial Library, and an Appomattox County resident, is at the top of that list. Others who rate a thank-you are Ron Wilson at the Appomattox Court House National Historical Park and Patty and Mike Ramsey.

Lowell Schreyer has been chasing the ghost of Joe Sweeney in present times, writing about Sweeney in 1997.[1] On numerous occasions, Schreyer generously shared his insights, as well as his unpublished Sweeney chronology.

Dale Cockrell very generously provided research notes gathered in the writing of his book, *Demons of Disorder*. A goodly amount of my exploration into early American minstrelsy comes from Cockrell's work.

Stuart Thayer did the same with information on the pre–Civil War American circus. Fred Dahlinger, director of the Robert L. Parkinson Library and Research Center at the Circus World Museum, introduced me to Thayer and provided an entree into the world of circus archives and research. Joan Barbarec at the Hertzberg Circus Collection helped other circus research along.

My raw data on early Australian banjo history came from newspaper clippings furnished by Gary Le Gallant. Further information came from John Whiteoak.

Research is a lonely pursuit, and I was fortunate to have the company of colleagues on many of my journeys. These included Jim Bollman, Pete Ross, John Hartford and Joe Ayers. Additional researchers aiding me in the United States were Allin Cottrell, Dena Epstein, Robert Winans, Charles Perdue, Clarke Buehling, Rip Lhamon, Eli Kaufman, Kym Rice, Kinney Rorrer of Danville Community College, Philip Gura and Joe Wilson.

Sheet music research was conducted at the Lester Levy collection of Johns Hopkins University and the Hay Library at Brown University.

Other institutions utilized include the Maryland Historical Society; Southern Historical Collection and North Carolina Collection at Davis Library of the University of North Carolina; Wadsworth Athenaeum; Historic New Orleans Collection; Theatre Arts Collection at the Harry Ransom Humanities Research Center of the University of Texas at Austin; Appomattox County Library; Rare Book, Music and Microforms Departments of the Boston Public Library; Bostonian Society; the Library Company of Philadelphia; Smith Reynolds Library at Wake Forrest University; Museum of the City of New York; Ohio Historical Society; and Cincinnati Historical Society. Thanks also to Jane Duggan of the Print Department at the Boston Public Library; Raymond Wemmlinger of the Hampden-Booth Theatre Library; Petie Bogen-Garrett at the Library of Virginia; Teresa Roane of the Valentine Museum; Gail R. Redmann, library director at the Historical Society of Washington, D.C.; Sandra Markham, chief librarian of the Albany Institute of History & Art; Annette Fern at the Harvard Theatre Collection; and the staff of the Theater Collection at the Free Library of Philadelphia.

In researching this book, I read through literally thousands of period newspapers, originals and on microfilm. Depositories for these periodicals include the Library of Virginia, Boston Public Library, University of Virginia, Jones Library, Richmond Public Library, Lynchburg Public Library, Martin Luther King Public Library, New York Public Library, American Antiquarian Society, Louisville Public Library, Free Library of Philadelphia, New Orleans Public Library, Tennessee State Archives, Troy Public Library, McClung Historical Collection-Knox County Public Library, University of Tennessee-Knoxville, Alabama State Archives, New York State Library, Mobile Public Library, Mississippi State Archives, Charleston Public Library, Savannah Public Library, University of South Carolina, University of Georgia, Library of Congress, University of North Carolina at Chapel Hill, Pennsylvania State Library, University of Texas, University of Kentucky, Oneida County Historical Society, Missouri Historical Society, New York Historical Society and Saratoga Springs Public Library. The following provided research assistance at the collections listed: Dr. Tony Medlin, Louisiana State University; Marianne Neal, Cayuga County Historical Society; Jessica Closser, Mercantile Library Collection; Deborah J. Ferrell, county historian, Wayne County, New York; Jessica Myer, Newark Public Library; Harold Witter, Skaneateles Historical Society and Onondaga Library; Christine M. Palmatier, Schoharie County Historical Society, New York; and Ann Roche, Goshen Library and Historical Society. Paul Mitchell at the University of North Carolina and the Davidson County Public Library facilitated loans of newspapers on microfilm. Pete Ross, Ulf Jagfors and the Center for Popular Music provided copies of articles in *The Cadenza* and *B.M.G.*

The majority of the information about minstrelsy in Britain was gathered during a visit to England in February 2000. I utilized the collections of the British Library, the Victoria and Albert's Theatre Museum, the Mander-Mitchenson Theatre Collection and Westminister Archives Center, and visited or spoke with collectors such as Cyril Wickham, Pete Stanley and Stan Gee. Additional information was obtained from the Folger Shakespeare Library, the Adelphi Theater website and Center for Research Libraries loans via the University of North Carolina at Chapel Hill. Sandy Semenoff culled the playbill collection of the Mitchell Library in Glasgow and Linda Greenwood, the Irish and local studies librarian, did the same at the Belfast Public Library, and Helen Kelly provided research assistance at the Dublin Public Library and the National Library of Ireland. Special thanks goes to Professor Kathy Castle of North London University and her graduate assistant, Dianne Robinson, for sharing their unpublished research into English blackface minstrelsy and for conducting further inquiries on my behalf at the Colindale Newspaper Library, Finsbury Library, Liverpool Public Library and Birmingham Central Library. Thanks also to Judy Martin and Anne Beauchamp for food, lodging and medical attention.

My journey through the subculture of Civil War scholarship began while an artist in residence at New River Community College. A forum conducted by Professor James I. Robertson, Jr., as well as the collections of the Newman Library at Virginia Tech launched me into accounts of the war. For musical information on popular songs in chronicles of the conflict, I thank my old friend Caroline Moseley of the Princeton University libraries. Banjoist Jeff Chumley pointed to published references that I had missed, and George Wunderlich of the Museum of Confederate Medicine provided general information both banjo and medical. Other information on Stuart's command came from the Southern Historical Collection at the University of North Carolina at Chapel Hill, the Virginia Historical Society and Special Collections at Duke University in Durham, North Carolina.

Wherever possible, I have turned to firsthand, period sources for the elements of this story. I have mined archival sources either underutilized, or never utilized, in this type of work. This book is built upon the research of previous writers, without whom this search for Joe Sweeney would have proved a lot longer and more difficult.

This information would be unreadable if it weren't for masterful editing by Vaughn Webb, Robert Winans and my long-suffering brother, Richard Carlin. Richard in particular spent many hours of his own time reshaping and revising my original manuscript. To them I owe big thanks.

Many proper names and song titles mentioned are found in historical accounts with multiple or alternative spellings. Wherever possible, I have chosen one way to spell these titles (such as Sweeney for Sweeny, Swiney, Sweney, etc.), except where I am directly quoting one of those accounts. In the later case, I have used whatever original spellings existed within the quotation.

Some information contained within these pages first appeared in lectures given on Joe Sweeney at various conferences and at the opening of the Musical Instrument Museum's exhibit "Banjo," as well as in the exhibit catalogues for the Blue Ridge Institute's "The Banjo in Virginia" and the Katonah Museum of Art's "The Birth of the Banjo." An early version of the chapter on Sam Sweeney first appeared in *Bluegrass Unlimited*. Thanks to Roddy Moore and Peter Szego for support.

Ultimately, this work is mine for better or for worse. I take all responsibility for the information contained and for all the conclusions reached. After 15-plus years immersed in this material, I hope that I have gained some enlightenment, which I share here for your enjoyment.

Table of Contents

Preface

Sweeney's relationship to minstrel playing is analogous to Earl Scruggs' relationship to bluegrass banjo. His influence was so great that the fact that he learned from blacks is nearly enough in itself to tie the whole tradition of minstrel banjo to contemporary folk black playing.[1]

The real history of minstrelsy in this country, were it to be honestly and comprehensively written, would touch in one way or another every form of popular music we have and on some part of our composed tradition.[2]

American music is not just black or white, it is a mixture of black and white influences, Anglo and African American. The interchange between the races that has resulted in most if not all of the great American popular musical movements may have started for all we know with the arrival of the first Africans. By the time America declared its independence from England and formed a new republic, the seeds were planted for the first popular mixture of white and black music. Called "minstrelsy" (or alternately, "blackface minstrelsy," "Negro minstrelsy," etc.), this musical phenomenon featured the portrayals of southern slaves by white performers. It pushed aside drama and entertainments brought from Great Britain to become the first national musical theatre during the first third of the nineteenth century. The roots of this theatrical movement—English and American plays with African and African American characters—will be discussed in Chapter One.

The banjo was a part of American minstrelsy from its very beginnings. Although the instrument itself was not a major force during the first ten years minstrel performers and songs entered the consciousness of the public, the banjo was used as an emblem for minstrelsy by songwriters and sheet music illustrators from its earliest days. This usage should come as no surprise, as the banjo, an instrument with African roots in its construction and playing style, was quickly altered to fit European melodies and uses.

When the banjo did finally move out of the rural south to join circus and theatrical blackface presentations, it spread like wildfire throughout America. The man primarily responsible for bringing the banjo to the attention of the public was a white Virginian, Joel Walker Sweeney.

Joe Sweeney was the Elvis Presley of his time, a white man who could sing like a black man, to borrow and paraphrase the words of Elvis Presley's mentor Sam Phillips. Sweeney served a parallel role in the 1840s to Jimmie Rodgers in the 1920s, Bill Monroe in the 1940s, and to Hank Williams or Elvis in the 1950s. In their heydays, these men of Anglo-American heritage "crossed the tracks" to sample African American music, adding to it white sounds of previous and current generations, and therefore creating something new and unusual out of their personal musical consciousness. At a time when African American music and musicians were unacceptable or inaccessible to main street America, these players provided a suitable version of black music for most listeners.

Considering how important was Joe Sweeney's role in the introduction of the African American banjo into mainstream Anglo-American society, modern day minstrel scholars have surprisingly all but left him out of their writings. Sweeney is dealt with in a perfunctory way in the five most recent book-length studies dealing with minstrelsy[3] (at the time of this writing), as well as in several "classic" works,[4] their authors all but ignoring his important contributions to American culture. This work rectifies their omissions, elevating Joe Sweeney to his rightful place in the minstrel and cultural pantheon. Besides providing the fullest biography of Sweeney's life to date and a list of his known appearances, this book thoroughly examines Joe Sweeney's role in the development of the physical banjo and his introduction of the instrument to America and Great Britain. I attempt, as best is possible, to lay to rest a century of fantasies and oft-repeated fallacies about Sweeney and the banjo, as well as promote a new understanding of his important role in the history of the instrument.

Up until this time, whatever celebrity Sweeney had came from his supposed development of the five-string banjo. According to those that knew him, Joe Sweeney added "the 5th string or thumb string to the banjo."[5] However, as I show in Chapter Eight, this assertion has been proven incorrect. Strangely enough, Joe Sweeney's role as a popularizer of the banjo is the more important one, and easier to prove.

Joe Sweeney was an Irish-American born midway between the cities of Richmond and Lynchburg in Virginia's south side. Learning the banjo from area slaves, Sweeney was among the first generation of native-born Anglo-Americans to play the instrument at southern community functions: dances, picnics, horse races, and the like. Joe Sweeney then took his act on the road, becoming a professional musician when "banjoist" was first becoming a career. Sweeney took the only route available to a banjo player wanting to earn a living from his music: He donned the burnt cork make-up of the nascent minstrel profession. Initially, Joe Sweeney played a song or two on the variety shows featured in the traveling American circus or in-between dramas of the theater. Eventually, he was a member of the early groups exploiting blackface songs, dances, and plays presented during an entire evening's concert. In the process, Joe Sweeney brought African Americans' songs and tunes, as well as their instrument, into American popular music.

ONE

African American Roots

Several old and reliable farmers in Appomattox related to me ... how Joe would hang around with the negroes, learning their rude songs and playing an accompaniment on this rude instrument, and how he used to construct others.... He finally made one, and getting hold of some strings ... very soon learned to play most any tune on it.[1]

West African slaves brought banjo prototypes to the New World, in the process introducing early versions of the instrument into Anglo American culture (see Chapter Twelve for a discussion of the banjo's physical development). In this chapter, I'll explore African American music in Joe Sweeney's birthplace of Southside Virginia and discover how the young Sweeney learned to play the banjo.

Early African American Banjoists

By the beginning of the 1800s, the banjo was already established in the United States, albeit as the provenance of African Americans. Joe Sweeney was raised around many of these black musicians, who are well documented in eighteenth and nineteenth century accounts of Virginia. A runaway slave advertisement from 1775 mentions the fugitive "plays exceedingly well on the Banger, and generally carries one with him."[2] Thomas Jefferson's famous essay on the state of Virginia features his often-quoted comment, "The instrument proper to them is the Banjar, which they brought hither from Africa."[3] And, at the end of the 1700s, Thomas Fairfax heard banjo playing by blacks in Richmond:

> After going to bed I was entertained with an agreeable serenade, by a black man who had his stand near the Tavern, and for the amusement of those of his colour, sung and played on the Banjoe [sic]. He appeared to be quite an adept on this African instrument, which tho it may not bear a comparison with the Guitar, is certainly Capable of Conveying much pleasure to a musical ear.... Its wild notes of melody seem to correspond with the state of Civilization where this species of music originated.[4]

Other period accounts imply the popularity of the instrument among African American canal workers. P.C. Sutphin wrote a letter to the Glasgow, Kentucky, *Times* relating that in the earlier part of the nineteenth century "the banjo had been quite common with the negro boatman of James river, whom I have often heard playing it while their batteaux were lying at the landing on the river at Lynchburg."[5] New Yorker James Kirke Paulding (August 22, 1779–April 6, 1860[6]), a famous author of his time and a friend of Washington Irving's, toured Virginia in 1816 and published the results in his *Letters from the South*. Paulding wrote, "In the evening I have seen [the Negroes] reclining in their boats on the canal at Richmond, playing on the banjo."[7] And Carey, an African American slave in John P. Kennedy's fictional account depicting life along the James during the first quarter of the nineteenth century,[8] played the "banjoe" as "he sings the inspirations of his own muse, weaving into song the past or present annals of the family. He is considered as a seer amongst the negroes on the estate."[9] So, not only did Carey play an African derived instrument, but he also composed historical songs about his patrons, much in the manner of a West African griot.

The banjo also seems to have been associated with a popular amusement, horse racing. This association between banjos and racing is a logical one, as the races, held twice a year in the spring and fall, were prime places of congregation for Virginians (and other southern residents as well). In the days before such a thing as a "professional country performer," banjo players both white and black had to take advantage of every opportunity to entertain in order to earn a living, no matter how difficult the circumstances. Titus, another griot-like African American banjoist, appeared before 1818 at the Richmond racetrack and mixed both African and Anglo influences in his songs:

> With an old slouched hat—a coat considerably the worse for wear—shoes which had not often known the value of a good polishing—banjo under arm and stick in hand—he marched over the hill to Fairfield, ... to him the great day—of the races.... He usually waited until the race was over before he commenced, and then he sang the incidents of the struggle for victory. Every circumstance was brought in—every gentleman who owned a horse was named in appropriate [?] and made a hero of just as Pindar [poet and chronicler of the ancient Greek Olympics][10] immortalized those who triumphed at the Olympic games. Only a few fragments of his inspirations survive for the admiration of mankind.—One of them is an entire piece, giving a true and graphic account of the capture of the "nigger gineral," as he calls him, Gabriel. A second contains an elaborate narrative of the acts and deeds of a certain individual who would otherwise have been lost to history, whom he designates as "Archie Mullen," whose story he commences by telling us that "he shot the devil," ...—and a third, which he evidently stole, it being nothing more nor less than the old English ballad, which describes the race between the "Bonny Grey Mare," and the "Noble Skewball."[11]

Another function for the African Virginian banjo was to accompany slave dancing.[12] Frances M. Butler draws a distinction between white and black dances, writing that while African Americans played for both audiences, the banjo was only used for slaves:

> The slave orchestras that played for white owners were usually composed of fiddlers and frequently a tambourine player. Slave dances were accompanied by the banjo, fiddle, quills, tambourine, bones, or, infrequently, a drum or pots and pans beaten like drums.[13]

Even as the instrument spread into Anglo American hands throughout the South, African Americans in Virginia continued to use the banjo for dances and entertainment. Slave narratives from Appomattox County (Mrs. Fannie Berry, born circa 1833–1842[14]), Southampton County (Mrs. Marriah Hines, born 1835[15]), Suffolk (Matilda Henrietta Perry, born 1852[16]), Charlotte County (Levi Pollard, born circa 1850[17]) and the Lynchburg area (Robert Williams, born 1843[18]) all connect the banjo and black dances in the decades before the Civil War.

African American banjoists were a common part of Joe Sweeney's milieu. It wasn't very long before their playing captured his attention, and he adopted the instrument as his own.

Learning to Play

Proving when the banjo was first conveyed into Anglo American hands is difficult. A case has been made for the transmission of the instrument from African Americans to indentured servants in the tidewater region of Virginia immediately following the Revolutionary War.[19] And another scholar has been investigating other early southern accounts of the banjo, especially in the mountains of Kentucky.[20] Oral history and other evidence suggests that there might have been some scattered cases of whites being interested in the banjo in the late eighteenth century. However, according to surviving documentation, the instrument did not receive widespread dispersal until many years later.

It is certain that Joe Sweeney learned to play some form of the banjo from local African Americans. Some historians believe that the slaves on Sweeney's family's "plantation" taught him to play. This scenario seems unlikely, because John Sweeney was a subsistence farmer, and tending his land did not require a sizeable number of workers. Joe's father owned two slaves,[21] and these were as likely to have been female household help as grown male laborers. Sweeney researcher George Collins gives a more believable explanation: "At 'Old Home,' the nearby plantation of the Flood family owned by [Major] Henry Flood [1755–1827; actually, the plantation's brick mansion was the home of Henry's son, Dr. Joel Walker Flood, Sr. (1789–1858), who owned 20 slaves in 1820, which grew to 121 African Americans over the next 30 years, on an estate valued at $50,450.00].... himself a violinist of ability, Joel came to know the Colonel's coachman ... from whom Joel learned much of the [banjo] and the music of the African."[22] Area resident Judge Robert Pore mentions the age of 12 as the start of Sweeney's banjo playing.[23] Others allude to him playing the banjo as a teenager (see Chapter Twelve for more information).

But, the question remains, was Sweeney the "first" white banjo player? In a memoir published in 1895, P.C. Sutphin supports the claim that Sweeney was the primary white musician to take up the instrument:

> When I was a mere boy ... going to school in Lynchburg, Virginia, I knew Mr. Sweeney well.... Sweeney had a fine natural musical gift, and played handsomely on any musical instrument that he took a fancy to. He was an expert violinist, and the last time I saw him, was chief violinist at a special dance party of some of the "elite" of Lynchburg.... It was about this time that he took a fancy to the banjo, which, before that, had only been in the hands of the negro.... To [Sweeney], so far as this instrument is concerned, belongs the credit only ... of being the first white person to play on it and introduce it into the society of the whites.[24]

This statement is hard to take seriously. First, its primary purpose is to prove that Joe Sweeney was not the inventor of the banjo, and that it had existed as an African American instrument before his involvement. Secondly, there are scattered mentions of other rural whites that *could* have been performing on the banjo around the same time as Sweeney.[25] At best, we can state that Joe Sweeney was among the first crop of Anglo American banjoists learning the instrument between 1800 and the mid– to late 1830s.

Even though we can't prove that Joel Walker Sweeney was the first white American to take up the banjo (a valueless argument at best), it can be stated that Joe Sweeney was a key player when the African American instrument developed into the form we know of today. Even if there was absolute proof for the existence of white banjoists before Sweeney, widespread dissemination into mainstream American culture is another matter. The bottom line is that when Sweeney was performing locally in Virginia during the mid–1830s, the banjo was still a novelty among white Americans.

Two

The Origins of Blackface Minstrelsy

The first actual signs of the budding life of this new theatrical form were found around 1800 in the comic songs sung in blackface at the circus and in the theatre. When rendered on the regular theatre program, they were inserted either between the acts of a play or between the separate sections of the whole bill.[1]

During the 1820s and 1830s, a form of popular entertainment developed in America called the minstrel show. White performers blackened their faces to present songs, dances, jokes, and skits supposedly based on rural slave life. This form of "blackface" grew out of centuries of theatrical and circus masking traditions from both sides of the Atlantic. Famous American thespians such as Edwin Forrest and Junius Booth as well as the English actor Samuel Cowell[2] played African Americans in character as a matter of course.[3] When Joe Sweeney made the move into professional music, blackface performing was the avenue he took. Because of Sweeney's involvement with minstrelsy, it's important to profile the early history of blackface in America and Great Britain.

1
What are the joys of white men here, what are his pleasures gay?
I want no joys, no ills I fear but on my bon-ja play
Chorus: I sing all day, I sleep all night
I have no care, my heart is light
I think not what to-mor-row bring
I'm happy so I sing

2
But white man's joys are not like mine
Though he look smart and gay
He great, he proud, he haughty, fine
While I my bon-ja play
3
I envy not the white man then
I'm poor, but I am gay
I'm glad at heart, I'm happy when
I on my bonja play.[4]

The Roots of American Minstrelsy

The roots of blackface entertainment lie in English theatrical tradition, reaching as far back as William Shakespeare's *Othello*. Shakespeare's "African" was followed onto the stage by plays such as Thomas Southerne's *Oronooko*, based on a novel about an African prince and first performed in 1685,[5] and *The Padlock*, premiered by Bickerstaff at the Drury Lane Theatre in 1768. Charles Dibdin (b. 1745)[6] wrote the music for the latter, and portrayed the extremely stereotypical Negro character of Mungo in the play. Dibdin is also responsible for other songs depicting African personages, including "The Negro and His Banjer" (the lyrics for which are printed at the beginning of this section), written for the drama *The Wags* and published around 1800.[7] These plays with African characters performed by white actors in blackface makeup transferred effortlessly to the nascent American theater. Beginning the

6

year after the play's London premiere, Lewis Hallam recreated Dibdin's Mungo for audiences in New York City. Some thirty-five years later, Hallam was still portraying the hapless African[8]; additional actors kept the play in the theaters through 1828.[9] *Oronooko* also traveled across the waters, showing to Baltimore theatergoers by December of 1783.[10] Around 1800, Boston audiences heard Mrs. Johann Christian Gottlieb Graupner, the wife of the Federal Street Theatre's orchestra leader,[11] render "The Song of the Negro Boy" at the conclusion of *Oronooko*'s second act.[12] Various other African characters graced American stages in the late eighteenth and early nineteenth centuries.[13]

1

Backside Albany dar Lake Shamplain
One little Pon half full a wa-ter
Plattburg dar too close upon de main
Town small he grow bigger doe here ar-ter
On Lake Shamplin Uncle Sam set he boat
An Mas-sa Macdonough he sail 'em
While Gen'ral Maccomb
Make Plattburg he home
Wid he army whose courage nebber fail 'em

2

Elebenth day September 1814
Gubner Probose wid he british army
Dress 'imself up make all tings clean
Cum to Plattburg tea party cortin
An he boat cum too
Arter Uncle Sam boat
Massa Donough look sharp out de winder
Ah, he always home
Catch fire too jiss like tiner

3

Bow wow wow den de cannon gin't roar
In Plattburg an all 'bout dat quarter
Gub'ner Probose try he han pon de shore
Wile he boat try he luck pon de water
Rul Massa Macdonough
Kick he boat in de head
Broke he heart, broke he shin, love he cuf in
An Gen'ral Macrumb
Start ole Probose home
Tor me soul den I muss laffin

4

Probose heart so heddef all behine
Powder, ball, cannon, tea pot an kittle
Sum say he cotch he cold, ad perish in he mind
Bloyg'd cat so much raw an cold vittle
Uncle Sam berry sorry
Two be sume for he pain
Wish he nuns imsef up well an arty
For Gen'ral Maccomb
An Massa Donough home
Wen he notion for nudder tea party

The first truly American blackface figure appeared in 1815, when, at Albany's Green Street Theater, Andrew Jackson (known as "Dummy") Allen (1788–October 30, 1853)[14] sang "Backside Albany" (see the lyrics above).[15] Called "the first black-dialect song known to have been published in the United States" by music business historian Russell Sanjek, "Backside Albany" borrowed its tune from the Irish air "Boyne Water."[16] The song told the story of a Great Lakes battle between the Americans and the British during the War of 1812. Sung by the character of a black sailor, "Backside Albany" was written by Michael "Micah" Hawkins, a thirty-eight-year-old grocer and hotelkeeper. Micah had learned to fiddle from his slave, Toney Clapp, and taught himself the rudiments of musical composition. Based in lower New York City,[17] Hawkins had seen slaves dancing and singing in the public market located near his place of business (Hawkins was the uncle of genre painter William Sidney Mount, who featured African American musicians, including a banjoist, in some of his most famous paintings).[18] With this song, America had at last found its voice, and other songs featuring American archetypes soon followed. Within these compositions, myths of the frontier, plantation, river, and railroad gained shape and form. At the same time that Allen was performing "Back Side of Albany," Hopkins Robinson was singing the song in Hawkins's home of New York City.[19]

Lubly Rose, Sambo cum
Don't you hear de Banjo tum, tum, tum!
Lubly Rose, Sambo cum

Sheet music cover for "Backside Albany" written by Micah Hawkins, deposited for copyright January 3, 1837 (Library of Congress).

> *Don't you hear de Banjo tum, tum, tum!*
> *Oh Rose! coal black Rose.*
> *I wish I may be cortched if I don't love Rose.*[20]

For the next fifteen years, blackface characters continued to grace American stages, and songs sung in burnt cork (white skinned performers would darken their faces using a paste made from mixing water with cork blackened by burning) trickled out of America's publishing houses. A Virginian, George Washington Dixon (circa 1801–March 2, 1862), introduced the (arguably) first American minstrel song, "Coal Black Rose," to the country. A native of Richmond,[21] Dixon began performing in the circus during the early 1820s.[22] Although he was singing "negro melodies" during 1827,[23] he is not documented as singing "Rose" until the summer of 1829, which is when the song was first published and enjoyed its initial popularity.[24] Several months later, following his early success singing "Coal Black Rose" in the theaters of New York City, George Dixon turned the song into the play titled *Love in a Cloud*.[25] "Coal Black Rose" quickly spread throughout America. A "Mr. McCafferty" presented the composition, along with other parts of Dixon's act, in Louisville during early 1830.[26] For the period of 1828 to 1831, the prominent Texas jurist, publisher, and statesman Robert McAlpin Williamson (circa 1806–December 22, 1859)[27] used the song to entertain his compatriots, "admirably adapted to the banjo which he handled like a professional," a surprising statement if true, considering that the banjo had not yet entered blackface performance.[28] The song remained in minstrelsy into the early 1840s, and was even performed on horseback.[29]

On the surface, "Coal Black Rose" is a simple love song sung by the African American "Sambo" as he battles for the attention of "Lubly Rosa" (see the sample verse above). The plot has Sambo showing up outside the residence of Rose, where he is invited inside to escape the cold and eat a meal. He then spies his rival Cuff, with whom he fights for Rose's affection. Sambo ultimately chases Cuffee away and rejects Rose because of her dalliance. There are frequent mentions of the banjo in the song's lyrics, and of southern foodstuffs such as hoe cak[e], possum, hominy, rice and sugar cane. It is hard to deduce if "Coal Black Rose" has any hidden meanings beyond this simple story.

> *1*
> *I've come to town to see you all*
> *I ask you how d'ye do?*
> *I'll sing a song not very long,*
> *A-bout my long tail blue*
> Chorus
> *Oh! for the long tail blue*
> *Oh! for the long tail blue*
> *I'll sing a song not very long,*
> *A-bout my long tail blue*[30]

"My Long Tail Blue" was another early minstrel song associated with George Dixon. The lyrics (see a sample verse and chorus above) describe a competition between the story's main character and T. D. Rice's Jim Crow persona (see below), an interesting parallel to the onstage rivalry between the performers behind the personages, Dixon and Rice. During the fall of 1833, a Mr. Burns, appearing in the Baltimore and Washington, D.C., area, performed "My Long Tail Blue" supposedly "written and sung by him in all the Southern Theatres"[31]; the song was so popular that Burns was still singing it at Baltimore's Front Street Theater during the second week of 1834.[32] The title of the composition refers to the type of tailcoat favored on Sundays by the "dandy" subject of the lyric, and the majority of its early sheet music publications feature a blackface character clothed in fancy evening dress prominently displayed on their covers. Interestingly, all music sheets extant date to 1836 or 1837, at least three years after the earliest documented performances of the song. This is indeed a mystery, for which no explanation has currently been found.[33]

Thomas Dartmouth Rice: Jump Jim Crow

1
Come listen all you galls and boys
I's jist from Tuckyhoe
I'm goin to sing a little song
My name is Jim Crow
Chorus: Weel about and turn about and do jis so
Eb'ry time I weel about and jump Jim Crow
2
Oh I'm a roarer on de Fiddle
And down in old Virginny
They say I play de skyentific
Like Massa Pagannini
3
I git 'pon a flat boat
I cotch de Uncle Sam
Den I went to see de place
Where dey kill'd Packenham
7
I wip my weight in wildcats
I eat an Alligator
And tear up more ground
Dan kifer 50 load of tater
8
I sit upon a Hornet's nest,
I dance upon my head,
I tie a Wiper [Viper] round my neck
And den I goes to bed.
9
Dere's Possum up de gumtree
An Raccoon in de hollow,
Wake Snakes for June bugs
Stole my half a dollar.
11
Oh de way dey bake de hoecake
In old Virginny neber tire
Dey put de doe upon de foot
An hole it to de fire.
15
I'm berry much afraid of later

Dis jumping will be no good
For while de Crow are dancing
De Wites will saw de wood
16
But if dey get honest
By sawing wood like slaves
Der'es an end to de business
Ob our friend Massa Hays
26
I went to Hoboken
To hab a promenade,
An dar I see de pretty gals,
Drinking Lemonade.
28
At de Swan cottage,
Is de place I tink,
Whar dey make dis'licious
An 'toxicating drink.
34
De great Nullification
And fuss in de South
Is now before Congress
To be tried by word ob mouth
36
Wid Jackson at de head
Dey soon de ting may settle
For ole Hickory is a man
Dat's tarnal full ob mettle
37
Should dey get to fighting
Perhaps de blacks will rise
For deir wish for freedom
Is shinning in deir eyes
39
I'm for freedom
An for Union altogether
Aldough I'm a black man
De white is call'd my broder[34]

The theatrical performer who dominated blackface in the 1830s was T.D. Rice. The subject of Rice's act was the first fully realized minstrel character with its own distinctive costume, personality, theme song and voice. Indeed, if it can be said that American minstrelsy had a specific starting point, Thanksgiving of 1832, during Rice's first New York appearance in his character of "Jim Crow," would be it.

Thomas Dartmouth Rice was a native of New York, born in that city's seventh ward on June 20, 1808.[35] Rice entered the world of the theater as a teenager, and, around the age of nineteen, played a lead at the Lafayette Theater.[36] For the next several years, Tom Rice portrayed a variety of characters, and gained experience knocking about the provinces in numerous productions. During the summer of 1829, at the same time that George Dixon was performing "Coal Black Rose," Rice joined the company of Samuel Drake, then alternating between stages in Cincinnati and Louisville.[37] It appears that in Louisville, on May 21, 1830, T.D. Rice performed in his character of Jim Crow for the first time.[38] Upon whom Rice based Jim depended on who is telling the story (and which of Rice's press releases they had read). Variously, Jim Crow was created from a street song heard by Rice in Cincinnati using the wardrobe of a Pittsburgh Negro,[39] or from a stable worker in the city of Jim Crow's first stage appearance:

> Back of the Louisville theatre was a livery-stable kept by a man named Crow. The actors could look into the stable-yard from the windows of their dressing-rooms, and were fond of watching the movements of an old and decrepit slave who was employed by the proprietor to do all sorts of odd jobs. As was the custom among the negroes, he had assumed his master's name, and called himself Jim Crow. He was very much deformed—the right shoulder was drawn up high, and the left leg was stiff and crooked at the knee, which gave him a painful but at the same time ludicrous limp. He was in the habit of crooning a queer old tune, to which he had applied words of his own. At the end of each verse he gave a peculiar step, "rocking de heel" in the manner since so general among the many generations of his imitators; and these were the words of his refrain: "Wheel about, turn about, Do jis so, An' ebery time I wheel about I jump Jim Crow."[40]

The first publication of Rice's new song seems to coincide with his arrival back east. "The Original Jim Crow," as circulated by New York publisher E. Riley and excerpted above, shows the latitude a stage character such as Crow allowed Tom Rice. It is ostensibly a composition in which Jim Crow of "Tuckyhoe" (a tributary of the James River in Virginia and the similarly named plantation on the waterway where Thomas Jefferson came of age) can boast of his abilities as a musician (comparing himself in verse two to the Italian virtuoso of the violin Nicolo Paganini) and a fighter (verses seven and eight). Rice uses verses such as twenty-six and twenty-eight to mention local landmarks familiar to the audience. There may even be some folkloric content, as verse nine and eleven signify southern songs and food ways. However, behind the mask of the blackface makeup, T.D. Rice used "Jim Crow" to make commentary on all manner of current events. Within the song's long and varied storyline, Crow visits the place where General Andrew Jackson defeated and killed British General Edward Pakenham in the War of 1812 (verse three), and returns to Jackson as president in verse thirty-six. Thomas Rice even takes on the issue of slavery in verses thirty-four to thirty-nine, although I doubt that Rice would sing these lyrics where Jim Crow's sympathies did not align with those of his audience.[41]

With Jim Crow, Rice had found his character, and his voice. Word of Thomas Rice and his new minstrel song began to build. Before debuting Jim in New York City, Rice toured him in the summer and fall of 1832 through Philadelphia, Baltimore, and Washington, D.C.[42] November 12, 1832, marked Jim Crow's arrival in New York City. For the two weeks until the momentous Thanksgiving Day, Rice "jumped" (as the song of "Jim Crow" describes) Jim Crow between dramas at the Bowery Theater.

By Monday, November 25, 1832, word had spread of Rice and his blackface song and dance. The audience jammed the auditorium, spilling out onto the stage and filling the wings of the theater. Junius Booth attempted to perform *Richard III*, but the spectators, impatient and unruly in their expectation of "Jim Crow," interrupted the performance with objects thrown onto the platform and by wandering about among the actors attempting to do their business. Tom Rice's performance during the intermission of the theater's production brought the house down, as reported in the *New York Courier*: "When Mr. Rice came on to sing his celebrated song of Jim Crow, they not only made him repeat it twenty times, but hemmed him in so that he actually had no room to perform the little dancing or turning about appertaining to the song."[43] It was such a famous debut that an engraving was made of the assembled multitudes around Rice; the theater would never be the same.

Jim Crow mania swept the nation. Just as Rice's first performances in New York were ending, other performers picked up Rice's song and additional actors presented his playlets. Crow became part of the shared vocabulary. There were stage Indians jumping Jim Crow,[44] militia attachments fifing Jim's melody[45] and the general population singing Rice's song in the streets.[46] T.D. Rice's brother George appeared at a rival New York City venue portraying Jim during the fall of 1837.[47] In Boston, a Mr. Eaton mixed his impression of Rice in with those of the most famous dramatic actors of the day.[48] There was the little Jim Crow, Miss Wray, "only seven years old," appearing in New York during February and March of 1835.[49] Between 1832 and 1837, myriad personalities throughout the United States and Great Britain mimicked Rice. Some of the reason for Jim Crow's popularity was the flexibility of the act. Various types of performers could adopt the character. The dance was accessible to anyone who attempted it, and the song singable by all strata of society. The "Jim Crow" composition lent itself to new verses, and was often altered to fit the circumstance or the unfolding events of the day.[50]

Even in his success as Jim Crow, Rice continued to offer songs and plays with characters other than Crow. While he leaned most heavily on Jim, Tom Rice was not unusual in varying his performances. Numerous entertainers of the 1830s, as differentiated from the minstrels of the 1840s, did not just perform blackface material. Instead, they included the popular blackface songs as a part of their evening's program. An actor might black up for a few selections, and then return in his normal color to play a different character. An equestrian could offer "Jim Crow on horseback," and then show off his trick riding skills. A few entertainers concentrated on minstrelsy, and those numbers grew as it became separated from other forms of amusement.

Rice remained the most famous minstrel performer through the 1830s. He maintained his popularity by retaining the elements the audience loved—the Jim Crow character, dance, and song—and placing these into new structures, stories, and plays. He set the pattern for later minstrels in parodying works from popular and high culture.[51] Rice continued touring the United States, with long runs in New York City bracketed by trips to Baltimore, Philadelphia, Washington, D.C., and Boston. Occasionally, Tom Rice forayed along the Atlantic coast into the South and the West. Rice also found fame among English audiences, touring Great Britain and possibly the continent.

Circus Minstrelsy

[The circus] would be more respectable, and more profitable if they would eschew frequent exhibitions of black characters. Singing of gross and meretricious songs beclouds the excellence of the equestrianism.[52]

Even though the dramatic stage provided some of the performers and format for early American Negro minstrelsy, there were other influences as well. An equally important masking convention was a part of circus history, both in England and in its American descendants. Audience (urban versus rural), performers (singing and dancing actors versus acting

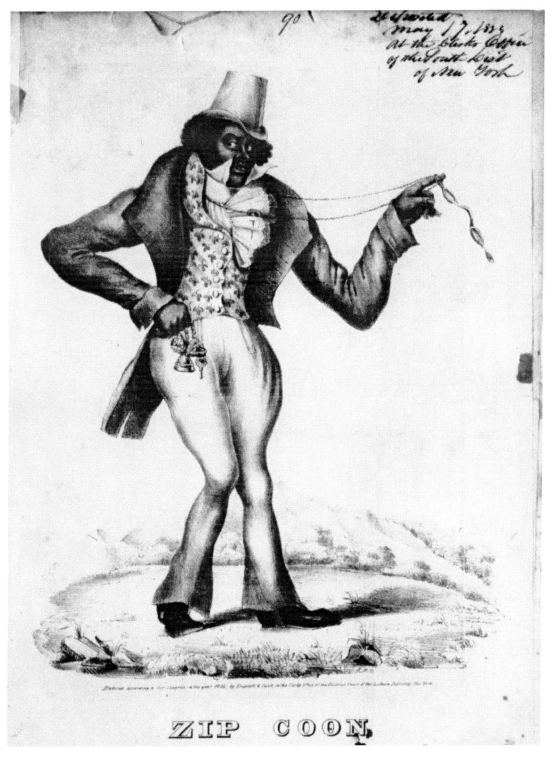

Sheet music cover for "Zip Coon" showing G.W. Dixon in the character of a "dandy."
J. L. Hewitt & Co., New York, deposited for copyright May 17, 1834 (Library of Congress).

musicians and dancers), or venue (theatres versus tent) differentiated theater from circus minstrelsy. However, these generalizations quickly break down when analyzing individual performers, time periods, and troupes.

During the end of the eighteenth and start of the nineteenth centuries, the English-style circus was just beginning to be introduced into the United States. Initially, these primarily equestrian shows relied on permanent facilities for their performances. Eventually, the American circus became mobile, using wagons and a tent to penetrate the most rural areas throughout the United States.

Bob Farrell is credited with being the first circus performer to sing in blackface the songs sweeping America—at the beginning of 1833. Farrell is also given the distinction of introducing "Zip Coon," which George Dixon appropriated, and "Claire De Kitchen" to American audiences.[53]

In the period before the War for Southern Independence, Southern city dwellers had the advantage of theatrical halls large enough to host entertainers on regular routes and managers who presented seasons of drama. On the other hand, rural Virginians outside of cities such as Richmond, Petersburg, Norfolk, and Lynchburg had the circus. Traveling by wagon and hauling the large canvas pavilion that J. Purdy Brown had introduced in 1825 (in 1826, Brown's was the first circus to tour Virginia), these troupes of equestrians, animal acts, and musical and theatrical performers followed established routes of commerce and transportation.[54]

Not surprisingly, Stuart Thayer's *Annals of the American Circus*, which chronicles the comings and goings of American shows before the Civil War, lists several circus performers that Joe Sweeney could possibly have witnessed first hand. One was Samuel H. Nichols (some historians have confused him with George Nichols), who began his career with various companies in 1829, first as a clown as was the case with many circus minstrels.[55] Nichols was working for J. Purdy Brown, who had a propensity for employing "Ethiopian" performers, during an 1830 Richmond appearance.[56] In March 1831, Sam was the first circus performer to sing "Jim Crow" (in New Orleans) while the song's originator was still touring the provinces.[57] This places Nichols in the earliest generation of minstrel singers, although he is not credited with performing in burnt cork. Minstrel historian T. Alston Brown gives credit to Nichols as the composer of "Zip Coon" and "Clare de Kitchen," although Bob Farrell also laid claim to that honor (see above).[58] Sam Nichols and Bob Farrell often worked together, and one may have appropriated the songs from the other. Joe Sweeney also might have seen T.D. Rice in his Jim Crow character. Rice possibly appeared in Richmond in November of 1833,[59] although another author claims the summer of 1834 as being the date of the earliest "Ethiopian opera" in town.[60]

Rice, Smith, and Coleman: American Minstrel Pioneers in Britain

As noted, British theatrical and circus masking traditions predate and influenced American minstrelsy. However, soon after its nascent beginnings, American performers began to tour Great Britain, planting the seeds for British Ethiopians.

With the same roots as the American "stage Negro," British "Ethiopianism" followed much the same history as its American counterpart. However, the British version of blackface minstrelsy jettisoned the more grotesque characterizations of African Americans found in American shows. The abolition of slavery in 1833 may have given Great Britains a different attitude toward the institution, lessening the need for such broad parody of blacks.[61] Whatever the cause, British audiences and performers took much more readily to the "refined" entertainments by American artists such as the Ethiopian Serenaders (see Chapter Seven), quickly usurping American minstrel formulas in the presentation of distinctly British material.

Although minstrelsy in Great Britain owes a large debt to Thomas Dartmouth Rice and his Jim Crow character, British blackface's prehistory began with the thespian Charles Mathews (1776–1835).[62] Mathews was a comic actor whose one-man show, "Mathews At Home," established his reputation in England and America. During an 1822 tour of the United States, the performer chanced upon an early African American theater company, the African Grove. Inspired by the evening's events, including interruptions of the actors' Shakespearean presentation by unruly white elements in the audience, he wrote a comic piece while still in America.[63] As early as 1823, in *A Trip to America*, Mathews used the composition "(O)Possum Up A Gum Tree" for his portrayal of a black individual.[64] When he returned to England, he brought the song and characterization with him.[65] Surprisingly, Mathews' arrangement appears to have come directly from slave society. Six years before Charles Mathews discovered the piece, the author James Kirke Paulding (August 22, 1779–April 6, 1860) heard the song sung by an African American on a trip through rural Virginia.[66]

But most historians agree that "Jim Crow" Rice had the same electrifying effect on Great Britain and her peoples as he had on America. A scant sixty years after Americans had broken away from the Empire, Rice took this first truly American development of English theatrical traditions back to Great Britain, announcing to audiences the independence of America's entertainment business. The length and number of Tom Rice's trips to Europe attest to his popularity in the Mother County as Rice's success continued in his own land.

Tom Rice's first English sojourn began on June 8, 1836, when he embarked for Britain to begin a month-long engagement at London's Surrey Theater that July.[67] After a prearranged visit to France during August,[68] Rice returned to London for a successful run through the fall, beginning with two months at the Surrey and then a move to the Adelphi Theater[69]; the management of the Surrey countered by offering up a counterfeit "Jim Crow."[70] Rice began to attract a "fashionable"[71] following, including members of the English nobility, some of whom made multiple visits to the theater.[72]

His run finally ended sometime in mid to late April of 1837,[73] and Rice departed London to tour Ireland and possibly Scotland.[74] After appearances in Dublin, Belfast,[75] Cork[76] and Limerick, Tom Rice returned to London, where, on June 18, he spoke of his success and warned of his imminent farewell. "I can have my own terms at any theater in London"; Tom Rice told the *Spirit of the Times*, "and although there are a great many counterfeit Jim Crows, they none of them *caw* to any purpose."[77]

The American newspapers raved about Rice's success in Great Britain, mentioning other Yankee thespians that had dominated English Theater during the season. The *New York Herald* summed it up by printing, "Forrest, Hamblin, Hill, Hackett, Rice, all went to England. 'Jim Crow' came out the best."[78] Rice himself drew comparisons to Thomas Hamblin when he improvised the following lyrics in performance:

> *Oh, Thomas Hamblin is arrived, who all New York does know*
> *To be better than the best in Hamlet and Othello*
> *Oh his Wirginius is fuss chop—his Brutus is'nt slow;*
> *But if he makes you weep too much, come back to see Jim Crow.*[79]

Success can be measured in many ways, and T.D. Rice achieved a number of the markers. He filled theaters, attracted the attention of both the nobility and the masses alike and spawned a large number of imitators. Rice also made a financial success, drawing upward of $600.00 for a single performance during his Irish sojourn.[80] *The Spirit of the Times* published that the tour, begun in mid–July, had already "realized" $15,000.00 by November's end.[81]

The reasons for Rice's overseas triumph paralleled those in his own country. The "Jim Crow" song proved extremely flexible in the adaptation of additional lyrics to fit any situation. This worked for Rice from the stage, as well as for his audience. Like many "hit" popular songs, "Jim Crow" was also easy for the audience to sing, and the "Jim Crow" dance lent itself to imitation. The *London Satirist* wrote critically how:

> Jim Crow is now sung in every nook and alley of the kingdom, from the aristocratic drawing-room of his Grace of Devonshire down to the hovels of the unwashed dustmen of Maiden-lane—for whom, by the bye, the song does not seem altogether unsuited; in fact, we may say that a Jim Crow mania has seized on all classes of the community; their eyes are now unable to see any beauty but in smutty faces, bow shins, splay feet, and lark heels; and no humor but in the unmeaning chuckle and idiot grin of a senseless nigger.[82]

There were horses trotting Rice's dance, and Spring Rice, the Chancellor of the Exchequer, was tagged with the "sobriquet" of "Jim Crow," which the English Mr. Rice was happy when rid of.[83]

Rice returned to England in December of 1838, opening at London's Adelphi Theater on December 10, performing there until at least the end of March 1839.[84] After a tour of provincial houses through the summer, Rice returned to the Adelphi on the theater's opening night of September 30. Interestingly, Tom Rice was paired that fall with James Henry Hackett (1800–1871), another American portraying character types. One of Hackett's favorite roles was as Nimrod Wildfire in *The Kentuckian*. The play also featured the blackface part of "Caesar ... a comic servant,"[85] a perfect role for Rice. The pair remained at the Adelphi until the third week of October,[86] when Rice once again "lit out for the provinces."[87] Rice returned to the Adelphi for a final week beginning December 18[88] and then made further tours in the northern provinces, before departing to America around the middle of March in 1840.[89]

After Rice, the next major American minstrel performers to tour England were two companions of Sweeney, John Smith and Thomas Coleman (see Chapter Three). Smith and Coleman's invasion began in November 1840, when they took over London's Surrey Theater, the same venue where Rice began four years earlier. From Monday, November 2 until the year's end,[90] "Yankee" Smith and "Piccaninny" Coleman (nicknames acquired in England[91]) filled the Surrey with delighted Londoners,[92] thereafter taking their show to provincial theaters for the remainder of their stay.[93]

Although their tour was much shorter in scope or duration (lasting into the spring of 1841) than either of those by Tom Rice, it had an equal impact. On the surface, the act of Smith and Coleman contained little that had not been seen before. "Zip Coon" and other well-known minstrel songs sat alongside dances shared with other performers. However, the secret to their success was their adaptation of the song "Jim Along Josey," which John Smith had developed into a dance rendition and a vehicle for contemporary verses, similar to what T.D. Rice had done with "Jim Crow."[94] Interestingly, the performer who claimed to have created the song, Edward R. "Ned" Harper (died circa 1860[95]), had toured Britain the previous year but had achieved only a modicum of success (for more about the song "Jim Along Josey," see Chapter Eleven).

Back in February of 1840, as Tom Rice was concluding his second foreign tour, the *Sunday Morning Atlas* sounded the arrival of Jim Crow's challenger:

Sheet music cover for "Jim Along Josey," showing John Smith in a ragged stage costume typical of early blackface minstrelsy, Firth & Hall, New York, deposited for copyright January 31, 1840 (Library of Congress).

Jim Crow has had its day—Public taste has "wheeled about." It has 'lighted upon "Jim Along Josey," which is now the rage. Jim Crow opened the door to a faithful representation of "Nigger" Character, and Jim along Josey has walked to, walking his predecessor out. The dynasty of the Crows is over—their cawing finished. There is another black Richmond in the field, and his is the Conqueror. The popularity of Jim along Josey is unbounded. Young Ladies play the melody and place it beside—shall we not say above—their favorite Rossini. The streets are vocal with it; men hum it, lads whistle it, and boys sing, squeak, or screech it, as they are blessed with musical voices, or cursed with defective musical organs. Even little unbreeched urchins attempt the thing, and precocious infants lisp the sweet sounds before those of "Pa!" and Ma![96]

The Surrey Theater jumped on "Josey's" popularity to promote Smith and Coleman, saying that "'Jim Along Josey!' has already acquired a greater popularity & created more excitement than the original 'Jim Crow' obtained during its extraordinary run—it will consequently be repeated," and that "Jim Crow completely 'wheeled about' by the rapid popularity of 'Jim Along Josey.'"[97] Coleman and Smith, like Rice before them, inspired many native imitators.

When Joe Sweeney entered minstrelsy in the 1830s, its conventions were already in place. As he performed throughout the United States and Great Britain, he followed blackface traditions in performance and practice. Joe also participated in the development of self-contained blackface minstrel groups, discussed further in Chapter Six's focus on the Virginia Minstrels. Sweeney brought to minstrelsy his knowledge of Southern blacks and the banjo, an instrument that was to effect major change in America's musical culture.

THREE

The Birth of a Banjoist

I have heard some noise and twanging on the banjo since the days of the Sweeneys, but it seems to me I have heard nothing from that instrument since then worthy of the name of music.[1]

Early Life

Joel Walker Sweeney (hereafter referred to by his professional name of Joe) was born in what was then Buckingham and, by his adulthood, Appomattox County, Virginia. The area looked remarkably similar to how it does today. With its gently rolling terrain, pine scrub forests, and streams in which to swim, it was an idyllic place in which to grow up. Tobacco was the main industry of this rural area that lay on the coach road between Richmond to the east and Lynchburg to the west. Between the time of Sweeney's birth and of his first ventures into the wider world, the population of the county was fairly stable, with blacks slightly outnumbering whites, approximately 10,000 to 7,400. This reflects the small number of slaves held by the average white resident, although a few slaveholders, such as the Flood Family, owned and operated large farming operations utilizing many slaves.

Joe Sweeney's grandfather was Moses Sweeney (circa 1755–1833). Born in Amherst County to the east of Appomattox, Moses came to the Appomattox area after serving in the Revolutionary War, settling in what was then part of Prince Edward County in 1785.[2] Possibly Moses came looking for unclaimed land and new opportunities, or he could have been joining his siblings who were already established in the growing area. Along with Moses Sweeney came his new wife and their six-year-old son John; a brother Charles (middle name perhaps Moses for his father) joined John around 1795, and there were possibly other siblings. The Sweeney family lived about one mile northeast of Appomattox Courthouse and the Appomattox River, along the Richmond/Lynchburg Stage Road.[3] Moses probably maintained a small farm, holding a few slaves to raise tobacco for income, and other crops and animals for food.

Moses' son John was a wheelwright (a good profession for someone living on the main road between Richmond and Lynchburg) and farmer. John married Tabitha(1) Virginia Baugh(s) (circa 1784–January 16, 1860).[4] Their oldest son, Joel Walker, was born sometime around 1810.[5] John and Tabitha's home, said to be a four-room frame dwelling, was supposedly not completed until Joe was five years old[6]; it is believed to have been just south of Moses' home, on the north side of the Appomattox River[7] and sat on one hundred forty-four acres of land.[8] John's brother Charles built his home just north of the couple around 1823. Although not wealthy, John's estate was eventually valued at $11,70.00, probably in land and buildings.[9]

Although neither the Sweeneys nor the Baughs are chronicled as having musical backgrounds, four of John and Tabitha's children played fiddle and/or banjo. In addition to Joe, this included Sam (1832–January 13, 1864), Richard Alexander, known as Dick (1828–February 10, 1859), and possibly Missouri A. (circa 1830–April 9, 1885).[10] Furthermore, Joe's cousins Robert Miller Sweeney (1826–1888) and his sister Polly (Mary) Ann Sweeney Patterson (1824–1892?) are supposed to have played both instruments. As the oldest in his generation, Joe may have taught all of his younger siblings and cousins to play, although they probably also learned some of their art from area blacks as well.

At the same time as rural Anglo Americans embraced the banjo, urban dwellers were developing a form of popular entertainment called the minstrel show. White performers blackened their faces to present songs, dances, jokes, and skits supposedly based on rural slave life. When Joe Sweeney made the move into professional music, blackface performing was the avenue he took.

Joe Sweeney's Early Performing Career

[Joe Sweeney] began by wandering through central Virginia, playing and singing for crowds during county court sessions. He was a one-man show, singing the doggeral [sic] he had learned from Negroes or had improvised from their tunes, dancing, reciting, and crowing, braying and roaring in imitation of animals. He not only played the banjo; he was equally accomplished on the violin. During this period he began blacking his face for these performances.[11]

It is said of Joe Sweeney that he not only blacked his face, but his neck, arms and feet as well and came on the stage in his bare feet, carrying a sawbuck, on which he sat, though he often played standing.[12]

Since the early 1830s, Joe Sweeney had been looking for opportunities to perform his music before a wider audience. As a fiddler as well as a banjoist, Sweeney surely played area dances, held in homes and in other informal circumstances. Anecdotal evidence suggests that Joe also played his banjo for guests at the Sunnyside Tavern, along the old coach road about twenty miles north of his home.[13] But these types of local appearances would have yielded little, if any, income for the musician. Theatrical and circus work, however, was another story. There were plenty of opportunities for the banjoist in these public venues in the developing blackface business.

> Come, all you Virginny gals, and listen to my noise;
> Neber do you wed wid de Carolina boys;
> For if dat you do, your portion will be:
> Cowheel and sugarcane, wid shangolango tea.
> Chorus: Mamzel ze marrel—ze bunkum sa!
> Mamzel ze marrel—ze bunkum sa!
> When you go a-couring, de pretty gals to see
> You kiss 'em and you hug 'em like de double rule ob free.
> De fust ting dey ax you when you are sitting down,
> Is, 'Fetch along de Johnny-cake—it's gitting rader brown.[14]

By the end of 1836, Sweeney had made the transition from local, amateur musician to professional, regional performer. On Monday, December 5, Joe Sweeney joined touring blackface singer James Sanford in Richmond to present "Negro Extravaganzas" at the Terpsichore Hall.[15] (See Chapter Ten for more about Sanford and Sweeney.) The advertising for the duo's weeklong engagement gives the sense that Sweeney was well known to Richmond audiences, suggesting that the banjoist had already been performing professionally at least for a year or two.[16] The whereabouts of Jim Sanford and Joe Sweeney are unknown for the next two and a half months, but by mid–February of 1837, Sweeney and Sanford were back in Richmond, appearing at the city's theatres.[17]

Following his performances in Richmond with Sanford, Sweeney appears to have been based in Virginia, and was not a member of any traveling show during much of 1837 and 1838. Lynchburg resident Newman Eubanks recalls hearing Sweeney play at the town's racetrack sometime in the spring or fall of 1837 or 1838.[18] (The races offered a good opportunity for busking, or picking up tips from the crowd. See Chapter One for more about horse racing and the banjo.) There were also many balls held around these occasions, and Joe Sweeney may have been employed as a dance musician as well.

Joe Sweeney's first documented circus performance came in the winter of 1839. For two weeks in February, the banjoist was advertised as appearing with the

Portrait of Joe Sweeney, circa 1850s.

Circus and Menagerie United in Charleston, South Carolina. (It is possible that Sweeney worked for Hobby during the touring that occurred before or after their stay in Charleston, but, unfortunately, he is not mentioned in any of the surviving newspaper advertisements.)[19] Joe Sweeney began his engagement the week of Tuesday, February 12. On February 13 and 19, Sweeney appeared in T. D. Rice's *Oh! Hush!* and portrayed Rice's character of "Pompey Smash" on Monday and Tuesday, February 18 and 19. Joe took his benefit on the 16 (meaning that all of that evening's receipts went to the banjoist).[20]

Following the Charleston appearance, Hobby's circus headed north and Sweeney eventually did the same. By April, the Virginia banjoist was in New York City,[21] and the whirlwind of success had just begun. For the next six years, Joe Sweeney would be away from his home, traveling as far away as the British Isles before returning to his Appomattox residence.

Minstrel Man in New York

When the regular drama broke down, ballet dancers, model artists, Hollick lecturers, negro singers, Ethiopian serenaders, and such like entertainments were the ones which took their place publicly for one portion of the community, as the Italian and French opera ... did for another.... Whether these amusements are less innocent than those offered by a well regulated theatre ... it is hardly necessary to discuss.[22]

Joe Sweeney arrived in New York in April 1839 to discover a City that was well acquainted with minstrelsy. Because New York was the winter home for many traveling shows as well as the place where numerous circuses assembled their troupes for summer touring, it served as an incubator for countless pre–Civil War minstrel acts. New York audiences had the opportunity to view a veritable Who's Who of early blackface, with the best of the established performers sharing the limelight with up and comers. Sweeney picked a good time for his first New York appearance. Although New Yorkers were in the third year of a financial depression, the panic of 1837 resulted in an explosion of middle-class businesses, such as theaters and museums. And these venues all needed talent such as the Virginia banjoist.[23]

Joe secured a weeklong engagement at the Old Italian Opera House on the corner of Leonard and Church Streets, about a half a block off Broadway. The National, as it was then named, was definitely not the best of the New York Houses, and the *New York Clipper* described it as "situated in an inconvenient and poor neighborhood."[24] Sweeney was not the only featured performer; over the course of the evening, two or three paired-down plays were bracketed by specialty acts such as Joe Sweeney. His banjo playing was placed in the same context as plate spinners, polka dancers, magicians, and other novelty acts. Perhaps the break provided by the banjoist was to allow the company to change costumes and scenery; it also gave the audience a change of pace. Luckily, Sweeney sang, played his banjo, and represented "Negro characters" from Virginia to full houses. It is hard to tell if the play *Tortesa, The Usurer* or Joe was the draw, although the *New York Herald* singled out "the great feature of the nigger [sic] is his playing upon the 'banjo' which is exceedingly well done and gave general satisfaction."[25]

On May 4, Sweeney returned to the stage, appearing at the Franklin Theatre.[26] Located on Chatham Square, this was a small venue and only four years old at the time.[27] Joe than vanishes until late November, which probably means that he signed on with a circus for spring, summer, and fall touring.

> THE AMPHITHEATRE [at the Bowery] from its peculiar construction, possesses this great advantage over the common Theatre and other places where the Olympian Games are exhibited: the performances takes [sic] place in the midst of the audience—inspiring a reciprocal enthusiasm between the Equestrian and the observer—not in perspective or at so great a distance from the spectator that the feats of the performers cannot be scrutinized. Every thing is done here in open sight, and every person within the walls can be comfortably seated, and witness all the entertainments.[28]

Upon his return to New York City, Joe Sweeney was employed at the Bowery Amphitheatre by June, Titus, Angevine & Company in support of the blackface singer John Smith (b. John Washington Smith, =1815–August 31, 1877).[29] A noted "Negro delineator" who performed with various traveling circuses as early as 1836, Smith was known for his presentation of the song "Jim Along Josey (see Chapter Eleven for more information about 'Josey')." His popularity was such that he was paid $100.00 for a month's tour with the June, Titus, circus company in late 1838, the highest paid performer in the show.

At the Amphitheatre, Sweeney sang "several of his original Virginia Banjo Extravaganzas"[30] and John Smith presented the character of "Ginger Blue."[31] The duo appeared together in "the laughable Afterpiece of The German Farmer."[32] Also appearing was the dancer Thomas Coleman, who, according to theatrical historian George Odell, "was a pupil of Smith's as early as June of that year, when he appeared at the Olympic Theatre in New York doing '"Jim Along Josey."'"[33] Coleman also was a student of Joe Sweeney's, learning the banjo from the Virginian during this period. He would perform with Sweeney in many different venues over the coming years.

After two weeks at the Bowery Amphitheatre, Joe Sweeney jumped ship, and was reunited with Jim Sanford at the Broadway Circus. Sanford played in Rice's *Oh! Hush!*[34] and Sweeney was advertised as providing "a correct delineation of the Old Virginia Nigger."[35] Presumably to celebrate Christmas, the whole company danced a traditional English Morris dance.[36] Through the end of the year, Sanford and Sweeney remained with the Broadway Circus, and Smith at the Bowery Amphitheatre.[37] Both drew large audiences to their performances.[38]

During Joe Sweeney's stints appearing in New York, a veritable flood of minstrels passed through the city's venues. Because the blackface dancers and singers needed accompanists, Sweeney often appeared in conjunction with some of minstrelsy's brightest stars. Dancer/singer John Diamond (1823–October 29, 1857)[39] was a New Yorker who first came to the attention of the public in April 1839.[40] On Saturday, January 18, 1840, he joined Joe Sweeney at the Broadway circus.[41] On the following Monday, their union caused quite a rush at the box office, as reported by the *New York Post*:

> This elegant establishment was excessively crowded last evening, and many disappointed of obtaining admission to witness the novelties produced on the occasion. Master Diamond was called out and compelled to repeat his negro dances five or six times.... The same entertainments will be repeated this evening [January 21].[42]

Sweeney accompanied the young dancer on the violin (which was his first instrument) as well as the banjo. Now advertised as "Master Diamond The Prince of Darkies!,"[43] the *New York Post* hailed him as "the greatest card of the day ... well worth going a mile to witness."[44]

Their success inspired circus entrepreneur P.T. Barnum, who was also managing the dancer, to try to lure Diamond and Sweeney to Philadelphia for a two-week engagement, offering slightly more for the popular dancer than his banjo accompanist. Diamond took the offer, but Sweeney continued at the Broadway Circus, playing the banjo behind his own singing and dancing, as well as that of other performers. Joe also took on an unidentified apprentice, who aided him in performances during the first week in February (for more about Diamond, Sweeney and Barnum, see Chapter Ten).[45]

Occasionally, the Virginia banjoist was "loaned out" to other theaters to help a thespian on his or her benefit night. Sweeney appeared January 10 at the Bowery Theatre to aid a Mr. Gates,[46] and again on March 9 to abet Mr. Champlin, the theater's treasurer. Sweeney's old partner John Smith, who had just left the Bowery Amphitheatre to rejoin him at the Broadway Circus, also came along.[47]

Rufus Welch and Jonas Bartlett, the proprietors of the circus on Broadway, had done well that winter. Minstrelsy played a large part in Welch & Bartlett's success, as the *Herald* also noted that the Ethiopian "species of entertainment appears to be the only favorite with the public.... Jim-along-Josey being all the go at the present."[48]

On March 23, in preparation for leaving New York, Welch & Bartlett, reorganized their show, keeping Smith, Sweeney, and Diamond.[49] During the circus's last week in the city, Joe Sweeney and John Smith were fully evident; the banjoist took his benefit the same night as an imported troupe of native Americans[50]; Smith's night was five days later on April 8.[51] Thomas Coleman did his best to imitate John Diamond (who had left the company) by dancing the Camptown Hornpipe, and added his own "twist," that of the "Grapevine" variety, which he would continue to perform with Sweeney in future appearances.[52] After a three-day stand in Brooklyn, the company set out for New England.

On Tour

Harrington's Museum does not fall off in the way of attractions. Joe Sweeney, Master Chestnut, and the Tattooed Man, are all there–banjoizing, extravaganzaizing, grapevinetwisting, lightfantastictoeing, &c, &c, &c.[53]

It was the spring of 1840, and any performer worth his or her salt was taking advantage of the good weather and out on tour. Joe Sweeney, singer John Smith, and dancer Thomas Coleman headed out of New York on their journey with the Broadway Circus. It must have been quite a sight to see the troupe, "employing more than 75 Men and Horses,"[54] with their equipment, livestock, and costumes boarding the steamboat the John W. Richmond for Providence. Upon their arrival, Welch & Bartlett showed on the "Dorrance street Lot" from April 15 through 17,[55] possibly losing some of their audience to a rival company from New York City managed by N.B. and T.V. Turner.[56] The troupe then spent the rest of the month working their way through Rhode Island and Massachusetts to Boston.[57]

Beginning on Tuesday, May 5, Welch & Bartlett occupied a "pavilion" on the Mansion House estate in Milk Street, Boston. Their tent stood in an ideal location, at the corner of Hawley "nearly opposite Riddle's carriage depository"[58] "just below the Old South Church"[59] in the city's downtown. The *Post* and *Transcript* ballyhooed the show, reminding readers that manager Rufus Welch will "bring out performers who will almost equal Whig politicians in turning somersets."[60] The circus actually opened a day late, because a large storm prevented the show from going forward.[61]

For the next month, the Welch & Bartlett captivated Boston audiences and introduced Joe Sweeney to the city. The *Boston Transcript* singled out John Smith as "the greatest Ethiopian character we ever saw."[62] The *Courier* praised the blackface trio of Smith, Sweeney, and Coleman, stating that:

> The specimens of negro extravaganza, too, are excellent in their way, and convulse the audience with laughter. They are said to afford very faithful pictures of "life among the Virginia niggers"; whether they do so or not, we are unable to say; but as they are well calculated to remove a wrinkle from the brow of care, we cannot but speak well of them in these times of general dulness [sic], when half the business community are desponding, and require some mental stimulus to make them laugh and feel merry.[63]

On Friday, May 15, Sweeney and Smith were hired out to the Tremont Theater, where they volunteered their services for the benefit of Sig. Hervio Nano.[64] A dwarf possessing a normal upper body but shrunken lower limbs, Hervio Nano appeared as a kind of human fly, creeping "around the edge of the upper boxes of the theatre, and even across the proscenium, more to the terror than amusement of his spectators."[65] Nano played New York's Bowery Theatre during Sweeney's winter residency in the city,[66] and joined the circus on Milk Street following his week at the Tremont.[67]

On May 25, Welch announced the imminent departure of his company from Boston, which he had been threatening almost from the beginning of their run. Finally, the engagement ended the week of June 1.

From the beginning, Welch & Bartlett drew large crowds,[68] averaging around 1,450 people for each of their first eleven evening shows, and 630 for each of three afternoon performances. Evenings ranged from 1,000 attendees all the way up to an overflowing house of 2,000 paid admissions. The circus was particularly proud that a large number of their admirers were ladies.[69] "Upwards of 30,000 persons have visited this public place of amusement during the last four weeks," boasted the local newspapers.[70] The banjoist and his compatriots

Sheet music cover for "Jumbo Jum," showing dancer John Smith and banjoist Joe Sweeney as seen at the New York Circus during their Boston run. Henry Prentiss, Boston, deposited for copyright July 28, 1840 (Library of Congress).

must have made a favorable impression on these many spectators, as Joe Sweeney was a pop-ular Boston attraction for the next several years.

On Sunday, June 6, Welch & Bartlett left Boston behind. The show headed northwest, eventually crossing Massachusetts toward engagements in New York state.[71] John Smith and Thomas Coleman, however, were not with the troupe on this journey. The blackface singer/dancer and his apprentice had chosen instead to head back to New York City for an engagement at the Chatham Theatre. On June 22, Smith sang "Jumbo Jum,"[72] a "negro bal-lad" which the firm of Henry Prentiss had published upon the end of his Boston engage-ment.[73] The printer also issued "Tell Me Josey Whar You Bin."[74] The cover drawing of "Jumbo Jum" by Robert Cooke depicted a frolic scene with caricatured renderings of African Americans, including a dancer accompanied by a banjoist playing what appears to be a gourd-bodied instrument.

At the end of their Chatham engagement, Smith and Coleman headed up river to rejoin the circus for an Albany run. For four days ending on the Fourth of July, the Broad-way Circus gave shows, their evening performances expanded to include two additional day-time shows to accommodate viewers on the Fourth.[75] Welch & Bartlett traveled the rest of July, August, and September, playing a series of one-nighters around northeastern New York state.[76]

When the newspapers decided to run full descriptions of the company (or, the circus chose to purchase the coverage), Sweeney, Smith, and Thomas Coleman were given promi-nent mention. An advertisement for the circus's performances on August 25 and 26, at the Auburn Garden in Auburn, outside of Rochester, New York, ballyhooed them as:

> J.W. Sweeny, the accomplished artist on the Banjo, will give a great variety of his enchanting Airs, Solos, and Virginian Ditties.... John Smith the most celebrated and popular representa-tive in the world of the Ethiopian Character. Will appear in several of his original extravagan-zas, duetts, songs and dances, introducing his Pupil, Master Coleman, in a great variety of extra double shuffle and old Wirginia Breakdowns, grapevine twist, etc., etc. The eccentricities of these delineators of the African race, must be witnessed to be believed. The attractions of this scene will be enhanced by Mr. Sweeny the Banjo Player.[77]

On September 3–5, the *Rochester Advertiser* recounted the performances another way, confusing Sweeney's middle name with Smith's in their description:

> Mr. John Smith, the great Delineator of the American Negro Character and Virginia Buffo Dancer. This gentleman's powers are so well known through the country, having last season travelled [sic] with the Bowery Amphitheatre, that it needs no comment. However, as a Darky said who had witnessed his performance lately, "the more I look at him, the worse I feel."
> Master Coleman, a Pupil of John Smith, and said to be an apt scholar. This youth is termed Dancing Tom, of Squash Hollow.
> Joseph Washington Sweeny, is a Virginian and known as the Virginia Banjo Player—This young man's execution on an Instrument of his own manufacture, convulses the heavens with laughter. This performance is enhanced by Smith and Coleman, who never fail to exert their utmost endeavors to please an enlightened and discriminating audience.[78]

The crowds came out in droves to see the Rochester shows, and the *Advertiser* singled out John Smith for praise.[79]

By October 10, Welch & Bartlett's show had circled around to Albany and, once again, Smith, Coleman, and Sweeney are singled out as "three of the most popular representatives of Ethiopian character in America." Then, there were repeat performances in Troy[80] before the circus headed south, showing at towns along the Hudson River on the way back to Man-hattan.[81]

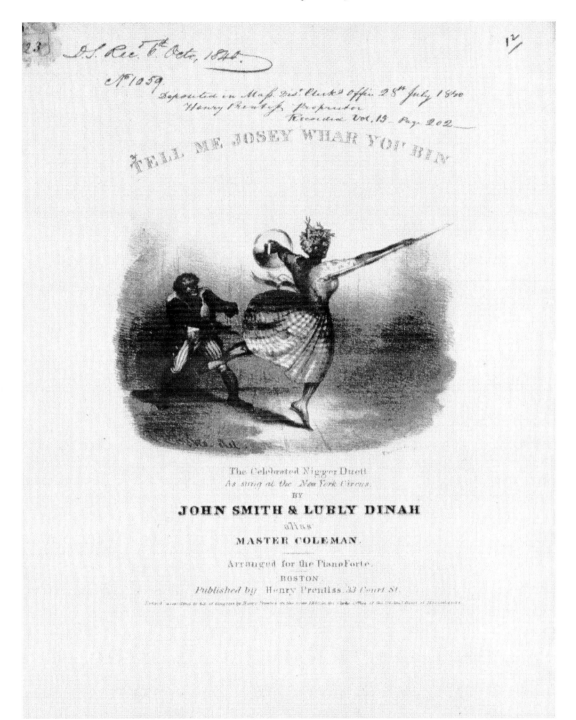

Sheet music cover, "Tell Me Josey Whar You Bin," picturing John Smith and "Lubly Dinah" (Master Coleman). "As sung at the New York Circus." Henry Prentiss, Boston, deposited for copyright July 25, 1840. Shows the cross-dressing common in early minstrelsy (Library of Congress).

On Friday, October 23, while appearing in Poughkeepsie, Welch & Bartlett once again advertised Smith, Coleman and Sweeney.[82] While nothing points to Joe being elsewhere, John Smith and Thomas Coleman began a successful tour of Great Britain on November 2.[83] In order for the duo to make the trans–Atlantic journey, they had probably deserted the show sometime at the beginning of the month. Perhaps to make up for the absence of John Smith and Thomas Coleman's dancing, William Chestnut joined the show at Peekskill as Sweeney's apprentice.[84] However, when Welch & Bartlett opened at the Old Bowery Theatre in Manhattan on November 16, Sweeney and Chestnut were not listed on the program.[85] Instead, Joe and his student took an engagement at the New Chatham Theatre from the second to the seventh in support of Junius Booth, the great "tragedian" of the day. Sweeney, as "the original professor of the Banjo," and Chestnut, "his surprising pupil," offered "the real Virginia music on the banjo," and "celebrated negro extravaganzas" in counterpart to Booth's Shakespearean offerings. Joe Sweeney and William Chestnut took their benefit on Friday, and on Sunday, left New York City.[86]

Star Performer

> Let 'em talk 'bout dar guitar and peranum Forte, mine's de rail conglomerated essence of perfection—de Southern Banjo.

During the spring of 1840 in Boston, Joe Sweeney appears to have had gained many fans, both for himself and for the banjo. So, it was no surprise that he and William Chestnut landed a booking at the Tremont Theater located in that city for Thanksgiving week and the first week in December 1840, or that they were able to transfer their Boston residency to another venue through the end of the year.[87] Throughout their time at the Tremont, Sweeney and Chestnut received good press, and were often highlighted on the playbills issued by the theater. On November 24 and 25, as well as on December 2, the duo was top billed on the broadsides used to ballyhoo that evening's shows.[88] The Tremont provided its own description, written in dialect, supposedly to reflect the authentic nature of the night's performance. From his selections, Master Chestnut is shown to be a dancer in the John Diamond mold:

> Look Hea!! I'm gwoin to cum de rail scientific, and if yer want to encourage native talent, give dis tall Virginny Nigger a lif. Let 'em talk 'bout dar guitar and peranum Forte, mine's de rail conglomerated essence of perfection—de Southern Banjo, and when him speak "he discourse most elegant music," as Mass Shakepole say—and I bet a pound of sassingers agin a Virginny hoe cake dat no white or brack nigger can hold a candle to this child. His Pupil Master Chestnut Will come de ole Virginy Breakdown, Smoke-House Dance, Grapevine Twist, and all that sort of thing, on dis occasion, Old Joe Sweeny He'll be dare sartin, and the Little Darky will be dare too, and no Mistake, so look out![89]

Some critics took issue with the presentation of minstrel performers in a "legitimate" theater. The Boston Courier commented on this disapproval while praising Sweeney's act. "However much may be the difference of opinion respecting the adaptation of the peculiar line to which Mr Sweeney belongs to the boards of a regular theatre," said the Courier,

> yet there is no mistake about the vis comica, of both this gentleman and his pupil. They are full of fun—their dancing and playing are excellent, and no one, of a tolerably quiet conscience, can resist a hearty laugh at their oddities.[90]

It may have been just a publicity ploy, but Joe and Will were advertised as only showing for a week, taking their benefit at week's end, and being re-engaged for the following six days.[91] The pair were also said to be departing "to fulfil [their] Southern engagements" at the end of that second week at the Tremont,[92] but, either these dates were flexible or not booked until after the first of the New Year. However, if these items faithfully reflect events, this would be another indicator of Sweeney and Chestnut's success in Boston.

After taking their benefit on Friday, December 4,[93] Sweeney and Chestnut moved over to Harrington's Museum, where Joe remained from Monday, December 7, until the year's end. Harrington's was one of many so-called "dime museums" that featured "oddities" such as those later made popular by P.T. Barnum at his American Museum in New York City. The presentation of live acts in the dime halls seems to have come into currency during the late 1830s and early 1840s. Productions were given in the "lecture rooms," or theaters located within the museum building. These ranged in size from small rostrums fronted by a few rows of seats to lavishly decorated rooms that held a thousand viewers. The acts as well varied in size and quality, from the types of variety bills found in the lowest beer halls to classy productions similar to those promoted within regular theaters.[94] A day or evening at these museums was less expensive than attending the theater or the circus. For example, when Sweeney played the Tremont, admission ranged from the gallery seats at twenty-five cents, to the pit at half a dollar, on up to the box seats at one dollar.[95] When Welch & Bartlett tempted Boston audiences, the cost of entry was fifty cents for boxes and half that for the pit.[96] Harrington's Museum charged only "25 cts.—Children under twelve years of age, half price" to see Joe Sweeney and Master Chestnut.[97]

Ventriloquist and magician "Professor" Jonathan Harrington was a fixture around Boston from the late 1820s until around 1871. Harrington had first attempted his own enterprise in 1834, when he leased the Boston Theatre on Federal Street for the season.[98] On May 4, 1840, Harrington tried again, opening his new facility on the premises of the New England Museum at 76 Court Street. However, the rival Boston Museum proved more popular with the public, and two years later, Jonathan Harrington's collection of curiosities was sold at auction.[99]

If the newspapers can be believed, Joe Sweeney and his pupil Chestnut were a continuing draw at Harrington's.[100] One could view the assembled collection of curios, see Sweeney and company's performance, and, at the same time, get a phrenological exam by Mr. Southworth.[101] There was a "great 'gittin' up stairs,"[102] and "extravaganzaizing, grapevinetwisting, lightfantastictoeing" while Sweeney and Chestnut were in the house.[103] Joe Sweeney's popularity was such that a competing venue falsely claimed his services.[104]

On the Road

Christmas time came, and the Museum was decorated for the holidays. Joe Sweeney's southern engagements were finally upon him, and so ended his Boston run the next day.[105] William Chestnut stayed on, dancing at the Tremont during January and February of 1841, sometimes accompanied by a "Mr. Newcomb from Ole Virginny" (a musician whose biography is lost to history) on the banjo.[106] By the spring, Sweeney and Chestnut were back together, appearing in Bartlett & Delavan's New York Circus.[107] In the New Year, Sweeney is rumored to have been in New Orleans, but no evidence has surfaced to substantiate this claim. (Colonel Collins lists a New Year's Day appearance by Sweeney in the *New Orleans Picayune*. However, a search of the *Picayune* [December 24, 1840–January 21, 1841] and *Bee* [January 1–6, 1841] yielded no information.)

His first known engagement that year was in Washington, D.C., where the banjoist followed T.D. Rice into the National Theatre. Joe played Washington from Friday, January 22 at least through Monday, January 25, as a stopover on his way South. Sweeney's performances gained the praise of critics, who wrote Sweeney's "singing, dancing, and performance of the negro character [were] not inferior, in the opinion of many, to those of Mr. Rice."[108] From there, Sweeney headed to Richmond, Petersburg, and other south side towns.[109]

But a short visit home was all Sweeney got. Success beckoned, and the banjoist headed north again. By March, the performer was at Baltimore's American Theatre. An interesting feature of the Front Street Theatre was accommodations for the "Colored" population, which occupied two galleries.[110] Sweeney's "Farewell Benefit" was held on Saturday, March 6.[111] The Virginia banjoist then went to New York City to join the New York Circus for the end of their winter show.

> If the Bowery Theatre should never open, unless as a church, it will be a happy thing for the morals of a large portion of society. More iniquity and wickedness have been perpetrated within its walls, than in all the other theatres of the country. If a hundred persons, as he says, are thrown out of the devil's employment, so much the better; let them go to work like honest people.[112]

Sweeney arrived for a week at the Bowery with the New York Circus on Thursday, March 18.[113] Many of his old compatriots from the Broadway Circus were in the Bowery Company. One equestrian in that show who would play an important role in the life of Joe Sweeney was Richard Sands (May 1814–February 24, 1861[114]). Sands would later lead the show that brought Sweeney to the British Isles.

The press greeted Sweeney's return to New York City as if it were the second coming. "The only banjo player in existence" proclaimed the *New York Post*.[115] The *Herald* was even more enthusiastic as it raved:

> The most eccentric and melodious of musical geniuses, "Old Joe Sweeny," as he is familiarly termed by the Bowery boys, showed his good natured countenance in the arena of the Bowery last evening, and astonished the audience with "Old Johnny Bouka," and several other of his celebrated Virginia ditties, accompanied by the banjo, in his usual masterly style.[116]

Playbills broadcasting his return announced:

> The Virginia Melodist, Joe Sweeney, just from his native soil, where he has been renovating on "hog and hominy," for the last three months, will make his first appearance this season, and introduce those never-to-be-forgotten JIGS, REELS, and BREAKDOWNS, with Vocal Accompaniments and new variations, only done by the rale [sic] niggers of the Old Dominion, except by "himself alone," being the only one yet that can give the "scientific touches to perfection, on the Southern Banjo." ... The whole to conclude with the laughable Scene of OH! HUSH! Or.—The Virginny Cupid! In the course of which, Mr. Sweeney will play several popular airs on the BANJO.[117]

Minstrelsy as such, and Joe Sweeney in particular, were gaining widespread enough popularity to prompt Martin Van Buren, former president of the United States, to attend Sweeney's performance on the eve of March 23. Sweeney and Van Buren drew a full house,[118] with the president entering to cheering and the waving of handkerchiefs.[119]

> Clar de Track, de steam's up, de Locomotive's coming.
> Look here White Folks;
> "Come one, come all, hear de Music ring,
> From de melodious Banja string."[120]

At the end of their New York run, Joe Sweeney and "his pupil" William Chestnut traveled to Baltimore to rejoin Bartlett & Delavan's New York Circus. From May 5[121] until June

SWEENY'S VIRGINIA MELODIES,
AS SUNG BY
J. W. SWEENY.

Cover for "Sweeny's Virginia Melodies" showing the performer in his stage costume and make-up. Henry Prentiss, Boston, 1841 (The Harvard Theatre Collection, Houghton Library).

5, Sweeney "the Unrivalled Banjo Player and Celebrated Vocalist"[122] sang his "old Virginia Ballads accompanied on the Banjo, and [was] assisted in the capering department by Master Chestnut, his scientific pupil in the Nigger line." Joe continued to show T.D. Rice's influence and popularity by performing *Oh! Hush!*[123] Few song titles or dances are named in the advertising placed with local newspapers, with the exception of "the New Grape Vine Twist," and "the Real Camptown Hornpipe," the latter accompanied by Sweeney on the violin.[124]

The evening of Wednesday, May 26, was chosen to benefit Joe Sweeney and the newspapers made much noise about it. The *Baltimore American* told readers that Sweeney "has no equal or arival [sic] in his peculiar art of African imitations"[125] and named him "the Ethiopian Paganini." The *Sun* concurred, possibly being the first to use the pun "Ban-Joe Sweeny" in advertising his feature, attesting "to the fidelity and humor of his negro delineations."[126]

Upon leaving Baltimore, the New York Circus traveled south to Washington, D.C., crossed the Potomac River to show in Georgetown. Then, as company member John Glenroy remembers, "by boat up the Potomac to Fredericksburg," and therefore through rural Virginia, opening in the capitol Richmond on June 28. Business had been so poor that Bartlett & Delavan sold the show back to Rufus Welch. Along with his partner Alvan Mann, Welch is first advertised as owner on July 5, the last day of the Richmond run.[127] Surprisingly, Joe Sweeney was not given any special mention emphasizing his ties to Virginia, nor his previous appearances in Richmond.

Then, it was on to Petersburg, Norfolk, and Portsmouth, where the members of the New York Circus once again boarded a ship for Baltimore.[128] Although this stay was only for a week, it is a testament to the popularity of the show that the circus was able to return to the Maryland city so soon after their previous stand. Considering how recently they had been seen by audiences in Baltimore, it was strange that the performers stuck to pretty much the same fare for the week of July 19 as they had used back in May. But, this did nothing to deter the spectators.[129] Joe Sweeney, identified as the "Virginia Minstrel"[130] or the "Virginia Melodist," is singled out in the press coverage and advertising.

For the rest of the summer, the New York Circus took to their wagons for a typical series of short stands throughout small hamlets in Pennsylvania. By the end of August, the circus had crossed over the border into New York state. The company reached Albany sometime during the third week in October[131] and ended their tour up river in Troy on October 23.[132] Welch opened at the Bowery Amphitheatre on Monday evening, October 25.[133] Sweeney and Chestnut are not mentioned in any of the publicity for the New York City run, and it must be assumed that the duo left the circus at this time.[134]

Back to Boston

I can see (Sweeney) in my mind now, as he stood upon the stage of Harrington's Museum, in striped pants and checked shirt, warbling old "Dandy Jim," etc., and playing the jig for John Diamond to dance by.... my recollections of seeing him dates back to about 1840 or 1842, this being the date your correspondent mentions.[135]

When Joe Sweeney and William Chestnut concluded their 1841 circus tour, Jonathan Harrington was ready for a repeat of their success from the previous year. Harrington contracted the team for an engagement during the week of Thanksgiving.[136] The weather wasn't very cooperative, but Sweeney's opening evening was greeted with a full house.[137]

At the end of two weeks, Joe Sweeney took his benefit[138] and moved over to the Tremont Circus a week later. With amusements at the museum, as well as two circuses in town, competition for the audience was intense. The Tremont, in close proximity to the location of the New York Circus (who had the minstrel dancer Dick Pelham in their employ[139]), attempted to draw away crowds by undercutting their prices.[140] The management also played on Sweeney's banjo playing, drawing comparisons to high art in poetics:

> Great Sweeny, hail! bending before thy shrine,
> I will essay thy skill to sing,
> For magic music thrills those cords of thine,
> Thou master of the Banjo-string.
> Let poets sing of Orpheus' famed lyre,
> Or Paganini's praises ring,
> More witching sweetness and melodious fire,
> Breathes softly from thy Banjo-string.[141]

At year's end, Sweeney's engagement was over,[142] and he left Boston for points south.

As 1841 concluded, Joe Sweeney's star continued to rise, as did that of the whole minstrel business. But, even as Sweeney experienced continued success, the number of Ethiopian imitators in general, and banjoists in specific, began to challenge Joe. There is no way to gauge Joe Sweeney's reaction to the rising popularity in the banjo that he had helped to foster, nor know how he felt as his students turned into the competition. One thing is for certain, that overseas markets had yet to be initiated into the American banjo, and Joe Sweeney was poised to be the one to do just that.

FOUR

On the Road in Great Britain

For some few years after [1839] the field of negro minstrelsy lay fallow. But about the year 1843 it suddenly sprang up with renewed vigour, as though the pause had done it good.... In the musical portion [of Sand's Company] the greatest attraction was supplied by Mr. Joseph Sweeney, "Negro Vocalist and Banjo Player." It was the first time the instrument was brought to the attention of the English public, and it "froze" on at once.[1]

When Joe Sweeney arrived in England during the late winter of 1842, he was performing for audiences well acquainted with American blackface performance, having seen some of America's best and most original. However, although they were familiar with the conventions of Rice et al, no one had presented the banjo and banjo songs in such a way as Sweeney did, and this uniqueness is where the Virginian was to have his biggest impact.

Joe Sweeney's first documented performances of 1842 were back in New York City with the rider Richard Sands at the Bowery Amphitheatre.[2] Sweeney joined the company that toured New England for June, Titus, Angevine & Company in 1841 as their "Circus and Caravan," and had been back in New York since mid–November.[3]

Joe stayed in New York from Monday, January 17,[4] until the end of the month, billed as bringing "this instrument to greater perfection than any other person in America."[5] William Chestnut appeared with Sweeney on at least two occasions during this stand. Another dancer, known as "the Buffalo Boy,"[6] John Van Brammer/Bramer,[7] made the group a trio.[8] Van Brammer replaced Chestnut as Sweeney's performing partner the following week, when the banjoist departed for Philadelphia.[9] On Tuesday or Wednesday, January 25 and 26 (or possibly both), Joe Sweeney took a benefit in preparation for his departure from New York. Sweeney's rising popularity resulted in printed announcements filled with superlatives.[10]

In Philadelphia on January 31, Sweeney and Van Brammer appeared with the New York Circus of Rufus Welch. It had become the Philadelphia Circus, and was in residence for the winter on Walnut Street, between Eighth and Ninth.[11] The circus must have thought highly of Joe Sweeney's abilities, because they already had the blackface singer John Smith on the bill.[12]

Back in New York, Sands had been preparing his circus for a tour of Great Britain since at least the beginning of the year.[13] On February 12, 1842, again with Richard Sands' company, Sweeney and Van Brammer performed for the last time in the United States. Then, it was off to England. New adventures and audiences lie ahead.[14]

This was an early opportunity for an American-style circus to show in the land of its ancestors. Although Isaac Van Amburgh, the American animal trainer, had been in British Isles since 1838, American circus performers were still a novelty.[15] As an added attraction,

Sands planned to introduce the canvas pavilion, developed in the United States, to British audiences.

Sands American Circus, with Joe Sweeney and Jack Van Brammer, boarded a ship in New York for the voyage to England. Although completely unverifiable, the following humorous story of the journey involves the banjoist and the dancer:

> During the voyage they encountered a most terrific storm, and everybody on board became panic-stricken. Indeed, so unrelentingly did the storm rage, that it was momentarily expected that all would be lost. Both Sweeney and Von Brimmer were frightened to such an extent, that the former asked the latter to pray, but he said, "Uncle Joe, I never prayed in my life, and don't know how, you pray, Uncle Joe." Well, said Sweeney, get on your knees, Jack. Both knelt down on the ship's deck, and Sweeney offered up a short, but seemingly effective prayer which ran thus: "O God, if Jack Von Brimmer and me has ever done anything wrong we ax your pardon." The storm at once ceased, and two hours later, Joe was playing the banjo, and Jack was doing a jig, both feeling so happy that the little prayer had been answered.[16]

Sweeney's British Tour

Sweeney landed at Liverpool with the Sands Circus troupe during March of 1842, and the company took up a month-long residence there, awaiting preparations of their rolling stock and portable amphitheater. From the beginning of their run, Sands' Circus tried to differentiate themselves from their European counterparts. They used "American" in their title and as often as possible in advertisements for the show: The horses were "American,"[17] the company was wholly made up of "American equestrians, voligeurs, and masters of the gymnastic art," and Sweeney was billed as "the American negro singer."[18] Although the equestrians got the most publicity, Sands pushed the fact that "Negro Songs accompanied on the Banjo" as well as "Wirginny Melodies and Breakdowns" were prominently featured,[19] unusual for British circuses of the time.

The reviews for Sands's Liverpool stay were overwhelmingly positive. After mentioning the large size of the audience, the *Courier and Commercial Advertiser* praised all the performers, and singled out Sweeney, saying that, "His instrumentation is excellent, and his self-possession, while the house was convulsed with laughter at his 'niggerisms,' was irresistibly comic. He was encored three times."[20] An unknown reporter commented, "Mr. Sweeny, with his banjo and Nigger songs, has become a prodigious favourite already, judging from the applause he receives from all parts of the house."[21] Another writer testified to the veracity of Sweeney and Van Brammer, adding, "that if they were not known to be of the 'pale faces,' they might pass off for genuine talented 'niggers.'"[22] During the company's final week of performances, *The Albion* hailed the American Circus and Joe Sweeny: "The entertainments of the American troop continue to attract crowded houses and to call forth loud approbation. The negro banjo-player nightly gains new popularity, and the numerous droll entertainments in which he appears are so many fresh provocations to laughter."[23]

On Sunday, April 24, their caravan and 2000-seat tents now ready, the Circus left Liverpool for St. Helens.[24] Liverpool, being a port city and one directly linked by ship to the United States, was predisposed toward American performers, especially the blackface minstrels. However, the American circus, with its portable pavilion, was designed to show in small, rural communities, which often had little or no contact with Americans and American entertainers, let alone the theaters of London. And, with the exception of Manchester and Leeds, Sands' show would go where none had gone before. It's hard to know who seemed stranger to whom, the performers to the audience or vice versa.

The show wended its way through many small towns, decamping in vacant lots or occasionally in a farmer's field. Notices in local newspapers appear from late April through the end of May, taking the circus through major centers including Manchester, Leeds, Nottingham, and Sheffield, along with smaller burgs. From here on, Sands Circus drops off the radar of surviving documentation. To be sure, the show toured northern England throughout the summer. They could have even made it to Scotland or other areas of the British Isles. One thing is definite, that by winter audiences in London got their first taste of Joe Sweeney's Ethiopian extravaganzas.

London

"Jim Crow Rice," with his amiable lady [daughter of Mr. Gladstane, proprietor of the Adelphi theatre, London] accompanied by two or three young "Crows," took their departure yesterday [sic] in the Great Western, seemingly in the best health and the highest spirits. We understand that several new pieces, adapted and expressly written for Mr. Rice's peculiar powers, will be produced during the ensuing season in London, and doubtless with as much success as the gentleman commanded on his former visit.[25]

Jim Crow in his New Place is another attempt to frame a piece for the purpose of Mr. Rice's personation. It is, perhaps, unfair to examine with any degree of rigour this style of farce, or to consider it otherwise than as a vehicle for the peculiarities of the actor. Even in this light, we cannot discover much merit of adaptation in the one-act labour of the concocter of Jumbo's Jum and his blunders.[26]

When Joel Sweeney arrived in London, T. D. Rice was already performing there. Rice had left New York City for his third (and last) British tour on November 17,[27] reaching England on December 7.[28] After a few weeks of relaxation and the renewing of old friendships, Rice was once more performing at London's Adelphi Theatre.[29]

Unlike Rice's two previous tours of Great Britain, this one went poorly. The press, in particular, was unusually unkind to Rice and Jim Crow. He opened with Yankee Notes For English Circulation, which the Spirit of the Times called "a comparative failure"[30] while another journal advised Rice "to keep his Yankee Notes in his pocket, they not being fit for English circulation."[31] When Tom Rice tried a comeback with Jim Crow in His New Place, the best the Atlas could call the play was a "vapid affair."[32] At the end of his run, the Theatrical Journal summed up the reviewers' reactions: "We are heartily tired of him and his unmeaning nigger songs." It was the beginning of the end for T. D. Rice. While he would continue to perform, Rice's time at center stage was concluding. After all, by the end of 1844, the Theatrical Journal would claim, "he has wheeled about and turned about 111,000 times."[33]

However, while Rice's star was beginning its decline, Sweeney's was on the way up. The newspapers in London compared the banjoist favorably to Tom Rice, preferring the Virginian's new (or, at least, new to them) form of minstrelsy. "Mr. Sweeney, a capital fellow, ... bids fair to be a formidable antagonist to Mr. Rice, of 'Jem [sic] Crow' notoriety," bragged John Bull.[34] Bell's Life called Sweeney "quite equal to our friend Rice, and somewhat more original,"[35] while back in America the Spirit of the Times noted that in London, "The great card just now is Sweeny, the Banjo player, who exceeds Jim Crow Rice, in popularity."[36]

Winter touring under canvas by horse and wagon made no sense in Britain's dreary weather. So, in early 1843, Richard Sands joined with the animal trainers Isaac A. Van Amburgh[37] and John Carter, taking up residency in London at the Royal Lyceum and English Opera House. Van Amburgh was one of the great characters in the early history of the American circus, famous for "training" his animals with a wallop on the head from a crowbar.

From 1838 until 1845, he appeared in Great Britain,[38] and became a favorite of Queen Victoria.[39]

On Friday, December 9, 1842, Van Amburgh entered London with a parade to publicize his upcoming shows at the Lyceum.[40] The Circus opened on Monday, January 16, combining the equestrians and minstrels of Sands' show with dramatic presentations starring Van Amburgh and Carter's lions and other animals, as well as a host of guest artists. Strangely, Jack Van Brammer is not mentioned in any publicity. Possibly his contract had run out and he was appearing elsewhere, or he was not considered enough of a draw to warrant a mention.[41] Interestingly, the acts showed on stage instead of in a normal ring set-up favored by the circus. Although unorthodox, it gave the audience a better view (according to the press) of the proceedings.[42]

Joseph Cave (October 1823–October 20, 1912)[43], a budding English Ethiopian, attended some of Sweeney's performances in London. In his autobiography, Cave describes Joe Sweeney's act at that time:

> In the musical portion [of Sands Company] the greatest attraction was supplied by Mr. Joseph Sweeney, "Negro Vocalist and Banjo Player." It was the first time the instrument was brought to the attention of the English public, and it "froze" on at once. Mr. Sweeney was accredited with its invention, and certainly he made it discourse most eloquently. This singer and instrumentalist discarded the usual "get up" of the former "niggers," who appeared in coats, vests, and smalls all tattered and torn—in short, veritable scarecrows—and attired himself in a costume at once spruce, picturesque, and characteristic, consisting of wide trousers, alternately striped white and red, a large fancifully coloured vest, a huge white collar on his shoulders, shirt sleeves, and a broad sombrero-looking straw hat…. Sweeney's manner and attire greatly aided his abilities as singer and dancer; it was, therefore, not long before he firmly fixed himself in public favour…. His dances were simple but fetching, and had the novelty about them of being accompanied by himself on the banjo.[44]

Cave's description highlights some of the differences between Joe Sweeney's act and those of other "Ethiopian delineators." Besides his main attraction of the banjo, Sweeney "discards" the "Jim Crow" costume for that more common to a circus performer. By inference, Joseph Cave also portrays Joe Sweeney's routine as less grotesque and stereotypical than other contemporary minstrels. This gave the Virginian an elegance that many other blackface actors lacked.

From the start, the London papers were unkind to Van Amburgh and Carter's attempts at animal dramas, complaining about the length and the wordiness of the dialogue. But Sweeney's song was "worth the price of admission."[45] Joe Sweeney also received compliments for the authenticity of his depictions.[46] Joe Sweeney continued to receive positive press into March.[47] On Wednesday, March 15, Van Brammer reappeared,[48] staying through the first week of the after season.[49]

After a final appearance on March 18, Van Amburgh headed for the North of England to spend the summer performing on the road.[50] Richard Sands stayed in London, leasing the Lyceum Theatre for another three weeks.[51]

In early April, the American Circus followed Van Amburgh out of London, but Joe Sweeney stayed on. Perhaps Sweeney's contract with June and Titus had expired, and, having been introduced to audiences through the circus's appearances during the previous year, the banjoist was ready to try England on his own. Joe was engaged by Mr. Davidge of the Surrey Theatre beginning on Easter Monday, performing there until the end of May.[52]

The first night, despite the holiday and good weather, the house was full and Sweeney was a favorite,[53] a response that continued throughout the week.[54] By the third week of his engagement, *The Dramatic and Musical Review* was able to print that:

LYCEUM ROYAL THEATRE
AND ENGLISH OPERA HOUSE.
AMERICAN AMPHITHEATRE

Under the PATRONAGE of
HER MOST GRACIOUS MAJESTY THE QUEEN.

REDUCED PRICES!

Dress Circle, 3s.   Upper Circle, 2s.   Pit 1s. 6d.   Gal. 1s.
Half-price to the Pit and Gallery at 9 o'Clock.
Private Boxes from £1. to £1 10s.

Last THREE NIGHTS.

On Thursday, April 6th, 1843,
And during the Week, the Performances will commence with the Favorite Burletta of

Mr. Sweeny, the Negro melodist, is a great favourite here, and deservedly so. His voice is a tenor of good compass, and the command he possesses over the instrument on which he accompanies himself is perfectly wonderful; at the same time, no effort is apparent in his execution, for he appears to be playing with the banjo instead of on it; add to this, an infinite fund of humour, which the assumption of the Negro gives such excellent opportunities for developing, and the laughable character of the melodies, and no one will be surprised to hear that the house echoes with laughter during his performance, or that he is encored four or five times every evening.[55]

During that time, the British music publishers D'Almaine and Company announced their publication of three of Joe Sweeney's songs. (D'Almaine and Company were instrument makers, music sellers, printers and publishers, located at 20 Soho Square in London from around 1834 until 1858. They were descended from various publishing concerns dating back to 1798.)[56] The cover illustrations are surprisingly realistic for the time, showing the obviously Anglo Sweeney wearing a tall, broad brimmed hat, a collared striped large sleeved shirt with a cravat around his neck, a checked vest, pants with wide dark stripes, dark shoes and dark make-up (compare this to Cave's description above). At the time, copyright law did not cover British sheet music, and so unauthorized editions of popular songs were common. In fact, at least one English "pirate" version of "Lucy Long" bearing Sweeney's name is known. In order to fight the illegal publications, the D'Almaine editions carry a warning about republication, as well as a facsimile of Joe Sweeney's signature, known to be accurate because it matches the only other extant document signed by the banjoist.

In his fourth week at the Surrey, Joe Sweeney "still continue[d] to prove an attraction,"[57] supposedly postponing the Virginian's planned trip to the hinterlands for another two weeks.[58] Saturday, May 27, was Sweeney's last night at the Surrey, and he departed London on his own for the provinces.[59] He left behind the seeds for British banjo playing. For the next two years, Joe Sweeney would expand his influence to the entire British Isles.

From Solo Star to Minstrel Troupe

During June of 1843, Joe Sweeney had been touring the English provinces, landing at the Adelphia Theatre in Edinburgh, Scotland, on Thursday, July 13.[60] Sweeney sang "His Popular Melodies, Accompanied by Himself on his Favourite Instrument the Banjo."[61] The theatre critic for the *Edinburgh Courant* commented on Sweeney's playing, "No one could have supposed, previous to hearing Mr Sweeny, that so much music could be extracted out of such an uncouth instrument."[62]

Just in time for Sweeney's benefit performance on July 24, ex–Virginia minstrel Frank Brower arrived in Edinburgh to join the company; he would perform with Sweeney until week's end (see Chapter Six for information about the Virginia Minstrels and Brower's early career). According to Dick Pelham, Brower and Sweeney then joined Cooke's Circus for other Scottish engagements.[63] Three weeks after their last show at the Adelphia, a poster for Monday, August 21, features a solo Frank Brower at the same theater in Edinburgh.[64]

What happened next is a mystery that is hard to unravel. American newspapers began carrying notices of Joe Sweeney's death. "Joe Sweeney, the celebrated Banjo player so well

Opposite: **Detail of Lyceum Theatre, London, program, April 6, 1843, from the "Last Three Nights" of dancer Jack Van Brammer and banjoist Joe Sweeney (by permission of the Folger Shakespeare Library).**

known throughout this country," reported the *New York Herald*, "has made an eternal bar rest. He died recently in London, whither he had gone on a starrling [sic] expedition. Alas."[65] But, Sweeney was very much alive. Had he suffered some unknown illness, or was Joe just touring the provinces, out of the eye of the major British and American publications? A playbill from his February 1844 stay in Liverpool, mentions that this reappearance is "after his long illness."[66] One possible explanation is that the press had confused Joe Sweeney with another member of Van Amburgh's Lyceum show, the acrobat John Aymar, who was killed during this time at the Jersey Theatre while executing a triple somersault, breaking his neck.[67]

When the Birmingham's Theatre Royal reopened on September 23,[68] Sweeney and Brower were back on the radar. From Monday, September 25, until Wednesday, October 4, "the Virginian Banjo and Bones" were a featured attraction. Their act combined elements of Sweeney's solo performances and the routines featured by Brower's former ensemble the Virginia Minstrels the previous spring.[69] However, unlike the Virginia Minstrels, who had developed their blackface act into a whole evening's concert, Joe Sweeney had continued to seek employment at theaters between the plays, or, as in Birmingham, on variety and circus bills containing multiple bits. Perhaps there were not enough performers capable of filling the roles of group members, or, Sweeney (who was not a songwriter like the Minstrels' Dan Emmett) lacked the depth of material for a whole group. A third possibility is that it was easier to continue presenting his act in familiar environments for promoters he already knew.

Reporters finally caught up to Joe Sweeney when he returned to London. "This celebrated banjo player is not dead," proclaimed the press, when he appeared in front of them at Batty's Amphitheatre.[70] His reported death was to continue to dog Joe Sweeney into 1844, when he wrote to the *Liverpool Chronicle* to correct this misimpression of his passing. In the only surviving document in his own voice, Sweeney writes:

> It having been reported that I had departed this life, you will oblige me by referring to any of the numerous and crowded audiences of the Theatre Royal as to the fact of my existence, and to assure my dear friend, the British public, that as long as I can live in the sunshine of its favour, which has hitherto been so bountifully bestowed upon me, I will not willingly quit this very agreeable world.
>
> The report of my death I find was only the prelude to a dramatic farce which is now [upset]ing at Belfast, Stockport, and other places where shallow pretenders are exhibiting as Banjo players in my name, to neither of which they have the least pretentions—I am, Sir, your obedient servant, J. W. Sweeny.[71]

This second paragraph, referring to "shallow pretenders" alludes to the slew of imitators (discussed in Chapter Thirteen) arising in the wake of Sweeney's success.

Sweeney and Brower presented London audiences with the same show that they had featured in Birmingham. When their engagement ended on Saturday, October 28,[72] an interesting item was printed that the banjoist was "to follow the example of Rice, and try the drama on his return to town, when he will appear in a character of a very novel nature though of a very common complexion."[73] Had this occurred (and it does not seem to have happened), it would have been a big change for the Virginian, possibly taking his career in

Opposite: Sheet music cover, "Where Did You Come From, Nock A Nigger Down," showing Joe Sweeney as he appeared "at the Theatre Royal English Opera House" in London during 1843. Note Sweeney's stage costume and signature at the lower right on each cover to testify to the authenticity and legality of this publication. D'Almaine, London, 1843 (British Library Reproductions).

a completely different direction. If Joe Sweeney had become an established character actor on the theatrical stage, the benefits could have been an increase in his livelihood and longevity in show business. Sweeney's place in minstrel history might have had better documentation and promotion during his lifetime, resulting in an increased visibility after his death.

Joe Sweeney had been a popular feature during Sands American Circus's Liverpool stands a year and a half previously, and he was welcomed back to the city in February 1844. On the tenth of the month, the banjoist opened as a part of a variety bill at Williamson Square's Theatre Royal.[74] On February 17, the *Liverpool Mail* reported of Sweeney, "He is an immense favourite with the 'Gods' and was three times encored."[75] Sweeney remained in Liverpool at the end of his engagement,[76] joining his old friends in the company of Richard Sands and Isaac Van Amburgh at the Amphitheatre sometime between Monday, February 25, and March 4.[77] Frank Brower rejoined Sweeney with his dancing and bones playing, drawing the comment that "But of all the amusements which the Amphitheatre now teems withal, commend us especially to the Nigger dance of Brower, accompanied by the banjo-playing of Sweeney.... Half-a-dozen encores ... nightly inflict their pleasurable pains on Brower; and Sweeney comes in for a large share of the uproarious applause of the audience."[78] Sweeney and his partner took their benefit on Monday, March 25, their program showing no change from the previous fall.[79] The show closed on March 30.[80]

After a spring tour with the reconstituted Virginia Minstrels in Ireland and Scotland (discussed in Chapter Six), Brower and Sweeney returned once again to Liverpool, the city of their biggest success. From Monday, July 22,[81] through Friday, August 16,[82] "THE GREAT ORIGINAL Banjo Player" and "the far-famed representative of the American Negro Character" held forth at the Royal Amphitheatre between the various theatrical presentations.[83] For Sweeney's benefit on July 31, the "English Jim Crow" John Dunn was added to the bill.[84] *The Albion* praised Sweeney and Brower,[85] and the *Liverpool Standard* mentioned the positive audience response given the pair. They took their benefit on August 14,[86] and moved over to the Theatre Royal for a few days during the last week of August.[87]

Brower then left for the United States.[88] For the moment, Joe Sweeney remained in Britain, soldiering on either as a solo or in conjunction with other performers. Supposedly, Joe was heading for London when he appeared Friday and Saturday, October 11 and 12, at Nottingham's Assembly Rooms.[89] The banjoist also rejoined Van Amburgh's Circus for area appearances[90] in Nottingham during December.[91] Sweeney then joined Richard Sands' traveling circus show at the beginning of 1845, which was featured at Liverpool's Theatre Royal and Modern Arena of Arts.[92] Sands opened on the week of January 13,[93] and Sweeney, billed once again as "the Original Banjo Player," appeared on the following Monday.[94]

During this engagement, Sweeney faced stiff competition from a British minstrel group, the Southern American Minstrels Woolcott, Robbins, Parker and Ring, who were working for William Batty at Astley's Royal Amphitheatre. Luckily, their run only overlapped Sweeney's for between one and two weeks (they opened around January 11 and left sometime during the week of January 27).[95] The programs of the American Minstrels show the influence of the Virginia Minstrels, featuring songs of Dan Emmett's such as "Dance, Boatman, Dance," "Old Dan Tucker," "Goin ober de Mountain" and "De Fine Old Coloured Gemman."

In Liverpool, Joe Sweeney once again received good press and a positive audience reception.[96] On Monday, January 27, Dick Pelham (see Chapter Six) joined Sweeney.[97] Joe Sweeney took his own benefit on Friday, February 7, abetted by Pelham, and Sands' circus company.[98] On Saturday, Sweeney and Pelham's last day in Liverpool, the duo "Personated ... Emancipated Niggers."[99]

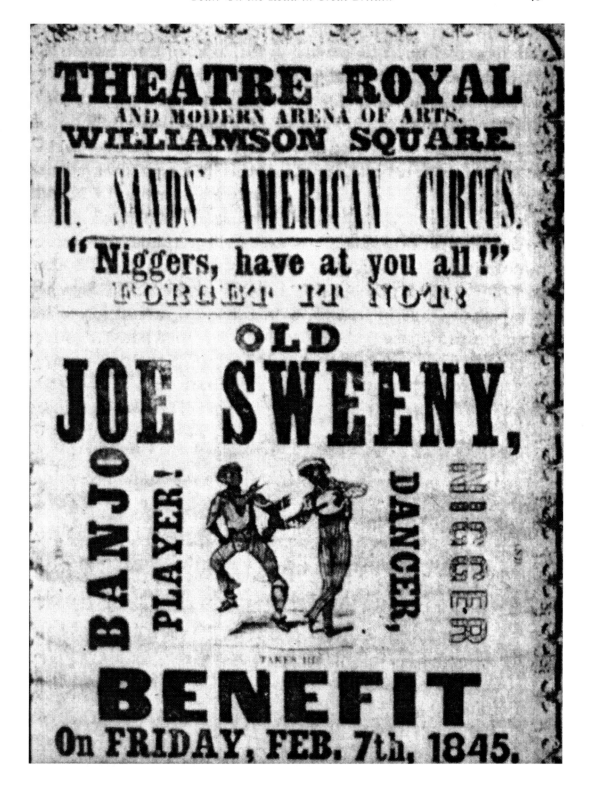

Detail of theatrical program, Theatre Royal, Liverpool, England, from February 7, 1845. The graphic shows the dancer Dick Pelham and the banjoist, Joe "Sweeny."

Joe Sweeney and Dick Pelham then went their separate ways. Joe left Sands and rejoined Van Amburgh, appearing in Sheffield at the end of the month.[100] Sweeney may have also played Nottingham, with or without Van Amburgh.[101] By the end of March, Joe Sweeney joined Mr. and Mrs. H. Webb in Birmingham. The Webbs were apparently based at Birmingham's Theatre Royal, and Mr. Webb (his first name is unknown) had been singing Ethiopian songs like "Jim Along Josey" and "Coal Black Rose" since 1841.[102] On Monday, April 7, Sweeney took his benefit and made his last appearances.[103] Sometime in the next month, Joe Sweeney concluded his British residency, and was back in the United States by the end of May 1845.[104]

> Joe Swinney (colored banjoist) was well known to a family that moved from a town, then called Germanton, to Banner Elk, in 1857, when I was only 3 yrs. old.
>   Following the Civil War, my school teacher, a Confederate soldier [Calvin Kime], just from in, or near, Germanton, told me that Joe Swinney had gone to London, plaid [sic] the banjo for Victoria and received from her as a present, a banjo worth, or that cost, $2,500.00.[105]

A number of stories have emerged from Joe Sweeney's years in the United Kingdom. Civil War historian Burke Davis claims that "Sweeney remained in England [after his tour with Sands in 1842–3] as a kind of strolling troubador, [sic] giving banjo concerts in the homes of the nobility," and performed for the Queen of England.[106] Cole amplified this assertion, writing that:

> Commanded to appear before [Queen Victoria's] court, [Joe Sweeney] so pleased Her Royal Highness she offered him a position as entertainer.... The Queen understood and heaped gifts upon the minstrel. Before he left London, the Queen had a suit made for him, the buttons which adorned it, being of gold.
>   There is said to be in existence a beautiful instrument that Her Majesty presented to the music maker, a banjo of rare wood inlaid with ivory. Other gifts which are still treasured by descendants are a money belt which shows clearly the imprint of gold coins from the royal treasury, and is now in the hands of D.A. Conner of Appomattox.[107]

However, no newspaper coverage or playbill has been discovered that would place Sweeney in the same theater as the Queen and nobility, or in any houses of the dukes and earls of Great Britain. It is most likely that, because Isaac Van Amburgh was a special favorite of Victoria's, historians have assumed that the Queen saw and admired Sweeney in his appearances with the company of the animal trainer. English theater historian George Rowell mentions that Van Amburgh and his lions first showed before the Queen during Christmastime of 1838. But Rowell lists no appearance of Van Amburgh's where both Sweeney and Victoria were in attendance. Another possibility is that Sweeney appeared in a command performance at Windsor Castle during a summer tour of the circus. The animal trainer did show in Windsor during July 1844 while the Queen was at the Castle, but she was in the late stages of a pregnancy, and did not attend. During this visit, Van Amburgh sent the clown Wallett over with two lion cubs to show the Queen, but Joe Sweeney is not mentioned as accompanying the animals. English theater historian George Rowell has written a book about the Queen's theatrical attendance based on Victoria's papers and journals kept in the Royal Archives. Nowhere in this work is Joe Sweeney, nor any other minstrel, mentioned. I was not allowed to examine the Royal Archives myself, but a search by the Deputy Registrar yielded no further information about the Queen and the banjoist.[108]

Davis also wrote that the English "tour was so lucrative that Joe soon returned home to retire," only resuming performing because he missed the spotlight.[109] This statement, and those about Queen Victoria showering the banjoist with money and gifts, seems fanciful at best. Although a money belt with a Sweeney provenance did at one time exist, neither suit nor a banjo like those described above survive.

Joe Sweeney, unlike T.D. Rice or the minstrel groups of the 1840s, worked for circus shows or on theatrical variety bills during his British sojourn. Given the financial limitations of dividing the take among a large number of acts, it would have been highly unusual if Sweeney had emerged from his three years overseas a wealthy man. And, rather than "retire" from performing when he was back in the United States, as we shall see, Joe Sweeney went immediately back to work.

However, historians have continued to reprint such stories about Joe Sweeney performing for the Queen. Why would anyone want to perpetuate such myths? The indirect descendants of Sweeney—from his sisters and cousins—have shown a propensity toward elevating their social status and that of their famous relative, so, perhaps this is a result of that impulse. Joe Sweeney (and other performers of the day) played in theaters labeled "Royal" throughout the British Isles, and this may have added to the confusion. Other minstrel performers, such at Tom Rice, did captivate British royalty, and were invited to their social events and into their homes. Perhaps Sweeney's supposed association with the royals was based on the actions of others. At best, Joe Sweeney may have indeed rendered his songs for Queen Victoria, and the evidence has yet to emerge.

FIVE

Back in the United States: Touring with a Minstrel Band and Final Days

Joe Sweeney was considered the greatest banjo player at that time.... At dancing the jig, the break-down and the old Virginia reel, he was among the best, and there was no one who could "cut the pigeon wing" like him.[1]

Joe Sweeney arrived back in the United States during May of 1845. Maybe he got home-sick, or had "played" out the venues in Great Britain. Possibly Frank Brower had contacted him or made a prior arrangement to work together.

Whatever the case, Sweeney was greeted by a confusing collection of minstrel groups with similar sounding names and rotating members. Newspapers and playbills from the decade list a dizzying array of bands, including any number of Minstrels, Melodists, Sere-naders, and Harmonists. They were African, Ethiopian, Guinea, Congo, Negro and Sable, United States, Columbian, Metropolitan, and Southern, from Virginia, Kentucky, Alabama, Carolina, and Georgia. They were juveniles and adults, men and women.

Sweeney accepted an engagement within the familiar confines of the circus with his old partner Francis Brower (see Chapter Four). Since the previous fall, when Frank Brower had been in New York City, the bones player had toured up and down the East Coast (Brower appeared during February 1845 with Robinson and Foster's National Circus for their last night in Savannah).[2] Upon the banjoist's return, Sweeney and Brower joined forces in New York City, appearing for the last few days of May at the New Bowery Theater.[3] Within twenty-four hours, the duo had crossed the Hudson River to Newark, joining up with the second unit of Welch & Mann's Mammoth Circus.[4] Perhaps arrangements had been made before his return from Europe, and Sweeney had reappeared in order to keep this commitment.

After a few days in Newark, the company boated up the Hudson to Albany, where Welch & Mann opened on Monday, June 9.[5] They faced competition from Howe's show.[6] To complicate matters further, the first unit of Welch & Mann's circus was touring the Rochester area, which featured banjoist Neil Jamieson, minstrel vocalist Tony Winnemore, and dancer John Diamond.[7] But Welch was well prepared, headlining Sweeney and Brower's unidentified "Band of Sable Minstrels" in their pavilion "capable of holding four thousand people."[8] Anyway, the Albany run was short, and Welch & Mann was on the road after two days, heading west along the top of New York State and into Canada.[9] Their tour ended back in the state capital on Saturday, October 4.[10]

When Welch & Mann sent their company to Brazil for the winter, Joe Sweeney and Frank Brower headed south. On Monday, December 1, "the great original Banjo Player ... having returned from a most successful tour through England, Ireland and Scotland," made an engagement to appear for a week between the acts at the Richmond Theater with his companion Brower.[11] It was then onto Joe's homecoming in Lynchburg. The newspaper played up his area associations by billing him as "a native born Virginian, reared in old Buckingham [soon to be Appomattox County]," and continued how:

> after an absence of several years in Europe, where he performed to the astonishment of the Crowned heads there, he has returned among us, and will make his original Virginia instrument gladden the hearts of our citizens and convulse their sides with laughter. He has with him Frank Brower the greatest Ethiopian extravaganza extant.—Go and see them tonight.[12]

This tour was the last for Sweeney and Brower as a duo. By the summer, Frank Brower was back with one of Welch & Mann's shows, joining forces with Neil Jamieson for tours during 1846 and 1847.

Sweeney, it appears, remained in the South. As the next fifteen years unfolded, Joe increasingly based himself in Appomattox. For the remainder of his life, records of his comings and goings diminish, making his bookings harder to track. Except for one suspicious reference, known listings of Joe Sweeney's appearances show him reaching no farther north than Baltimore.

From the scant information available, it is difficult to judge the extant of Sweeney's touring. He may have been constantly on the road or laid over at home for extended periods. Additionally, he would increasingly depend upon his brothers and other local performers to help him fulfill engagements. Recognizing the popularity of minstrel groups over soloists, Joe formed one by the later part of the 1840s.

If Sweeney wouldn't come to New York and the center of minstrelsy, the minstrels would come to him. It was just a short hop from Washington, D.C., to Richmond, Petersburg, and Lynchburg. This proximity created many opportunities for reunions between Joe and his compatriots in minstrelsy, and for the banjoist to be honored by up-and-coming performers.

> For the last four or five days the boys, (and some of the men, too,) of our town, have stood tip-toe to see Sweeny, the celebrated Banjo player. Rumor has had him in five miles of Milton, [this/last?] week, at least—and night after night had been fixed upon for him to "show" in Milton—Last Tuesday night brought with it a grand hoax—report was current [that] Sweeny had sent a Message to the landlord of our Hotel that he would be here precisely at 8 o'clock, P.M. and that he wished to find the Tavern Hall brilliant [?] his arrival, as he wished to give a touch of his music. A little after dark, accordingly some wag, who'd doubtly gave the Tavern keeper a significant wink, 'lighted [up] the hall and rang the bell—and such a rush! is [?] made for the Tavern by the show-going folks [?] hooped and hallowed "Sweeny's come!" The darkies ran hither and tither to collect four pence debts, by why of "raising the wind." to go to the show. "Where's Sweeny?"—was now the tumultuous cry of the congregated crow. "Who keeps the door?" enquired [?]—"Take my quarter and let me in," roared another "It's a water haul, by thunder," shouted a third—we believe the whole crowd dispersed, finally satisfied that they were gentenly hoaxed. Who did it is a mystery.[13]

During 1846, Joe Sweeney traveled Virginia's south side as a soloist, performing courthouse shows in conjunction with a magician named Averett. He is reported as playing during the Halifax and Charlotte courts "to crowded houses with great applause," and may have made it into North Carolina as well. In fact, just the rumor of an appearance at the Hotel Tavern Hall in Milton, North Carolina, caused a large crowd to gather and nearly riot (see above).[14] The banjoist and the magician also appeared at Petersburg's Mechanic's Hall, just south of Richmond and due east of his Appomattox home, for two days in early September. During this appearance, the press played up Joe's return to the South: "after an absence of several years, during which time he has not only played in all the Cities of the North, but has been received with the most enthusiastic applause on the other side of the Atlantic, having visited most of the towns and cities of Great Britain."[15] Perhaps he continued the same pattern for 1847, but references to his performances for the year have not yet emerged. The next mention of Sweeney occurs in mid–1848, when he provided "a band of Music" for the Fourth of July celebration at Appomattox Courthouse, then still known as Clover Hill.[16]

By the fall of 1848, Sweeney had put together a minstrel company, and toured the area around his home. One of the performers was another local, tambourinist William Parrow (circa 1828–November 29, 1870).[17] Parrow was playing in blackface as early as the previous year, when he appeared in Lynchburg as a member of "The Sable Melodists." Other members of Parrow's former group included Cool White (aka: John Hodges, July 28, 1821–April 23, 1891), and, although not mentioned in the newspaper coverage, anecdotal evidence places Joe Sweeney's two brothers, Dick and Sam, with The Sable Melodists as well.[18]

The two other members of Sweeney's troupe were the bones player Master Berry and "J. A. Sweeney" on violin.[19] This member of Joe's family (if indeed this fiddler were really a Sweeney), most logically would be Joe's younger brother Richard Alexander. (Advertisements from later that year list the violinist as "Mr. A. Sweeney, old Joe's brother," which would presumably mean "Alex," that is, Richard Alexander.) Just twenty years old, Dick was never known as a fiddler, but possibly was taught the minimal skills necessary by his sibling to convince an audience.[20]

Joe Sweeney's younger brother Dick Sweeney, portrait done probably in the 1850s and copied in 1890.

For three days during the week of September 18, 1848, "Old Joe Sweeny, as he is familiarly called," brought his "band of Virginia Minstrels" to Mechanics' Hall in Petersburg.[21] On Friday and Saturday, Joe took "his celebrated band of Sable Harmonists" north to Richmond's Odd Fellows' Hall.[22] And, in October, Sweeney's Sable Harmonists occupied the Masonic Hall of Lynchburg, where he and Parrow were well known. "The most conspicuous members of the band are the celebrated and Ral personifiers [sic] of the Southern negro," wrote the Lynchburg Virginian:

Wm. Parrow and old Virginia Joe Sweeny, the later of whom is said to the best performer on the banjo that the world has ever produced. The music which flows from this instrument, when he is playing a solo, is at least equal, if not superior, to that of any which we have ever heard on the piano. Parrow's performances on the Tamborine are truly wonderful, and he richly deserves the reputation which he has acquired for himself, of being the most correct delineator of the negro character in the United States, not only in his actions and laughter-provoking speeches, but in his personal appearance.

By this time, Joe Sweeney had added a fifth member to his troupe, dancer J. [possibly John[23]] Sherman. Bill Parrow was advertised as bringing Sherman "from the North" to join the company.[24]

According to the Virginia papers, the troupe was beginning a southern tour, heading towards New Orleans, although there is no documentary evidence for their appearing south of Charleston.[25] On November 1 and 2, "For Only Two Nights, ... The Band Of Sable Harmonists" with Joe Sweeney at the helm, held forth in the City Hall of North Carolina's capital, Raleigh.[26] It's also possible that a performance in Chapel Hill occurred during this tour. According to Dr. Kemp P. Battle, the author of a University of North Carolina chronicle, Sweeney and company's influence was felt for several years. Following their concert, the banjo and the bones were taken up by students to accompany such minstrel favorites as "'Old Uncle Ned,' [Stephen Foster, 1848] 'I'm Come From Alabama,' [Stephen Foster, circa 1848] 'A Little More Cider,' [Hart Austin, 1853] 'Dearest Mae,' [James Power of the Harmoneons, 1847, see Chapter Nine] 'We'll Have A Little Dance,' [1848] and 'Rosin, the Beau.'"[27]

Three weeks later, Sweeney and his group occupied Temperance Hall in coastal Charleston, South Carolina. They joined with another band of "Sable Harmonists," the "Original Southern Troupe," for these shows.[28] This other similarly named minstrel band dates back at least to September 1846, when their banjoist William Fish appeared for three days with "a company of 'Sable Harmonists'" at the St. Louis Theater.[29] The two Charleston papers heaped superlatives on the heads of the combined troupe, and one assumes that the run was a successful one.[30] Unfortunately, no itineraries or coverage exists for the rest of Sweeney's tour.

For the first half of 1849, Joe Sweeney's group was back on home turf. Sweeney had assumed the billing previously used by the "other" Sable Harmonists ("Original Great Southern Band of"), and added one of their members, flutist R. Moore, into his company. Joe had given up on his brother becoming a fiddler, instead assuming the violin duties himself and moving Dick to second banjo. The Sables' program at Petersburg's Odd Fellows Hall January 29, 30, and 31 reflected the metamorphosis that minstrelsy was undergoing. Along with the usual "Negro Melodies, Rapartees [sic], Witicizms [sic] and Plantation Dancing and Singing" were "Selections from the best composers, Parodies from the most popular Operas" and "Burlesque Polkas."[31] This shift was also apparent several months later, when Sweeney's minstrels also appeared in "white character," meaning that non-blackface, non-minstrel material was also a part of their presentation.

Once again, the Lynchburg newspaper ballyhooed Joe Sweeney and his tambourine-playing partner Bill Parrow to the public, while noting that the audience had been thin for their previous engagement. Joe was still fiddling with his band, and, as the only other musician mentioned is Parrow, it is unsure if the group's membership was the same (another Lynchburg appearance, this time in July at the Universalist Church, also fails to give Sweeney and Parrow's group member's individual faces).[32] It is likely that Sweeney and Parrow hired whichever local residents and family members they could corral to fill out the band.

When the Sable Minstrels performed in Tennessee at the end of 1849, Parrow's name was at the top of the advertisements, with Sweeney on banjo, D.A. Gates on bells, and J.M. Melton on flute, and the group was moving further away from the style of blackface entertainment pioneered by Joe Sweeney and his ilk—if they appeared in blackface at all. Most of the surviving advertisement call Parrow's group the "Harmoneans," relating their "concert" to more of a musical variety show than one of the minstrel variety. And, obviously, the only instrument exclusive to the minstrel show in the Harmoneans was the banjo.[33] There were still ties to the minstrel shows of the Virginia variety, as "the whole [evening was] to conclude with the Plantation Festival."[34] However, at least with this ensemble, Bill Parrow was becoming more and more like the "minstrels" (ie: singing groups) for which these bands were namesakes.

The tour went in the westward direction, as Parrow's troupe played Knoxville November 12 to 14, heading through "lower East Tennessee" before performing in Nashville[35] a month later. There, Parrow's group joined forces with the Ventriloquist Col. I.B. Hardy to benefit the local Protestant Orphan Asylum, and raised $110.10 for the orphans.[36] Joe Sweeney may have been a part of Parrow's band for their Tennessee sojourn. One advertisement triumphs "Sweeny, the great Banjo player" as one of Parrow's associates,[37] while others indicate that the Sweeney mentioned was Joe's brother Richard.[38]

> Mr. Editor:—The dull times of Lynchburg have been broken in upon most unceremoniously during the last week by that arch-enemy of ennui—Bill Parrow. Has he not respect for the phelinks [sic] of our quiet and sober (in the morning) Lynchburgers [sic]? He and Old Joe Sweeney have ruthlessly broken in upon our established sobriety and quiet, in a manner that has provoked the ire of the father of Blues to an irreconcilable extent. What is to be done with him? Bill Parrow has done the same thing, to the writer's certain knowledge, in Richmond, Petersburg, Norfolk and Portsmouth, in times past, (but not so long ago as to be forgotten) and the citizens of these cities felt it incumbent upon them as lovers of peace and order, to give him some kind of expression to the public feeling. I propose that he be treated in like manner by us, in this way:—.... Parrow has, by unexampled industry, worked himself up to the highest point in his profession, and he has returned to his old home, not so much to win the money of his friends, as to prove to them the good result of industry and perserverance [sic] [signed] Paul Pry.[39]

By 1850, Joel Walker Sweeney was settling into his life in Appomattox County, Virginia. He joined the local militia, and was elected First Lieutenant of Company Six, First Battalion of the 174th Regiment at the end of April. Sweeney was promoted two years later, and he finished out his three years of service in 1853.[40] When the census was gathered in late July, Joe was noted as living with his parents, along with his brothers Alexander (i.e., Dick) and Sampson (Sam). All the brothers were listed as "musician."[41]

No appearances by Sweeney are documented during 1850, with the next known engagements occurring in January 1851 in nearby Richmond. As the years progressed, it becomes increasingly evident that Joe was playing any area gigs he could, solo if he could manage or with whatever group he could assemble. Luckily, both his brothers were capable musicians and performers, and often were available for his employ.

Sweeney and Bill Parrow had once again joined forces, bringing their "Celebrated Band of Virginia Minstrels" to the Richmond Theater several times at the end of January and in early February 1851.[42] Besides Parrow and the eldest Sweeney, the group included Joe's two brothers and possibly Frank Johnson. "Their Celebrated Operatic Extravaganzas" were in the form of the evolving "minstrel show." Parrow is reported to have led his own group with John Lacy, Tim Hays, and John P. Smith (see below) on bones at area appearances during the same year, although there is no documentation to support this contention.[43]

It is also probable that Joe Sweeney performed in Danville, Virginia, during the 1850s. Harry Wooding, a prominent figure in Danville politics, remembers seeing the banjoist, along with his brother Richard "and two others," perform in the Masonic Hall. The show Wooding describes is similar to the performances of the original Virginia Minstrels, with Sweeney's company of fiddle, banjo, tambourine, and bones sitting in "split bottom chairs ... [with] no curtains or scenery."[44]

After this Richmond appearance, it is almost two years until Sweeney again surfaces, this time in Baton Rouge, Louisiana. There must have been performances for several months on either side of his engagement, but no advertisements or newspaper accounts have been found. "Old Joe Sweeny and His Original Virginia Minstrels," personnel unnamed, gave two shows at Baton Rouge's Harney House Saloon on December 28 and 29, 1852.[45] Meanwhile, Bill Parrow was leading his "Jenny Lind Minstrels" at Lynchburg's Masonic Hall on January 14, 1853, without Joe's assistance.[46]

Joe Sweeney hadn't given up on touring, but there aren't many known appearances for the banjoist from the mid–1850s. Sweeney made the short trip to Washington, D.C., in August 1854. Calling his group the Virginia Minstrels, he played the Odd Fellows' Hall from Thursday through Saturday, August 17 to 19. Guitarist D.C. Price shared the bill, but it is unclear if he was a part of Sweeney's group.[47] Thursday and Friday of the following week, Sweeney occupied Baltimore's Carroll Hall. Correctly billed as "his first appearance in this city for thirteen years," Joe Sweeney and Newcomb's "Southern Serenaders" (i.e. Campbell's Minstrels) played to benefit George W. Harvey. Sweeney "appear[ed] in some of his original and unrivalled [sic] Solos, giving a history of his trip across the Atlantic to and through England, and his return to Old Virginia."[48] The following week, "Old Joe Sweeney, the Pagunini [sic] of banjo players," played Petersburg.[49]

One other account has surfaced relating to Sweeney during this period. In the fall of 1855, S.S. Sanford left his main minstrel company in Philadelphia and took a touring ensemble South. At Lynchburg's Dudley Hall, "Mr. Sweeney, The Old Virginia Banjoist," joined Sanford, R.J. Turner, and Vicenzo Amici on Turner's benefit night. Obviously, Joe Sweeney was still a local draw, and was regarded by Sanford as an honored guest.[50]

Meanwhile, Bill Parrow continued to pursue bookings without the help of his Sweeney neighbors. He appears to have stayed close to home with His Southern Burlesque Opera Troupe, as he was now calling his ensemble, with numerous performances in 1854 at halls in Lynchburg, Richmond, and Petersburg.[51] In 1855, Parrow folded his organization into "Jullien's Minstrels." The next year, Joe Sweeney rejoined Bill Parrow's troupe, then up to ten members.[52] Besides Parrow, this included R. Jean Buckley (aka: Alexander W. Moody; born November 24, 1834),[53] a banjoist and guitarist from Williamsburg, Virginia; and Frank Weston (see below), tambo, from the old group. The Julliens appeared on March 9 and 10, 1857, at the Masonic Hall in Edgefield, South Carolina. After discussing the decent size and good reaction of the audience, the *Advertiser* reviewed the performance:

> The entertainment of last night was extremely rich. "Old Bob Ridley" and the "Rail Road Smash-up" were abundantly amusing. Mr. [R.J.] Buckley, in "The Grave of Uncle True," did admirably; and Bill Parrow was good in every thing. Old Joe Sweeny with his Banjo was, as usual, perfectly in town. Indeed the entire performances were uncommonly fine, and deserve to be heard by every one. With one or two exceptions the evening was marked by good order; and the acting was in good taste in every respect. Ho! For the Julliens to-night![54]

Parrow's Original Jullien Minstrels were working their way north, and arrived in mid–April in the border city of Charlotte, North Carolina, for two performances, and then traveled to Salisbury.[55] Parrow and Sweeney arrived back home in Lynchburg in May, with four nights at Dudley Hall. To beef up attendance, they employed two standard (and long-lived) schemes. First, they advertised that the troupe was "now en route North, prior to their departure for Australia." This was probably just a ploy to build excitement, as there is no evidence that the troupe ever toured down under. Second, on their last night in Lynchburg, the Minstrels offered patrons a special bonus by giving away "Two Hundred Dollars worth of Valuable Presents."[56] After closing in Lynchburg, it was immediately on to Richmond's Metropolitan Hall for six nights. The Enquirer noted, "Old Joe Sweeney, king of Banjo players, ... and Parrow's famous song of 'run nigger, run,' is of itself worth the price of admission."[57] On Monday, June 1, the Julliens again presented a "Gift Concert," offering double the amount of "watches, bracelets, breastpins, rings and other jewelry" given away in Lynchburg. The Troupe also presented T.D. Rice's "Opera of 'O Hush!'"[58] The following evening's performance was given in "Joint Benefit of Old Joe Sweeney, The originator of the Banjo and Frank Weston, The favorite 'Brudder Bones.'"[59] Weston, the stage name for John Pemberton Smith (August 3, 1832–November 12, 1897), was born in Richmond and had possibly worked with Sweeney and Parrow on and off since the 1840s.[60]

By early November 1857, Joe had apparently left Jullien's Minstrels to reorganize his own "Opera Troupe," recruiting the brothers Harry and W. Penn Lehr as well as Paul Berger from the Melodeon Star Troupe, along with their compatriot in Kunkel's Minstrels, Billy Birch.[61] This could have been the same group, with the addition of Sweeney, billed as "Billy Birch's Ethiopian Minstrels" which played Richmond's Metropolitan Hall and Phoenix Hall in Petersburg during the first two weeks of October.[62] The only documented appearance for this collection of performers was November 5 through 7, at Lynchburg's Dudley Hall.[63]

By the end of 1857, Joe and Bill Parrow were back together for a tour of Georgia. On Wednesday and Thursday, December 16 and 17, "Old Joe Sweeny & Co. Great Burlesque Opera Troupe! And Southern Minstrels!" appeared in Atlanta[64] and made a New Year's engagement in Columbus, Georgia. This band, "Parrow & Sweeney's Great Southern Burlesque Opera Troupe," was a thinly disguised group of Sweeney (Joe, Dick, and Sam) and Parrow (Bill and "Mast.") family members.[65]

> Sweeney, as a negro delineator, was inimitable. He knew the negro well and was perfectly natural.... One of his performances always excited applause.... His habits were improvident and he was the subject of many temptations. He lived a life of unselfish generosity and died in poverty.[66]
>
> Negro minstrelsy has scarcely reached the perfection or the purity of which all musical effort is susceptible, simply because the great majority of those who attempt to make that branch of musical attainment a profession, forget to study the peculiarity of the negro character. That is full of music and rich wit; and is as susceptible of correct delineation as are the peculiarities of any people.[67]
>
> The heyday of [minstrelsy] has passed, and none now prosper except the very best.[68]

The three Sweeney brothers and their company reappear during the fall and winter of 1858–59. Winter was not the best time for a minstrel group to be heading north, especially one based in southern Virginia. Perhaps a theater owner had made them an enticing offer, or there were bills to be paid that needed immediate attention. Regardless of the reason, the Sweeney boys departed for Washington, D.C. They stopped in Fredericksburg on the way, giving their performances for "crowded audiences at the Planters' House" Hotel before leasing the Citizens' Hall for Saturday, November 20, 1858.[69] By this time, the three Sweeneys carried seven other entertainers, including the Virginian R. Jean Buckley with whom Joe had worked in the Jullien's (see above), and Frank Johnson, rumored to be with the Virginia banjoist in 1851. George Herbert, Mr. Woodland, Tim Morris, Mons Sol, and D.C. Boyd rounded out the troupe.[70]

The following Monday, Old Joe Sweeney's Burlesque Opera Troupe began its Washington, D.C., engagement at Melodeon Hall on the south side of Pennsylvania Avenue between ninth and tenth streets.[71] Saturday, November 27, was Dick Sweeney's benefit night.[72] By Monday, December 20, the Sweeneys had traveled down the peninsula to Norfolk[73] and then, during the last week of the year, the Burlesque Opera Troupe, as Joe and company were being billed, was in Petersburg. Dick was heralded as "The Champion Banjoist of the World!," and attendance was good. "Their motto is 'fun without vulgarity;'" wrote *The Press*, "so all who wish to enjoy a little innocent amusement, will not fail to be present."[74]

However, problems began to occur in the New Year. In Baltimore, unusually cold weather caused the gas fixtures in the theater to freeze, and the Minstrels first performance on Tuesday, January 11, 1859, had to be canceled. Fortunately, only one night was missed, and the show ran for the remainder of the week.[75] The Sweeney troupe then returned to Washington, where they performed until at least Thursday, January 27, when advertisements ceased.[76] On February 10, suddenly and seemingly unexpectedly, the middle brother Dick Sweeney passed away at a Washington boarding house. The newspapers reported the cause as "a brief illness, ... from hemorrhage of the lungs," which could have been caused by a long-term disease such as tuberculosis or lung cancer.[77] Dick was the third family member to die within the same number of years; the brothers' paternal grandmother had passed away in 1856, and the Sweeneys had lost their father, John, on December 16, 1857, "by a fall."[78] This could not have been an easy time for his surviving brothers. With the exception of a benefit for Joe and Sam Sweeney in memory of Dick on Tuesday, February 15,[79] there are no other documented performances for this group. Nor are there any further known joint appearances by the two remaining minstrel siblings.

> A desultory talk springs up, mainly about the Harper's Ferry affair. Billy Ivvins swears that an attempt will be made to rescue "old Brown."
> By the time we reach a snug little bachelor establishment, the stars are sparkling in the skies, and we are warm as toasts from the rapid two mile walk. Supper is soon served. We partake of it sparingly and go to Farmville to hear old Joe Sweeny. We find that the old fellow has let down; but he is welcome to our small change for the sake of what he used to be when he was young and in his prime.
> After the concert is over we repair to the Randolph House.... it is the night before election day.... We return to the bachelor establishment, and about eleven o'clock sit down to a magnificent flat-back supper.[80]

Joe Sweeney returned home to Appomattox and continued to sporadically perform in the general area. He is known to have appeared in conjunction with a "Mr. Shakespeare, the Vocalist and Ventriloquist, and delineator of character" at Petersburg's Phoenix Hall on Saturday, November 5, 1859. This "benefit" night for Joe cost only twenty cents to attend, five cents lower than the usual lowest price for presentations of this type.[81] Anecdotal evidence also suggested that he also performed in Farmville around this time. It is interesting that the viewers felt that the skills of the banjoist were in decline, as perhaps Joe was already showing the signs of the illness that would take his life the following year (conflicting facts within the narrative make it unclear if this concert occurred in 1860, as claimed, or in 1859; see above).[82]

The year 1860 was not a good one for the Sweeney family. With war clouds looming on the horizon, rather than joining another minstrel troupe, Sam was staying close to home. Joe and Sam's mother, Tabitha Sweeney, died of old age on January 16[83] and by the time of the census in July of that year, both Joe and Sam Sweeney, listed as "Bangerman" (meaning banjo player), were living alongside their sisters Missouri and Elizabeth in the household of Elizabeth's husband, Allen Conner.[84]

Joe's health had been failing over the last year. With both of his parents gone and Richard's death having broken up the brother's minstrel band, Joe Sweeney's support system had weakened. His fame was receding and his music was passing from fashion. Perhaps he had contracted yellow or typhoid fever, or an infection of some sort.[85] Finally, on October 29 of 1860, Sweeney succumbed to "dropsy," probably related to long-term heart failure, and, without any mention in the entertainment papers, he died at the age of fifty.[86] It would take another twenty or thirty years for historians to begin to assemble the history of the banjo in early minstrelsy. Joel Walker Sweeney left behind no wife or progeny to uphold his memory, and the majority of artifacts he had saved from his career were quickly dispersed or lost to minstrel historians.

SIX

The Virginia Minstrels and the Dawn of the Minstrel Show

Clar de Track, de steam's up, de Locomotive's coming. Look here White Folks; "Come one, come all, hear de Music ring From de melodious Banja string."[1]

This chapter explores the history of the groundbreaking group that helped give minstrelsy its name, the Virginia Minstrels. Not only were these musicians professional associates of Sweeney, Joe even belonged to the group during their last tour.

As Joe Sweeney began his initial performances in Britain's capital city, four musicians made their first appearances as a band in New York City. These humble beginnings were to lead to a revolution in minstrelsy, one that was to soon follow Sweeney to Great Britain.

One of the downfalls in the minstrel business was a performer's dependence on circus and theater owners for employment. It was hard enough to make a living as a member of a traveling show. For the majority of blackface singers, musicians, and dancers, long periods of unemployment were a reality of the business. So, whether by design or by accident, when four performers—Billy Whitlock, Dan Emmett, Frank Brower, and Dick Pelham—banded together as "Virginia Minstrels" in the winter of 1843 for a series of New York appearances, a new wave of minstrelsy was inaugurated.

Regardless of whose idea it was, using fiddle, banjo, tambourine and bones to present songs, dances, imitations and skits in a freestanding program revolutionized the blackface business. Two outcomes of the new blackface groups and their Ethiopian shows, as Dale Cockrell has written, were the independence from circus and theatrical shows and the rise in the salaries for performers. Minstrel groups could now present entertainments lasting the whole evening, and reap a larger portion of each night's take. Some even kept their own theaters for months or even years at a time. Additionally, groups would soon take advantage of the increased mobility that the railroads brought to rural America. By 1850, blackface minstrels could be seen in every corner of the United States. In the process, the minstrel band pushed out solo performers and smaller performing aggregations.

The Early Careers of Whitlock, Pelham, Emmett, and Brower

Among the most curious, as well as the most pleasing musical novelties lately presented to the public, is the Band of Whitlock, the incomparable banjo player, assisted by Emmit, the very Paganini of violin players; Brower, who performs upon a pair of Bone Castinets equal to the divine Fanny; and Pelham, who also thumps and jingles his tamborine with infinite address.

The instrumental performance of this Band is entirely original, being composed of the usual accompaniments of a Southern congo medley, and played with a skill and melody not equalled by any other four instruments that can be brought together. Emmit has a perfect library of negro music, which his ready ear has enabled him to collect in various places in the South, many pieces of which are the most exquisite musical gems in existence. Scarcely one of them has ever been published, or even heard, in this part of the country, before. The harmony and skill with which the banjo, violin, castinets, and tamborine are blended by these truly original minstrels, in their Ethiopian characters, is a redeeming feature to this species of amusement, and cannot fail of making it acceptable to the most refined and sensitive audience.[2]

The Virginia Minstrels brought together four talented performers. Billy Whitlock was born three years after Sweeney, in 1813.[3] Like many minstrel performers, nothing is known for certain about his early life. Whitlock is first documented in 1835 as working for the *New York Herald* newspaper as a printer and typesetter[4] and possibly appearing in a production of T.D. Rice's *Oh! Hush!*, at the Patriot House on New York's Chatham Square. Whitlock continued to work as a printer through 1835 and 1836, concurrently appearing (presumably singing blackface songs) occasionally at the theaters in Richmond Hill.[5]

As will be explored in Chapter Thirteen, Billy Whitlock learned the rudiments of banjo playing from Sweeney in 1837 while he was touring Virginia as a circus performer. Three years later, show promoter P.T. Barnum paired Whitlock with dancer John Diamond, who had just appeared at the Broadway Circus with Joe Sweeney.[6] When Sweeney left with the troupe for their spring tour, John Diamond stayed behind, and so needed another traveling partner. Barnum hired the next best thing to the Virginian banjoist, Sweeney's "first pupil" William Whitlock.

From late March through August 1840, Whitlock worked with Diamond in New York City and on the road. Their April 8 performance at the Bowery Amphitheatre was a grand sendoff for a week of dates arranged in Providence by Barnum,[7] where Whitlock played "Settin on a Rail," and Sweeney's "Jenny get yer hoe cake done."[8] Barnum next sent Whitlock and Diamond to Connecticut to perform in New Haven and Hartford, Boston's National Theatre (overlapping their friend Joe Sweeney's run by a few a days) and Philadelphia, among other places.[9] Billy Whitlock appeared in the character of Sambo Squash[10] "accompanying himself on dat terror to all Pianos, Harps, and Organs ... dat Melodious Instrument de Banjo" and played "Jinny git your Hoe Cake done!," "Sittin' on a Rail" and "Jim Along Josey," which had all been part of his New York performances.[11] The last documented performances of Billy Whitlock and John Diamond together are at the Chatham Theatre in August.[12] Barnum had grown deeply disheartened with New York, and decided to take Diamond west on tour (see Chapter Ten for more about Billy Whitlock, John Diamond and Barnum).[13]

Billy Whitlock stayed in New York City and began an association with blackface singer and dancer and female impersonator Dan Gardner (October 25, 1816–October 7, 1880).[14] The duo's act quickly solidified, with Whitlock taking the role of the male banjoist and Gardner as the female focus of his attentions. Whitlock and Gardner called their piece "The Serenade," in which "Sambo Squash" (Billy) played his banjo attempting to gain the affections of "Dear Fanny" (Dan). Billy Whitlock sang his (and Sweeney's) standards, "Jenny get the Hoe-Cake done" and "Jim Along Josey."[15]

After breaking with Gardner in December of 1840, Billy Whitlock remained in the city and continued to perform. There was evidently enough work to support the banjoist without traveling, and Billy preferred to stay in his birthplace. He worked in a variety of settings in the early months of 1841. There are no documented performances for Billy Whitlock during

Sheet music cover for "Whitlock's Collection of Ethiopian Melodies." Strangely, the illustration depicts Joe Sweeney rather than his pupil Billy Whitlock and is "borrowed" from the English sheet music cover of "Lucy Long" (reproduced elsewhere in this volume). C.G. Christman, New York, 1846.

the touring season of 1841; perhaps he joined a circus company or returned to his profession of printer. During the winter and spring of 1841–1842, Billy was back playing banjo for the second "John Diamond" (aka: Francis Lynch) at the Chatham Theater and the Bowery Amphitheatre during Sweeney's 1841 stay at the Amphitheatre.[16] The duo continued to work together in 1842, with Lynch now billed as "Frank Diamond" to differentiate the dancer from the "original" John Diamond. Later that spring, Whitlock accompanied the "real" Diamond from May 22 until June 4 at the American Museum[17], but then returned to working with Lynch/Diamond at Barnum's Museum in early June. Billy Whitlock received good reviews for his banjo playing; the New York Herald stated that "Whitlock is quite equal if not superior to Sweeney,"[18] an attack on the Virginia banjoist that Joel could not defend from Britain. This comment was just the beginning of the fight for preeminence over the banjo.

Dancer Richard Ward Pell (February 13, 1815–October 8, 1876), known professionally as Dick Pelham,[19] was the second New Yorker in the Virginia Minstrels and well known to Billy Whitlock. He had been performing in New York and with various traveling circuses and companies since at least 1835. Such was his fame that he had made a guest appearance with Joe Sweeney at the Broadway Circus on Saturday, January 11, 1840.[20]

One of the highlights of Pelham's 1840 New York season was a "match dance"[21] between him and the original John Diamond. The night of Thursday, February 13, Pelham and Diamond met at the Chatham Theatre for the dance-off, the winner to receive $500.00. These events were more spectacle than contest, with both contestants reaping the benefit of the publicity generated by their dual engagement. As compiled from various publications:

> The house was so crowded at 10 o'clock, that a friend of ours could not obtain sight of the stage. Master Diamond is said to have "flaxed out" young Pelham, who claims to be "de mos science nigga!" The tunes "chawed up" on the occasion, were "Juba"—"For I'm gwine to the Alabarme"—"Go Way, nigga,"—"Jimmy, is [sic, Jenny, get] yer hoecake done?"—"Shinbone Alley," etc., etc. The judges awarded the purse to the little darkies, as being the best performance in the general variety of negro dances; but accorded to Pelham the praise of excelling in some particulars.[22]

The two other Virginia Minstrels, fiddler/banjoist Dan Emmett and bones player/singer/dancer Frank Brower, had met as performers in the Cincinnati Circus. This company was a partnership between the equestrians C. J. Rogers, John Mateer, and J. W. Jackson, and the ringmaster, clown, and juggler John Shay. The Cincinnati Circus played its hometown and toured the Midwest and South for two seasons in 1840 and 1841. Emmett was originally just a member of the orchestra, while Baltimorean[23] Francis Marion Brower (November 30, 1823–June 4, 1874)[24] was hired to provide blackface entertainment as a singer, comedian, and all-around performer.

On Friday, April 24, 1840, the troupe opened in Cincinnati for a week and a half run.[25] Then, the performers began with an easy trip through southeastern Ohio, before crossing the Ohio River into West (then Western) Virginia in early July. By August, they were in the mountains along the Virginia/Tennessee/North Carolina border region.[26] Sometime during the several weeks spent along the Clinch River in Southwest Virginia, Dan Emmett discovered an itinerant banjoist who could provide appropriate music to accompany the dancing of Frank Brower. As C.J. Rogers recollected almost thirty-five years later:

> While we were traveling in Western Virginia [Emmitt] found a banjo player by the name of "Ferguson," who was a very ignorant person, and "negger all over" except in color. Emmitt wanted us to engage him, but my partners objected to increasing our expenses. We were only giving an afternoon performance that day, on account of a long route ahead; the wagons were

about starting, when Emmitt ran up, shouting: "Ferguson will work on canvas, and play the banjo, for ten dollars a month." I answered, "Tell him to jump on a wagon," which he did.[27]

"Ferguson," the mythical banjoist Dan Emmett met in "Western Virginia" has remained a cipher. If Mr. Ferguson (his first name is unknown to this day; only the initial "A." survives of his given name) was indeed from the Kanawha Valley, he could have learned the banjo from Eastern Virginia slaves imported to work for the salt industry at places such as Kanawha Salines on the Kanawha River. In 1840, the area's slave population stood at 2,500 individuals, versus a total 10,000 white inhabitants.[28] Then again, Ferguson may have hopped a steamboat in Cincinnati and become stranded where Dan Emmett found him. Mr. Ferguson could have been a down-on-his-luck minstrel performer in what were then the western states. A third possibility is that in an area of show business rife with myth-making, Rogers may have made up the whole story in order to give a greater air of authenticity to the musician.

Regardless of his origins, Ferguson was a welcome addition to the company, and the act he formed with Brower more than doubled the attraction of the two men on their own. When the Cincinnati Circus reached Lexington, Kentucky, on September 21,[29] just in time for race week, "'Ferguson' was the greatest drawing card we had," recalled Rogers, "and 'Brower and Ferguson' were the talk of the town."[30] After a few more rural dates, the circus entered Louisville. For two and a half weeks, from October 1 through the 17, the Cincinnati Circus pitched their tent in an empty lot.[31] As in Lexington, horse races were being held in Louisville from at least October 6 through 10, allowing the circus to take advantage of the crowds drawn by the event.[32]

Besides one poster from their opening in Cincinnati, the only surviving broadsides (and, therefore, the only surviving in-depth description of performers and performances) are from the Louisville run. The appearance on Monday, October 12, benefited "Mr. Ferguson The Celebrated Banjo player and Master Brower The negro dancer and singer," as the two blackface entertainers were billed. The poster proclaimed:

> De Banjo Music, On dis tickler kasion will be displayed in all its varieties And de Toe and Heel genus will be Wonderfully Dewellopt...."Jinney git your hoe cake done." By Master Brower.... Mr. Ferguson will play upon the Banjo and sing Miss Lucy Long.... Messrs. Brower and Ferguson Will introduce de Banjo wid de Toe and Hell Science and conclude with Old Char. Accompanied by Brower wid de Bones. The whole to conclude with the German Farmer.... Sam Smash, Ferguson. Pompey: Brower.[33]

Once again, Sweeney's song "Jenny Get Your Hoe Cake Done" makes its appearance in the hands of another singer, while Joe Sweeney would adopt another of Ferguson and Brower's songs, "Lucy Long," several years later (It seems unusual that Ferguson would include "Lucy Long" in his performance, as it appears that the song had not yet entered into widespread circulation. See Chapter Eleven for a further discussion of "Lucy Long.").

The circus left Louisville on October 17 and departed for Indianapolis, where their season ended on October 22.[34] The owners must have felt the season to be a success, as they laid the groundwork for a similar tour in 1841. The circus packed up for the winter, and Frank Brower returned to Philadelphia.[35]

With the spring races on in Cincinnati,[36] the circus erected their pavilion on the corner of Ninth and Vine streets. Brower had returned from the previous season. They opened on Friday, April 23, with Frank Brower singing John Smith's hit of "Jim Along Josey" (see Chapters Two and Eleven for more information), and dancing the "Negro Extravaganza" of "Zip Coon." The "Colored" population was admitted at the half price of twenty-five cents.[37]

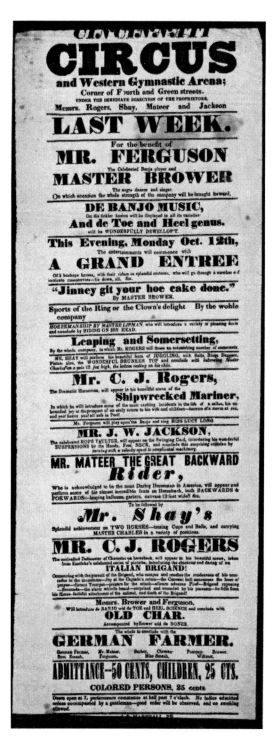

Playbill, Cincinnati Circus, October 12, 1840, performance in Louisville, Kentucky. Banjoist Ferguson and dancer Frank Brower are prominently featured on Ferguson's benefit night.

When Frank Brower took his benefit on Friday, he was joined by "Mr. J. Kelly, The celebrated Negro Dancer and Singer" and the dancer "Master George Gates." Brower sang Sweeney's "Whar did you come from," and danced "his 'Wirginny Breaks,'" Kelly sang "Jim Along Josey," and all danced, with Kelly and Brower specializing in "the Grand Grape Vine Twist."

Ferguson, too, was back temporarily to help out in the performance. The banjoist again featured "Lucy Long," as well as a song associated with orchestra member Dan Emmett, "Hard Times."[38] But, when the Circus closed the following day and left on tour, Ferguson had other plans. He apparently left the Cincinnati Circus and took his banjo to join Fogg & Stickney's concern, although exactly when this occurred is unclear. However, by July 4 when Rogers and company reached Lynchburg, their advertisements were trumpeting a new banjo player, none other than circus band member Dan Emmett. Ferguson continued to work with Fogg & Stickney as they toured the Midwest and South through at least October, but then at the end of that month his name mysteriously disappears from the record—never to be seen again. Rogers remembered, "Ferguson went South, and died of cholera,"[39] and perhaps that's what happened (for more about Ferguson, see Chapter Ten). Ferguson's banjo student, Dan Emmett, had been coaxed from the orchestra of the Cincinnati Circus to take the departing banjoist's place. Emmett was to create songwriting history almost twenty years after his initial triumphs in minstrelsy with his composition, "I Wish I Was in Dixie's Land," the original title of the song best known as "Dixie."

> I wish I was in de land ob cot-ton,
> Cim-mon seed an san-dy bot-tom,
> Look a-way look 'way
> a-way, Dixie Land,
> In Dix-ie land whar I was born in,
> Ear-ly on one fros-ty morn-nin,
> Look a-way look 'way,
> a-way Dixie Land,
> Chorus: Den I wish I was in Dix-ie,
> Hoo-ray, Hoo-ray,

In Dix-ie's land, we'll took our stand,
To lib an die in Dix-ie,
a-way, a-way, a-way down south in Dix-ie,
a-way, a-way, a-way down south in Dix-ie.[40]

Daniel Decatur Emmett (October 29, 1815–1904)[41] was born in Mount Vernon, Ohio. His family had come to the hamlet northeast of Columbus in 1806.[42] Emmett settled in Cincinnati, where he worked (as did Whitlock) in the printing trade. In 1834, Dan enlisted in the army, although he was not yet twenty-one, and therefore ineligible for service. It seems that the military offered the young man an opportunity to follow a musical career, as he used his service to practice drumming. Dan also learned to play fife in the army and later published instructors for both instruments. By the summer of 1835, he was found to be underage, and on July 8, Emmett was discharged.[43] Some minstrel performers reported that Dan Emmett divided his time, as did Billy Whitlock, working as a printer in the wintertime and playing during the summer in circus bands.[44] However, there is no documentation of his participation in circus life until 1840, when he played in the band for the Cincinnati Circus. Mount Vernon residents remember Dan playing for local dances (he was also a fiddler) during the late 1830s, but, again, this is anecdotal.[45]

During that 1840 season, Dan Emmett had studied Ferguson's banjo playing. Emmett either took lessons from the banjoist, or "picked it up" by watching the other man's performances. By July 4, 1841 Dan,

Playbill, with detail, for the Menagerie and Circus in their appearance in Charleston, South Carolina, on February 2, 1842. The dancer and banjoist are Frank Brower and Dan Emmett, who would go on to make up half of the Virginia Minstrels group.

as owner Charles Rogers recalled, "after a good deal of persuasion, agreed to ... assist Frank [Brower] in the ring with the banjo."[46] When the Western Gymnastic Arena opened near the Western Hotel in Sweeney's old stomping grounds of Lynchburg, both Brower and Emmett were given full billing.[47]

Unlike the previous year, when Rogers and his partners only got as far into the southern states as western Virginia, the 1841 tour was to take the circus all the way across the bottom of Virginia and down the coast through North and South Carolina and Georgia.[48] Seeing that they were showing in areas familiar with the banjo, it took some nerve for the Cincinnati Circus to advertise Emmett as playing "the Virginia Banjo." Or, maybe this was just smart publicity, considering where they were performing. Regardless that Dan Emmett was born in Ohio and Frank Brower was a northerner, the audiences could not have failed to have been delighted when "Messrs. Brower and Emmitt [had] their grand Corn Husking, Grapevine Twisting, Apple Cutting, five Mile out of the Town Jig and Banjo Concert."[49]

Upon their arrival in Charleston, the tour and indeed the history of Cincinnati Circus itself drew to a close. Frank Brower sang "Sich A Gittin Up Stairs," and danced the "Camp Town Hornpipe." For Sweeney's song "Old Tar River," Frank Brower joined Dan Emmett on the bones, an instrument which Frank had used as early as the previous fall.[50] Brower and Emmett removed their burnt cork in order to perform a "Pantomime called The Frolicsome Har-equin, Or, the Militia turned Statues!!" As living statuary, a common act for their time, Dan portrayed "Big Bill, the Fifer," and Frank "Little Clem, the Drummer."[51] After a stint in Savannah (October 16 through 25), the Cincinnati Circus disbanded.[52]

At the end of October 1841, Brower and Emmett made it back to Charleston, attaching themselves to the circus from the Bowery Amphitheatre in New York City, where they were first announced as members on January 17, 1842. Frank Brower joined with other company members to present T.D. Rice's *Oh! Hush!* For the first two weeks, advertisements did not mention Dan Emmett; perhaps he was playing in the orchestra. Finally, on Friday, January 28, Emmett strummed his banjo in accompaniment to Brower's dancing.[53] At the month's end, the circus headed north for a summer of touring up through western Pennsylvania and New York State.[54]

Emmett and Brower next appeared with the Philadelphia Circus at the end of September and in early October. They stayed with this show through November 19, adding the young dancer Master Pierce to their performances.[55] At the end of November, Frank brought his friend Dan to New York City for the first time. The duo set up shop with Pierce on November 28 at the Franklin Theater,[56] which they used as their base of operations through the first week of the New Year. Dan Emmett and Frank Brower also worked with various Ethiopian performers at Nathan A. Howe's Amphitheatre of the Republic at 37 Bowery, often traveling between both venues on the same evening.[57] Both Emmett and Brower received high marks, with Dan being compared to Sweeney in much the same way as Whitlock. *The Herald* wrote that, "Emmit's banjo playing is fully equal to Jo Sweeney's, and far ahead of any other now in the United States."[58] Emmett's last mention in the newspapers was on Friday, January 13, when he played the character of "old Dan Tucker."[59]

After this success, for slightly over two weeks, Dan Emmett and Frank Brower sat idle. They may have been playing small houses that did not merit mention in the newspapers or on broadside posters, or taking a much-needed break. Historians, utilizing the writings of both men, paint a picture of two out-of-work artists desperately casting about for engagements. Other blackface entertainers, including their future partners Whitlock and Pelham,[60] were continuing to perform; perhaps the market was flooded with talent, as many bills were filled with large numbers of performers. However, Emmett and Brower's problems were about to come to an end, and, in the course of their banding with Dick Pelham and Billy Whitlock, an entire form of amusement was to gain a new name, and blackface entertainments were to move into whole evenings' concerts.

The Virginia Minstrels

1
I come to town de ud-der night
I hear de noise an saw de fight
De watch-man was a run-nin roun
Cry-in Old Dan Tuck-er's come to town
Chorus: So get out de way! Old Dan Tucker
Your to late to come to sup-per
2
Tucker is a nice old man,
He use to ride our darby ram;
He sent him whizzen down de hill,
If he had'nt got up he'd lay dar still.
3
Here's my razor in good order
Magnum bonum—jis hab bought 'er
Sheep shell oats, Tucker shell de corn,
I'll shabe you soon as de water get warm.
4
Ole Dan Tucker an I got drunk.

He fell in de fire an kick up a chunk,
De charcoal got inside he shoe
Lor bless you honey how de ashes flew.
5
Down de road foremost de stump,
Massa make me work de pump;
I pump so hard I broke de sucker,
Dar was work for ole Dan Tucker.
6
I went to town to buy some goods
I lost myself in a piece of woods,
De night was dark I had to suffer,
It froze de heel of Daniel Tucker.
7
Tucker was a hardened sinner,
He nebber said his grace at dinner;
De ole sow squeel, de pigs did squall
He 'hole hog wid de tail and all.[61]

Exactly who had the idea to form the Virginia Minstrels is unknown; both Whitlock and Emmett took credit for coming up with the idea of joining forces, but this was many years after the fact, when the group's fame and importance was already established. Whatever the circumstances, it appears that the Virginia Minstrels first tried out their combination on Tuesday, January 31, 1843, when Dick Pelham was taking his benefit at the Chatham Theater. A poster for the evening, while mentioning a number of Dan Emmett's songs (all are by Emmett except for "Miss Lucy Long" and possibly "Why, Don't Forget!), proclaims that during the second part of the program:

> the Old Virginny Minstrels Will appear in a Grand Concert. "Prince Albert and Victoria Looking on All de Time," "Old Dan Tucker," "Gwine Over de Mountain," "Nebber Do to Gib It Up So," "What Would Uncle Gabriel Say?" "Why, Don't Forget!!" "Miss Lucy Long." De whole to conclude wid "Tearing up de stage—knocking all de putty out o' de cracks"— Piney-wood heart breakers—Knockin' de breff out o' bards, aunt-so-fowth—by Dick Pelham and Frank Brower. Accompanied by de music ob dose King Dan Emmit and Billy Whitlock.[62]

The group was not yet a permanent aggregation, as the following evening, Whitlock joined Andrew Jackson Allen, Harry Mestayer, Dan Gardner, and (probably Richard) Pelham at the Bowery Amphitheatre.[63] At this point, *The Sporting Whip* began carrying notices of the Minstrels' comings and going, reporting on Saturday, February 4 about the Virginia Minstrels' evening "Concert" at the Second Ward Hotel, as well as the news that the band "is going to England."[64]

The first real performances of the Virginia Minstrels occurred the week of February 6 at the Bowery Amphitheatre. It was obvious that their act was still under development, because the band was a part of the larger show. For example, Pelham participated in an

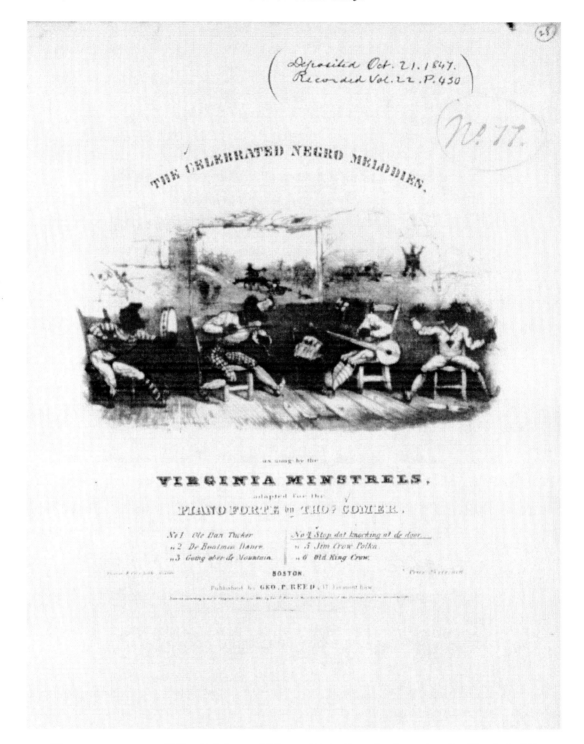

Sheet music cover, "The Celebrated Negro Melodies, As Sung by the Virginia Minstrels," (left to right) Dick Pelham on tambourine, Dan Emmett on fiddle, Billy Whitlock on banjo and Frank Brower on bones. Geo. P. Reed, Boston, deposited for copyright October 21, 1847. Probably a reprint of the original (Library of Congress).

equestrian act, "Dan Tucker on Horseback."[65] After four days off, the Virginia Minstrels, also calling themselves "Old Dan Tucker & Co.," gave their second New York concert to a full house "in the large hall over Luscomb and Sanborn's 'Cornucopia,' and Benjamin's popular hotel" at 28 Park Row.[66] From then until the first day in March, the Olympic Circus at the Park Theater employed Dan Tucker's boys as a part of the evening's festivities.[67] Interestingly, the theater's owner didn't think that four blackface minstrels were enough, so the trio of singer-comedian S.W. Hoyt, banjoist William Chestnut, and dancer John Diamond were also on the bill.[68] For their benefit night March 1, "Dan Tucker On Horseback" was expanded to include Brower and Whitlock. Billy Whitlock gave a "Negro Lecture on Locomotives," Brower defined Bankruptcy Laws, "A Brief Battering at the Blues" was done by Richard Pelham, and Dan Emmett offered up some "Conundrums."[69] *The New York Sporting Whip* heralded the last New York appearance of the Minstrels at "a house in Bleeker Street," plugged the upcoming tour of New England, and an engagement with Van Amburgh in London, although the animal trainer left the British capital before the Minstrels would arrive and Sweeney was firmly ensconced at the English Opera House.[70]

The *New York Courier* encapsulated the New York success of the Virginia Minstrels:

> The harmony and skill with which the banjo, violin, castanets [sic], and tamborine [sic] are blended by these truly original minstrels, in their Ethiopian characters, is a redeeming feature to this species of amusement, and cannot fail of making it acceptable to the most refined and sensitive audience.[71]

It wasn't as if other bands of minstrels with similar ideas didn't or couldn't have existed before or concurrently with the birth of the Virginia Minstrels. E.P. Christy (November 28, 1815–May 21, 1862) claimed to have assembled a band in 1842 (see Chapter Nine for more information).[72] It really doesn't matter who was in the original minstrel band. As with Sweeney, it was the performers with the widest ranging influence that counted in defining the style. Other bands may have been performing in small, provincial venues, but, as was shown with Tom Rice, nothing mattered until you opened in New York City. The Virginia Minstrels set the format and the standard for the other minstrel groups to copy.

And copy they did. Although the John Diamond, William Chestnut, S.W. Hoyt trio never adopted a group title, they incurred the criticism of *The New York Sporting Whip* for shamelessly aping the Minstrels' successful formula. The individual performers had been on the scene since 1840, and had pooled their talents at Welch's Olympic Circus in late January.[73] An unidentified writer lambasted John Diamond and company. "They are wretched dancers, miserable banjoists, and no singers at all," said *The Sporting Whip*, "envious of the success of 'Old Dan Tucker & Co.' have exerted themselves to induce the public to believe they are the real Virginia Minstrels; but signally failed, as they deserve." On another occasion, when Harry Mestayer was added on the violin, *The Whip* added, "We hope they may succeed; but at present we see no opening for them."[74]

A more serious threat to the Virginia Minstrels was the quartet of dancer and now banjoist Frank Diamond, Harry Mestayer on violin, T.G. Booth on bones, and a Mr. (probably Sam) Richardson on the tambourine. On Friday, February 27, the *New York Herald* reported that Diamond, Mestayer, Booth and Richardson were now "The four Kentucky minstrels," a tag that would reappear in the New York newspapers on March 1 for the remainder of the performers' time in the City.[75] The group spent a week at the Chatham Theater, where their repertoire—"Old Dan Tucker," "Dance de Boatman," "Lucy Long," "Colored Gentleman" —reflected the Kentucky Minstrels' debt to the Virginia band.[76] In fact, the imitation was so complete and the confusion so great that the *New York Herald* listed the Kentucky Minstrels as "Virginia Minstrels."[77] The group would carry the "Virginia" moniker with them when they left New York after their Chatham engagement,[78] following the Virginia Minstrels to Boston, where it appears that the Kentucky group worked for a short time at Howe's circus[79] before moving over to the National Theater.[80] After their run at the National, which lasted for about a week at the end of March and in early April,[81] they toured the same Massachusetts circuit as the Virginia Minstrels in a blatant attempt to capitalize on the success of Emmett's group.[82]

1

Johnny come from Chickasaw,
De dardes fool I ebber saw;
He put his shirt outside his coat,
An tied his breeches roun his throat.
Chorus: So walk along John!
Walk along John!
Walk along John! high for de Sun,
Aint you might glad you day's work done.

2

Johnny went to Tenessee,
He grin de possum up a tree;
He grin an fotch his body down,
An leff de tail for anudder roun.

3

Behind de hen cook on my knees,
I tink I hear old Johnny sneeze;
Goose chew tobackur duck drink wine,
De brack snake sleep wid de punkin vine.

4

Johnny's chees was nine years old,
De skippers gittin mighty bold;

A long tail rat in a bucket of souse,
Jist come from de white folks house.

5

Johnny's rooster had a fit,
De niggs all thot he's die of it;
De fedders flew out his tail flew in,
Den he jump up an crowed agin.

6

Walk 'long Johnny de got drunk,
He fell in de fire an kick de chunk;
De charcoal got inside his shoe,
Lawd bress y'e how de ashes flew.

7

Johnny lay on de rail road track,
He tied de engine on his back;
He pair'd his corn wid a rail road wheel,
It gib 'im de tooth ache in de heel.

8

Way down south on beaver creek,
Old Johnny grew about ten feet;
He went to bed, but 'twas no use,
His leg hung out for de chicken roose.[83]

Meanwhile, the real Virginia Minstrels could finally consistently fill an evening with their capers. They performed in early March in Boston for a week beginning on Tuesday, March 7, and then began a short tour, but, after the first stop, March 15 in Charlestown,[84] it was back to Boston for more full houses and thunderous encores.[85] They would continue to alternate shows in Boston with appearances in its suburbs. By the time the Virginia Minstrels reached Worcester on Monday, March 20, for three appearances, their posters indicated that the band had taken the raw materials of Dan Emmett's songs and elements from the solo acts of each of the four and woven it into a full concert. This synthesis would serve as the blueprint for subsequent groups to follow and build upon for years to come.

After promising attendees that their show would be "'Moral, Chaste and Elegant!' ... entirely free from every objectionable feature," the Virginia Minstrels "delineated in a masterly and chaste manner, the Sports and Pastimes of the Virginia Colored Race, through the medium of Songs, Refrain and Ditties, as sung by the Southern Slaves, at all their Merry meetings, such as the gathering in of the Cotton and Sugar Crops, Corn Huskings, Slave Weddings and Junketings." Then, in direct contrast to their contention that this was an authentic presentation of Southern Blacks, they assured viewers that "The Songs are all new and original, being composed and arranged expressly for them, by their Leader—Old Dan Emmit." Here in one statement is the great combination/contradiction of minstrelsy. On one hand, the representation of slave life is supposed to be accurate and based on first hand experiences by the performers. On the other, due to the demands of show business, the material needed to be new and unique, forcing the composition of new songs, dances, and routines by these groups. However, the contention that Emmett (or some other group member) "composed" all their songs is a bit contrived. According to research by scholars such as Hans Nathan, Dale Cockrell, and William Mahar, a number of the supposed "new and original" songs are really reworkings of older lyrics, or new lyrics set to preexisting tunes.

A sample program from Worcester shows just how far the band had come in a month and a half. They opened with a number of vocal selections, most written by Dan Emmett. First, came their "theme song," "Old Dan Tucker, a Virginian Refrain, in which is described the ups and downs of Negro life [see lyrics above]," and "Goin Ober De Mountain," both claimed by Emmett and published under his name by Charles H. Keith of Boston in 1843. After a solo by Whitlock on Sweeney's "Where did you come from," the whole group sang another song of Joel Sweeney's, "Old Tar River." Emmett rendered "Never do to give it up so," also included by Keith in *Old Dan Emmit's Original Banjo Melodies* (see lyrics, following), and then Whitlock closed the first part with his "Locomotive Lecture, ... in which he describes his visit to the Wild Animals, his scrape with his Sweet heart, and show the white folks how the Niggers raise steam." During the second part of the concert, all four sang "Uncle Gabriel" and "Boatman Dance [whose lyrics are printed below]," followed by Whitlock parroting Sweeney again with "Jenny get your Hoe Cake Done." The group then sang Emmett's sequel to "Dan Tucker," "Walk along John [the song's lyrics are printed above]." Dan Emmett picked up the banjo, accompanying "'Fine Old Colored Gemmanin' in a manner that will make all guitar players turn pale with delight." Dick Pelham led a series of "conundrums,"[86] including "Why are the ladies here to-night like children whose sorrow is suddenly turned to joy? Because they laugh in tiers."[87] This prompted *The Daily Mail* to respond with "Why are the Virginia Minstrels like slaves on the coast of Africa? Because they make their money by *taking off* the negroes."[88] The Virginia Minstrels concluded the evening with the song, "Lucy Long."[89]

During their tour of New England, Nathan Howe, who had closed his New York amphitheater, attempted to engage the Virginia Minstrels for his Boston show. Emmett claims that Howe refused to hire the group at the price requested,[90] bringing up the Kentucky Minstrels instead.[91] However, Nathan Howe reconsidered his decision after losing his audience to Emmett, Brower, Whitlock and Pelham's appearances. On Thursday, March 23, Howe summoned Emmett's band back from Worcester to appear at the Tremont in Boston, now converted for the Great Olympic Circus.[92] Once again the Minstrels were integrated into the Circus' performances. Frank Brower and Billy Whitlock joined Whitlock's former performing partner Dan Gardner in a blackface play that recalled the old Whitlock/Gardner act. Dick Pelham, Brower, and Dan Emmett participated in a reprise of "Dan Tucker on Horseback," with the rider Henry Madigan playing Dan. Even though the Circus left Boston at the end of the month, the management of the Tremont kept the Virginia Minstrels on the bill into April.[93] Emmett and Company then returned to New York to prepare for a trip to England.

1	2
De old Jim riv-er I float down	*De old log rake me aft and fore*
I run my bac-ker boat up-on de groun	*An leff my cook-house on de shore*
De drift log come wid a rush-in din	*I tho't it would'nt do to gib it up so*
An stove both ends ob de ole boat in	*So I scull mysef ashore wid de ole banjo*
Chorus: It will neb-ber do to gib it up so!	*3*
It will neb-ber do to gib it up so!	*I lite on de sand an feel sorter glad*
It will neb-ber do to gib it up Old Mis-ter Brown	*I looks at de banjo an feels bery mad*
It will neb-ber do to gib it up so!	*I walks up de bank dat slick as glass*
	Up went my heels an I lite upon de grass

4   5
It will nebber do to gib it up so Mr. Brown,   *Nigger on de wood-pile barkin like a dog,*
I jump up agin an stood upon de groun;   *Toad in de mill-pond sittin on a log,*
I haul de boat out high an dry up de bank,   *Possum up a gum tree, sarcy, fat an dirty;*
Den float down de ribber wid de backer on a plank. *Come kiss me gals or I'll run like turkey.*[94]

Off to England

After their benefit at the Park Theater in New York City on April 17, the Virginia Minstrels departed for Great Britain, sailing for Liverpool on April 21.[95] Although they may have performed as early as May 21,[96] the first newspaper advertisements for the Virginia Minstrels' English tour appeared on Wednesday, May 24. For their "Ethiopian Concert" at Liverpool's Music Hall, they boasted somewhat truthfully that "None of their songs have ever been sung in Europe, having been procured at great toil and expense, from the slaves themselves."[97] By Saturday, the first review appeared, detailing their performances and the audiences' reactions. After quoting the playbill and complaining about the "pretty considerable sum" being charged for admission, which did not seem to deter the audience, the writer commented favorably on the show and those in attendance. The band appears to have presented a program similar to that developed in the United States. The reviewer concluded that, "Those who wish to enjoy a hearty laugh can have their inclination gratified by attending the performances of the Virginian minstrels." This boded well for their upcoming engagements. The reviewer did raise one red flag that would dog the Minstrels throughout the next two months. British audiences seemed to have a problem with Emmett and company's "queer action(s), grimaces, and manner of their singing" which was supposed to represent the characteristics of the African American slave. The nature of the Americans' performances proved puzzling and problematic to English audiences for the remainder of the tour.[98]

The Virginia Minstrels continued to "delineate ... the Sports and Pastimes of the Virginia Coloured Race" to Liverpool audiences through Saturday, June 3.[99] It was then on to Manchester for a week of shows at the Athenaeum concert-room.[100] The Minstrels were smart enough to heed the advice of the Liverpool critics, and dropped the admission price.[101] They received further good notices,[102] although the alien aspects, "the violent contortions of their limbs," of the Minstrels' show were again highlighted.[103] The reviewer particularly singled out the dancing of the Virginia Minstrels:

> The first is, the Slave Match Dance, as performed during the holidays in the southern states by the male slaves, in the presence of their master overseers and other whites, who urge the negroes to their utmost skill by making small presents to the negro who can stand the most fatigue or remain upon the board for the longest time. The second is the celebrated Slave Marriage Dance, as performed by the most expert dancer on the plantation, he being held in high favour by the rest of the slaves for his skill in the heel and toe science. The third is the Corn Husking Jig, in which the most expert dancer is selected. After the gathering in of the corn crop, and whilst both male and female slaves are being employed in husking corn, he amuses them by his antics and grimaces to the music of the banjo, as played by some worn-out slave, whose age alone prevents him from joining in more arduous work.[104]

For a second week, they moved over to the Queen's Theatre in Spring Gardens,[105] and then, to London where they opened on Monday, June 19.[106]

In the British capital, the Virginia Minstrels worked for the illusionist Professor Anderson, the "Wizard of the North," who had taken the Adelphi Theatre for the after season (theater companies generally spent the summers, "after" the regular "season," touring provincial houses, therefore leaving the big city venues open to other ventures) starting on Easter Monday, April 17.[107] The Virginia Minstrels drew good houses,[108] so Anderson engaged the band for a total of four weeks.[109] Once again, the critics were positive about the Virginia Minstrels, identifying the humor in the performances as their strong point.[110] Three reviewers used the image of Rice, aka "Jim Crow," to describe the Minstrels' act. One played on the strangeness of their portrayal, writing "They sing with rare comic humour, ask odd conundrums, and dance in most peculiar style."[111] Another emphasized Brower's playing of the bones, a feature popular among English audiences, while suggesting the dance numbers "might well be omitted."[112] A third dismissed the uniqueness of the group, calling them "no other than four Jim Crows" and that "One was always too much for us."[113]

Luckily, one program survives from the month the Virginia Minstrels spent in London. "Accompanying themselves on instruments of a peculiar nature, which, in their hands, discourse most exquisite music," they continued to amplify their identification with the lives of Southern slaves. "The subject of each [song] ascribing the manner in which the slaves celebrate their holidays, which commence at the gathering-in of the sugar and cotton crops ... [is] a true copy of Ethiopian life." For their English appearances, the Virginia Minstrels had kept the basic contents of the American concerts, dividing the two parts into three and shuffling them around a bit. Otherwise, their act was the same, at least on paper.[114]

Dan Emmett states that the Minstrels were financially strapped during their entire existence, with their English tour being no exception. The "last straw" was the lack of profits from the contract with Professor Anderson. Although Anderson claimed to have paid the Minstrels 100 pounds per week, Emmett contends the Wizard stiffed the group.[115] The Virginia Minstrels, a tentative union at best, then dissolved. The time the band had been together was slightly more than five months, but their influence would be long lasting. Musicians flocked to music stores, purchasing banjos and tambourines in large numbers.

Their lack of financial success drove the Minstrels apart. Billy Whitlock, seemingly self-centered, pragmatic, and always looking for the immediate return, had been at odds with Emmett, the artist. Since their voyage from America, Whitlock had been challenging Dan for the leadership of the band. Billy left England first, and in no time, Whitlock was back at performing in New York City. The banjoist joined with T.G. Booth and Henry Mestayer of the Kentucky Minstrels, as well as Barney Williams, sometimes using the name of Booth and Mestayer's old band.[116] By mid–September, Billy Whitlock had brazenly adopted the moniker of his former group, the Virginia Minstrels. However, this was shortlived, and, by early October, theater historian George Odell writes, "the [Whitlock] Virginia Minstrels seemed to have disintegrated into separate individualities."[117]

Almost immediately, Richard Pelham was able to translate his abilities as a singer and dancer into English success. Pelham had closely modeled himself on the American T.D. Rice, which worked well with British audiences. By August 28, Dick Pelham had rejoined Emmett at London's Surrey Theatre.[118] The duo, billed as "the Sable Minstrels," performed some of the Virginia Minstrels' repertoire on and off for three weeks. Emmett played the banjo, and both danced.[119] London's Sadler's Wells Theatre subsequently hired Dick Pelham for a successful run. Pelham claims that this engagement lasted two months,[120] but documentation exists for only half of that time. Surviving programs and newspaper coverage show the minstrel dusting off older pieces in his repertoire such as "Ginger Blue" and "The Racoon Hunt." Pelham also borrowed Joel Sweeney's "Whar did you cum frum" from Billy Whitlock,[121] as well as Whitlock's "Locomotive Lecture."[122] Dick portrayed Brower's Negro drummer,[123] sang "Lucy Long"[124] and "Jim Along Josey," as well as dancing a variety of steps.[125] All appealed to the London critics, and one wrote that:

Another Jim Crow has found his way to this country,—a Mr. Pelham, who personates the nigger tribe in a very novel manner; his dancing is of a most singular description, and very superior to any other who has tried this line of character. He appears to be very young, although his performance appears to give general satisfaction.[126]

Chorus: *High row, de boat-men row*
Float-in down de ri-ver de O-hi-o
1
De boat-men dance, de boat-men sing
De boat-me up to eb-ry ting
An when de boat men gets on shore
He spends his cash as works for more
Refrain: *Den dance de boat-men dance*
O dance de boat-men dance
O dance all night till broad day-light
An go home wid de gals in the mor-ning
2
De oyster boat should keep de shore,
De fishin smack should venture more,
De Schooner sails before de wind,
De steamboat leaves a streak behind
3
I went on board de odder day
To see what de boatmen had to say;
Dar I let my passion loose
An dey cram me in de calaboose.

4
I've come dis time, I'll come no more,
Let me loose I'll go on shore;
For dey whole hoss, an dey a bully crew
Wid a hoosier mate an a captin too.
5
When you go to de boatmen's ball,
Dance wid my wife, or don t dance at all;
Sky blue jacket an tarpaulin hat,
Look out my boys for de nine tail cat.
6
De boatman is a thrifty man,
Dars none can do as de boatman can;
I neber see a putty gal in my life
But dat she was a boatman's wife.
7
When de boatman blows his horn,
Look out old man your hog is gone;
He cotch my sheep, he cotch my shoat,
Den put em in a bag an toat em to de boat.[127]

Pelham was soon to have other offers to consider. In late March or early April, he was hired to play at Dublin's Theatre Royal. Either Mr. J. Calcraft, the manager, requested a band rather than a solo act, or Dick saw the prospect to make more money utilizing a group of performers. Whatever the motivation, there was an opportunity to reconvene his old colleagues. Brower had just finished a Liverpool engagement with Joe Sweeney and Emmett was playing in nearby Bolton, so, the three musicians gathered in Liverpool. With Whitlock having returned to America, Sweeney was recruited to play the banjo, moving Emmett back to the fiddle. Because of Sweeney's greater fame, he was billed as the "leader."[128]

Perhaps Pelham was inspired to reform the troupe by the number of minstrel groups cropping up in Great Britain, some even using the name of the defunct Virginia Minstrels. The first "fake" Virginia Minstrels appear to have been in Ludlow in August of 1843.[129] No members of the group are known, so it is hard to say if the counterfeit "Virginia Minstrels" who appeared in October at Hull's Victoria Rooms and in Birmingham were one and the same. They definitely wanted the public to believe they were the real Minstrels, because their program is identical to that of the original band. A third appearance, in August of 1844 at Sheffield, does reveal that phony group's identities as "Inkersall, Vango, Waring and Morton," which doesn't match the one known member of the Hull/Birmingham band ("Mr. Burton").[130]

Whatever was in Dick Pelham's mind, the Virginia Minstrels opened in Dublin on April 24, a Wednesday. This collection from their solo and duo shows was longer than the usual "d'entracte," but did not fill a full evening. *Freeman's Journal* detailed the first night in its pages, giving the usual review, mixed with praise and gentle condemnation for the strange goings-on.[131] The Minstrels' Dublin run closed with their benefit on Tuesday, May 7; Frank Brower gave his Locomotive Lecture, Dick Pelham danced a "Corn Husking Jig," and "The Marriage Festival Dance" was by Brower, with music by Emmett and Sweeney.[132]

The Virginia Minstrels must have been extremely popular, as, in the wake of their appearance in Dublin, the music director of the Theatre Royal, violinist Richard Michael Levey (ne: O'Shaughnessy) wrote and had published a piece immortalizing the band. "The Banjo Quadrilles for the Piano Forte, Selected from the most celebrated Negro Melodies," featured the four movements "Sweeny," "Brower," "Pelham" and "Emmit."[133]

The rest of the week, the Minstrels supposedly played Cork, although no publicity from that city has yet emerged.[134] On Monday, May 13, they opened their week in Belfast.[135] Joe Sweeney had been advertised as "the Original Banjo Player" in Dublin,[136] and his billing in Belfast was expanded to include "the first that ever brought that Instrument before the Public."[137] As in Dublin, the Minstrels did well in Belfast, as "the attendance was very large, and the loud plaudits which followed the fall of the curtain, testified the admiration of the audience at the very amusing entertainment of the evening."[138] "Several of their pieces were loudly encored."[139]

A week and a day in Glasgow, Scotland, was next on the schedule. Although they appeared on the same program, the playbills began listing Joe Sweeney as separate from "The Virginia Minstrels" Pelham, Emmett, and Brower. On Friday, Dick Pelham was featured in a Shakespearean parody, the "Masquerade Ball, Or Tickets On/Or Tick" (it is listed both ways), with Pelham as:

> Sambo Hit-'Em-Hard, a negro doorkeeper, Spruce Pink and his Love—Mr. Emmit and Mrs. Wood Joe Break-Em-All, the Virginia Paganini, J.W. Sweeny. The whole to conclude with the excellent farce (written expressly for the purpose of illustrating the American negro character) entitled The Virginia Mummy. Ginger Blue, a regular Virginia nigger, with the usual characteristics of his race, and an uncommon love of wittles—Mr. F.M. Brower.[140]

For Saturday and Monday, June 1 and 3, Joe Sweeney's name is conspicuously absent from the Theatre Royal playbills. Emmett moved back over to the banjo and all three Virginia Minstrels are listed as dancing, with Pelham given the most ink:

> Mr. R.W. Pelham, who will show de science of de heel-and-toe caperbilities [sic], surprising to de white folks and sartin deth to all fresh-water niggers. Den kums de neber-to-be-forgotten and unkonkerable jig, by R.W. Pelham, which has exterminated, laid on de shelf, and driven into retirement all de ober heelologists in de East, West, Norf and Souf. Sich a set of double-shuffles, Long Island trouble, heel-and-toe tormenters, and dandy-nigger flourishes, you nebber did see! verifying de truth ob Massa Charley Dickens, when he sez: "De right leg, de leff leg, de hind leg, and all de odder legs will be brought to bear on dat 'ticular 'casion." Music on de banjo by D.D. Emmit. So clare de track and let genus perspire.[141]

No explanation has been given by Dick Pelham, nor is there any evidence in newspaper accounts, of why Sweeney was missing those last two days in Glasgow. Was it illness, a dispute over money, or some other disagreement that kept Joe Sweeney from the theater? Whatever the reason, it wasn't serious enough to prevent Sweeney from rejoining the Virginia Minstrels for their Edinburgh engagement. In that city, from the fourth or fifth until at least Saturday the eighth, the Virginia Minstrels returned to the concert format. With the exception of the songs by the Irish singer, Mr. W.G. Ross, the Minstrels themselves performed the entire evening at the Waterloo Rooms.

The program followed the same format as previous concerts by the Virginia Minstrels and included many of the same highlights. Emmett kept his trademark pieces, "Old Dan Tucker," sung by Frank Brower, and "The Fine Old Coloured Gemman" and added to them five of his other "compositions." "De Wild Goose Nation," first published in 1844, was dedicated to T.D. Rice, because it borrowed the tune from Rice's song "Gumbo Chaff." Another claimed by Dan Emmett and sung by Dick Pelham, "My Old Aunt Sally," was a variation on the English composer Charles Dibdin's late Eighteenth Century song "Peggy Perkins." A third, "Master John and Uncle Jess," is unknown. Interestingly, with the exception of "Lucy Long," Sweeney did not perform his own publications, choosing instead to sing two published by Emmett. "Old Joe," published in 1844 and credited to Brower, was included in a second collection of *Old Dan Emmits Original Banjo Melodies*. A variation of Joe Sweeney's "De Ole Jaw Bone," "Walk, Jaw Bone," was included in the same publication.[142]

The *Edinburgh Post* hailed the Virginia Minstrels as "the most perfect representation of negro character we have ever seen." Four days later, it further praised the performances, noting:

> We know no means more certain of exciting the risible muscles than hearing and seeing these entertainments. They keep the audience in a roar of laughter from first to last. But although the absurd predominates more especially in the eccentricities of Brower, Pelham, and Emmit; yet the banjo melodies of Mr Sweeny are full of simple beauty, and while they provoke laughter, also excite admiration at the admirable skill and taste of the player. Mr Brower's contortions and evolutions are truly negroesque, and his dancing seems nothing short of an inspiration of St Vitus. His imitation of the peculiar noises of a railway engine in motion, is perfectly unique and marvellously [sic] exact. This feat was loudly encoured.[143]

It was then back to Glasgow for the end of their spring tour. The Minstrels had been so successful in that city that they had to return to satisfy the audiences, and their first reappearance, at City Hall on Saturday, June 15, drew 2,100 people.[144] Another reason for their return could have been to present the full-length concert that they hadn't the time to give during the Minstrels' theatrical presentations. The running order was juggled, and new pieces substituted for others used in Edinburgh. Pelham rendered "Old Mr. Brown, who was cast away on the James River, and saved himself by sculling the boat to land with the old banjo" ("Nebber Do to Gib It Up So") and Emmett's "Boatman's Dance," Sweeney returned to his own material with "Old Tar River" and "Jenny, Get Your Hoe-Cake Done," with Brower and Pelham combining on Joe's "Take Your Time, Miss Lucy Long."

Some other pieces performed by the Minstrels included "Dandy Jim from Caroline," which had first been published in America under the Virginia Minstrels name in 1843 without author credit. Emmett later claimed that he wrote it "while on ... passage to England." As with many of Dan Emmett's pieces used by the Virginia Minstrels, it wasn't Emmett who sang it, but group member Joe Sweeney.[145] "Dandy Jim" was one of the songs from Emmett's *Celebrated Negro Melodies or Songs of the Virginny Banjoist* printed by Sweeney's English publisher, D'Almaine, in 1844. Additional songs that had been featured by the Minstrels and Emmett in their British appearances put onto music sheets included "Old Dan Tucker," "The Boatman's Dance," "Gwine ober de Mountains," "My Old Aunt Sally," "Walk Along John," "Walk-Jaw-Bone," "Fine Old Color'd Gemman" and "Nebber Do to Gib It up So."

Although billed as their only appearance, the Virginia Minstrels were back at Glasgow's City Hall on Thursday, June 20, ending their engagement and tour at that venue on Saturday.[146] Even though playbills hinted at a continuation of the Virginia Minstrels performances on the continent,[147] the ensemble then disbanded. Richard Pelham wrote that Emmett spent a few weeks at Cooke's Circus before heading back to the United States.

Dan Emmett and Frank Brower were back at the Bowery Amphitheatre in New York City by October 7, 1844, where they were still leading a band one month later.[148] Dick Pelham remained in Britain, where he became an important promoter of Ethiopian minstrelsy. Pelham continued to perform as well, appearing in November 1844 in Newcastle.[149] He eventually retired to become an agent for other minstrels (for more on Pelham's subsequent life in England, see Chapter Seven).

The Virginia Minstrels were only together for a short period, the original quartet for around five months and the group with Sweeney on banjo about two months. However, their effect was long lasting. They not only gave minstrelsy its name, the Virginia Minstrels spawned a myriad of sound-alike groups, both in the United States and abroad. Even if Emmett, Whitlock, Brower and Pelham hadn't been key "players" in the development of blackface minstrelsy, their association with Joe Sweeney—Sweeney trained Billy Whitlock, the banjoist with the Virginia Minstrels, as well as partnering with various group members both before and after Joe performed under their aegis—makes them key to his story.

Minstrel Groups After the Virginia Minstrels

In the aftermath of the Virginia Minstrels, a multitude of groups with a myriad of names formed to take advantage of the demand for ensembles. Solo performers saw the financial advantages to joining with three or more other like minded blackface entertainers in the move toward minstrel bands. While numerous players continued to travel the country from engagement to engagement, some minstrel leaders chose to purchase or lease permanent homes for their productions. Companies like Christy's, Wood's and Buckley's stayed at one building for months at a time in locales like New York City and Philadelphia. By the 1850s, stationary minstrel troupes became a powerful theatrical force, with ensembles numbering from ten to twelve performers.

In fact, at least two of the former Virginia Minstrels (Frank Brower and Dan Emmett) would work in these expanded minstrel shows. And Dan Emmett would have somewhat of a comeback when he penned one of blackface's (and American popular music's) biggest hits.

According to blackface historian T. Alston Brown, the first "cheap" theater in New York City designed for minstrel performances was the Melodeon at 53 Bowery. Opened on November 24, 1846, by Charles T. White (June 4, 1821–January 4, 1891), one paid half to a fourth of the going rate for a normal evening at the theater to attend shows there. Between its opening and April of 1854, the theater had been leveled by fire and rebuilt several times.[150] Performers in White's groups included banjoist Billy Coleman (circa 1829–June 4, 1867[151]) and original Virginia Minstrel alumni Dan Emmett.[152] Emmett had known Charlie White since Dan's return from Great Britain, and, between the end of 1849 and the close of White's Melodeon, Emmett served as banjoist, company member and co-proprietor.[153]

Another minstrel group based in New York City was Christy's Minstrels (see Chapter Nine and above). In the spring of 1846, Christy's took up permanent residence in Mechanics Hall at 472 Broadway.[154] Irishman R.M. Hooley (April 13, 1822–September 8, 1893[155]) and William A. Porter (May 4, 1822–January 18, 1906[156]) had joined Edwin Christy, George Christy and Tom Vaughan by the time Edwin had moved his band from Buffalo to New York. Opening on February 15, 1847, and remaining in that location until July 15, 1854, Edwin Christy and his various employees made Mechanics Hall one of the most famous minstrel theaters during its time. By the fall of 1847, Holey was out and banjoist Earl Horton Pierce (1823–June 5, 1859[157]) and C. Abbott were in. Porter didn't last much longer, and at the end of the year, was replaced by J.W. Raynor (March 31, 1823–April 5, 1900[158]), another Irish-born blackface performer. At the same time, banjoists Tom Briggs (see Chapter Seven) and S.A. Wells of the Sable Harmonists were also incorporated into the group.[159]

On September 20, 1854, Christy's Minstrels left for California, where they stayed only a short time before returning to New York City.[160] Edwin Christy then retired from minstrelsy. He had amassed a significant fortune from promoting minstrel shows, and used his

money to support an elegant lifestyle in New York City. Newspaper writers relished reporting his comings and goings, and in January of 1857 proclaimed that Christy:

> recently made a great dash in the streets with a magnificent sleigh, which attracted unusual
> attention, from its splendor and the beauty of the prancing stud of snow white horses, to
> which it was attached. In the summer he drives out in an elegant carriage, behind two splen-
> did bays, with a fine large coach-dog running under the carriage. He is quite a connoisseur in
> horseflesh, and in driving out alternates between his bay and white horses. In his promenade
> he is accompanied by a large bull terrier, a splendid specimen of the canine race. His wealth is
> prodigious, and as he has been economical and laborious while earning it, he feels authorized
> to spend it freely. He may be frequently seen in the dress circle of the Italian Opera, and is
> always the observed of all observers.[161]

In October 1853, before the Christy's Minstrels departed for California, George Christy
left the employ of his stepfather and entered into a partnership with Henry Wood (see Chapter Nine). Wood had taken over Fellow's Opera House and Hall of Lyrics, built at 444 Broadway for Jerome B. Fellow's (or Fellowe's) Ethiopian Operatic Troupe, a group founded by Earl
Pierce and Fellow in 1850. Pierce had departed the Christy's Minstrels before George Christy
(in April 1850), hiring a troupe that included Moody Stanwood of the Ethiopian Serenaders on
accordion (see Chapter Seven).[162] Fellow's Opera House opened on November 6, 1850, and was
consequently taken over by Henry Wood in 1851.[163] Within several years, the Opera House burnt
to the ground. During the next seven years, Wood and Christy utilized a number of venues in
New York City, as well as touring their troupe. Among the New York members of their company were Tom Briggs and Sam Wells,[164] who had come over from Edwin Christy's band, as well
as Dan Bryant (see Chapter Nine) and ex–Virginia Minstrel Frank Brower.[165] This partnership
continued until May 1858, at which time George Christy reformed the Christy's Minstrels.[166]

Like his stepfather, George Christy profited from keeping his company in one locale.
Although the price of admission was kept to twenty-five cents, the gross receipts for 2,792
performances amounted to $317, 589.30. The net resulted in profits of over $160,000.00
for the producers of Wood and Christy's Minstrels. George Christy himself drew a salary
of $19,168.00, an astonishing figure for the time.[167]

Many other minstrel troupes used New York City as a base of operations in between
tours. For example, Peel's Campbell Minstrels (see Chapter Nine) of 1858—Matt Peel and
thirteen other performers in black—held court at the old Wood and Christy's hall at 444
Broadway during the spring and summer of 1858.[168] Dan Bryant, who succeeded Christy's
Minstrels at Mechanic's Hall between 1857 and the end of the Civil War led another group
appearing in New York. The most significant occurrence during Bryant's occupation of 472
Broadway was the introduction of Daniel Emmett's most famous composition, now known
as "Dixie." On April 4, 1859, Bryant's company debuted Emmett's song, which was to become
an anthem of the Confederate cause. Although historians have recently questioned whether
Dan Emmett "wrote" or "borrowed" the song, "I Wish I Was in Dixie's Land" remains the
composition that helped to establish the Bryant's and Emmett's reputation.[169]

Philadelphia's first stand-alone purpose-built minstrel theater premiered during 1853,
when Sam Sanford opened the Twelfth Street Opera House. Sanford (see Chapters Seven
and Nine) was the former manager of Buckley's New Orleans Serenaders.[170] When his building was destroyed by fire in December of that year, Sanford took to the road, returning to
Philadelphia for a long-term residency at the Eleventh Street replacement. Jim Carter's Jullien Minstrels had occupied the hall during 1854, abandoning it when receipts didn't surpass expenses. Sanford's troupe moved in to their new home during April of 1855, remaining,
for the most part, until 1862.[171]

Virginia Minstrel Frank Brower, a native of Philadelphia, came back to his hometown to work for Sam Sanford at various times in the late 1850s.[172] Brower variously appeared in two of Tom Rice's plays, playing "Ginger Blue in *The Virginia Mummy*"[173] and Cuff in *Oh! Hush!*[174] as well as parodying the animal trainer Van Amburgh[175] (as "Von Humbug"). On a number of occasions, Frank Brower also performed in conjunction with Dan Gardner.[176]

The freestanding minstrel theaters encouraged the growth and establishment of blackface minstrelsy. The larger troupes provided a more stable economic environment as well as steady employment for many performers. Minstrelsy's success in the 1850s and 1860s led to its long term health in the post–Civil War period, assuring that blackface would be a staple of American (and worldwide) entertainment well into the twentieth century.

SEVEN

Ethiopian Serenaders:
British Minstrelsy After Sweeney

The English Serenader's Lament[1]

1

Come listen kind friends while my tale I re-late
And I thin when you hear it you'll pity my fate
I, a prodigy was in the musical way
Now my friends all assert that poor Tom's had his day
Thos Foreign invaders with outlandish sounds
I can hear ev'ry where while I'm going my rounds
They're encourag'd and fed by e-very grade
While true native genius must pine in the shade
Chorus: Then pity poor Tom who was born in a land
Where talent if native they wont understand
...

3

Once I-talian Signora's our spirits could cheer
Then I'm free to confess there was something to hear
Even Poor Pagannini on our bounty grew fat
He could play on one string there was merit in that
The Statesmen may boast while the sage makes pro-
    fession
And philosophers call this an age of progression
It's an age of de-ception in ac-tions and tones
Coun-terfeit Niggers of Banjo's and Bones

4

To Englishmen sure it's a shame and disgrace
To compel "Lovely Woman" to blacken her face
Even dear Jenny Lind I'm afraid after all
Must consent to appear as a "Buffalo Gal"
If Rainforth or Romer will live by their tones
They must take my advice and come out on the
    bones
For all classes are touched high, low and the middle
And the Banjo has quite circumvented the fiddle

5

The other day as I 0'er my misfortunes did pore
I met a sweep's Lady who feelingly swore
As she saw I was starving she'd give me a meal
If I'd tune the old Fiddle and play Lucy Neal
Although conscience said no, my stomach said yes
And the tune that I played—perhaps some of you'll
    guess
It was poor Mary Ann, but I altered the time
And with tears in her eyes she exclaims its "diwine"

    Once Rice, Sweeney and the Virginia Minstrels had created a minstrel conscious British society, it opened the door for other American groups interested in touring Great Britain. This also encouraged more homegrown talent to try their hand at blackface entertainment.

    The first British group with any longevity appears to be the American Southern Minstrels. Comprised of a "Mr. Robins on a Tuckahoe Violin, Mr. Woolcott, on the Longo [sic] Banjo, Mr. Parker, on the Bone Castanets, [and] Mr. Ring, on the Cohea Tambourine,"[2] their programs, instrumentation and the like were a direct copy of the original Virginia Minstrels. The American Southern Minstrels (alternately, "The American Minstrels," "Southern Minstrels," or "Southern American Minstrels") first performance that I have been able to document occurred on February 7, 1844, or thereabouts, in the north of England at Gainsboro's Theater.[3] This minstrel group was in London at Batty's Amphitheatre on January 5, 1845, until at least January 11.[4]

    Luckily, the move toward a more genteel minstrel repertoire and performance style in

76

the United States coincided with the audience's taste in the mother country. As Michael Pickering has written about the British Isles, "minstrelsy also began to shift in tone from an earthy robustness and frenzied excitement towards an appeal in refinement and senti-mentalism. Also detected during this phase is an incipient process of adaptation to the tra-ditions and characteristics of English popular culture, and the early signs of a growth of distinctly English features."[5] Two of these more sedate minstrel troupes included two bands of "Ethiopian Serenaders." One was affiliated with Richard Pelham, the former Virginia Min-strel and companion of Joe Sweeney who had made quite a name for himself in Britain. The other featured those former Sweeney associates the Buckley family.

> I took the hint from the performance of Pell and the others at the St. James's.... One of us had been a street singer before, another a street fiddler, another had sung nigger-songs in public-houses, ... The banjo is the hardest to learn of the lot.
> The first came out at St. James Theatre.... After them sprang up the "Lantum Serenaders," and the "Ohio Serenaders," the "South Carolina Serenaders," the "Kentucky Minstrels," and many other schools of them; but Pell's gang was at the top of the tree.[6]

Dick Pelham was not immune to the accomplishments of Virginia Minstrel want-a-bees. The only group member to remain as an expatriate, Pelham had successfully toured Britain after the Minstrel's final disbanding. As we have seen in Chapters Four and Six, first, Dick Pelham joined with the remaining members of his former band, or, allied himself with great American Ethiopians such as Joe Sweeney.

After all his contemporaries returned home, Pelham assembled, trained and toured groups of British minstrels. For example, Dick Pelham brought the "Sable Bros" to Belfast's Theatre Royal in November of 1845. The group's members included C. Brennie on banjo, W. Williamson on tambourine, W. Green on violin, J. Secole on triangle and H. Dwight on bone castanets.[7] Pelham also promoted American minstrels in Britain, and its a good guess that his brother Gilbert (circa 1825–December 21, 1872[8]), now returned to his given name of Pell, came with his band the Ethiopian Serenaders under the management of Dick.

January 21, 1846, marked the first British appearance of the Ethiopian Serenaders: Pell on bones and dancing, George A. Harrington on banjo (d. January, 1859[9]), Bostonian G. Warren White on banjo (1816–March, 1886[10]), Moody G. Stanwood on accordion and Fran-cis Germon on tambourine (d. 1850s[11]). Each had some performing experience, with Gilbert Pell probably the most seasoned in front of an audience. Francis C. Germon is documented singing "Sittin' on a Rail" at a Taunton, Massachusetts, concert in December 1839.[12] And accordionist Stanwood was playing in public, although probably not in blackface, as early as a September 25, 1840, concert in Boston.[13]

Odell first notes the Ethiopian Serenaders, also known in their premiere days as the Boston Minstrels, as appearing in New York City on June 1, 1843, four months after the debut of the Virginia Minstrels.[14] The Ethiopian Serenaders spent the fall of 1843 in the South, appearing twice in Richmond, at the Concert Room of the Exchange Hotel and at the Theater in November,[15] and again in March 1844.[16] The group was back in New York City by the end of June, playing various venues throughout the summer and early fall.[17] The publicity for an October appearance mentioned that they had recently appeared at the White House; it also mentioned the addition of White to the band.[18]

At the same time the Virginia Minstrels were trying to prove their authenticity by the grotesqueness of their portrayals, the Ethiopian Serenaders betrayed their roots as a vocal group in the manner of the Hutchinson Family singers. From the beginning, parodies of popular songs took a prominent place in their entertainments. A program from September

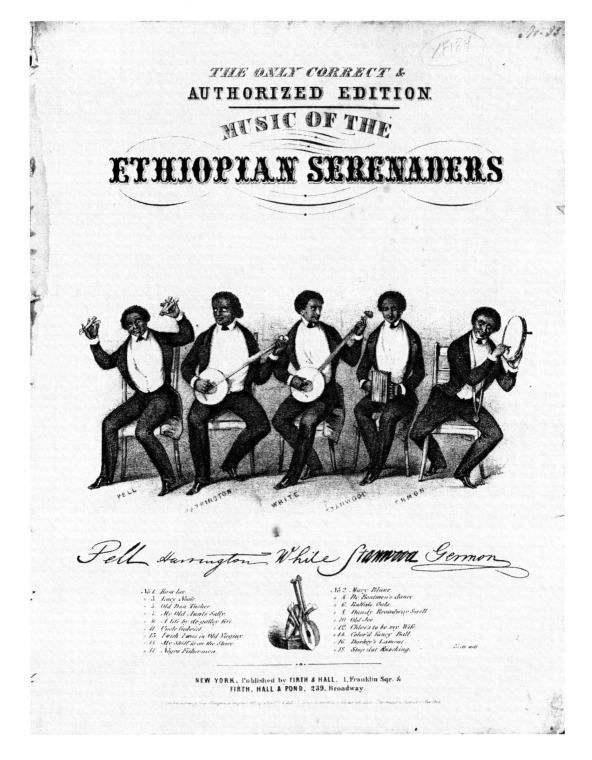

Sheet music cover, "Music of the Ethiopian Serenaders," Gilbert Pell, George Harrington, Warren White, Moody Stanwood and Frank Germon. Note the tuxedos and realistic facial features. Firth, Hall & Pond, New York, 1842.

1843 lists the spoof of "Come, soldiers, come" entitled "Come darkies sing," and "'Echo,' from the opera of the Americas."[19] The following year, the Serenaders featured lampoons of the "Old Granite State" by the Hutchinson Family and "Lila's a Lady."[20] By the time the Ethiopian Serenaders reached England, tuxedos had replaced the "appropriate costume[s]" of Southern slaves,[21] and the rough edges had been knocked off of their music as well. Although a New York reviewer took the Serenaders to task for being "too elegant" and untrue to Southern blacks,[22] this refinement of minstrelsy brought the Ethiopian Serenaders success in Britain, along with a host of imitators, and helped to change American minstrelsy, preparing it for the sentimental songs of Stephen Foster.

When the Ethiopian Serenaders arrived in London, they first went to the Hanover Square Concert Rooms, then to the St. James Theatre,[23] to the Vauxhall Gardens and eventually to Evan's Song and Supper Rooms. *The Era* felt them to be the best of their type.[24] Their tour extended into 1847, taking them to Brighton, Liverpool and Dublin.[25]

Songs associated with the Serenaders began almost immediately to appear in British publications during their first year abroad, in books such as Barlow's *Nigger Melodist, Songs of the Ethiopian Serenaders and Celebrated Banjo Players*,[26] and *The Real Virginny Melodist*. Sheet music bearing their name came out in both England and America during 1847.[27]

> An improvised troupe of Negro Minstrels called the Ethiopian Serenaders and consisting of five males and three females, all with blackened faces, occupied the stage. The name had been unfairly annexed from that of the more noted Ethiopian Serenaders from America performing at the ST James' Theatre.[28]

Concurrent with the tour that Dick Pelham had set up for his brother Gilbert and the Serenaders in Britain, Pelham seems to have kept his own band, the Ethiopian Delineators, on the road. The group was surely made up of Brits, and included two banjos, violin, tambourine and bones.[29] As the demand was high for minstrels, Richard Pelham wanted to supply as many venues as he could. After all, if he didn't, others would step in to claim the engagements. Indeed, documents claiming to publicize Pelham's group could have indeed been promoting knock-offs of the popular Serenaders. Bands bearing the "Ethiopian Delineators" name played Brighton in May[30] and London's Lyceum at August's end in 1846.[31] Dick Pelham's group seems to have been in Liverpool at the Lord Nelson Street Concert Hall in late June and early July,[32] although his name, misspelled (perhaps purposely) as "Richard Ward Phelam," is in an advertisement for an booking at Birkenhead's Craven Rooms at the same time. This group's members included F. Blewett, B. Roberts, W. Sandford, R. Jerome and T. Leicester, "late of the Theatre Royal, Williamson-square, Liverpool."[33]

If the Ethiopian Delineators weren't trying to cash in on the Ethiopian Serenaders' popularity, others were surely riding their coattails. A group posing in Dublin as "Virginia Minstrels" became "Ethiopian Serenaders" Lee, Millicent, King, Neal and Harroway for a Sunderland run in August 1846.[34] Another band of Serenaders were in Bristol during July 1847, and even had a "Sweeney" among their members Palmer, Walford, Bowter and Sefton.[35] A third "Ethiopian Serenaders," with Roberts, May, Daniels, Sherwood and Fortescue, played Mechanics Hall in Nottingham during November 1846[36] and Norwich's Theatre Royal during the first week of 1847. From a surviving playbill, we know that, along with their name, the ensemble's repertoire was also taken from the Serenaders.[37] Roberts, a concertina, tambourine player and "Comic Vocalist," along with Fortescue on bones, later joined with banjoists Goulding and Collins, and Dalzelle on concertina in the Ethiopian Harmonists. While slightly modifying "Serenaders" to "Harmonists," they obviously still wanted audiences to associate their group with the original, as they also advertised "Late of the celebrated Serenaders of the St. James's Theatre." This group played Dublin's Music Hall in November and December 1847, and featured the forward-looking banjo duets of "American Quickstep," "Yankee Doodle, with new effects," and "Irish Melodies."[38]

There were even female versions of the Ethiopian Serenaders. An "improvised" group including five men and three women using the name of the Americans appeared during 1846 in London at the Marylebone Theatre (see above).[39] The "Buffalo Girls, or, Female Ethiopian Serenaders" (named for the popular minstrel song), were in York during May 1847,[40] and the Female American Serenaders appeared in London at the Adelphi and the St. James's Assembly Rooms during May and July of the same year.[41]

British craftsmen would also make their own distinctive contributions to the American minstrel banjo. By 1860, Henry Solomon & Company of London offered instruments in eight different styles. The simplest cost 3 shillings, 6, with their fanciest "No. 8" a "full size, pearl mounted [banjo] with vellum [skin] head and tuning screws richly inlaid" for 1 pound, 8 shillings, 6. Probably the best known of the early English banjo makers was William Temlett (died May 2, 1904). Beginning in 1846, Temlett ran a workshop at 95 Union Street in Southeast London, where he made the very English six and seven string instruments (with added bass and drone strings). In the 1880s, Temlett became best known as a pioneering maker of the "zither banjo," a closed-back instrument with the fifth string running through a tunnel in the neck to the headstock.[42]

The members of the original Ethiopian Serenaders returned to Great Britain in 1849. By this time, the group had split in two. The majority of the members continued under the name Dumbolton's Ethiopian Serenaders to distinguish them from the earlier band. Besides White and Stanwood, there was a Mr. Howard who had been recruited upon the Serenaders' return to the United States after their first tour, Mr. Parker, possibly from the Southern American Minstrels, Jerry Bryant of the famous Bryant minstrel family[43] and Sam A. Wells (circa 1826–August 27, 1864[44]; see the previous chapter for more information). They were documented in Dublin during February and March in 1849,[45] returning to the United States by July of the year.[46]

At the same time, Dick Pelham had his brother Gilbert lead a group of seven minstrels, at least some of them Americans. Pell's group played London in the spring,[47] Dublin in July[48] and Edinburgh in August and September.[49] Besides Gilbert Pell, among their number were the banjoist Tom Briggs and the dancer "Juba."

Thomas F. Briggs (circa 1824–October 23, 1854[50]) garnered Joe Sweeney's knowledge of the banjo from Joe's student Billy Whitlock.[51] In the two years before coming to Great Britain, Briggs had worked around New York City with a number of well-known minstrel groups, including the Western and Southern Band of Sable Harmonists[52] and Christy's Minstrels (see Chapter Six).[53] William Henry "Juba" Lane was familiar to British audiences through his promotion by the author Charles Dickens. During an American tour early in 1842,[54] Dickens had seen Lane dancing at a hall located within the Five Points neighborhood of New York City. Upon his return to England, Dickens included a description of the dancer in his *American Notes*.[55] Juba, an African American, began moving into minstrel performances during the same year, making him one of the select few black Ethiopians.[56] Match dances were common places where non-affiliated, non-professional performers could appear, and allowed Lane entry into performances previously restricted to whites. Juba is mentioned competing against John Diamond in 1843[57] and again against one of the men using the Diamond name in 1844.[58] According to T. Alston Brown, Juba was working for Charles White at his discount theater, the Melodeon, in the two years before moving to England.[59]

Another group based in America that influenced early British minstrel bands were the expatriate Buckley family. These are the same Buckleys whose father conducted Harrington's orchestra during Joe Sweeney's appearances and whose banjoist, George Swaine Buckley, learned the instrument from Sweeney during that time (see Chapter Thirteen for more information). According to group member Samuel S. Sanford (January 1, 1821–December 31, 1905[60]), the New Orleans Serenaders sailed on the John P. Harwood.[61] They arrived in Liverpool on January 17, 1847, and played their first engagement at that city's Royal Assembly Rooms on Great George Street January 28.[62] It was then off to London for appearances at the Adelphi and then, for the month of March, at the Princess Theatre.[63] In London, they went "head to head" with the Ethiopian Serenaders, then holding forth at the St. James Theatre.[64] They moved to another hall, staying in London for another month or so, during which time Queen Victoria and her children attended a performance.[65] The Buckleys moved on to Dublin, where they joined forces with the English Ethiopian singer Henry Russell[66] and went to Shields, Newcastle, and Ripon and then to Edinburgh, Scotland.[67] The New Orleans Serenaders performed in Glasgow in December into 1848, with Russell on his own back in London by early March.[68] The group played Yorkshire at winter's end, and, after brief stays in London, headed north to Birmingham, where they appeared at the end of

New Orleans Ethiopian Serenaders, broadside for their last night at the Music Hall, Dublin, Ireland, June 7, 1847. This poster features a woodcut of the five-piece band, at that time (left to right) Sam S. Sanford on tambourine, James Buckley and Fred Buckley on violins, George Swaine Buckley on banjo and J. C. Rainer on bones (a previous owner of the poster has switched George Buckley and Rainer in the handwritten labeling). Notice the evening dress worn by the group, and the inclusion of a "Burlesque, Italian Opera" performed by the company along with the usual minstrel fare.

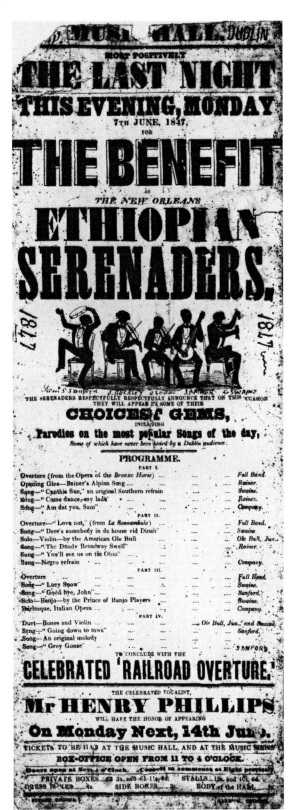

June with Charles Dickens in a benefit for the Shakespeare Endowment Fund. It was back to
Edinburgh, and, their tour ended during the early fall in Liverpool. The New Orleans Serenaders then returned to the United States via New York City.[69]

The upshot of groups like the Ethiopian Serenaders and Buckley's New Orleans Serenaders was the introduction of a new repertoire and sensibility to the minstrel stage. These
were the second generation of performers, brought up within the milieu and trained by
other minstrels. No longer would composers be seeking African American material. Instead,
the songs and bits would come from the minds of Anglo Americans. The blackface mask
would be retained to present parodies of highbrow culture and sentimental renderings of
Southern life, far removed from the slave experience.

1

A-way down in de Ken-tuck brake
dar-key lib, dey call him Jake,
He pick up-on de ban-jo string,
De am de song dat he would sing.
Chorus: Ree-ro my true lub,
O come a-long my dar-lin,
So fare you well, my Di-nah gal,
I'm gwine o-ber de moun-tains.

2

Come my lub an go wid me,
I'm gwine away to Tennessee;
A hoss an cart shall put you roun,
Walk up hill an foot it down.

3

One kind kiss before we part,
One more kiss would break my heart;
Hitch your hoss up to a rail,
Make him fast both head and tail.

4

I fed my hoss in a popular trough,
De old hoss catch de hoopin cough,
I lick him wid a hick'ry stick
He paw de groun an begin to kick.

5

I hitch him to a swingin limb
De ole hoss cut a pidgeon-wing;
Den I rote de tanner a letter
I though de hoss was getting no better.

6

De tanner made me dis reply
'I want de hoss-hide when he die,'
De tanner he was well enuff,
De hoss-hide was ole an tuff.

7

De ole hoss die, I dig a hole,
I cover him up both body an soul,
De tanner come but soon he found,
De hoss was too deep under ground.[70]

By 1850, blackface minstrelsy, modeled on the American performers, had become
ingrained into British society. It had moved into the streets, with vendors peddling song
sheets such as "Buffalo gals, come out to-night" and "Jim along Josey."[71] The Punch and
Judy shows as well utilized "Jim Crow" characters singing Rice's signature composition,[72]
and blackface clowns joined the other minstrel performers on London's thoroughfares.[73]

As one strolled about London, full bands imitating the original Virginia Minstrels and
Ethiopian Serenaders would entertain the passers-by, hoping for a handout. The strains of
"Buffalo Gals," "Going ober de Mountain," "Dandy Jim of Carolina" and other favorites of
the last ten years drifted over alleys and avenues. Many bands moved between the streets
and public houses or "cheap concert-room [s], such as the Albion, Ratcliffe-highway, or the
Ship and Camel, Bermondsey." Sometimes, as one street performer recollected, they'd get
lucky and be hired to "serenade people, such as at weddings or anything of that sort."[74]

"As soon as I could get in to vamp the tunes on the banjo a little," recalled the player,

> I went at it, too.... First of all we formed a school of three—two banjos and a tambourine,
> and after that we added a bones and a fiddle.... The first songs we came out with were "Old
> Joe," "Dan Tucker," and "Going ober de Mountain," and "O come along, you sandy boys."
> Our opening chorus was "The Wild Racoon Track," and we finished up with the "Railway
> Overture," and it was more like the railway than music, for it was all thumping and whistling,
> for nobody knowed [sic] how to play the banjo then.

Sometimes, when we are engaged for it, we go to concert-rooms and do the nigger-statues, which is the same as the tableaux vivants. We illustrate the adventures of Pompey, or the life of a negro slave.[75]

These bands at the same time reflected and also led this change, both in Great Britain and in the United States. Of course, only rarely does change occur suddenly and unequivocally. Single performers and duos continued to present the older repertoire and styles, and the elder statesmen of minstrelsy were still very much in the public eye. As the years progressed, English, Irish and Scottish Ethiopians would add some unique British touches to the procedures borrowed from the Americans. But that is outside the reach of this investigation.

EIGHT

The Banjo in Australia

The myth of isolation is a popular (as well as false) one when describing the spread of the banjo into the American south. The commonly held belief is that Southerners were so isolated from the urban north that minstrelsy had little effect below the Mason-Dixon line. Instead, southern banjoists were left to develop their own repertoire and playing styles. Nothing could be further from the truth, since minstrel banjoists were penetrating even the remotest corners of the southern United States as early as 1840 (see Chapters Six and Nine) and vestiges of the minstrel repertoire and playing style are found throughout southern traditional music.

This myth is just as incorrect when considering the faraway continent of Australia. The story of the American banjo's spread from the United States and Great Britain to the former English colony can be read in period newspaper articles and advertisements (provided to me by Gary Le Gallant), and through the writings of Australian scholars Richard Waterhouse and John Whiteoak. In my investigation into these sources, it's apparent that some of the same cultural forces at work in the United States were present in Australia. And while the continent initially lagged behind America, Australian banjo trends eventually came to parallel those in the United States and Great Britain.

Part of the reason for the early exposure given the banjo in Australia was well-developed routes of transportation. In the nineteenth century, excellent lines of communication existed between Australia and the United States. The gold rushes encouraged the immigration of American miners and helped to create an audience with a disposable income. Therefore, hit plays and minstrel troupes with banjoists followed in close pursuit of the émigrés, reaching Australian viewers within twelve months of their initial staging in America.[1] As mentioned in Chapter Five, Joe Sweeney and William Parrow used the believable ruse of an impending Australian tour in order to boost attendance at their American concerts. With the approach of the Civil War, an increasing number of American (and British) groups took advantage of improved methods of transportation to try their luck with the Australian market.

Blythe Waterland's Serenaders

1
As I was lumb'ring down de street,
down de street, down de street,
A hand-some gal I chanc'd to meet;
Oh! She was fair to view.
Chorus: Buffalo gals, cant you come out to-night?

cant you come out to-night? cant you come out to-
  night?
Buffalo gals, cant you come out to-night?
And dance by de light ob de moon.
2
I ax'd her would she hab some talk,

hab some talk, hab some talk,
Her feet cover'd up de whole side walk
As she stood close by me.

3
I ax'd her would she hab a dance,
hab a dance, hab a dance,

I taught dat I might get a chance,
To shake a foot wid her.
4
I'd like to make dat gal my wife,
gal my wife, gal my wife,
I'd be hap-py all my life,
If I had her by me.[2]

The first appearance of the "American banjo" in Sydney was in the hands of a British member of the Blythe Waterland minstrel troupe, James W. Reading (much of the basic information within this chapter was initially published in two articles by Gary Le Gallant, "Minstrelsy and the Banjo in Australia: The Beginnings," and "Minstrelsy in Australia: A Brief Overview").[3] The Waterland Company had been assembled in England and brought to Australia in late 1849 by Henry Burton, well known for his work with the early Australian circus.[4] Blythe Waterland (Burton's "nom de minstrel") opened his Sydney season at the Royal Hotel on April 1, 1850. His group left Sydney for northern performances in May, splitting into two troupes upon Burton's return during the next month.

Howard's Celebrated And Original Company of Serenaders, as the breakaway company called themselves, were one of the groups to avail themselves of opportunities for entertainers in Australia's gold fields.[5] With an unknown banjoist,[6] they also played some of the same locales as the primary group, now led by the banjoist Reading. The *Melbourne Argus* noted that "two parties of Ethiopians hav(e) suddenly invaded us; making this whole town alive with the notes of the banjo and the rattle of the bones."[7] Unfortunately, the presence of two similar bands created a great deal of confusion in the minds of the public. Waterland and Reading deemed it necessary to alert their audiences to what the promoters saw as the fallacious nature of the "other" minstrel group. Advertising for Waterhouse trumpeted that "[we are] not in any way connected with the Messrs. Howard, or any other parties who may term themselves the Ethiopian Serenaders, and most respectfully ... apprise the [public] that [we] are the original performers on the American Banjo, and the first to introduce the gems of Negro Melody to the public of New South Wales."[8]

By July, Waterland & Reading's Band of Ethiopian Serenaders, as the reformed group was now being labeled, had opened in Melbourne at the Royal Hotel. On July 12, the *Melbourne Daily News* praised James Reading: "The Banjo was uncommonly well played and can produce a tone little inferior to the harp—decidedly superior to any guitar." It was then across the water to Launceston, Tasmania, where the group resided during September at the Cornwell Assembly Rooms. When they returned to Sydney in October during the Races, the *Sydney Morning Herald* luckily saw fit to print their concert program. This included J.W. Reading's renditions of "Buffalo Gals," published under the name "Lubly Fan Will You Cum Out To Night?" as early as 1844,[9] Stephen Foster's "Oh, Susannah" (published in 1848, see Chapter Eleven) and "Lynchburg Town" (see Chapter Fourteen). Reading additionally rendered his imitation of Church Bells on the banjo. It was also during this time that a songbook, *No. 1 of 'Songs of the Serenaders' containing 12 Ethiopian Melodies* was published. James Reading then joined up with a Mr. Hyde for a series of year-end performances in Sydney, where he added Dan Emmett's "Dandy Jim [From Carolina]" (see Chapter Seven), as well as "Ole Grey Goose" to his repertoire.[10]

Another early banjoist in Australia to claim the title of "first" was Troy Knight. Although he seems to have been British, his origins are undocumented by this author. Knight showed during 1850 with a local troupe of "Ethiopian Serenaders" at the Theatre Royal in Geelong. This was shortly before the Howard and Waterland troupes had appeared in Melbourne.

Billed as the "celebrated banjoist," Knight also performed as a vocalist on such decidedly
non-blackface songs as "[The Lament of] The Irish Emigrant,"[11] "Fanny Gray" (written in
the 1830s),[12] and Jenny Lind's hit of that year, "By the Sad Sea Waves."[13] Troy Knight also
played the bones as well as on the banjo. Forgiving this lack of focus, the critic of the *Geelong Advertiser* noted that, "Unlike most of our own colonial 'Ethiopians,' Mr Knight really
brings music out of the primitive instrument the banjo, and does it too with a lightness
and swiftness of touch, absolutely astonishing."[14]

Following his Geelong performances described above, Knight next appeared at the
Queen's Theatre, Melbourne[15] in August 1850. Troy Knight spent September at the Royal
Olympic Theatre and the Cornwell Assembly Rooms in Launceston, Tasmania and at the
Longford/Blenheim Hotel. During this period, Knight performed such pieces as "Carry me
back to Ole Virginny" (not the better known James Bland composition, but an earlier proto-
song performed by the American Christy Minstrels in 1847[16]), along with Dan Emmett's
"De Boatman Dance" and "Ole Dan Tucker," (see Chapters Four, Six and Seven). The light
classical "Canzonett" from "The Firefly,"[17] and "Rosa May," an 1848 composition claimed
by Francis Germon of the Ethiopian Serenaders (see Chapter Seven) were also a part of his
repertoire.[18] Additionally, Troy Knight duplicated Reading's cover of "Susannah Don't You
Cry ["Oh, Susannah"]," as well as the other musician's simulation of church bells on the
banjo.[19]

Knight also helped in the spread of the banjo in Australia. He taught lessons while
based in Launceston and integrated some of his students into his own productions. One
could learn the instrument in twelve lessons, promised Mr. Knight, for the lowly cost of 2
guineas. He could even supply students with a banjo if necessary.[20]

Troy Knight had his own imitators, as a Mr. Howson (possibly one of Knight's students) was in the same territories as Knight in 1851, playing the banjo with the Turon Minstrels.[21] Other banjoists followed Knight onto local stages. By the following year, at least two
other minstrel groups appeared in Australia featuring the instrument, the American Black
Serenaders[22] and the Ethiopian Juvenile Serenaders.[23]

The New York Serenaders

1
I cum from Lousianna,
Wid de banjo on my knee;
I'm bound for Alabama,
My own true lub to see.
It thaw all night de week I left,
De hailstone dey war dry;
De sun so hot I froze alive,
Susannah, don't you cry.
Chorus: Oh! Susannah, you must not cry for me,
I'm cum from Louisianna wid de banjo on my knee.
2
I stepp'd on board de lightengraph,
An steer it by de trigger,
My finger slip it bustified,
And kill a tousand nigger.
And den it was, my dearest lub,
I tought dat I shoud die,
I shut my ears to keep my breff,

Susannah don't you cry.
3
I had a dream to-morrow night,
When all de tings war still,
I tought I see Susannah
Coming by de mill.
She wore de robe ob mourning,
And de tears war in her eye,
Says I, here am your true lub,
Susannah don't you cry.
4
I soon will be in de ole Mobile,
And dare I'll look around,
Oh, should I find Susannah,
I shall sink into de ground.
But if I do not find her
Dis child will surely dire,
And when I'm cold and in my grave,
Susannah don't you cry.[24]

The first American minstrel ensemble to appear in Australia including a banjoist was the New York Serenaders, who arrived in early 1851. The Serenaders were in the midst of a world tour that had taken them throughout Mexico, South American, the west coast of the United States and the Islands of the Pacific. When the group arrived in Sydney from Hobart, Tasmania in late June, it had two banjoists in the persons of C. Cushing, first banjo, and J.E. Kitts, second banjo.[25]

By the time of their thirty-sixth concert at the Royal Hotel on September 26, James Reading (see above) had replaced Cushing as the group's primary banjoist. From that instance until his benefit at the end of November, Reading had added Joe Sweeney's "Jenny get your Hoe Cake done" 'discussed in Chapter Eleven,' the 1844 composition "Juliana Johnson" from the Congo Melodists[26] and Stephen Foster's recent song "My Brudder Gum."[27] The New York Serenaders were popular enough with Australians to warrant the publication of a number of minstrel songs under their name by H. Marsh and Company of Sydney.[28]

Other American groups followed in the 1850s. Rainer's Ethiopian Serenaders featured a "Characteristic [African American] Banjo Trio" along with "Solo-Banjo with oddities, absurdities, comicalities, profundities, contradictories, incongruities, [and] probabilities."[29] Totten's Harmoneons appeared in Melbourne in 1854, with M.B. Clark and a Mr. Baker, banjoists, playing Dan Emmett's "Hard Times" (see Chapter Six).[30] And The New Orleans Serenaders included banjoist George A. Harrington, lately of the Ethiopian Serenaders (see Chapter Seven), who played and sang "Lucy Long" (see Chapter Three, Four, Six, Eleven and Thirteen), Sweeney's "Johnny Boker" (see Chapters Eleven), and "Come back, Stephen" (see Chapter Fourteen) during shows staged in Sydney during February 1851 and March 1852.[31]

The banjo as well was continuing its spread among Australians. In 1853, a local Melbourne troupe was led by a banjoist named Barlow,[32] and other bands spun off of the original Waterland troupe. All of the Australian minstrel troupes gave performances and taught lessons, and were the first groups to tour extensively throughout the gold fields and outlying districts.

The following years gave rise to local amateur Ethiopian Serenader concerts as well as the creation of the New South Wales Christy Minstrels. The native Christy group was a feature of the Sydney scene for many years, appearing at various holiday picnics and social functions. Of course, all the banjoists up to this time exclusively utilized the "original" African derived banjo method of down picking, called in the period "stroke style," which we now know as frailing or clawhammer.

Christy Minstrels

The 1860s began with the English Christy's troupe making their presence known on the continent. Led by Anthony Nish, a Brit who had worked with a number of American ensembles, Christy's opened in Melbourne at the Queen's Theatre Royal in February 1863. After four years touring the country, they disbanded in late 1866.[33] Their banjoists were Joe Brown (January 2, 1830–October 25, 1883), an American member of the group better known as a "jig" dancer,[34] or H. Leslie,[35] and Wash Norton. Norton (born in New Orleans February 22, 1839, died in California November 16, 1899) had been a member of Boston's Ordway Aeolians and Bryant's Minstrels.[36]

By the time the Christy Minstrels had come over from England in the 1860s, the banjo was a relatively commonplace instrument in Australia. At the end of the nineteenth century, blackface characters with banjos were well known down under.

As Richard Waterhouse states in *From Minstrel Show to Vaudeville,*

> The establishment of a regular steamship service between San Francisco, Sydney and Melbourne in 1871 gave American entertainers fast, comfortable and cheap access to an affluent and expanding Australian market. American minstrel companies flocked to Australia as never before and the colonies became simply an extension of the western circuit.[37]

Even though minstrel troupes with banjoists continued to tour throughout the 1860s and 1870s, the banjo was no longer a novel asset. In fact, a reviewer of Emerson's California Minstrels' opening Melbourne performance in 1873 stated bluntly that the "banjo eccentricities might have been dispensed with without prejudice to the merits of the performance."[38]

The Georgia Minstrels

The second wave of the banjo's Australian invasion was led by two competing bands of African American "Georgia Minstrels." The first to appear in Australia, "featuring real negroes from the slave states," were Sheridan Corbyn's troupe that appeared at the School of Arts in Sydney at the end of 1876.[39] However, the company did poor business in Sydney, thereby leaving in early January 1877 for country towns in New South Wales and Victoria.[40] Their banjoist was George H. Carter, who specialized in the "guitar style" (ie: finger picking solos that had replaced the "stroke" or down picking style) on such pieces as "Home Sweet Home" with variations that earned him multiple encores.[41] This group lasted at least until the end of the year.

The more successful of the two ensembles was Charles Barney Hicks' Georgia Minstrels. The Hicks troupe had come off a yearlong tour of the American west coast that included Oregon, California, British Columbia and fourteen weeks in San Francisco. Hicks first appeared in New Zealand, Melbourne and Adelaide before opening in Hobart during late July 1877.[42] Even after the conclusion of their tour, banjoist Hosea Easton was to remain in Australia as a major influence on Australian players.

Easton was born in Hartford, Connecticut, in 1857.[43] His "Talking Banjo" was a feature with Hick's troupe in Australia throughout the spring of 1878, although Hosea also played dramatic parts in "Uncle Tom's Cabin" and the like.[44] By 1882, Hosea Easton was appearing with R.B. Lewis's Mastodon Star Minstrels,[45] and in 1887, with Hugo's Buffalo Minstrels.[46] He was a member of a reformed Hicks troupe "in his refined Banjo Solos" from 1889–1891.[47] Easton also taught a number of musicians to play, including Australia's preeminent classic style player in the 1880s, Bessie Campbell.[48]

Easton continued to mix his banjo playing with comedy and dramatic roles throughout the 1890s. Hosea Easton died in Sydney of jaw cancer in 1899 and was buried in his adopted country within The General Cemetery of Waverley. His obituary in the *Sydney Mail* called Easton "One of the last Australian survivors of the old-time coloured minstrel companies ... a remarkable banjo player."[49]

By the end of the 1800s, the five-string banjo was firmly ensconced in Australia. Several early cylinder recordings featured Australian banjoists,[50] instruments were readily available for sale, and a number of major cities featured one or more banjo clubs. Other styles such as old-time and bluegrass would have an effect on Australian banjo[51] playing in the twentieth century, but all musicians owe a debt to the traveling minstrel banjoists of the nineteenth century.

NINE

Minstrel Touring in the American South

The second week I was threatened with ... formidable opposition, in the shape of a Christy Minstrel troupe of wonderful popularity in the Freemason's Hall, which was unfortunately situated on the opposite side of the street, right in front of my theatre. There was an iron balcony running across the theatre from wall to wall over the front portico. I gave orders to my scenic artist to get canvas for the length of the balcony and high enough to admit of life-size figures painted on it.

I instructed him to paint a Minstrel Troupe on it, and underneath "The Howe Troupe of Christy Minstrels Every Night!" I then called the company together, told them my intention, and asked them to oblige me by blacking their faces and dressing for a series of minstrel performances, after "Hamlet" in the second week. I even persuaded the band to black and sit on the stage.

We called a rehearsal next day, and by Saturday night I had improvised a negro minstrel entertainment of such capacity and numbers (forty members, including the band) that with the mammoth streamer outside and the fact of there being no hitch in the performance within, perfectly swamped the lot on the other side, who gave up after the fourth night and left the field to me.[1]

* * *

A production of "Monte Christo" failed to attract satisfactory audiences in Richmond, Virginia, until the enterprising manager engaged a band of Ethiopian minstrels to play between acts.[2]

In the later half of the 1840s, as transportation improved and minstrelsy flourished, more troupes began the trek south in search of new audiences. During minstrelsy's first golden age between 1845 and 1860, famous blackface performers from the Buckley Family to S.S. Sanford, Matt Peel's Campbell's to J.H. Haverly and Billy Birch to Kunkel's Nightingales all appeared in Virginia. In 1859 Joe Sweeney's youngest brother Sam, as part of a circus troupe, played to audiences all the way from Alexandria to Bristol (see Chapter Fourteen). Clearly professional banjo concerts were reaching all parts of Virginia (and the South) by the outbreak of the Civil War. This invasion of banjo-containing minstrel groups could not but help the spread of the instrument throughout the American South.

While some minstrels, like Sanford, became entrepreneurs, acquiring buildings and managing troupes of ten or twelve performers in large northern cities like New York and Philadelphia (see Chapter Six for more information), others, like Sweeney, incessantly roamed the country following the eternal gig. As the minstrel troupes became separate units, leasing local halls to give an entire evening's entertainment, they, too journeyed below the Mason-Dixon line.

Some of the most important ensembles to play a role in the spread of Ethiopian music throughout the South were those led by Edwin P. Christy and his associates. Christy had made the claim that his troupe was the first in minstrelsy, predating even the Virginia Min-strels (see Chapter Six). This does not appear to be the case. Although English thespian H.P. Grattan offered first hand information of seeing the Christy trio featuring Edwin, George N. Harrington Christy (November 6, 1827–May 12, 1868), and Tom Vaughn/Vaughan (September 5, 1823–September 3, 1875) on banjo, violin, tambourine, triangle and bones at a Buffalo saloon and at the Buffalo theater during the last third of 1842, Hans Nathan, in his book length study of the Virginia Minstrels, points out that Grattan's first American appearances date to the spring of 1843, so that his recollection of the year must be faulty. Additionally, the earliest Vaughan, a banjoist born in New York City who had appeared in November of 1841 with Joe Sweeney's compatriots John Smith and Thomas Coleman, could have been in Buffalo seems to have been after the Virginia Minstrels' New York debut.[3]

Although they failed in their claim as the "first" minstrel group, Christy's band was still an important player in pre–Civil War minstrelsy. Edwin's company helped to introduce the early songs of Stephen Foster to the music-buying public and, because a 1960s "folk" group decided to use the name "the New Christy Minstrels," Christy's band became syn-onymous with minstrelsy in the minds of late twentieth century Americans.[4]

Edwin Christy first took his group on tour in late 1843. Adopting the name of the absent Virginia Minstrels, Christy left Buffalo with his stepson George and Tom Vaughan at the core of his group, making the American Theater in New Orleans by the end of November. The group had evidently a lot to learn, because an unknown newspaper writer called them "a complete humbug as regards the Negro, Ethiopian characters, which they attempt to take, as they know nothing about it; if they do they don't show any."[5] Regardless of their reviews, Christy's stayed in New Orleans into December,[6] and then helped to bring in the New Year at the Royal Street Theater in Mobile.[7] The group then returned north to New York State for the remainder of 1844 and 1845.

George Christy benefited from blackface leadership as well. Edwin's stepson left his father's employ at the end of October 1853, and quickly formed an alliance with Henry Wood, the brother of New York Mayor Fernando Wood.[8] Following a fire that destroyed their home theatre at 444 Broadway in New York City, Wood & Christy's Minstrels were sent south on tour. They appeared in Savannah and Nashville during May 1855.[9] Mean-while, Edwin Christy had left for California in September 1854, leaving J.W. Raynor (March 31, 1823–April 5, 1900[10]) behind to lead another Christy Minstrels group.[11] With both Raynor and George Christy's ensembles touring the South with similar schedules in the mid–1850s, it becomes impossible to differentiate one from the other. So, the "Christy's Minstrels" that appeared during July 1855 in Baton Rouge and Plaquemine, Louisiana, could have been Raynor's band, George Christy's group, or a third unrelated poseur.[12] The same holds true for the Christy's troupe that appeared in Petersburg, Virginia, in January 1856 and 1857.[13] Raynor's band of Christy Minstrels, co-managed by banjoist Earl Horton Pierce (1823–June 5, 1859[14]) was in Vicksburg, Mississippi, at the end of September 1856,[15] and in Mobile dur-ing October of the same year.[16] After George Christy and Henry Wood split, George con-tinued touring the South, appearing in Natchez at the end of February and in Petersburg in March 1859.[17]

In the 1840s, groups or musicians affiliated with banjoist William Roark made frequent Southern tours. A member of Boston's Guinea Minstrels (a Virginia Minstrels' knockoff) back in 1843[18] and the Carolina Minstrels who appeared in New York City during the fall of 1844,[19] Roark first showed in the South at the end of 1849. Bill Roark's group, the Sable Harmonizers, was in New Orleans during November and December of 1849, and journeyed to Vicksburg for performances in mid–January 1850.[20] The membership of Roark's band—

G.G. Temple, W.N. Chambers, J.M. Foons and R. Moore—all had previous experience play-ing below the Mason-Dixon line. Moore had been with one of the Sable Harmonists groups who appeared in Savannah during October 1847.[21] R. Moore had shared the stage with Joe Sweeney as a member of his ensemble.[22] Chambers, Foons/Foens/Foans, and possibly Tem-ple were members of "the Original Band of Sable Melodists" who played New Orleans dur-ing December 1848 and January 1849.[23]

Southern audiences of the late 1840s and 1850s also got an eye and earful of the two groups using the name Campbell's Minstrels. Matt Peel and Luke West led one Campbell's group; Dan Bryant and his successor, William W. Newcomb, led the other.

Matt Peel Flannery (January 5, 1830–May 4, 1859[24]) was a life-long resident of the New York borough of Brooklyn.[25] Peel entered minstrelsy in 1840, and during 1850, he formed an alliance with Joseph Donnelly Murphy (January 11, 1823–January 1, 1884[26]) and Luke West (real name William Sheppard; 1826–May 26, 1854[27]) in a troupe known as Murphy, West and Peel.[28] Dan Bryant, aka: Daniel Webster O'Brien (May 9, 1833–April 10, 1875) was born in Troy, New York, and followed his brother Jerry (June 11, 1828–April 8, 1861[29]) into minstrelsy.[30] In 1847, Jerry O'Brien helped to form the original Campbell's Minstrels, with Raymond Henry Mestayer on violin, J.P. Carter on banjo and William Donaldson on tambourine.[31] Before his membership in Campbell's Minstrels, William Newcomb was the tambourinist with the Boston Sable Harmonists[32] and, in 1851, a dancer with Fellow's Minstrels in New York City.[33]

Murphy, Peel and West's group made southern tours during the winter months of each year between 1850 and 1852. Their itinerary resembled that of other groups, who traveled down the east coast, performing at the coastal towns en route to New Orleans. Groups then either worked their way north in reverse order, or up the Mississippi and back across the upper South. During those years, Peel and West appeared before audiences in Savannah, Columbus, Nashville, Baton Rouge, and Vicksburg.[34] William Newcomb is first mentioned as a member of Campbell's Minstrels in December 1853, when they appeared at Temper-ance Hall in Columbus, Georgia.[35] After Dan Bryant's departure from the Campbell's in 1857,[36] Newcomb forged a partnership with the banjoist H.S. Ramsey (July 12, 1828–Sep-tember 9, 1871[37]), and continued to appear in the South through the end of the decade.[38]

As one can imagine, the existence of two groups with the same moniker created a great deal of confusion among audiences, and criticism from the local media in the cities visited by the minstrels. There were even times when the two competing groups were booked into opposing venues in a city for the same time period.

A humorous story is told of the advance men for two different minstrel companies com-peting to rent a hall in Montgomery, Alabama. Although it does not pit one Campbell's troupe against another, it does involve one of the Campbell's Minstrels groups. It represents what must have occurred as the Peel ensemble and the Bryant band went head to head:

> [Watkin's company was] making preparations to appear [in Montgomery] when they discov-ered there was "another Richmond in the field"—Campbell's Minstrels, who were working toward the same spot. It was a question of which advance courier arrived first to secure the Hall. Coolidge of the Watkins troupe embarked on the Montgomery stage and found himself in company with Dr. Jones, agent for the Minstrels. All through the night, muffled in their overcoats, they eyed each other suspiciously, as silent as the grave. Meanwhile Watkins telegraphed to the Montgomery Hall owner to hold it in his name. After a two-day's delay a reply came refusing the company the booking. They held the fort for three more nights at Columbus.... Coolidge secured a smaller hall at Montgomery and the company started.[39]

The Baton Rouge, Louisiana *Comet* raised the question of "which are the *genuine* Camp-bells?"

> Will somebody inform us how it is that the "Campbell Minstrels" perform in New Orleans and Nathez [sic] at the same time. The *Free Trader* is blowing at them there, at the same time that the New Orleans papers are puffing their excellent performances at the Odd Fellow's Hall.
>
> A band of minstrels have obtained some celebrity under this name, and a thousand companies at once spring into existence with the same title. There is [sic] libellers and counterfeiters abroad and somebody should be sued for slander.[40]

Ultimately, even though Peel, West, Dan Bryant and Newcomb had all been members of the Campbell's Minstrels, the usage of the same name by two groups was not beneficial to either one.

Between 1850 and 1860, the Buckley's former employee S.S. Sanford (see Chapter Seven) also frequently toured the south. As the New Orleans Opera and Ballet Troupe, Sam Sanford's groups made southern jaunts during the last halves of 1851 and 1852. During the first months of 1854, Sanford played Metropolitan Hall in Richmond, Norfolk, Petersburg[41] and Masonic Hall in Lynchburg, where minstrel-loving officials waved the local theater tariff.[42] Sanford's group included dancer Richard H. Sliter (died May 21, 1861[43]), banjoist J. Albert Allen, J.W. Holman, J. Lynch, Joe Kavanagh, W. Pearson "Punch" Collins (circa 1826–November 1, 1881[44]), J.C. Rainer (from Buckley's group), Herr Leibenstein and the banjoist W.J. Rudolph (1826–September 5, 1881).[45] After leaving Sanford's employ, Dick Sliter was back "down south" at the end of 1857, playing Nashville and Richmond's Metropolitan with the Empire Minstrels, on "their first Southern tour."[46]

George Kunkel (circa 1823–January 25, 1885) led another northern group that repeatedly toured the South. A native of Green Castle, Pennsylvania, Kunkel began in minstrelsy during 1844,[47] forming the Nightingale Ethiopian Serenaders as early as 1848. During that year, they appeared twice in Richmond, once in the summer and again in the fall. The Nightingale Serenaders was back in the South for tours in 1849 and during the end of 1852 and the first three months of 1853, called Kunkel's Nightingale Operatic Troupe in its later appearances.

Throughout the first half of the 1850s, George Kunkel appears to have been following a similar pattern of touring, occupying coastal cities on his way south to New Orleans, and then journeying up the Mississippi to Memphis and across Tennessee on his way back north. The September 1853 Richmond visit was advertised as the Opera Troupe's "Eighth Annual."[48] Their 1854 Washington, D.C., appearances drew as large an audience as the thespian Edwin Forrest, which *The Spirit of the Times* was not sure "this fact is a credit to us."[49] Audiences in Richmond, Petersburg and Lynchburg witnessed various songs, dances, and plays by members of Kunkel's group, including Harriet Beecher Stowe's *Uncle Tom's Cabin* and the T.D. Rice piece, *Oh! Hush!*[50] Some of their performances were to help raise funds for the new Washington Monument. Kunkel's southern touring continued into 1855.[51]

Both the Lehr brothers and Paul Berger (circa 1827–October 8, 1894[52]) left Kunkel for the Melodeon Minstrels Star Troupe.[53] In the late fall of 1856, the Melodeons came through Virginia on tour. When the group played Phoenix Hall in Petersburg around the middle of the month, the newspapers called Harry Lehr "droll and comical" and "a capital actor" on his benefit night. His brother, W.P. sang "that new popular melody, 'My Mary Ann,'" and Paul Berger's "ballads" were well received.[54] The Melodeon Minstrels spent the week of November 17 in Lynchburg. On November 21, Mr. J. Conrad took his benefit, "On which occasion [Joe's brother] Dick Sweeny will give his 'Rock Susannah' Banjo Duett."[55]

Minstrelsy in the Circus

The horses soon must cut, and Her-Vio Nano he must go,
To bide the public taste with Messrs. Diamond and Crow,
Turn about and wheel about, etc.
There was a time when standing on The head was all the go,
But t'other end is righted—we're Again upon the toe.
Turn about and wheel about, etc.[56]

In previous chapters, we have mentioned a number of circus companies and theaters that included minstrels during their southern tours. Even though minstrel performers had begun moving out of the circus, first to the "after show" (ie: as a separate performance in an adjacent tent) and thence to separate touring units, many equestrian troupes still carried blackface performers. Stuart Thayer, in his compilation of pre–Civil War circus touring schedules, lists eleven owners traveling the South between 1843 and 1850 carrying minstrels. Many showed in Lynchburg, just west of Joe Sweeney's home. Some performers who had begun their careers with the circus, often as clowns or stand-up performers, had switched to Ethiopian impressions during the first flush of T.D. Rice's success. Others doubled in both capacities, and a third group switched back and forth between the two. Now, with minstrel groups dominating the form, these same entertainers joined blackface bands or reverted back to their traditional circus roles.

One of these was William Worrell, whose earliest documented performance as a minstrel was with the New York Circus United. Between 1843 and 1851, Worrell was in the south with various circuses companies every year but one. William Worrell worked with a Mr. Walters on banjo for Robinson & Foster's National Circus in 1843, and with Samuel Stickney's New Orleans Circus in the company of T.G. Booth of the Kentucky Minstrels and William Chestnut in 1844. By 1846, Worrell was listed as a clown with Stone & McCollum's Great Western Circus, then back with Stickney in 1847 and 1848.[57]

Samuel Stickney's show seems particularly "minstrel-friendly," especially when lodged at their winter quarters in New Orleans. Between 1845 and 1848, Stickney carried a band of "Sable Harmonists." For the most part, this was *not* Sweeney's group, as the name had replaced "Virginia Minstrels" as the most popular identifier for minstrel groups. Indeed, as noted above, the rapidly changing membership and interchangeable names used by minstrel bands makes it difficult to track the itinerary of any aggregation.

Frank Brower, Sweeney's old touring companion and ex–Virginia Minstrel, worked with banjoist Neil Jamieson in Welch's National Circus. In 1846 and 1847, they toured Kentucky and West Virginia. By 1851, Brower had resorted to playing clown roles with Robinson & Eldred's New York Circus and Jamieson was a ringmaster for Welch. Frank Brower's fellow Minstrel Dan Emmett had also returned to circus work. During 1847 and 1848, Emmett worked alongside "Bandana" Brown for Spalding's North American Circus in Kentucky, Tennessee, Louisiana and other Mississippi River towns under the management of former minstrel John Smith.

Other minstrels joined the circus as well. George Hoyt, the banjoist and dancer, spent the winter of 1844 with James Raymond's Olympic Circus in coastal Virginia, fiddler Harry Mestayer toured Northern Kentucky with Spalding's show, and John Diamond worked southern river towns with Dan Rice's Circus in 1849 and in 1850 with Samuel B. Burgess's American Circus. And the duo of John Smith and Thomas Coleman, apart or together, worked the south for Stone & McCollum's Great Western Circus between 1846 and 1850. Two of those years, they showed on Sweeney's home turf.[58]

Vocalist John Smith had spent much of the previous years when Joe Sweeney was in Great Britain working the Southern States. Stuart Thayer reports that Smith performed during at least part of the 1842 season with Aaron Turner's Columbian Circus,[59] and Mary Toulmin places the "pioneer in the field of blackface minstrelsy" in Mobile during a good portion of March 1843. Banjoist R. Nash accompanied Smith for much of his stay there, with Jack Alden stepping in for Nash on Smith's benefit night of March 25.[60] Poor Alden had been stranded in Montgomery, Alabama, two months earlier, when the ventriloquist Johnson had skipped town with the proceeds from their joint engagement.[61] Rather than switching to clowning as some circus minstrels had done, John Smith then moved into management. The minstrel singer had an association with Spaulding's circus during 1847 and 1848, moving during the winter of the later year to Stone & McCollum's outfit, where Smith remained through the end of the decade.[62]

Other circuses carried whole minstrel troupes, the minstrels preferring the guaranteed income of a season with one show to the autonomy of making their own touring arrangements. Often groups would join the circus for a part of a winter show, or make a guest appearance in a large city such as New Orleans. Dick Myers's Virginia Serenaders came to South Carolina for Robinson & Foster's winter show in 1844, and the group possibly stayed on for all of the 1845 season.[63] Myer's group was again in the south without a circus affiliation during October 1849, when they spent at least several weeks in Savannah, Georgia.[64] Another band using the Virginia Serenader name played Lynchburg and the south during 1847 as a part of Banigan & Kelly's Zoological Exhibition.[65] And Harry Mestayer had the nerve to compare himself to Dick "Ole Bull" Myers by calling his band "the Ole Bull Band of Serenaders" when playing one of Richmond's theaters in early 1845 (Myers, of course, had himself appropriated the name from the original "Ole Bull," a Norwegian violinist). Thomas Coleman, "pupil of Joe Sweeny," was on banjo, John Smith was their dancer, Sam Johnson played triangle, and W.B. Donaldson beat the jawbone.[66]

The Economics of Minstrelsy

1
O! whar is de spot dat we was born on,
Whar is de spot dat we was born on,
Whar O! whar is de spot dat we was born on,
Way down in de Caroline State
When we go back dar to hoe de corn,
We'll lib in de house whar we was born,
Sing to Mas-sa night and morn,
Case ole Mas-sa's bery great
Chorus: And it's by and by we do hope to meet him,
By and by we do hope to meet him,
Way down in de Car'line State,
And it's by and by we do hope to meet him,
Way down in de Car'line State.
2
O! dar libs Fadder dar libs Modder,
Dar libs Sister and dar libs Brudder,
Case ole Massa's got no older,
To hoe de corn in de Car'line State;
O! de nigger lubs home dar if Massa don't cross 'em
De cane-brake grow and de corntop blossom,

Whar de coon and de little fat possum
Mass hunt till de moon shine late.
3
O! we used to hab the fun on de ole Plantation,
We used to hab de fun on de ole Plantation,
We used to hab de fun on de ole Plantation,
Way down in de Car'line State;
O! we dance and sing when de days work's ober,
Lib like de coons in de field ob clobber,
Sing to Massa case he's sober,
And he's bery rich and great.
4
O! when we go back Massa'll be so bery glad den,
O! so hab de grand time oh! De best we eber had den,
We work no more in de field so hard den,
Way down in de Car'line State;
O! Fadder bery glad when he know dat it be us,
Modder bery glad too case she can see us,
Dey say dat Massa's agwine to free us,
Case ole Massa's bery great.[67]

Sheet music cover, "Harmoneons Carolina Melodies," showing the band members in their blackface stage characters. The band includes (left to right) James Power on bones, Marshall Pike (in female character) on triangle, L.V.H. Crosby on violin, Frank Lynch on banjo and John Power on tambourine. Martin & Beals, Boston, 1846.

What was it like for a minstrel group like that led by Sweeney touring the South in the late 1840s? There is little information that survives to indicate the economics and procedures for such a venture. Luckily, an account book from a Southern jaunt by the "Harmoneons" has recently surfaced. Using it in conjunction with newspaper accounts and publications by the band, a picture emerges for a small portion of a minstrel's life.[68]

The roots of the Harmoneons go back to at least 1840, when Bostonians Marshall S. Pike (May 20, 1818–February 13, 1901)[69] and L.V.H. Crosby (circa 1824–March 26, 1884)[70] had their song collection, *Harmoneons Carolina Melodies*, published. The songs of Pike and Crosby, both productive writers together and apart, would form the basis for the repertoire of the Harmoneons throughout the decade (Crosby was also a fine painter, whose best-known accomplishment was a rendering some years later of Mrs. O'Leary's cow starting the great Chicago fire).[71] Sometime over the next several years, the Power brothers James (circa 1826–January 5, 1890)[72] and Jonathan joined the group, with Frank Lynch making the Harmoneons a quintet in 1845. Lynch had left the Kentucky Minstrels sometime in the summer of 1843, and appeared between that time and his joining the Harmoneons in conjunction with various artists at Barnum's two museums in New York City. (A "Lynch" appeared with Nelson Kneass's Ethiopian Opera Company in November of 1845; if this is Frank, then, his membership in the Harmoneons dates to the end of that year.)[73] On the cover of Crosby's 1840 publication, *Harmoneons Carolina Melodies*, the members of the band are pictured in their blackface stage personas. James Power on bones was "Honey," Pike on triangle was the female character "Fanny," fiddler Crosby was "Pomp," Lynch the banjoist was "Gumbo," and Jonathan Power's tambourinist was "Sambo."[74]

In 1846, one further addition to the group's personnel was J. Simmonds Davis, who served during that year as lyricist for Crosby's *Melodies of the Harmoneons*. Strangely, the cover of that collection depicts only four Harmoneons. Possibly, this reflects the types of songs included, which are the sentimental sort sung by quartets rather than the more robust minstrel material. Although the musicians are not identified, Davis and Crosby must be two of the group. Perhaps Pike had gone solo and Lynch was not needed for the non-minstrel material.[75] Regardless of shifts within the band, by the time of their southern tour of 1846–7, the group once again included all six members.[76]

Traveling south from Baltimore,[77] the Harmoneons began their Richmond engagement on Friday, December 4, when they gave "a Grand Musical Soiree at the Exchange Hall." As the group presented programs in both black and white (i.e.: without the burnt cork makeup) face, this evening's performance of "Glees, Quartettes, Trios, Melodies and Chorusses [sic]" was "exclusively in Citizen's Dress" (i.e.: formal evening clothes).[78] A similar program was given on their last night, Monday, December 7.[79] The Harmoneons remained in Virginia's capital, opening at the 500 seat Odd Fellows Hall two days later, on which occasion they added "Ethiopic" (i.e.: blackface) "Performances."[80] Large audiences attended their concerts, and the *Richmond Enquirer* singled out Marshall Pike's female impersonations as an attraction.[81] By Christmas week, the Harmoneons, as an incentive toward repeat business, had cut their admission price in half.[82]

This must have worked, for as the New Year dawned, the Harmoneons were still occupying the Odd Fellows Hall, and this is where the account book begins. The group entered 1847 with $774.10 "cash on hand" in their coffers. Within the first several days of the year, an additional $119.00 came in, one supposes from admissions. However, various expenses drained their account of $601.25. This includes payments to each band member, one assumes for living expenses, as well as newspaper advertising ($22.25), printing ($168.00) and posting ($36.00) of playbills, washing ($22.00) and purchase of stage clothes ($53.00), "mending instruments" ($5.00), and the costs associated with renting the hall ($139.00).[83] Houses continued to be good, keeping the Harmoneons in Richmond throughout early January.[84] "Citizens Dress" performances were given on Tuesday, January 5, Thursday, January 7, and Monday, January 11, 1847,[85] with the group appearing in blackface on January 8. Their last night at the Odd Fellows Hall was on January 11, where they also utilized "Piano Forte accompaniments."[86]

But, how well did the group do financially? Between January 4 and 11, the Harmoneons took in $378.15. There were more newspaper advertisements to purchase for Charlottesville, Brownsville, and Boston, as well as a piano to be moved. Washing needed doing, personal expenses kept accruing, there were halls to be rented, playbills to disperse, and railroad tickets to buy for Petersburg. The group also spent money on "Servants" ($5.25) and for "negro clothing" ($5.00), one supposes to use on stage. All in all, $453.51 was depleted against their receipts. Although some costs were associated with other appearances, the week in Richmond was still not a strong engagement.[87]

From Richmond, the Harmoneons went to Petersburg's Mechanics Hall for four days. They performed Wednesday through Saturday, January 13 to 16, bringing on "Grand Ethiopian Operatic Performances ... With the introduction of Violins, Banjos, Tamborines, Castanets, Triangle, Fancy Dances" for their last day.[88] Exactly $91.20 was collected in Petersburg. After various expenses were paid, including hotel bills, the Harmoneons had spent $102.71.[89]

Next, they traveled on Sunday to Norfolk, where the group took the Theater from Monday, January 18, until Friday, January 29. Ethiopian and "Operatic" performances were given equal billing for advertisements placed in the *Norfolk-Portsmouth Beacon*, which also mentioned Pike's "Female Characters." Bad weather hounded the band and may have caused the lengthening of their engagement. The newspaper lauded the Harmoneons' performances, and singled out their singing: "There is a peculiar sweetness in their Melodies, a purity of harmony in their blending of voices, and a richness in the whole variety of vocal and instrumental performances, which cannot but engage the admiration of all who have music in their souls." The writer also appealed to Pike and Crosby "to favor us with some of [your] favorite compositions in citizen's dress before taking leave of Norfolk." The Harmoneons took their "leave" on Friday, January 29,[90] having taken in $295.40, but, spending $491.38, including 25 cents for "Strings."[91]

The Harmoneons returned to Petersburg on Saturday, but Mechanic's Hall was occupied by a group of "Shakers."[92] After making arrangements to take the hall the following Friday, it was back to Richmond because, one assumes, it was important to take as few days off as possible. "A new Operatic Piece, entitled "The Sable Coquette; or, Rivalry Out-Did!" was presented on Tuesday, February 2, in Virginia's capital.[93] By this time, the group's accounts had slipped into the red.[94] The group must have soldiered onward thinking that their fortunes would improve. After presenting their act in Petersburg on Friday and Saturday,[95] the Harmoneons retook Odds Fellows' Hall for the five days prior to the trip back north.[96] After their Friday evening performance in Richmond, they beat a hasty retreat to Fredericksburg, showing on Saturday, February 13. By the time the Harmoneons had opened in Washington, D.C., they were $23.99 in debt. One of the most interesting items in the account book is the purchase of a "Banjo" for $5.00 in Richmond. Does this mean that the group's banjo needed replacing, if indeed they had brought one at all? It certainly showed that a banjo of some sort could be purchased in Richmond in early 1847.[97]

The account book continues through February and March, as the Harmoneons continued to travel north. They opened in the nation's capital on Lent, Wednesday, February

Above and opposite: Two sheet music covers, "Melodies of the Harmoneons," show-ing the group in "white face" or evening dress, one with four members, and the other with five members (James Power, John Power, Frank Lynch, T.G. Prendergast and F.A. Reynolds). C. Bradlee & Company, 1846, and G.P. Reed, Boston, 1851. (Library of Congress).

17, at that city's Odd Fellows' Saloon,[98] then took a short engagement in Georgetown at the college.[99] Thursday evening, February 25, the Harmoneons returned to the Odd Fellows through the end of the week.[100] March 1 and 2, the band played the new Temperance Hall, "on E street," to help defray the cost of the building,[101] thenceforth back and forth to Laurel, Maryland, (by stage) Saturday, March 6[102] and, on the following Monday, March 8, lend-ing their talents to aid the Ladies of the German Evangelical Church fund raiser at the Odd Fellows' Hall.[103] From March 11 through 13, while awaiting the availability of their Baltimore venue, they rented "the elegant saloon upon the avenue, occupied as a Daguerrean Gallery, and known as Concert Hall," at the cost of $15.00 for their final performances in Washington.[104]

The group bought "Cork" on February 17 (twice for 25 cents each time), a "Tambourine" the following day ($1.62) and again on March 13 (perhaps John Powers was hard on the instrument), as well as more strings (75 cents) on the same date. Heading for Baltimore, the ensemble was still slightly below the break-even point, lacking $115.56 to meet tour expenses.[105] The Assembly Rooms became available on Monday, March 15, where the Harmoneons followed a troupe of Swiss bell ringers. For their four days in Baltimore, the band challenged a minstrel legend for an audience. Frank Brower, backed by banjoist Neil Jamieson, was working at the Front Street Amphitheatre, along with the up and coming minstrel clown, Dan Rice.[106] The Harmoneons made $120.50 for the four nights in Baltimore, but spent $149.67, adding another $29.17 to their debt.[107]

Then, traveling through Philadelphia, on March 19, the Harmoneons performed in a Hall occupying the Indian Queen Hotel, possibly in Burlington, N. J. On Monday, March 22, they were at the Congress Hall (in Philadelphia?), and bought yet *another* tambourine. They played Wilmington during the last days of March, and this is where the journal ends. In all, after losing another $16.05, the tour was $160.78 in the red.[108]

1
O! la-dy sweetest la-dy,
Soft slum-bers round thee twine,
Sleep on for thou art dream-ing
Of music that's di-vine.
2
Thy fa-thers roof pro-tects thee,
O! would that it were mine,

Sleep on for thou are dreaming
Of music that's di-vine.
3
No sound shall break thy slumbers,
But let my song be thine,
Sleep on for thou art dreaming
Of music that's divine.[109]

It is puzzling that the Harmoneons could lose over $900.00 during just three months of performing. After all, this was the group that Walt Whitman had written so positively about during 1846. In his article, "True American Singing," Whitman said that "their negro singing altogether proves how shiningly golden talent can be spread over a subject generally considered 'low' ... there exists something really great about them."[110] The White House thought highly enough of them to have the Harmoneons play for President James K. Polk in the same period as their 1846–47 tour.[111]

So, why did they continue to tour with such loses? Perhaps sheet music sales helped support the shows. After all, group members L.V.H. Crosby and Marshall S. Pike were prolific writers, with many published songs to their credit. Crosby even authored a "New Series, Songs of the Harmoneons" for publication in Richmond during the summer following their tour,[112] possibly in reaction to sales during his group's appearances earlier in 1847. James Power and Frank Lynch had put the words of others to music, and would also financially gain from music sales.

It is also possible that this was an atypical schedule, and, that, under normal circumstances, the group was a moneymaker. The Boston Harmoneons must have done better up north or on other tours, otherwise, they couldn't have existed for over ten years. One wonders why they did so poorly during the first months of 1847. Could they have "played out" these areas, i.e.: performed too frequently within too short a space of time? Was their mixture of quartet singing and Ethiopianisms not to the liking of their audiences? Weather surely played a factor, because rain and snow is mentioned as having a negative effect on attendance in some of the newspaper coverage.

The whole method of scheduling performances, arranging for the hall on short notice, staying in one place until the audiences stopped coming, or, being bumped from a hall if the previous act was holding over, could have an extremely negative effect on cash flow and attendance. If a group wasn't popular one place, they could move on, but, as in Baltimore, sometimes the minstrels couldn't gain access to a hall. The choice of performing at a loss, or not performing at a bigger loss, was not a good one. One hopes that Sweeney's bands fared better.

TEN

P.T. Barnum's Black Face Adventures

Black face minstrelsy emerged at a time when America was establishing its own national identity and individual Americans were using their membership in the rising middle class as an excuse to redefine themselves. Early minstrelsy had it share of class-jumping characters. Of all the larger than life personalities using minstrelsy to launch their new social and economic status, none was bigger than P.T. Barnum.

Circus Days

We have had another Circus with us, and although it was so close on the heels of the extensive one that preceded it, we were astonished to find hundreds going in, and shelling out their half dollars, and some their dollars, as they went in by families!—We think it would be fair in all conscience, for Physicians and dealers in Dry Goods, and Family Groceries, who have small accounts against hundreds of families, who refuse to meet them, to select the accounts of all who attend circuses, and hand them over to an officer for collection. If they can muster up money to go into these dirty and demoralizing exhibitions every time they come along—say several times in each season—they ought to be *made* to muster up money to pay their just debts![1]

We have had a Circus here for several days, much to the annoyance of many peaceable citizens, and, we fear, much to the injury of the manners and morals of youth. In addition to the ordinary evils of such exhibitions, there have been, we understand, some disorders and breaches of the peace which have required the intervention of magistrates. If the Selectmen would refuse their license for such exhibitions, we are persuaded they would merely promote the public good, but would have the satisfaction of learning that their refusal accorded with the feelings and wishes of their constituents.[2]

He was born Phineas Taylor Barnum in Bethel, Connecticut, on July 5, 1810. From a young age, P.T. showed a natural feel for business by successfully running his family's country store. Unfortunately, Barnum's father lacked his son's flair for business and died penniless when P.T. was just fifteen years old.[3]

Barnum's first exposure to show business was through his contact with Hackaliah Bailey, an early promoter and exhibitor of exotic animals in America. During Bailey's frequent visits to Bethel, he assailed Barnum with stories of his shows and tours.[4] This made a deep impression on the young Phineas. Further fueling P.T.'s interest in traveling companies was his proximity to numerous entertainers, as many early American circus promoters were headquartered in Barnum's home state of Connecticut. (This concentration of entertainers was peculiar, as while the state allowed the showmen to locate their base of operations there, Connecticut didn't allow the circus companies to exhibit within the state's boundaries due to the low opinion some held of these shows). These included Aaron Turner (circa 1790–1854) of Danbury, born within hailing distance of Barnum's birthplace.[5] P.T. would apprentice himself to Turner at the age of twenty-four and with Turner's circus have his first contact with the burgeoning blackface business.

In the spring of 1836, Aaron Turner opened his Old Columbian Circus in Massachusetts.[6] Following these initials performances, Turner's goal was to head south, arriving by the fall in northern Virginia. On the bill was Robert White, who had presented "a variety of Negro songs and Extravaganzas" in the theaters of New York City and Boston.[7] Also along for the trip was Turner's protégé P.T. Barnum, serving as treasurer for Aaron's company.[8] Before joining Aaron Turner's concern, Barnum had been trying his hand at show business, first exhibiting Joice Heth, supposedly General Washington's ex-slave, and then promoting an Italian plate spinner named Signor Antonio Vivalla at the Franklin Theater in New York City. After Heth's death, Barnum brought Vivalla to Aaron Turner. In exchange for the Italian's services, as well as serving as treasurer, secretary and ticket seller for the Old Columbian Circus, Phineas Taylor Barnum received a percentage of the profits from the tour.[9]

The Old Columbian Circus opened on September 29 across the Potomac from Washington, D.C., in Alexandria, Virginia, and then slowly wended its way to Richmond. White performed his songs in a "Pavillion [sic] Adjoining the Circus," and the circus "crowed" that his "representations of the Negro Character ... surpass those of the far famed Rice."[10]

At the end of October, Turner's Circus had reached Warrentown (now Warrenton) in North Carolina,[11] where Barnum endeavored to strike out on his own. Phineas Barnum felt that he could make his own success apart from Aaron Turner. Many years later, Barnum wrote in his memoirs:

> My engagement expired with a profit to myself of $1,200[12] I now separated from the circus company, taking Vivalla, James Sanford, (a negro singer and dancer,) several musicians, horses, wagons, and a small canvas tent with which I intended to begin a traveling exhibition of my own. My company started and Turner took me on the way in his own carriage some twenty miles. We parted reluctantly and my friend wished me every success in my new venture."[13]

James Sanford (or Sandford, as it is spelled both ways, real name Blandford), according to Edwin Le Roy Rice, was born in Baltimore around 1814, dying in Philadelphia in 1855.[14] Sanford is reported as living in Albany around 1830, keeping the company of boxers, billiard players and circus people.[15] He represented himself as performing in New York City before joining up with Barnum,[16] and in 1843 was a founding member of the Virginia Serenaders, an early minstrel group.[17] Barnum took his one wagon show south and west to Rocky Mount Falls,[18] and then onward to the state capital of Raleigh, taking the same route to be later followed by Aaron Turner.

In South Carolina during late November, Jim Sanford abruptly left the promoter's employ. Sanford had gotten a better offer. As previously noted (see Chapter Three), on Monday, December 5, 1836, James Sanford joined Joel Sweeney in Richmond to present "Negro Extravaganzas" at the Terpsichore Hall.[19] It is tempting to assume that Sweeney had been with Sanford while the Negro delineator was working for P.T. Barnum, but there is no documentation to back this up.

Barnum surprised all by filling in for the departing minstrel, donning the burnt cork makeup to sing "Zip Coon" and other minstrel favorites.[20] But, Phineas wasn't to fill that role for long. Meeting up with Turner's disbanding troupe in Columbia, South Carolina, P.T. hired Bob White as his new minstrel singer.[21] The unfortunate White also deserted the unlucky Barnum, drowning while the company was crossing a river, supposedly in Frankfort, Kentucky, by the spring of 1837. Barnum was once again Ethiopian-less![22] Ultimately, P. T. Barnum had no more success with his circus company as with his earlier entertainment ventures, and he disbanded his traveling show during May after arriving in Nashville, Tennessee.[23] But, Barnum was not finished with show business or blackface entertainment. He continued to present Ethiopian entertainers, both in the roles of manager and promoter.

Mining Diamonds

P.T. Barnum's next foray into blackface minstrelsy was as the manager of the dancer John Diamond. Barnum discovered the New Yorker Diamond (1823–October 29, 1857[24]), first presenting him in April 1839.[25] Then supposedly sixteen or seventeen, John Diamond was advertised at the National and Franklin Theaters as only twelve years old to make him all the more spectacular as a dancer to the audience. During this time period it is unclear who accompanied Diamond's act, as a violinist identified only as the "Green Mountain Boy" provided the music for some of his New York engagements and a Mr. B.B. Boyce, of whom I have located no information, accompanied John Diamond on "banjoe" in Boston later that year.[26] By January 1840, John Diamond was back in New York City, joining Joe Sweeney at the Broadway circus (see Chapter Three).[27]

Barnum began to have some success booking his charge outside of the city. Stints in Philadelphia[28] were followed by a major tour in New England. As Joe Sweeney had his own plans, a new accompanist and performing partner was needed. So, Barnum got the next best thing to the Virginian banjoist, Sweeney's "first pupil" William Whitlock. On March 25, 1840, Diamond took his benefit at the Broadway Circus, for the first time backed up by Billy Whitlock on the banjo.[29] Some additional area dates followed before Barnum sent them off for a week of engagements in Providence, Rhode Island (see Chapter Six for more information).[30]

Back in New York, P.T. Barnum had been casting around for additional ways to make a living. He rented the Vauxhall Garden and promoted John Diamond and Billy Whitlock as an attraction in late July and early August of 1840.[31] After several months with no apparent financial success, Barnum grew discouraged and discontinued this venture, deciding instead to take Diamond west on tour.[32]

Unfortunately, P.T. Barnum's luck still had not changed. Even though he had experienced short-term gains, Barnum still hadn't discovered the secret to long-term economic success. The promoter writes in his autobiography of traveling to "Buffalo, Toronto, Detroit, Chicago, Ottawa, Springfield," and places in between with Diamond, steadily losing money and the confidence of the other members in his ensemble. When P.T. and John Diamond caught a steamboat in St. Louis bound for New Orleans, only a solitary fiddler remained with them from the original group that had left New York City.

Upon reaching the Crescent City on the day after New Year's, 1841,[33] Barnum placed Diamond at the St. Charles Theater, where, on Saturday, January 16, the dancer appeared for the first time.[34] P.T. Barnum used the ruse of a dance competition to draw a crowd, and the fortunes of Barnum and Diamond took a turn for the better. Sol Smith, the manager of the rival New American Theater at the corner of Poydras and St. Francis Streets, had to admit that, although the St. Charles was having a poor season, Diamond was a good draw. "[The] two nights of a brilliant star which burst out upon the boards of the 'temple' of the legitimate, bearing the sparkling name of Diamond," wrote Smith to a Mr. Woolf, "[was] a nigger dancer, whose benefit was good."[35]

Master Diamond continued at the St. Charles at least until the end of the month.[36] P.T. Barnum then took John Diamond to Vicksburg, Jackson and Mobile, where the dancer appeared during the last week of February. By this time, the eighteen-year-old Diamond had developed quite a sophisticated stage routine. As described in a playbill from his run at the New Theatre:

> Master Diamond will introduce his original Negro Speech in Congress, Long Island Break-down and Smoke-House Dance—making the greatest display of heel and toegenus [sic] ever witness[ed]. Challenge: Master Diamond, who delineates the Ethiopian character superior to any other white person, hereby challenges any person in the world to a trial of skill at Negro Dancing, in all its varieties, for a wager of from $200 to $1000.... After which, Master Diamond, Ethiopian Extravaganza of Jim-a-Long-Josey, with new and original verses.[37]

But these engagements had not been without incident. Diamond, perhaps under the influence of the "wide open" nature of New Orleans, had been feeling his youthful oats, disappearing from Barnum for periods, overdrawing on his account and spending it on prostitutes and other illegitimate pastimes. P.T. Barnum, realizing that the dancer would need to perform in order to earn the money to support these extracurricular activities, was fearful that another promoter would snare John Diamond's services. To ward off their advances, Barnum warned both the concerns of Fogg & Stickney, as well as Noah M. Ludlow and Sol Smith, against hiring Diamond. This worked, albeit temporarily, as John Diamond sheepishly returned to Barnum, now back in New Orleans, during the first week of March.[38] But, within a short time, Barnum and his young charge were again at odds. Finally, Phineas Barnum had had enough. He washed his hands of the young man and left for the journey back north.

P.T. Barnum journeyed back up the Mississippi to the Ohio River, arriving in Pittsburgh on March 30. There Barnum found one of his company's deserters, a youth named Francis "Frank" Lynch, in the company of C.D. Jenkins, an erstwhile banjoist and minstrel performer. The couple was working the local museum, with Lynch using the name of "John Diamond." P.T. Barnum initiated legal proceedings against Jenkins and Lynch, first having the banjoist arrested, and then trying and winning a judgment against the duo for the fallacious use of the name Diamond.[39]

Either Jenkins was not easily dissuaded or Barnum, having won the case, decided to leave the banjoist alone. Or, possibly P.T. Barnum, no longer associated with the "real" John Diamond, was reaping some financial benefit from Lynch's impersonation (the most likely possibility, see below). In any event, C.D. Jenkins and Master "Frank Lynch" Diamond once again took to the stage, opening at Baltimore's National Theatre in mid–May of 1841, where Jenkins sang "Settin' on a Rail."[40]

Meanwhile, Barnum was still struggling to stay afloat financially. He sold copies of "Sears' Pictorial Illustrations of the Bible," and decided to try leasing the Vauxhall Saloon for another summer. From June 14 until September 25,[41] he valiantly attempted to earn a profit by presenting a variety of minstrel entertainers. One was Barney Williams (July 20, 1824–April 25, 1876).[42] Although better known as an Irish character comedian (he was born Bernard O'Flaherty in Ireland),[43] Williams began his career as a dancer in blackface. J. Alston Brown reports O'Flaherty/Williams performing as early as 1835,[44] even though this seems a bit unlikely due to his age. Brown also erroneously claims that Barney Williams worked in New York City with John Diamond in the fall of 1839, when Diamond is documented as appearing in Boston.[45]

Another of Barnum's employees was the former Diamond impersonator Master Frank Lynch. For the last month of Barnum's lease,[46] P.T. leaned heavily on Lynch and the sort of "match dances" (i.e.: competitions) that Barnum had staged so successfully with the original John Diamond. On August 25, P.T. Barnum offered $500.00 to anyone who could best Frank Lynch at stepping.[47]

It didn't take long for someone to rise to the challenge. The following evening, *another* dancer using Diamond's name competed with Lynch at the Vauxhall, but, unfortunately, the outcome was not reported. Jenkins provided the banjo accompaniment on that occasion.[48] On Wednesday, September 1, with the purse having shrunk by tenfold, Diamond was again challenged, this time by "Master Miles, a butcher boy, well known as a regular break-down dancer," and "the Catherine Market Roarer."[49] This time, the *New York Herald* did report the results, as the judges favored Master Diamond.[50] These shenanigans continued throughout the next three weeks.[51] The "pièce-de-la-résistance" was a face-off between Diamond and "Mr. Blythe, a North River boatman," on September 17 for the sum of $200.00. When the smoke cleared at the Little Drury (formerly the Franklin) Theatre, Blythe had triumphed over Diamond. A rematch was scheduled at the Vauxhall on September 23 with much hoopla, but, alas, the results could not be found in the New York newspapers.[52]

Meanwhile, the "original" John Diamond had stayed in New Orleans and joined the circus of Fogg & Stickney. The Boston-born Samuel Peck Stickney (1808–March 20, 1877) was one of America's oldest equestrians, having first exhibited with Price & Simpson in 1823. His partnership with Jeremiah P. Fogg, from Westchester County, New York, ran from 1828 to 1842, an unusually long association by the standards of the circus business. The two had begun their relationship when Fogg, a non-performer, was handling the business for Isaac Quick's Washington Circus for whom Stickney was riding.[53]

When Fogg & Stickney opened their season in Mobile on March 16, Diamond was with them. Fogg & Stickney's Circus then returned to New Orleans, leaving sometime at the end of April or the beginning of May to travel up river to St. Louis, where their Missouri stand was to begin.[54]

Regardless, when Fogg & Stickney reached St. Louis, Diamond departed to perform for Sol Smith's partner Noah Ludlow. This was just the latest in maneuvers between the two organizations that had begun early in 1841. Sol Smith had contracted with Fogg & Stickney's circus from either December 1840 or January 1841 through the end of March to prevent them from competing with Smith and Ludlow in New Orleans.[55] To that end, Sol Smith straightaway shipped the circus off to Natchez until the end of January.[56]

Almost immediately, problems developed between Jeremiah Fogg and Sol Smith. The circus had only broken even in Natchez,[57] and business didn't improve when they returned to New Orleans in February.[58] When the contract between the two concerns expired, Fogg & Stickney immediately violated the terms of that agreement by showing in New Orleans under their own canvas. Ludlow and Smith were granted an injunction against their former employees,[59] which resulted in physical threats being leveled at Sol Smith by Sam Stickney.[60] Just when it looked as though the battle was over, Fogg & Stickney headed for St. Louis, breaching another term of their contract with Smith.[61] In a ruse designed to circumvent the terms of their deal, Fogg had the clown Green B. Johnson manage his troupe.[62] Unfortunately for Fogg & Stickney, this didn't fool Sol Smith, who immediately instructed Ludlow to offer John Diamond an engagement upon the latter's arrival, thereby robbing

Fogg of his leading attraction.[63] Smith also sent his own equestrian company from New Orleans to preempt Stickney's riders.[64]

It is unclear if Sam Stickney's circus ever appeared in St. Louis that spring, as no newspaper coverage or advertisements mentioning the show has emerged from the period.[65] Noah Ludlow could have used the courts to prevent Fogg & Stickney's St. Louis performances, but, again, no documentation for that course of action has yet to appear.

As one can imagine, the air was thick with acrimony as John Diamond made his first St. Louis appearances for Ludlow. From Friday, May 28, until Saturday, June 12, Diamond sang "Jim along Josey," and danced a variety of "Virginny Breakdowns."[66] For his benefit night, Friday, June 11, John Diamond parodied the Austrian dancer Fanny Elssler, then touring America, in blackface and played "the Negro Door Keeper."[67] When Ludlow and Smith's circus left St. Louis, Diamond remained with them. He is mentioned by a Nashville paper for the stay in that city from September 27 until October 9,[68] but was back in New Orleans by the end of October.[69]

As noted in Chapter Six, the mysterious banjoist Ferguson was working as a member of Fogg & Stickney's troupe during their summer tour and that he journeyed with them when the circus returned to New Orleans in October 1842, contracted to appear at Caldwell's St. Charles Theatre. John Diamond joined up with Ferguson, and the duo appeared together on Monday and Tuesday, October 25 and 26. For these two days, Ferguson covered Joel Sweeney's "Whar did you come from," and, possibly in another attempt to cash in on Sweeney's success, presented other "Wirginny songs."[70]

John Diamond continued to perform in New Orleans, switching his alliance back and forth between Caldwell's St. Charles Theatre and the American, controlled by Sol Smith.[71] Diamond persisted in his errant ways, reacting to an insult at a ball by stabbing the instigator three times with a penknife.[72] Not surprisingly, charges were pressed and John Diamond landed in jail.[73]

Within a month, the dancer was back in action. This time he teamed up with Sweeney's old performing partner James Sanford. The pair spent New Years at the St. Charles before moving to Mobile during the second week of January.[74] Perhaps Sol Smith had the last laugh, as he wrote a friend that Caldwell's hiring of Fogg & Stickney had "resulted in a miserable failure."[75]

> Instead of mongrel shows, fit to be witnessed by gaping country bumpkins, such as Howes has favored his visitors with Welch gives us facsimiles of the purely classic sports of Sparta.... One may enter the place without being jostled by cheek-peddling boys, or annoyed by the foul stench arising from filthy garments, peanuts, mutton pies, &c., nor are one's ears pained by obscene language, or boisterous vulgarity.... From the enormous company we select Gossin, Franklin, McFarland, and Diamond as the most capable.... and Diamond [is] the king of negro dancers, Apropos, speaking of Diamond, we recommend to Mr. Hoyt the propriety of remaining in the background and silent while John is dancing . His buffoonery is not needed at those times, though it is well enough at others.[76]

Since Sands American Circus had sailed from New York with Joe Sweeney as a company member in early 1842, Billy Whitlock had stayed in New York City. There was evidently enough work to support the banjoist without traveling, and Billy preferred to stay in the city of his birth. From February 22 until March 2, Whitlock supported Frank Lynch, now billed as "Frank Diamond" to differentiate the dancer from the "original" John Diamond, at the Bowery Amphitheatre, where the team had been working earlier in the month.[77] Lynch and Whitlock then moved to Barnum's latest venture, and his first to achieve financial stability, the American Museum on March 5,[78] ending the month at the Chatham Theater for a week's run through early April.[79] It was then to the Franklin Theater during the first full week of April with Barney Williams,[80] and finally back to the American Museum at month's end.[81]

The waters get muddied at this point, because the original John Diamond took the opportunity to return to the north, appearing to stop at the Arch Street Theater in Philadelphia to share the stage with James Sanford[82] before arriving in New York City.[83] Coverage of minstrel performances does not always differentiate between Frank Lynch and John Diamond, with Billy Whitlock confusing the matter further by appearing with both dancers. It is John Diamond who opened at the American Museum on May 14, supported by the instrumentalist R. (probably Richard) Myers.[84] Diamond appeared with Whitlock on banjo at the Museum from May 22 until June 4.[85] It is surprising that Barnum would employ John Diamond at all, considering his past experiences with the dancer. But, I suppose that Barnum was willing to put aside his earlier problems with Diamond if the performer could make the Museum money. But, unfortunately, Diamond's behavior had not made a change for the better, and by June 4, John Diamond was out and Frank Lynch Diamond, possessing "none of [John Diamond's] bad habit[s]," was back with Billy Whitlock at P.T. Barnum's Museum. From June until the end of September, Whitlock and Lynch moved between several New York venues, from the American Museum to the Bowery Theater and back to the Museum.[86] Billy Whitlock went back to the Chatham for the first of November to accompany Jim Sanford,[87] while either Mr. Alden or C.D. Jenkins backed Frank Lynch on the banjo.[88]

P.T. Barnum went on to become one of America's most successful promoters of the mid– and late–nineteenth century. After staging concerts with the Swedish singer Jenny Lind and exhibiting the midget Tom Thumb, Barnum's name became synonymous with the expanded three-ring American circus. Phineas Barnum retired a wealthy man, having learned many lessons about promotion and the entertainment business from his early experiences in minstrelsy.

ELEVEN

Sweeney's Repertoire

The authenticity of their performances and material was a selling point for early black-face minstrels. The player's tunes and songs were supposedly derived from those of plantation blacks. Recently, works like William Mahar's *Behind the Blackface Mask* have sought to clarify this influence, and study other references for early minstrel compositions. To investigate the songs of Joe Sweeney, this chapter will draw upon studies like *Mask* and period documentation to determine the origins, "originality" and "Southerness" of Sweeney's material. The chapter will also examine Joe Sweeney's role as a composer of early minstrel songs.

Considering how important Joe Sweeney is to the history of the banjo, we know precious few of the pieces that he performed. Perhaps this problem is due to the nature of minstrelsy. As a solo or duo circus and theatrical entertainer, Sweeney only sang a handful of songs each night. The same would have been true in his later years as a member of a minstrel group. Joe Sweeney never gave a full evening's concert that has been reported in a newspaper or on a playbill. Reminiscences of the banjoist fail to reproduce more than a handful of compositions. And, only fourteen different song sheets bearing Joe Sweeney's name survive.

Sweeney may be typical of most blackface minstrels. However, some of Joe's peers, like Dan Emmett, lent their names to a significant body of work. Others, such as banjoist James Buckley, published whole collections of minstrel pieces that, by inference, they performed. Since Joe Sweeney played such a major role in the introduction of the banjo into American popular culture, one wishes that he had left behind a greater indication of his repertoire.

Jonny Boker

1
As I went up to Lynchburg town
I broke my yoke on de coaling ground
I drove from dare to bow ling spring
And tried for to mend my yoke and ring
Chorus: O Jonny Boker
Help dat nigger
Do Jonny Boker do
2
I drove from dare to Wright's ole shop
Hollered to my driver and told him to stop
Says I Mr Wright have you got a yoke
He seized his bellows and blew up a smoke

3
Says I Mr Wright habat long for to stay
He cotched up his hammer knocked right away
Soon as he mended my staple and ring
Says I Mr Wright do you charge any thing
4
Says he to me I neber charge
Unless de job is werry large
For little jobs dat is so small
I neber charge any ting at all
5
I drove from dar to Anthony's Mill
And tried to pull up dat are hill

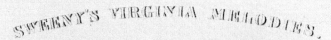

Sheet music cover for "Jonny Boker" showing a caricature of the banjoist J.W. Sweeney in the rural situations described within this song. The cover for "Boker" depicts Wright's blacksmith shop as well as "De Broken Yoke" that serves as the song's premise. Henry Prentiss, Boston, 1840.

I whipped my steers and pushed my cart
But all I could do I couldn't make a start
6
I put my shoulder to the wheel
Upon de ground I placed my heel
Den we make a mighty strain
But all our efforts prove in vain
7
Dare cum a waggoner driving by
I sat on de ground and 'gan for to cry
Says us to him some pity take

And help me up for conscience sake
8
Says he to me I will help thee
He tok out his horses No, 3
I wiped from my eyes the folling tears
He hitched his horses before my steers
9
Den to me he did much please
He pulled me up wid so much ease
His horses were so big and strong
De way dey pulled dis nigger along.

(The lyrics to Sweeney's songs are reproduced as they appear in the original sheet music publications in an attempt to give a more precise indication of his repertoire. This has been done with the understanding that some of the language in common usage during the period of minstrelsy's initial introduction may offend our modern sensibilities. Under no circumstance is the author endorsing nor encouraging the use of such language without a thorough explanation of the period from which it comes.)

The earliest song Joe Sweeney is documented as performing is "Jonny Boker, Or, De Broken Yoke in De Coaling Ground." Unlike many minstrel songs that fictitiously claim only African American heritage, "Jonny Boker" has a provenance definitively rooted in the South. On April 5, 1905, a recollection by Mr. Newman Eubank was printed in the *Lynchburg News* giving a history of "Jonny Boker," along with its lyrics. Eubank, a teenager in Lynchburg at the time of Joe Sweeney's ascent to stardom, related the song's background:

> To be true to history I must give you the origin and occasion of this song. It was composed by Billy Moon and sung by Joe Sweeney when he first started out in life. They were contemporaries, born between 1815 and 1820. The first I ever heard of Joe Sweeney was about the year 1837 or '38, when he sang this song accompanied by his banjo, on the race track of Lynchburg, which is now a part of Rivermont.[1]

Although some minstrel songs refer to current events and popular figures of the day, they usually portray stereotypes and story lines common to the canon. However, it turns out that "Jonny Boker" is about a real journey between the community of Spout Spring and the city of Lynchburg. And, while the actual incident may have been fabricated, the places named did exist and the details given in the song jibe with possible fact.

As Mr. Eubank begins the story, Billy Moon, "loaded his ox-cart with sheaf oats and started to Lynchburgh [sic] by the old stage road. The coaling ground was that district of the county to the right of the road coming this way between Glover's old stand and Concord Depot."[2] This route defines the proposed Appomattox County boundaries, "thence a straight line to the Stage Road ('Clover Hill to Concord to Lynchburg')[3], opposite Sam'l Glover's, thence a straight line to the beginning, the two last lines to be run as to leave said Glover in Campbell County."[4] The Concord Depot was fourteen miles from Lynchburg on the South Side Railroad.[5] Eubank continues, "It had been denuded of all timber to make charcoal for Ross' Iron Works, then located on James River below Robertson's Mill."[6] The Iron Works, also known as Oxford Furnace, was just across the Little Beaver Creek, south of the current highway near Oxford Furnace Road/Route 662. There have actually been three furnaces built in the area. An anonymous author of the historic marker relates how the business began as a bloomery forge in the period of 1768 to 1772, utilizing outside capital. Local lore has it that James Callaway constructed this first blast furnace one mile south before the Revolution. David Ross of Petersburg obtained the land and fashioned the second furnace on a different creek branch by the end of 1776. Thomas Jefferson was among the fans of the iron produced by Ross. From around 1836 until 1875, during the time of the events portrayed in "Jonny Boker," Ross's heir William Ross ran a third furnace.[7] Newman Eubank continues in his commentary that,

> The Bolling Spring was a tavern kept by a man named Minter. It is now owned by Captain Pettigrew's estate, the father-in-law of Captain L.F. Lucado. Mr. Wright was a wheelwright, and was the father of John P. Wright who with Edmund Logwood ran a broker's shop in Lynchburg when you and I first went to Lynchburg. After the War, he edited a Republican paper in Lynchburg.[8]

The Bolling family lived along the route taken in Campbell County. "Mr. Wright" is possibly John P. Wright, whose shop was in Madison Heights, on the current Wright's Shop Road off of Route 622.[9] In Newman Eubank's version of "Jonny Boker," Moon rode by Anthony's Mill, eventually making it into "Thurman's" (possibly "Thurmond's see *Historical Notes*). "After the narration of his being helped up the hill at Anthony's Mill, I have lost the thread of the tale until he got to Lynchburg," concludes Eubank. "[William Moon] described in verse Beaver [the Oxford Furnace area] and 'Possum Creek [which modern day Route 460 crosses east of Lynchburg], and even Sandy Hook [in Southwest Lynchburg], where he struck [the] James River again."[10]

The historical record contains many mentions of Billy or William Moon. They may all be the same person, or many different personages with the same moniker. Newman Eubank remembers Moon as a resident of Campbell County, living just below the Spout Spring near the Appomattox County line. Sweeney researcher George Collins reports that Moon was killed at Lowry, in Bedford County, Virginia, by a train on the N&W line,[11] but this has not been confirmed.[12] Mary Louise Gills, writing about the area, enthuses that "Billy was a great wag, and something of a poet."[13]

If one can believe Newman Eubank (and there is no reason to doubt him), Joe Sweeney carried "Jonny Booker" with him from Virginia into minstrelsy. Sweeney performed the song in Boston during December 1840,[14] the month that Henry Prentiss published his song for the first time.[15] Joe continued to sing the piece in the United States into 1842,[16] and brought it along to England, where his last known airing of the "Jonny Boker" was in the spring of 1843.[17]

Even though Joe Sweeney, by all appearances, dropped "Jonny Boker" from his repertoire, the song continued to be associated with the banjoist. When James Buckley's *New Banjo Method* instruction manual was published in 1860, "Boker" had been relabeled as "Joe Sweeney's Jig."[18] This early part of his stage repertoire had, by that time, gained such a strong Sweeney association as to take on his name.

Jim Along Josey

1
Oh! I'se from Luci-an-na as you all know
Dar where Jim along Josey's all de go
Dem niggers all rise when de bell does ring
And dis is de song dat dey sing
Chorus: Hey get a-long get along Josey
Hey get a-long Jim a long Joe!
2
Oh! When I gets dat new coat which I expects to
   hab soon

Likewise a new pair tight knee'd trousalon
Den I walks up and down Broadway wid my
   Susanna
And de white folks will take me to be Santa Anna

3
My sister Rose de oder night did dream
Dat she was floating up and down de stream
And when she woke she began to cry
And de white cat picked out de black cat's eye

Sheet music cover of "Jim Along Josey" showing Edmund R. Harper as Josey in his play "The Free Nigger of New York." Munro & May, London, circa 1838–1841.

4

Now way down south not very far off
A Bullfrog died wid de hoping cough
And de oder side of Mississippi as you must know
Dare's where I was christen'd Jim along Joe

5

De new York niggers tink dey're fine
Because dey drink de genuine
De southern niggers dey lib on mush
And when dey laugh dey say Oh Hush

6

I'me de nigger that don't mind my troubles
Because dey are noting more dan bubbles
De ambition that dis nigger feels
Is showing de science of his heels

7

De fust President we eber had was Gen'ral Washing-
ton
And de one we've got now is Martin Van Buren
But altho' Gen'ral Washington's dead
As long as de country stands his name shall float
ahead.

The second known piece to have entered Joe Sweeney's earliest performing repertoire did so in 1839. "Jim Along Josey" was associated with several other blackface performers before Sweeney added it to his own shows.

Around 1838, Ned Harper introduced the "Jim Along Josey" song to audiences attending the drama "The Free Nigger of New York." Around the same time, notes circus historian John Dingess, John Smith performed "Jim Along Josey" with the Ohio-based Menagerie and Circus United at the former Pavilion Theater building on the corner of Seventh and Main Streets in Cincinnati.[19] Without further evidence, it is unclear which performer originated this song. What is clear is that Smith staked out his ownership by frequently singing "Josey" throughout the late winter and early spring of 1839 at New York's Bowery Amphitheatre.[20] John Smith subsequently claimed the composition, publishing it in New York City through Firth and Hall by March 1840 (Some scholars have made some claim for the "John N. Smith" listed on the cover as a separate John Smith. Edwin LeRoy Rice, author of the groundbreaking *Monarchs of Minstrelsy*, lists the two Smiths as one and the same. With the exception of some conflicting data concerning an English tour, there is no information currently available that allows the separation of John W. and John N. I must conclude that the "N." is a typo on the part of the printer). Smith had his biggest success with "Jim Along Josey" during an English tour at the end of 1840 and the first third of 1841,[21] even challenging and defeating T.D. Rice's "Jim Crow" in a kind of metaphysical match dance (see Chapter Two).[22] "Josey" went on to become one of the big hits of minstrelsy, performed by a myriad of minstrels from 1838 to 1845. The first known banjo instruction book, *The Complete Preceptor for the Banjo*, of 1851, included the piece nestled among other hits of early blackface.[23]

Joe Sweeney first shared the stage with John Smith when Smith returned to the Bowery Amphitheatre in the fall of 1839 for its winter run. After two weeks at the Bowery, Joe Sweeney jumped ship to the Broadway Circus. Now in competition with Smith, Joe Sweeney took up the "Jim Along Josey" song as his own.[24] Sweeney continued using the song into 1840,[25] and Prentiss included it in a bound edition of Joe's pieces at the end of 1841.[26]

Although the song does boast a catchy melody, "Josey" is fairly standard in its lyrical content. A character song in the mold of "Jim Crow," "Zip Coon," and others of its ilk, "Jim Along Jo" sings and dances his story. He's from Louisiana on the western side of the Mississippi River, gets treated poorly walking with his gal in New York City, and wants to show his dance to audiences. The song utilizes a number of floating stanzas (i.e.: those found in other songs), name checks Rice's "Oh! Hush!" and offers a commentary on the president (see the lyrics reprinted above).[27]

Jenny Get Your Hoe Cake Done

1
De hen and chickens went to roost
De hawk flew down and bit de goose
He bit de ole hen in de back
I really believe dat am a fac
Chorus: Oh, Jenny get de hoecake done my dear
Oh, Jenny get de hoecake done, love!
2
As I was gwain long de road
Pon a stump dar sat a toad
De tadpole winked at Pollewog's dauter
An kick'd de bull frog plump in de water
3
High heel boot widout any strap
Hand me down my leghorn hat
Ise gwain to de Astor house to dine
I won't be back till past half nine
4
Massa and Missus gwain away
Left home fore de break ob day
Den you har de white folks say
Stan clar and let de banjo play
5
Apple cider, an percimmon beer
Christmas comes but once a year
Ginger puddin and punkin pie
Gray cat kick out black cat's eye
6
Massa an Misse promise me

When dey died to set me free
Now dey boss am dead and gone
Left ole Sambo hoeing out corn
7
Old Massa, and Misse is gone away
Da left home one morning gest about day
And den you har dat nigger say
Gi me down de banjo and let de nigger play!
8
You eat my sugar, and drink my tea
And run about de old field and talk about me
Dare was a nigger in de gutter and he turned right
    about
And up stept Jo and got his tooth nocked out
9
Dare was a frog jumped out de spring
It was so cold he couldn't sing
He tied his tail to a hickory stump
He rared an pitched but he couldn't make a jump
10
The old hen and chickens at the stack
An old hawk flew down amongst de pack
And struck de old hen whack middle ob de back
And I really do believe dat tis a fact
11
Now white folks, I'd hab you to know
Dare is no music like de old banjo
And if you want to hear it ring
Jist watch dis finger on de string.

During his second professional year based in New York City, Joe Sweeney came into his own. Along with switching over to a first generation "modern" banjo, Sweeney "introduced" his first fully realized minstrel composition. The verses of "Jenny Get Your Hoe Cake Done" make reference to New York's Astor family (Astor house, verse three), southern Christmas traditions (verse five, "Apple cider, an persimmon beer") and the banjo (verses four, seven, and eleven; see the lyrics reprinted above).[28] On the surface, the song is a simple Uncle Remus story of slaves witnessing animals exhibiting human traits. William Mahar, in his examination of the early minstrel repertoire, makes a case for the animal imagery in this and other Sweeney songs reflecting the rural lifestyle of southern slaves.[28] The exploits of animals in these pieces could just as well be a code to disguise slave behavior from the greater white world, or, by extension, an acceptable way for the masked minstrels to make comments on society as a whole.

Mahar also attempts to decode other meanings from "Jenny." He writes that "Jenny Get Your Hoe Cake Done"

> describes a bread loaf prepared in an oven adjacent to the main cooking hearth in a typical Virginia cookhouse, the hoe being used to remove the cake from the oven. Slaves often used the name "Jenny" as a code word in the expression "goin to set the floor with Jenny tonight" to disguise the social plans African American women made and avoid tipping off the "missus."[29]

"Jenny Get Your Hoe Cake Done" first appeared in Joe Sweeney's repertoire during the early months of 1840, when the New York firm of Firth and Hall submitted the sheet

Sheet music cover for "Jenny Get Your Hoe Cake Done," showing the banjoist performing at the Broadway Circus in New York City. Notice his stage costume, the possible gourd banjo and dancing board under his feet. Firth & Hall, New York, NY, 1840.

Sheet music cover, "Jenny Get Your Hocake Done" showing Joe Sweeney as he appeared "at the Theatre Royal English Opera House" in London during 1843. D'Almaine, London, 1843 (British Library Reproductions).

music for copyright.[30] John Diamond and Dick Pelham "match danced" to the piece (reported as "Jimmy, is yer hoecake done?"), possibly accompanied by Sweeney, during February. (Although Joe Sweeney wasn't performing with Diamond at his regular appearances on this date, the duo were partners right before and after this engagement.)[31]

Joe Sweeney regularly featured this song during the next four years. Audiences in Boston,[32] Baltimore[33] and Washington, D.C.,[34] were delighted with the piece. In 1841, Prentiss republished "Jenny" in a new edition of Joe's hits from the year before. The bound version featuring nine songs was titled "Sweeny's Banjo Melodies," even though, as before, the music was only for the piano. In addition to the four compositions issued in 1840, Prentiss included four from their association with John Smith—two that they had previously published—and "Jenny Get Your Hoe Cake Done," already in print in New York under Sweeney's name.[35]

Sweeney presented "Jenny Get Your Hoe Cake Done" to British audiences in 1843 and 1844.[36] The banjoist thrilled fans of the Virginia Minstrels by playing it for the band's engagement at Glasgow's City Hall in June 1844. "Jenny" was published a third time, when the British firm of D'Almaine and Company made the words with piano accompaniment available to aspiring banjoists and fans alike.[37]

Whar Did You Cum From? (Knock A Nigger Down)

1
Some folks say dat a niggar wont steal!
But I cotch one in my corn field
So I ask him bout dat corn as he call me a liar
So I up wid my foot and I kick him in de fire
Chorus: O whar did you cum from knock a niggar down
O whar did you come from knock a nigger down
2
I went for to mow down in de field
A black snake bit me 'pon my heel
To cut my dirt, den I tought it best
So I run slap up 'gainst a hornet's nest
3
O my red strip'd shirt and red cravat
Oh hand me down my leghorn hat
I was ask'd out one night for to dine
But don't cum back till de clock strike nine
4
I cum from old Wirginny one bery fine day
De riber was froze and I skate all de way
I hab de Banjo under my arm playin dis tune

Dat de niggers used to dance de light of de moon
5
As your young Wag'ner jus begun
You'll quickly find you'll hab no fun
Den you crack de whip and you crack so loud
Dat you jar de niggers head like a thunder cloud
6
As I look'd ober on yonder hill
Dare I saw my uncle Bill
Says I uncle Bill how does you do
Says he, I'm well and how is you
7
Wid a stiff shirt collar wid three rows of stitches
Tight kneed boots and square toe breeches
De rain cum wet, de sun cum dry me
Go 'way black man don't cum nigh me
8
De Alligator cum from Tuscaloo
All for to fight de Rangaroo
Dey fight till dey smash their noses down
Den up agin and take anoder round.

This compilation of "floating verses" was published around the same time as "Jenny Get Your Hoe Cake Done." Prentiss in Boston and D'Almaine in Great Britain ("Where Did You Come From, Nock A Nigger down.")[38] also republished the song at the same time as "Jenny." "Whar Did You Cum From?" stayed alongside "Jenny Get Your Hoe Cake Done" in Sweeney's performances through at least the summer of 1843.[39]

Sheet music cover for "Whar Did You Cum From?" showing Joe Sweeney as he appeared at the Broadway Circus in a rural scene. Firth & Hall, New York, 1840 (Peter Szego Collection).

Ole Virginny Break Down

1
Way down in ole Virginny
Dar I hear de fiddle ring
All de time dis nigger Jo
Play pon de Banjo String
Chorus: I got up in de morning
I go to de kitchen
To get a chunck ob fire
For to go a fishing
2
My mamma was a wolf
My daddy was a tiger
I am what you call
De Ole Virginny Nigger
Half fire half smoke
A little touch of thunder
I am what you call
De eighth wonder
3
I got up in de morning
Bout broke ob day
I went to de riber
My canoe gone away

When I got to de riber
De riber rader wide
I look ober yonder
My canoe on toder side
4
Last Saturday night
De nigger went a hunting
De dog run de wooler
And de wooler run de tiger
De tiger run de stiff neck
Stiff neck run de debil
And day all run together (Spoken)
And de nigger run rite arter em
5
I went to de mill
For to see de miller
Says I ole Mr Miller
Aint you got a chor tobacco
De miller had three dogs
One de name was Jowler
De oder ole Ranger
And de oder ole (Hard Times).

Sweeney's acquaintance, Judge Fernando Farrar, described "His old Virginia break-down, a jig tune, he danced, and made his own music with his banjo hung around his neck with a string."[40] Referred to by music historians as a "roarer" song, the words boast about the toughness and fighting skills of the singer. Published in 1840 and 1841 in by Prentiss, Joe Sweeney featured it throughout New York State tour of 1840[41] and in Boston at the end of the year[42]

Ole Tare River

1
Way down in North Carolina [interlude]
On de banks of Ole Tare River [interlude]
I go from dar to Alabama [interlude]
For to see my ole Aunt Hannah [interlude]
2
Raccoon and possum got in a fray
Fought all night untill de next day
When de day broke de Pos cut to de hollow
Old Coon says I guess I better follow
3
Da met next on de top ob de hill
For to settle dis great diffikil
Possum seized de Coon by de tail
Make him wish he was on a rail
4
Ole nigger cum along wid his dog
Possum cut for de hollow log

Coon he looked and saw dat nig
So up de tree he den dig dig

5
De ole dog watch, smelt all around
He found the Coon jest lef de ground
Den he bark rit up de tree
De ole Coon says you cant ketch me

6
De ole dog bark, de nigger blow his horn
Ole Coon begin to tink he was gone
Ole nigger cum he cast up his eye
On a big limb dat coon did lie

7
Nigger went to work and cut de tree down
De ole Coon he could not be found
De Coon cut stick he was afraid ob de dog
He run slap in anoder hollow log

The sheet music for "Ole Tare River" shows a caricature of the banjoist J. W. Sweeney in the rural situations described within this song. The cover of "Tare River" has the banjoist defending himself against an alligator with a banjo like those made by William Boucher, Jr., of Baltimore. Henry Prentiss, Boston, 1840.

8	9
De Pos says Coon get out ob dis log	*Now Miss Dinah I'm going to leave you*
Lay rite still for I believe I hear de dog	*And when I'm gone don t let it grieve you*
De nigger den cum and stopt up de hole	*First to the window den to de door*
And day couldn t get out to save dar souls	*Looking for to see de banjo.*

Another song that William Mahar identifies as describing rural southern life (a raccoon hunt) is "Ole Tare River." Mahar definitively links the piece to African American music in its use of call-and-response, the irregularity of verse structure and the musical dialogue that occurs between voice and banjo.[43]

"Ole Tare River" makes its first appearance during December 1840, when Prentiss published it in sheet music form. Joe Sweeney's first documented performance of the song was at a Baltimore appearance in March 1841, where it was given the added subtitle of "Joe Sweeny's [sic] Farewell."[44] Sweeney favored the song just before leaving New York for England in early 1842,[45] and continued to sing "Tare River" with Sands American Circus during their 1842 tour.[46] D'Almaine saw fit to reprint the song for the British Isles in the spring of 1843. Joe Sweeney was still singing "Ole Tare River" in Great Britain in June of 1844.[47]

Mahar also documents the song's long life in minstrelsy. He writes of "frequent appearances" in playbills, songsters and citations between 1843 and 1851.[48]

Old Dunbow Sound You' Horn

Not much is known about "Old Dunbow Sound You' Horn." I have been unable to locate lyrics for the song. There are only three mentions for Sweeney's performances of "Old Dunbow," one in December 1840 for Boston,[49] in Baltimore for March 1841 and with Cooke's Circus in Scotland during August 1843 ("Jumbo Sound Your Bone").[50]

Lucy Long

1	3
Oh, I jist come out before you	*Oh Miss Lucy's teeth is grinning*
To sing a little song	*Just like an ear ob corn*
I plays it on de Ban-jo	*And her eyes dey look so winning!*
And dey calls it Lu-cy Long	*Oh would I'd ne'er been born*
Chorus: Oh! take your time Miss Lu-cy	4
Take your time Miss Lu-cy Long	*I axed her for to marry*
Oh! take your time Miss Lucy	*Myself de toder day*
Take your time Miss Lu-cy Long	*She said sh'd rather tarry*
2	*So I let her habe her way*
Miss Lucy she is handsome	5
And Miss Lucy she is tall	*If she makes a scolding wife*
To see her dance Cachucha	*As sure as she was born*
Is death to Niggers all	*I'll tote her down to Georgia*
	And trade her off for Corn.

Opposite: Sheet music cover, "Lucy Long," showing Joe Sweeney as he appeared "at the Theatre Royal English Opera House" in London during 1843. D'Almaine, London, 1843 (British Library Reproductions).

"Lucy Long" was another popular minstrel piece, like "Jim Along Josey," that Joe Sweeney adopted from another musician. The banjoist particularly featured and claimed the comic song during his three years in the British Isles. "Lucy Long" is an especially interesting choice for Sweeney's performances because the composition is structured for a male/female duo, with the female part taken by a cross-dressing male player in blackface.[51] Joe could have only used "Lucy Long" when in concert with another minstrel.

Stuart Thayer writes that Dan Gardner, a long time circus performer who specialized in blackface female impersonation, sang and danced the "Lucy Long" character song as early as 1836.[52] Surprisingly, Thayer leaves this incident out of his exhaustive *Annals of the American Circus*. But, the story just gets stranger. Dan Gardner's brother-in-law, the aforementioned Billy Whitlock (a banjo student of Sweeney), claimed to have thought up the rather simple tune of "Lucy Long" in 1838, with the words being supplied by fellow minstrel T.G. Booth.[53] If Gardner sang the song in 1836, Whitlock couldn't have written the piece in 1838. And, if Thayer is mistaken, and Gardner didn't know the song two years before Whitlock claimed to have written it, why hasn't a documented pre–1842 performance of the song by Whitlock surfaced?

Notably, the mysterious banjoist Ferguson, in conjunction with future Virginia Minstrel Frank Brower, was singing "Lucy Long" as early as the fall of 1840. Dan Gardner was probably the banjoist's source for "Lucy," a fact suggested by Ferguson's inclusion of the "German Farmer" in his performance, another of Gardner's pieces.[54]

Joe introduced "his new negro song of 'Lucy Long,' [which] contain[ed] more humor than any thing of the kind ever produced, not excepting Jim-a-long Josey" in New York during January of 1842.[55] Although the song dates back at least to Dan Gardner, Sweeney presents it as "new" and as "his" own. Interestingly, John Alden was singing "Lucy Long" in New York City at the Arcadian Circus at the same time.[56] Regardless of the competition, Joe sang "Lucy Long" as his signature song throughout this New York run.[57]

Joe Sweeney continued to feature "Lucy Long" during his first two years in Great Britain.[58] D'Almaine and Company announced its publication in the spring of 1843, and another British firm soon issued a "bootleg" edition with Sweeney's name prominently featured on the cover.[59]

De Ole Jaw Bone

1
De Jaw Bone hung on de kitchen wall
Jaw Bone is ber-ry tall
De Jaw Bone ring Jaw Bone sing
Jaw Bone tell me ev-ry ting
Chorus: Walk Jaw Bone wid your turkey too
Neb-er mind dat bu-ger bu
2
De lute string blue it will not do
I want a string to tie my shoe
A cotton it will not do
A cotton string will break into
3
As I was cum from Tennessee
My hoss got mired up to his knee
I whipped him till I saw de blood
Den he hauled me out ob de mud

4
There was a little man he had a little hoss
Went to de riber couldn't get across
I fed my hors in de poplar troff
Ole Cow died ob de hooppin coff
5
De niggers at de south don t dress berry well
Day walk about and try for to cut a swell
In de night day meet for to play
Dance all night until de next day
6
Jay Bird pon a swinging limb
Winked at me I winked at him
Cotched up a stone hit him on de shin
And dats de way we sucked him in.

"De Ole Jaw Bone" was one of three songs published in Boston during December 1840 that were attributed to Sweeney. It reached greater fame when included in an 1844 collection of *Old Dan Emmits Original Banjo Melodies* (as "Walk, Jaw Bone").[60] Although lyrics are about rural life, William Mahar shows that the song originated in Italian opera, coming into American music by way of English stage and folk song.[61] Strangely, there are no printed announcements of Joe Sweeney's using the song in America; a lone mention appeared in May 1842 in conjunction with Sweeney's engagement with Sands American Circus in Leeds, England.[62] Because of the song's prior history and a lack of documented performances by Sweeney, his role in the composition of this piece is unclear.

Other Compositions Performed by Joe Sweeney

Throughout Sweeney's career, he undoubtedly performed a myriad of other songs and tunes. Of those mentioned in memoirs, most can be dismissed as the result of faulty recollections. Pieces such as "Zip Coon"[63] were such big hits that someone writing years later of their Sweeney encounter would often associate such memorable tunes with the banjoist. Another group of titles—"De Smoke House Breakdown,"[64] "Breakdown Rendezvous"[65] and "Old Joe's Trip to England"[66]—are just that, tantalizing titles mentioned once in passing in a newspaper or on a playbill. A third group dates from Joe Sweeney's short stint with the Virginia Minstrels. For their 1844 tour, Sweeney often sang songs "composed" by group member Dan Emmett rather then drawing upon his own repertoire. These included "Old Joe," credited to Frank Brower,[67] and "Dandy Jim from Caroline," which had first been published in America under the Virginia Minstrels name in 1843 without author credit. Emmett later strangely claimed that he wrote it "while on ... passage to England" after its initial publication.[68] Both had been published in 1844, "Old Joe" as a part of *Old Dan Emmits Original Banjo Melodies* and "Dandy Jim" in *Celebrated Negro Melodies or Songs of the Virginny Banjoist*, by Sweeney's English publisher, D'Almaine. Lastly, there were publications under Joe Sweeney's name. Included in Prentiss's bound edition of "Sweeny's Banjo Melodies" was "Ginger Blue."[69] While there is a great probability that Joe sang this song because of its popularity, no documentation supports this possibility.

The Change in Minstrel Material

By the 1850s, the songs from the decade of Joe Sweeney's initial success were considered nostalgic at best. The rough and rowdy material of Sweeney's younger years had been replaced by parodies of popular and light operatic material and the nostalgic, sentimental songs best signified in the work of Stephen Foster. This change is best explained in an account by Fernando R. Farrar. Writing under his stage name of "Johnnie Reb," Farrar's recollections, while jumbling the facts of the performances he viewed[70] mirrors the essential changes that the blackface minstrel repertoire was undergoing at the time:

> I saw Joe Sweeney for the first time about 1842, while I was at school at Prince Edward Courthouse. He and his brother Sam were together. Joe led on the violin and Sam played the banjo. Both had good voices, especially Sam, a rich, full baritone of great sweetness and power. Even at this distant day I can recall some of the tunes they sang—"Old Dan Tucker," "Do Johnnie Booker," "Julianna Johnson," "Oh, Susana" [published in 1848], "The Blue-Tailed Fly," "Jim Crack Corn, and I Don't Care."

When I saw the brothers again the character of the music had somewhat changed, and was much more sentimental and sympathetic. They rendered such pieces as "Dearest May," [sic], "Dearest Mae," James Power, 1847] "Rosa Lee," "Annie of the Vale," "Nellie was a Lady," and "Ellen Bayne."[71]

The Repertoire of Joe Sweeney

During his lifetime, Joe Sweeney is only documented as performing a handful of songs. Of the sixteen pieces associated with the Virginia banjoist, eight of them either have insufficient information for discussion, or they do not appear to have been a part of Sweeney's core repertoire. Of the eight remaining discussed two originated with other performers ("Jim Along Josey" and "Lucy Long"), and two were derivatives of other pieces ("Whar Did You Cum From? (Knock a Nigger Down)" and "De Ole Jaw Bone"). Only four ("Jenny Get Your Hoe Cake Done," "Ole Tare River" "Jonny Boker" and possibly "Ole Virginny Break Down") have ties to rural southern slave life, and could be original slave songs or new compositions, possibly by Joe Sweeney, based on African American tradition. Joe Sweeney did not have as extensive an influence on minstrel repertoire as did his contemporaries like Dan Emmett. However, Sweeney did help in the spread of two early minstrel hits and added four important compositions to the early minstrel canon.

TWELVE

Joel Walker Sweeney and the "Invention" of the 5-String Banjo

I see it erroneously stated that Joe Sweeney was inventor of the banjo. There never was a greater mistake. My father was born in 1777, and I have often heard him say that it was a well-known instrument with the Negroes in the country. My recollection extends back [to 1830]. My father had an old Negro, Davey, who was an expert banjo player.... The banjo and the Negro came to Virginia together.

—E. Newman Eubank[1]

Joe Sweeney has more often than not been directly tied to the development of the banjo from a rude plantation instrument into a musical tool. Decades of banjo historians have insisted that Joe Sweeney added the short, drone string and the frame body. This chapter will attempt to trace these assertions back to their source, and prove that the attributes ascribed to Sweeney were in place long before his involvement with the instrument.

Judge Robert Bolling Pore/Poore (1841–1910) first voiced the contention in print that Sweeney was the inventor of the "5th" string. Pore, then the Appomattox County attorney, grew up a mile from the Sweeney family and knew Joe as a child (a cousin to Joe Sweeney's neighbor Joel Flood, Pore also served with the Sweeneys in the conflict between the north and south).[2] Judge Pore gave this account of how Joe Sweeney began at the age of twelve to learn music "on the violin and four-string gourd":

> At a very early age he developed a great love for music and became when still a boy of 12 years old quite a proficient on the banjo and violin. As he grew and became proficient in the use of tools he undertook to make his own instruments and by the time he was 21 years of age and free from his father's control he had added the 5th string or thumb string to the banjo.[3]

We'll deal with the statement that Sweeney "undertook to make his own instruments" later. Judge Pore's belief that Joe Sweeney "added the 5th or thumb string to the banjo" has been debated "ad infinitum." Unfortunately, a contemporary of Pore's, also from Appomattox, rebutted his assertion by stating, "I am confidant that Sweeney added the bass string."[4] This statement can be and has been read several ways, with some scholars interpreting "bass string" for the lowest pitched string on the banjo (ie: the fourth string) and others believing the writer meant the "5th string" because of the drone's position on the instrument. Needless to say, when the banjo came to the United States before Sweeney's birth, it already had the thumb string in place. Early African American banjos, in paintings such as "The Old Plantation" (see below), are pictured with a short, "thumb" string.

The African American Roots of the American Banjo

De banjo am de greatest thing,
dat ever you did know,
And when de darkey hear de sound,
It shakes de heel an' toe,
It was raised in old Wirginny,
down in Louisiana State,
A-bout ten thousand years ago, for so de people state.
Chorus: Ah, Oh, Oh, Oh,
did you ever go to be!
De banjo am de wonderfullest thing you ever see.[5]

West African slaves undoubtedly brought their version of the banjo with them to America. The griots of West Africa, singers of praise and historical songs, play a semi-spiked lute called variously halam, xalam, hodou, tinbit, and ngoni, which some believe is among the

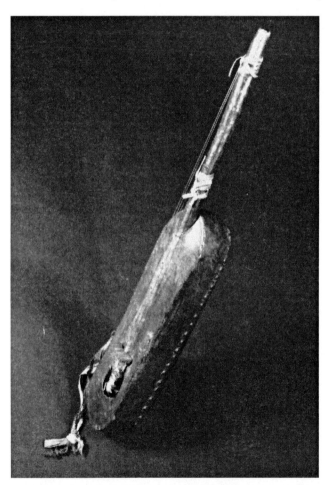

banjo's ancestors. These lutes feature a hollowed out trough-like wooden body with a cow skin stretched over the opening for a soundboard. A round dowel-like neck is inserted into one end and emerges through a hole cut in the head toward the other end onto which the bridge and horsehair strings are anchored. There are two or more noting and a number of drone strings tied to the neck with pieces of rawhide. Other banjo-like folk instruments, like the akonting, have been identified as possible African banjo prototypes as well.[6] There are strong links between griots with banjoists in Virginia, which is not surprising because the earliest slaves came to the area from West Africa. Unfortunately, there is a gap in our knowledge between the griot lutes of West Africa and those found in America. Whether actual instruments crossed the ocean with Africans, or their memory was kept alive in the minds of slaves, when proto-banjos began to be noticed in what was to become the United States, all the basic elements that make a banjo a banjo—the membranous soundboard, short drone string played with the thumb, the frailing and finger picking playing methods—were in place.

Xalam, one of the West African ancestors of the banjo. Wooden body, with wooden dowel neck inserted in the skin soundboard and strings tied to the neck with rawhide (photograph by Peter Szego, Peter Szego Collection)

The best evidence points to African American players constructing their own instruments based on old world prototypes. Descriptions vary as to the number of strings, but most evoke a gourd instrument, with a membranous skinhead. Why gourds replaced wood for the banjo's body is only speculation. Perhaps gourds were plentiful and did not need as much preparation as wood. The griot instrument makers use a lumber with special properties for both the construction of the balaphone (a wooden keyed xylophone) and the body of the lutes. This tree may not have been available in colonial America.[7] Another theory is that some African folk instruments that did use gourds in their construction, such as the akonting, are a more direct antecedent of the banjo.

Several paintings depict African American banjoists during Joe Sweeney's youth. These include James Warrell's "The Banjo Man," a portrayal completed in Richmond, Virginia by the artist in 1813.[8] The clearest representation of an early American banjo is in "The Old Plantation," mentioned above. The artist shows what appears to be a gourd-bodied instrument and a flat, European guitar or cittern-style neck, strung with three long and one short strings arranged as on a modern banjo. This depiction seems to have been made in the first part of the nineteenth century.[9] Recently, a Caribbean instrument has been located in a Parisian museum that mimics the construction details depicted in "The Old Plantation." This "banza" appears to be from the same time period as its American cousin, therefore reinforcing the prevalence for these construction details.[10]

There are numerous written accounts describing the pre–Sweeney banjo as well. The Rev. Jonathan Boucher, who had lived in Virginia and Maryland before returning to England in 1775, made some comments about the instrument in his *Boucher's Glossary of Archaic and Provincial Words* (published in 1832). He noted that in Virginia and Maryland:

> The favourite and almost only instrument in use among the slaves there was a bandore, or as they pronounced the word, banjer. Its body was a large hollow gourd, with a long handle attached to it, strung with catgut, and played on with fingers. Its sound is a dull, heavy, grumbling murmur; yet it is not without something like melody, nor incapable of inspiring cheerfulness and myrth. Negroes ... are always awakened and alive at the sound of the banjer.[11]

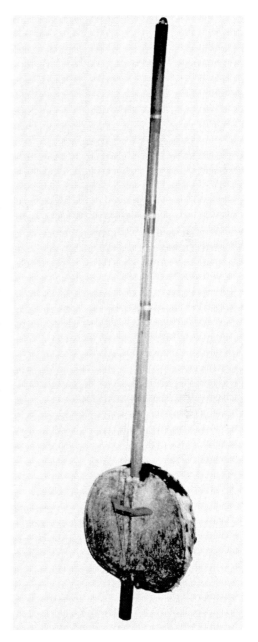

West African Akonting, a spike-lute with gourd body, skin soundboard and wooden dowel-like neck. Three strings. One of the possible ancestors of the American banjo (photograph by and courtesy Ulf Jagfors).

So, some form of the banjo, with a gourd body, long neck and gut strings, was in Virginia by at least the late eighteenth century, albeit in the hands of African American slaves.

An unidentified late nineteenth century correspondent from Appomattox writing to the *Richmond Dispatch* echoes the description above when he gave some clues as to the banjo's early form in the area of Sweeney's birth:

> The first [banjo] I ever saw was made in this way: A large gourd covered with a raw sheep-skin served for the drum, and the strings were made of horse-hair, pulled from a white horse's tail. It had only four strings. My father's carriage-driver was a banjo-player. He played two or three changeless tunes on one cord [sic].[12]

And P.C. Sutphin, who grew up in Lynchburg, reinforces the construction details for banjos in Joe Sweeney's area described above, by stating that:

> The original negro banjo ... was usually a large gourd with a drum head of sheep skin or coon skin, and four twisted horse hair strings, with bridge, pegs, etc., usual to the banjo now.[13]

Robert Pore agrees with these descriptions of area instruments at the time of Sweeney's learning the banjo—with gourd bodies, sheep or coonskin sounding board and four strings of horsehair (like the griot lutes, see above)—when he says that Sweeney learned on a "four-string gourd."

Joe Sweeney has also been given credit for the "improvement" of replacing the African American banjo's gourd body with a circular wooden hoop. In 1890, George William Inge (circa 1856–April 25, 1929), whose father then owned the Sweeney estate, said that:

> several old and reliable farmers in Appomattox related to me ... [Sweeney] first improved on the gourd by stretching a sheepskin over a common meal sifter and attaching a flat neck.[14]

This contention is easily rebutted, or at least contradicted, by another area resident, P.C. Sutphin, who reports a prototypical round rim sound box before Joe Sweeney's involvement with the instrument:

> Sometimes, the rim would be made of maple, or the rim of a sugar box, would be used.... the banjo ... was quite common with the negro, or at least the boatmen just named, before Mr. Sweeney was know as a performer on it, and it is even probable years before he was born.[15]

Therefore, the *idea* of a short drone string survived from Africa and the frame body, while not in widespread use, was an alternative construction method already being tried by the early nineteenth century. Joe Sweeney may have used and refined these concepts before carrying them into the mainstream, but he definitely did not invent them.

But, what of Pore's statement about Joe making banjos? Manufactured instruments did not become available until the mid–1840s, and so musicians would either have to find someone to make an instrument for them or make their own.

There is the possibility that Sweeney made some of his first instruments in the manner of African Americans. In a 1940 article by Mrs. J.O. Cole for the *Lynchburg News*, Sweeney's great-niece, Mrs. William Pitzer Gills, repeats the following fanciful family story of Joe making banjos (here from his mother's housecats) at the age of seven:

> As a child Sweeney wanted to express his soul in music in some sort of fashion and as he had no instrument he made one. The two Sweeney house cats—one black and the other white—were victims to this urge for expression. They mysteriously departed from this earth and only when the hide of the black cat appeared stretched over an old gourd frame, ornamented with hairs from the tail and mane of the old family gray mare, did the gruesome truth come out.

Mrs. Sweeney promptly consigned this instrument to the flames and doubtless chastized [*sic*] Joe. But the urge remained and little time passed before the white cat was offered on the altar of melody. This time the crude banjo was not destroyed by Mrs. Sweeney, who was a woman of good sense and saw that Joe's craving meant something. From that time on, he had help and some encouragement.[16]

So, despite Pore's contention that Sweeney redesigned the banjo, Joe's first instruments undoubtedly echoed those of the slaves around him, as Mrs. Gills' story, however fanciful, suggests.

Even though Joe Sweeney made his own instruments in the story recounted above, other evidence that Sweeney made his early banjos is contradictory. Various advertisements, such as one from a Richmond Theater in 1837, describe Sweeney as playing "on a real Banjo, made by himself."[17] However, when Billy Whitlock came to Virginia in 1837, Joe did not make Whitlock a banjo, but "had one made for him."[18] So, it remains unclear who made Joe's instruments.

Questions about the early development of the American banjo remain, however. How did the banjo change in Sweeney's hands, or, what changes did it undergo during Joe Sweeney's reign? When was the round, drum-like body substituted permanently for a gourd? In 1840, Joe Sweeney's earliest known musical publications appeared, "Jenny Get Your Hoe Cake Done" and "Whar Did You Cum From?"; on their covers, the banjoist is depicted holding an instrument with a gourd-shaped body, the soundboard attached with stitching to the gourd, with six pegs on a guitar-like head stock. Later that same year Henry Prentiss of Boston brought out "Jonny Boker, Or, De Broken Yoke in De Coaling ground," the cover of which portrays a black (or blackface) banjoist and instrument with a scroll-shaped head stock, a round head, and a long neck. This sideways violin peg box resembles those used by Baltimore banjo maker William Boucher from 1845 onward. During the same time period, Prentiss published "De Old Jaw Bone," which featured a more caricaturish cover drawing of a black man with a gourd-shaped banjo. Finally, as the cover to "Sweeny's Virginia Melodies" at the end of 1840, Prentiss represents Joe Sweeney holding an early frame construction banjo, with a "Boucher-style" headstock. From that point on, Sweeney (and most other banjoists as well) were pictured holding the "modern" banjo. It did not matter that these illustrations were not completely accurate in their portrayal of Sweeney and his instruments. As far as the majority of Americans were concerned, 1840 marked the transition from gourd to frame construction for banjos. If Sweeney was not the first to use this improvement, then, he was among the first crop of frame banjoists.

Besides period illustrations and descriptions, one instrument that belonged to the Sweeney family survives to this day. This Sweeney banjo, with a homemade left-handed neck and Boucher-made rim, resided with Polly Ann Sweeney Patterson, one of Joe's musical cousins. Polly gave the banjo to John Durrum, another Sweeney relative, from whom George Inge procured the instrument for John Henning. In the late nineteenth century, Professor John E. Henning was a one-time banjo, mandolin and guitar instructor at Chicago's YMCA and Central College, and writer for a small journal regarding the those instruments. The Sweeney banjo almost disappeared, as it was temporarily lost in shipping from Appomattox to Inge. Along with the instrument, Joe's sister Elizabeth Conner lent Inge and Henning photographic portraits of her three musical brothers. Some years later, the Henning family relocated to California, bringing with them the Sweeney banjo and family photographs. Upon the death of Professor Henning, his widow donated these items to the Los Angeles County Museum, where they still reside today.

Family lore identifies Polly as a left-handed banjo player, which would explain the left-

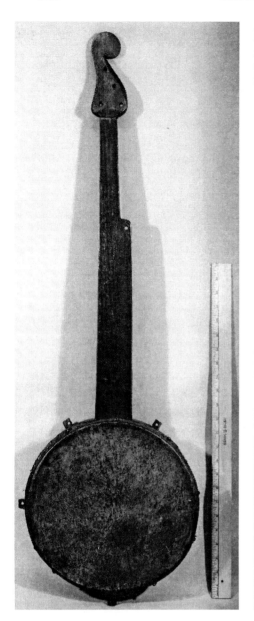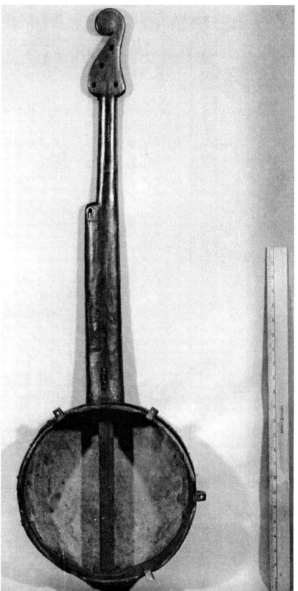

This so-called "Joe Sweeney banjo" was acquired by Professor Henning from a member of the extended Sweeney family and donated after his death to the Los Angeles County Museum. It features a pot in all probability by William Boucher and a homemade, left-handed neck. Two photographs, front and back views.

handed neck on the instrument.[19] Inge describes this as the banjo Joe made for an overseas sojourn in the 1840s, and "that it is the first instrument to which [Sweeney] added the fifth string, and also the one upon which he first played in public."[20]

If this was the banjo that Joe Sweeney "first played in public" and used for his tours of Great Britain, then possibly it resembles the "copy" belonging to English banjoist Joseph Cave. In his reminiscences, Cave describes his "Sweeney" banjo thusly:

The banjo which came into my possession was a very different instrument to those of the present day.... Mine was rather rudely constructed, consisting of nothing more than a hoop about four inches wide, with a piece of vellum fastened on with brass-headed nails, and a light staff of wood running through the tambourine-like body forming the finger-board. There were four larger strings and a smaller one, always tuned to the octave of the key the instrument was tuned in.[21]

Both the Cave banjo and the Sweeney family banjo have five strings (four long, one short) and a skin soundboard "tacked" (i.e.: attached with nails) onto the rim. So does the banjo pictured on the cover of "Sweeney's Virginia Melodies" published before his trip to England. Additionally, the "Virginia Melodies" banjo has a Boucher-like headstock, as does the family banjo. So, the family banjo *resembles* the instrument Joe Sweeney "first played in public" with a bent wood rim around 1840. However, this instrument bears no similarity to the banjo Joe Sweeney is holding on English sheet music covers. And, unless Sweeney was left-handed (which his cousin who owned the instrument was and Joe does not seem to have been) and Boucher was making banjos by 1840 (which he doesn't appear to have been doing), this instrument was not used by the Virginia banjoist during his three years in Britain. Although there is little evidence proving Joe Sweeney's connection to the instrument besides family lore, the most believable story is that Joe assembled the banjo for his cousin at some later date, fashioning and/or fastening the crude neck to a Boucher rim.

All of this evidence points to Joe Sweeney's role as a disseminator and popularizer of the new frame construction, five string instrument. Unfortunately, it is impossible to prove that Joe had any role in "improving" or making banjos in any number.

The Banjo in the Mass Market

With the addition of a round, drum-like body replacing the homegrown gourd, the banjo became easier to produce. Banjo manufacturers as opposed to builders of single instruments began to emerge by 1844, when New York City cabinetmaker John Stevens advertised himself as a "Banjo Maker."[22] Furthermore, anyone with a background in woodworking or cabinetry could fashion a banjo upon request, and many did, before and after the demand for banjos reached critical mass.

Throughout the 1840s and 1850s, the number of instruments made in small factories increased to meet demand to a veritable explosion. One brand popular in the upper south, particularly in Virginia, was that sold by a Baltimore music dealer, William Boucher, Jr.[23] Trade routes brought raw materials used by cabinet and instrument makers up the Shenandoah Valley of Virginia to Baltimore, and instruments in the reverse direction. It was during Boucher's reign that the method of fastening the head to the hoop changed from tacks to drum tightening hardware. When Sweeney fashioned a crude neck to a rim for use by his left-handed cousin, Joe utilized a discarded body from Boucher's factory (see above; for a more complete history of banjo manufacturing, see Bollman and Gura's book cited above).

Of all the pre–Civil War banjos that survive to this day, a good third of them bear the hallmarks of William Boucher, Jr. George Wunderlich, a contemporary maker of nineteenth century reproduction banjos, has accumulated a list of around 150 pre-war banjos, of which William Boucher marketed forty-three.[24] This attests to both the size of Boucher's operation, along with the popularity of his instruments. Besides the sideways violin peg box with its decorative wooden beehive described above, the banjos marked with the heel stamp of "W. Boucher, Jr. Baltimore" featured a single piece of scalloped bent oak for the rim, a limited number (usually six) of head fastening brackets or tacked heads, double heads on some instruments, faux wood graining, and laminated necks cut on the side facing the player to indicate noting positions.

Most of Boucher's instruments utilize the type of head fastening hardware borrowed from snare drums that have become standard on the modern banjo. Originally, drumheads were held on with ropes. Metal tensioning rods were first patented for drums in Europe during 1837, and were put to use on snare drums during the 1840s and 1850s. However, American drum makers neglected these ideas and kept using rope-tensioners through the Civil War and beyond. This is ironic, as banjo makers picked up the European-style hardware as early as the 1840s. Boucher used both of these technologies, employing tensioning rods for his banjos and ropes for his drums.[25]

The Bouchers trace their origins to the Alsace-Lorraine region of France. The family left for adjoining German soil sometime around 1800 because of political and religious turmoil. Johann Friedrich Wilhelm Esprit Boucher, Sr. (1790–1858,[26] known in this country by the anglicized name of William Boucher),[27] was a maker of violins,[28] banjos,[29] drums and guitars whose name appears in advertisements and exhibition catalogues between 1840 and 1858.[30] William Sr., probably had some musical education as well, as family members recall him as a professional singer.[31] By 1840, when he appears on the United States census for the first time, Boucher had relocated to the city of Baltimore.[32]

Interestingly, along with Philadelphia and New York City, Baltimore was a center for nineteenth century American instrument manufacturing, although local makers focused the marketing of their output to the immediate area. And, like Boucher, a goodly number of these builders were of German extraction with familial and old-world associations. These included piano companies such as William Knabe and Charles Stieff, and drum fabricators like C.H.C. Eisenbrandt.[33] In fact, there were area drum companies as early as 1794,[34] and other local instrument workshops at least twenty years prior to that date.[35] Eventually, the friendships between the various German wind, drum and stringed instrument makers seems to have resulted in a large number of symbiotic business relationships, with instruments imported or made by one concern being labeled and sold through another.[36]

While William Boucher, Sr., was undoubtedly a fine builder with a good reputation among his German colleagues in the new world, it was his son William Jr., that established the business that is renowned to this day among banjo and drum collectors. William Boucher, Jr., was born in Hanover (it is uncertain whether in the city or the kingdom) on September 12, 1822.[37] William Jr.'s passport from Mannheim in the Grand Duchy of Baden was issued in 1845; at that time the younger Boucher was making musical instruments.[38] William Boucher, Jr., first shows up in Baltimore several years later, and is listed as a "music dealer" either located near or sharing his father's shop on Holliday close to its intersection with Baltimore Street.[39] By the 1850 census, William Jr., and his family were residing in Baltimore's Fourth Ward,[40] with a shop at 32/38 East Baltimore Street through the decade.[41] Unlike most of his contemporaries, the younger Boucher quickly moved his family out of his place of business and into dwellings located in the city's best neighborhoods.[42]

The Boucher family's establishments were found within a triangular six-block area where most of Baltimore's instrument makers and music publishers were located.[43] One of those, C.H.C. Eisenbrandt, was probably the one to encourage the Bouchers to relocate to Baltimore, as William Jr. used a building once occupied by Eisenbrandt and later established himself near Eisenbrandt's shop on West Baltimore Street.[44]

Many of Baltimore's craftsmen shared their living quarters with their business, as many "manufacturers" were in reality hand making and importing much of their product. Early

American music expert Lloyd P. Farrar believes that the Bouchers followed this pattern. Farrar wrote to the banjo collector Peter Szego that:

> It is fully possible that non-mechanized instrument making (hand cutting, carving, and setting up for gluing) could have been done readily in either of the Boucher homes on East or West Baltimore Street. I don't think, however that they could have done the steaming and bending of the ⁵⁄₁₆" slabs of wood typically found in drums and other shells of the period within the house, and probably there was no facility for power tools even though shops next to Jones Falls did enjoy water-power drives for looms, lathes, power saws, etc. But there were unlimited numbers of wood fabricators in Baltimore at the time who could have done some sub-contracting, and there also were many brass and iron mechanics then active to support manufacture of fine furniture and pianos/organs.[45]

So, while William Boucher, Sr., concentrated his efforts on making instruments himself, William Jr., quickly moved into a supervisory position in his instrument business. Some parts of his banjo making he contracted out, and the pieces he did make, if we can use the example of other Baltimore instrument companies, were probably the work of slaves or indentured servants.[46]

By the 1850s, William Boucher, Jr., was well on his way to financial success. Boucher was able to advertise himself as an "Importer and Manufacturer of all kinds of Musical Instruments." Besides selling strings for "Guitar, Banjo and Double Bass" William Jr., sold "Guitars, Violins, Banjos, [and] Drums," and also "Bands supplied with all styles of Brass Instruments on reasonable terms."[47]

Like his father, William Boucher, Jr., must have pursued music, although on more of an amateur basis. He published at least three musical compositions. In 1857, the firm of Miller & Beacham, Baltimore, printed the "Shamrock Waltz"[48] and George Willig, an area publisher with German roots,[49] issued the "Verbena Waltz," dedicated to Boucher's first wife "Miss Magdalena A. O'Brien."[50] In 1865, the year he married his second wife, he dedicated the "Josephine Waltz" to her.[51]

It took manufacturers such as Boucher in Baltimore and James Ashborn in Connecticut to convert the early frame construction banjos into the form that, with the twentieth century addition of a removable resonator or closed back, we know of today. In the period leading up to the Civil War, makers introduced improved tuning machines and added guitar frets to the fingerboard.

At the dawn of the last decade before the Civil War, the banjo had become an integral part of American culture. On his Mugwumps website, Michael Holmes identifies around sixty instrument makers at work in the United States during the thirty-five years before the War. Although not all banjo makers came from this group (and most of these craftsmen didn't make banjos), when the professional production of banjos began in the mid–1840s, both musical instrument and woodworking shops began turning out banjos. By using the research of Holmes, Bollman and Gura mentioned above, who examined the catalogues of industrial fairs, local histories and business directories for northern cities such as New York, Philadelphia, Boston and their suburbs, as well as western outposts like St. Louis and San Francisco, combined with some errant bits and pieces, I have identified thirty-five banjo makers in addition to the Bouchers. Eleven of these were active in the 1840s and the remainder began production in the 1850s.[52] Judging from the known number of surviving instruments made before the Civil War, these banjo producers were mostly hand fabricating their five stringers in small shops. None of these builders had an impact on the banjo business equivalent to William Boucher, Jr.

In 1850, J.W. Randolph, a dealer of "Books, Stationery, Music and Musical Instruments and Fancy Goods," could advertise to his Richmond, Virginia, constituents that a "Banjo Preceptor, with Christy's Minstrels' Songs, pa, .25; [and] "Banjos, from $3 to $10" were available for purchase.[53] P.H. Taylor's Music Store, of the same Southern city, was selling banjos by the end of the 1850s.[54]

Besides the avalanche of sheet music containing minstrel songs arranged for the home vocalist and pianist, books containing "complete" collections of Ethiopian songs, such as *Nigger Melodies* by Cornish, Lamport & Company, were flooding the market.[55] In 1855, the first "real" banjo instructor was published by Oliver Ditson of Boston, supposedly authored by Tom Briggs. Phil Rice's *Method for the Banjo* in 1858 and James Buckley's *New Banjo Method* of 1860, all available through Ditson, followed this.[56] Although only one piece attributed to Sweeney ("Joe Sweeney's Jig," aka: "Jonny Boker") was contained in Buckley, many other early minstrel classics could be learned by the aspiring banjoist from these instructors. With or without new sheet music and instruction manuals, Sweeney's legacy continued to be felt.

By the end of slavery, musicians were imitating store-bought instruments rather than fashioning more organic creations. "When we made a banjo," remembered one ex-slave,

> we would first of all catch what we called a ground hog, known in the north as a woodchuck. After tanning his hide, it would be stretched over a piece of timber fashioned like a cheese box, and you couldn't tell the difference in sound between that homely affair and a handsome store bought one.[57]

Another imitation of a manufactured banjo from Sweeney's area was featured in the Ferrum College exhibit *The Banjo in Virginia* and in *America's Instrument*. This long neck double tack-head (skin coverings nailed on both the front and back of the rim assembly) is about 32 inches long and is labeled as "made by D.P. Diuguid, Lynchburg, VA." The Diuguids were the founders of the second oldest funeral home in the United States and a prominent area family. David Patterson Diuguid (August 25, 1818–July 4, 1864) was the oldest of three children born to Sampson D. (October 29, 1795–February 15, 1856) and Martha Bradley Patterson Diuguid (April 10, 1798–September 5, 1848). Like many engaged in the woodworking trade in areas lacking funeral services, Sampson Diuguid had first made caskets, and went on in 1820 to found the Diuguid Funeral Home. Surviving account books for the business list various items of furniture as well as coffins, but there are unfortunately no mentions of any banjos. I can only assume that this was a one-off instrument made for a customer, family member or possibly by David Diuguid for himself to play.[58]

After the war, the instrument continued to evolve through the end of the century, becoming sturdier, louder and brighter in order to meet the expanding needs of concertizing. Various metal tonal systems were adapted to the round rim to achieve these goals, with each company championing their version of this "improvement" over all others. Banjos became fancier looking as well. Perhaps in an effort to make the instrument more attractive to the public or to appear more impressive on stage, materials such as shell, pearl, precious metals and wood marquetry were added to adorn the banjo. Influences from the Victorian decorative arts found elsewhere in American culture were incorporated into banjo ornamentation. The most expensive instruments, many created for trade shows and far out of the reach for all but the wealthiest Americans, were wondrous creations. They featured carved necks, with fingerboards and rims covered in costly materials depicting the natural world, animals and astronomical bodies, as well as characters from mythology and the supernatural.

As the United States became industrialized, the nature of selling music changed as well, spawning large music distributors for sheet music and musical instruments. These businesses developed the marketplace and increased the demand for banjos, especially those aimed at the common man and woman. Industrialization also made possible enhanced production methods, cutting manufacturing time and increasing the number of instruments produced.

Professional banjo performers and instructors such as the Dobson Brothers allied themselves with instrument companies, or became manufacturers themselves. Henry C. Dobson began teaching the banjo in New York City during 1853, attempting to introduce the instrument to the wealthy residents of the city. He made his first banjo in 1851.[59] Philadelphia banjo maker S.S. Stewart was the largest and the best of these mass market makers, churning out instruments at an impressive rate. Boston makers such as Fairbanks and Cole (both alone and together) soon grabbed the top end of the market (instruments for professionals and the wealthy). Myriad cut-rate makers filled the bottom end. Stewart managed to combine the attributes of both consumer segments, merging quality with quantity.

Sweeney seems to first have been recognized as an important figure in the history and development of the banjo during the last decade of the nineteenth century. This rise of interest in Joe Sweeney coincided with an attempt at the legitimization of the banjo, through publications by manufacturers such as S.S. Stewart and in journals like *The Cadenza*. At that time, those involved with the promotion of the banjo—players, teachers, publishers and manufacturers—were trying to differentiate the instrument from its folk roots and "elevate," if you will, the banjo to increase its sales and popularity. It was during this period, at the height of the "classic" banjo craze, that George W. Inge, born in Appomattox during the last years of Joel Sweeney's life, acquired the Sweeney family instrument, as well as the only known photograph of the performer. Inge also interviewed surviving family members about their relative. "This information is reliable," claimed Inge in a letter to Professor John Henning, "coming as it does from responsible parties and from his sisters."[60] In an attempt to establish a pedigree for the then popular instrument, Professor Henning, an instructor of stringed music in Chicago, published George Inge's research in a series of articles for his magazine, *The Chicago Trio*. Henning's articles on the Sweeneys form the basis for much that has been written since about the banjoist and his family (see above for more about the Sweeney banjo, Inge and Henning).

Since the 1890s, discussions of Joe Sweeney's accomplishments have continued unabated. Several others have followed Inge and Henning in telling the story of "the Minstrel of Appomattox," including Vera Thomas of Lynchburg and Colonel George Collins of the American Banjo Fraternity. Just past the new millennium, Sweeney continues to be a figure that inspires interest and arguments about just what was his role in the banjo's early history.

THIRTEEN

Sweeney's Influence

As noted earlier, Joe Sweeney learned the banjo at a time when it was evolving from a gourd slave instrument into a mainstream manufactured music maker. He may have even participated in its evolution, bringing construction ideas out of the rural south to the industrial north. Besides being falsely credited for "inventing" the fifth string and hoop construction, Sweeney has also received much press as the first Anglo American banjoist. This chapter will investigate that claim, and in the process, discuss many early minstrel banjo players, some of who learned directly from Joe Sweeney.

The Banjo in Blackface

Mr. Everard will then introduce the old Virginia Banjo! and sing, Jim Along Josey, Coal Black Rose, and dis old Nigger will conclude by making the old Banjo walk and talk.[1]

Joe Sweeney's most important achievement was the introduction of an "improved" African American instrument into popular culture. Sweeney taught or performed alongside the most important first generation banjoists in early minstrelsy. The extent of his influence cannot be understated. This section, will introduce some of those early Anglo American minstrel banjoists, tell their stories and how they relate to Joe Sweeney's chronicle, and also investigate the contention that Sweeney was the first to bring the banjo into blackface minstrelsy, and therefore into mainstream consciousness.

Picayune Butler's come to Town

1
I come to town dis ve-ry day,
And brought my Ban-jo long to play,
Yah ha,
I raise my notes to such a sound,
Dat it clear'd my heel right off de ground,
Yah, ha.
Chorus: Pic-ay-une But-ler's comin, comin,
Pic-ay-une But-ler's come to town....
2
About some twenty years ago,
Old Butler reigned wid his old Banjo,
Ah, ah.
Twas a gourd, three string'd, and an old pine stick,
But when he hit it he made it speak,

Ah, ah.
3
Picayune Butler gwine to rise,
And meet his friends up in de skies,
Ah, ah,
Some thing else am mighty true,
De Banjo gwine to be dar too,
Ah, ah.
4
Now ladies all I'll had you know,
Dar is no music like de old Banjo,
Ah, ah,
And when you want to hear it ring,
Just watch dese fingers on de string,
Ah, ah.[2]

138

There has been much debate about who was the first banjoist in minstrelsy. Joe Sweeney was performing regionally by the end of 1836, and first appeared in New York City, the seat (if you will) of minstrelsy, in April 1839. Were there other performers using the banjo on stage before that time?

One early banjoist was circus performer and founding member of the Virginia Minstrels William "Billy" Whitlock (see Chapter Six). At the beginning of 1837, Whitlock ran away to join Waring and Raymond's circus. Waring, Raymond and Company had been wintering on the Georgia coast since the first weeks of the year. Billy remembers joining them in early March, as the troupe prepared to load up the wagons and leave the port city of Savannah for their long and slow tour north, but he could have been in Georgia as early as the first weeks of January.[3] After spending late March and early April in Georgia, the circus wagons traversed South Carolina, heading into North Carolina for shows in late April or early May of the year. By June, they were in Virginia, and at Lynchburg by the June 7.[4] Somehow, Joe Sweeney and Whitlock became acquainted, and, improbably, during Billy's short stay, Sweeney taught him the rudiments of banjo playing. One can envision Whitlock, a native of New York City, bragging to Joe about the theatrical scene and opportunities for an aspiring blackface minstrel in the north. From Wednesday until the week's end, Billy Whitlock spent his days with Sweeney, and his nights performing for local audiences.[5] Luckily, William Whitlock left behind an unpublished autobiography. Upon his death on March 29, 1878,[6] the *New York Clipper* entertainment magazine paraphrased parts of Whitlock's chronicle.[7] The *Clipper* described the men's meetings:

> Up to that time, Whitlock had never seen a banjo. During his four days stay in Lynchburg, Sweeney had one made for him, and taught him a tune—"Settin' on a Rail" [a song about a raccoon hunt], which was very popular. He now devoted his spare time to mastering the banjo. Every night during his journey South, when he was not playing, he would quietly steal off to some negro hut to hear the darkies sing and see them dance, taking with him a jug of whiskey to make them all the merrier. Thus he got his accurate knowledge of the peculiarities of plantation and cornfield negroes.[8]

It is tempting to ascribe Whitlock's tale as a fantasy, fabricated many years after the supposed events to assure Billy's place in minstrel history. This ascription seems unlikely for a number of reasons. First, Billy Whitlock had a long history of working with Joe Sweeney during the heyday of early minstrelsy, and so had no need to invent this meeting. Second, Whitlock is repeatedly billed as "pupil of the celebrated Sweeny" in advertisements for his appearances.[9] John Glenroy, a circus performer who knew both men, calls Billy "the second banjo player in the states (with Sweeney being the first), and a pupil of Sweeney."[10] Additionally, judging from his autobiography and the writings of others who knew him, Whitlock had a tremendous ego, and this story places him in the subservient position, one that he would never intentionally claim. While his visiting with blacks reeks of exaggeration, his learning the banjo from Sweeney seems plausible.

Regardless, the two must have made an interesting pair, the New Yorker and the Virginian. Whitlock caught Joel Sweeney at an ideal time in the latter's career. Sweeney had not yet entered full-time show business, and was still open about sharing his secrets. A scant five years later, Joe would be guarding his instrument and playing techniques, wary of those competitors who had risen up to emulate his early success.

Was Whitlock playing the banjo in New York before Sweeney's first appearances in the spring of 1839? City directories show that Billy returned to the printing profession during 1839 and 1840, and had not yet gone full-time into performing. Although some writers have reported Whitlock beating Sweeney to New York stages with the banjo,[11] I have found no documentation for Billy Whitlock playing the banjo in the city before January 1840, nine months after Joe Sweeney's debut.[12] Finally, the presentation of Whitlock in advertisements as the pupil of Sweeney in itself indicates that Joe Sweeney had already established a reputation as a banjoist in New York with which the ad writer expected the reader to be familiar.

Another earlier instrumentalist and a compatriot of Billy Whitlock and Joe Sweeney in the Virginia Minstrels was Dan Emmett. As had been mentioned previously, Emmett began learning banjo from the mysterious A. Ferguson sometime during August 1840. That date is also the earliest known performance for Ferguson.[13] Dan Emmett didn't perform in public on the banjo until the following summer. So, this eliminates both Ferguson and Emmett as contenders for the title of first minstrel banjoist.

Of all the candidates, the most likely is John B. "Picayune" Butler (died November 18, 1864, in New York City),[14] a Creole banjoist from New Orleans.[15] However, little is known about Butler, because his early career went largely uncovered by the day's newspapers. In fact, only two first hand accounts have surfaced, both from the banjoist's later years. One anecdote comes from the great post–Civil War banjoist and banjo instructor Frank B. Converse. In 1851, while still learning the instrument, Converse's hometown of Elmira, New York, was visited by a minstrel troupe including Butler. Many years later, Frank Converse remembered John Butler:

> Heralded as the greatest banjo player in the world, and the only acknowledged rival of the two most prominent banjoists of the period—Tom Briggs, then playing with E.P. Christy's Minstrels in New York, and "Hi" S. Rumsey.... As Butler's company remained in town several days, I had many opportunities for hearing him—not only in his solos, but often listening unobserved below his hotel window. As he played with the thimble, [i.e.: a finger pick worn on the finger that strikes the strings] his execution—unlike anything I had ever heard, powerful and brilliant—strongly impressed me, and in my enthusiasm I thought him the most favored mortal on earth....
>
> Butler's playing, while effective, was far from artistic, and his repertoire [was] limited chiefly to jigs, reels, walk-arounds and his comic songs. He was of medium height, rather heavily built, of a genial disposition, playing his solos sitting and in a "make-up" similar to that now worn by our comic solo players.... patched, ill-fitting plantation get-up of old boots, exaggerated collar, slouch hat, etc ... sitting with one leg thrown across the other as he played and sang.[16]

Six years later, Butler participated as a contestant in "the first banjo concert given in America," held at New York's Old Chinese Assembly Rooms, 539 Broadway. On Monday, October 19, 1857, Butler competed against Phil Rice (died December 4, 1857[17]), the banjo teacher of the renowned classical musician and composer Sigismond Thalberg and author of a banjo method published the following year,[18] and Charles Plummer.[19] At the end of the evening, the competition had come down to Butler and Plummer. As Charles Morrell witnessed:

> Billy Blair came before the audience and announced Pic. Butler, and when he made his appearance you should have heard the reception he got. I thought the roof would fall off, but it was plainly seen that he was a little under the influence of liquor; so much so, that he broke two strings during his trial. That, with the other cause weakened his turn considerably ... [and] The prize was awarded to Charles Plummer.[20]

Picayune Butler himself is a problematic candidate as the first banjoist in minstrelsy. If his documented prominence dates to the 1850s, he is an unlikely nominee for having been the one to embed the banjo into minstrelsy over a decade earlier. While these quotes

Poster for a Banjo Contest at the Chinese Assembly Rooms, on Broadway in New York City, October 19, 1857. This is the competition featuring Picayune Butler and described within the text (Peter Szego Collection).

provide insight into Butler's personality, they provide no evidence of his primacy on the banjo.

Besides Butler, little evidence suggests that many others actually played the banjo in the early years of minstrelsy (of course, the banjo could already be found within the "folk" music of rural African and Anglo Americans). At best, a small number of performers may have been using the instrument to lend credence to their act, with still fewer possessing even basic skills on the banjo. It took Sweeney to excite others about the instrument, and to inspire a first generation of minstrel players. Joe Sweeney was the first real banjoist in minstrelsy (i.e., he was accomplished on the instrument), the first professional to have learned directly from African Americans, and the one that got everyone interested in using the banjo for more than just a prop.

A Rush to the Banjo

Joe Sweeney's appearances spurred a rush to the banjo by many white performers playing in blackface. Sweeney somehow offered a connection to the instrument that African

Americans, denied access to public venues such as theaters and circuses, had been previously unable to provide the greater public. From our vantage point 150 years later, it is impossible to know whether it was his interpretation of black playing styles, the sonic improvements made by himself or others to his instrument, his charismatic stage presence, or, simply his white skin that sold America on this music.

Besides Billy Whitlock and Sweeney's apprentices William Chestnut and Thomas Coleman (discussed in Chapter Three), Joe also provided a model for members of the English expatriate Buckley family. James Buckley, Sr.,[21] was the literal father of one of the preeminent American minstrel troupes. Buckley (1803–April 27, 1872)[22] was born in Manchester, England, and came to the United States with his English-born sons in 1839.[23] Three of the Buckley boys became performers. Although *Monarchs of Minstrelsy* prints that he led the orchestra at Harrington's in 1840,[24] it seems likely that James Buckley was first there in 1841, because one of his sons also appears as a "vocalist" on the program with Joe Sweeney.[25]

"Master Buckley" joined Sweeney, Chestnut, and O'Connell during their second week at Harrington's. In spite of James's offspring only being identified in advertisements as "Master Buckley," it seems logical that George Swayne/Swaine (August, 1829–June 25, 1879) would have been the son sharing the stage with Sweeney. George Swaine is the son named by Edwin Rice in his history of minstrelsy and George Buckley is also the one identified by other historians as learning the banjo from Sweeney.[26] In a move that Joe Sweeney must have found aggravating, George even used the performing moniker "Sweeney" well into 1846.[27] The real Sweeney must have regretted having associated with the opportunistic Buckleys in the first place.

Portrait of George Swaine Buckley in his makeup, wig and stage costume. Note Buckley's right hand, in the "frailing" hand position. He is playing a fretted banjo with an extra large rim, possibly twenty brackets and two thumb strings.

By the fall of 1843, in the aftermath of the Virginia Minstrels, James Buckley had organized his own group. Originally called the Congo Melodists, Minstrels or Serenaders, it featured James and his ten-year-old son, Fred (October 12, 1833–September 12, 1864), on violins.[28] By the spring of 1845, when the group was in Philadelphia, it had been renamed the Ethiopian Serenaders (not be confused with the *other* group/groups of the same name).[29]

The New Orleans Ethiopian Serenaders, as the Buckleys billed their band, eventually came to include father James "Burke" Buckley, James' eldest son Richard Bishop (1826–June 6, 1867), who sang and played the "Chinese fiddle," middle son George, a multi-instrumentalist specializing in the banjo, and Fred, aka "Master Ole Bull," on violin.

Buckley's Ethiopian Serenaders spent much of 1845 and 1846 in the southern states, just one of the minstrel troupes to help expose southerners to minstrelsy and to the minstrel banjo style. Along the way, they managed to perform for both the great orator Henry Clay, as well as President Tyler.[30] The group had the continuing audacity, made more brazen by the familiarity of south side Virginia audiences with Joe Sweeney, to bill teen-aged George Buckley as "Sweeny, the great Banjo-Player" and "the far famed and only original Banjo player."[31] Although an indicator of the high regard in which Joe Sweeney's playing was held, this could only have drawn the banjoist's ire when this deception came to his attention. The company played a number of river towns, and, in Nashville on October 14, 1846, the *Republican Banner* singled out George Buckley's banjo playing, reprinting the words of a Kentucky newspaper that he "went so far in his solos, beyond anyone we ever heard on it, that it was incredible to [the audience] that the instrument was a banjo."[32] It was also remarkable that the just-turned seventeen-year-old had achieved such virtuosity (see Chapter Seven for more information on the Buckley family).

One last musician who claimed in later years to have known the Virginian was New Yorker Fred P. Mather. A banjo maker during the 1860s, Mather learned "how to 'bring down my thumb'" from the Virginia banjoist.[33]

The Banjo in Mid-Nineteenth Century America

The *Courrier des Etats Unis* says that Thalberg is learning to play on the banjo. He has taken ten lessons, and acknowledges that he has made considerable progress already. We commend Mr. Thalberg; a banjo solo would be a refreshing variation in his concerts; after he has been giving the piano fits on some air with so many variations that nobody can tell whether it is the Grand march in Norma or Yankee Doodle, "Root Hog or die" on the banjo would be a delightful relief.[34]

Once Joe Sweeney had brought the banjo into blackface minstrelsy, a whole generation of instrumentalists inspired by Sweeney or his students sprung up. This impact was particularly true after 1843, when the Virginia Minstrels spawned a plethora of groups. Every minstrel group needed at least one banjoist; some ensembles boasted two. In addition to Joe Sweeney's "students" George S. Buckley, William Chestnut, Thomas Coleman,[35] and Billy Whitlock, there were Whitlock's apprentices Tom Briggs (circa 1824–October 23, 1854)[36] and Frank Lynch/John Diamond, along with Billy's companion, Dan Emmett, who was taught by the mysterious Ferguson. They joined early banjoist "Picayune" Butler and Sweeney's competitors Mr. B.B. Boyce,[37] Mr. Newcomb,[38] Charles D. Jenkins, and Neil Jamieson.

There are a further twenty documented names (and who knows how many unknown others) of banjoists performing with minstrel groups before 1850. This assemblage of musicians includes a number whose influence reached far beyond their performances. Edwin P. Christy (November 28, 1815–May 21, 1862) was one of the best-known and successful promoters of the 1850s. Tom Vaughn/Vaughan (September 5, 1823–September 3, 1875), Christy's first banjoist, and Earl Horton Pierce (1823–June 5, 1859),[39] a later star for Christy, George A. Harrington (died January 1859[40]), and Bostonian G. Warren White (1816–March, 1886[41]) of the Ethiopian Serenaders, Virginia Serenader James P. Carter, William B. Donaldson (October 13, 1822–April 16, 1873)[42] of Campbell's Minstrels, and George W. Hoyt of the African Minstrels all gained prominence within the first generation of minstrel ensembles. William Roark/Rouke worked with many leaders, eventually assembling his own aggregation. Joe Sweeney employed William B. Fish (died July 29, 1875)[43], and Phil Rice was the author of a highly influential banjo tutor. Other names found in early chronicles of minstrelsy—Everard, Frost, Master Charles, J. Thomas, Tom Wilson, R. Nash, Jack Alden/Olden, D. W. Lull, Jim Carpenter, Frank Stanton/Stanford—remain just names, without significant details attached. One thing is for sure; the Virginia banjoist was no longer alone in his field.

One of the indicators for the banjo's popularity was the spread of the instrument to all corners of American society. One banjoist was Edwin Thomas Booth (1833–1893), a member of the famous theatrical family. His father, Junius Brutus Booth (1796–1852), was an English-born American thespian well known for his Shakespearean portrayals.[44] Edwin's actor brothers included John Wilkes Booth, whose notoriety came from his assassination of President Abraham Lincoln.

Edwin Booth learned music around the age of thirteen, according to biographer Stanley Kimmel. As Kimmel relates:

> Edwin began at a school for boys and girls directed by spinster Susan Hyde in a section of Baltimore known as Old Town.... An old Negro taught him to play the banjo and a Signor Picioli gave him instruction on the violin.[45]

Soon afterwards, Edwin Booth began traveling the theatrical circuit as caretaker for the tippling Junius.[46] The elder Booth was fond of Edwin's music,[47] and one tale has the young Booth appealing to Junius to forsake the barroom by offering to sing and play minstrel songs for him.[48] Even though he liked his son's music, Junius thought little of Edwin's acting abilities. When a manager suggested to the elder Booth that he and his son might appear together, Junius replied that Edwin could play the banjo between the acts![49] In 1852, the Booths went west and Edwin Booth took along his banjo.[50] Several accounts mention Edwin informally entertaining with his music.[51]

An oft repeated and fanciful story has Junius Booth visited backstage at Charles Thorne's New York City theater by his friend and fellow actor Edwin Forrest, for whom Edwin Booth was named. As fellow thespian John Ellsler remembered the incident:

> Edwin was playing his banjo one morning in the room occupied by his father, when, in response to a knock at the door and the invitation to come in, Edwin Forrest appeared in the doorway. At a motion made by his father, the boy was about to put away his instrument, but Mr. Forrest objected, asking in a thunderous tone, "Edwin, do you play 'Nellie Bly'?" "Yes, sir," was the reply. "Play 'Nellie Bly' then." Our dignified tragedian of later days did so. "Do you play a Negro jig, Edwin?" As he played, Forrest began to shake one foot and then the other,—the elder Booth followed suit, and before long, these two great tragedians were dancing a "breakdown" in true Virginia style.[52]

When could this incident have occurred? "Nelly Bly" was published no earlier than 1849,[53] and Edwin's first acting appearances were in Boston during that same year[54] and in New York City in the fall of 1850.[55] Unfortunately, theater historian Ireland shows no New York runs by Forrest from September 1849 through September of 1851.[56] Forrest's biographer Richard Moody places the incident during the spring of 1843.[57] Junius Booth played New York's Park Theater during that spring, and so the incident could have well occurred then.[58] However, Edwin would have only been ten years old, and, supposedly was neither playing the banjo nor traveling with his father at that time.

Sweeney's Influence on British Minstrelsy

A gentleman with a coloured face and a banjo sang some "nigger melodies," which were applauded and encored *ad nauseam*, to the great retardation of the progress of the piece.[59]

Mr. Marble is not one of those ebony-faced, banjo-playing, carpet-trowsered niggers, with whom we have been lately brought into such frequent contact.[60]

Performers as well in Great Britain and Ireland took to the banjo through seeing Joe Sweeney's performances. Between Sweeney's arrival in the spring of 1842 and his departure for America three years later, his performances inspired a post–Jim Crow generation of blackface minstrels. Unlike Rice and his followers, those influenced by Joe Sweeney included the banjo in their presentations.

Two early British banjoists who were directly motivated by Joe Sweeney's stage show were Joseph Cave and Edmund Mackney. Joe Cave had already been performing in blackface, and hearing Sweeney play during his first London appearances with Sands and Van Amburgh's circus influenced Cave to take up the banjo:

I shall never forget how my ears tingled and my mouth watered when I heard the tum, tum, tum of that blessed banjo. I thought to myself, if I could get one, there would be nothing between me and absolute affluence but—the learning how to play it. I knew it was hopeless to think of getting a banjo in England—I might as well have cried for the moon. I fancied it would be equally impossible to obtain one in America, as I had heard Mr. Sweeney had the only example in existence, which he had made himself, and that was at the moment lying across his chest as he stood on the stage of the theatre.

Cave turned to an old acquaintance, Charley Rivers (billed as "Rivea," possibly because it sounded more exotic), for help. Rivers, along with his brothers, were English-born equestrians who had plied their trade in America during 1840 and 1841, returning to Britain with Joe Sweeney and Sands Circus.[61] Cave contacted Charley, and asked him about obtaining a banjo:

"I shouldn't think you could get one," answered he. "You see Sweeney has only appeared in New York a comparatively short time, and he keeps his banjo a secret for fear anyone should copy it. Why, at every performance he has his man at the prompt entrance with the case, and as soon as he comes off he puts the banjo in that case and locks it."

"Look here, Joe," said Charley, "a little while before we left New York I found out that the property man of the theatre in which we had been playing had seen quite enough of the construction of the instrument to enable him to make copies of it, so I bought one from him, meaning to use it only as an amusement at home, and not in any way professionally; indeed, I shouldn't think of that now, for only a day or two ago Sweeney said on the stage that, if he knew of anybody in the company having one of the copies of his invention, that party should quit or he would leave himself. Now, Joe, ... the instrument I've got is very little use to me; so if you'll promise not to say where you got it I'll give it to you."

I had little difficulty in procuring the three songs [the assumption is that he's referring to the three songs published in England under Sweeney's name; see Chapters Four and Eleven], and then set to work to study the whole bag of tricks; the ditties were simple, and, with application and determination to conquer, I didn't find it monstrous hard to master the accompaniments.[62]

Cave's recollections provide much valuable information. He indicates how rare banjos were even in America, as the banjo had not yet become a "manufactured" item, but each was still a "one-off" hand-made affair. Strangely, his first banjo is not the instrument pictured on Cave's subsequent sheet music covers, which has more features of a guitar than a banjo. This discrepancy, of course, could have been a reflection of the illustrators' ignorance

Sheet music cover for "Sweet Lucy Neal" featuring J.H. Cave, "The Celebrated American Banjo Player." Note the evening dress and the banjo with a sound hole. "American" refers to the derivation of the banjo, not to the birthplace of the banjoist. Duncombe, London, England, nd.

rather than the actual structure of his instrument. It is also apparent from Sweeney's comments that, contrary to his earlier willingness to share the instrument and the skills necessary in playing it with any interested party, the banjoist had became possessive, afraid of imitators and vindictive toward those who attempted to mimic him.

Another would-be British banjoist, Edmund W. Mackney (February 11, 1825–March 26, 1909),[63] also attended Sweeney's London performances. A teacher and performer in the late nineteenth century, Mackney first learned Sweeney's pieces and, then, had a copy of his banjo made. William Temlett, a British banjo maker during the same period, recounted how Mackney:

> heard ... the ever famous Joe Sweeney, who brought the banjo to this country, and that whom there has never been a better artist. Sweeney's beautifully clean, neat and appropriate playing and his singing of the songs (probably forgotten or never heard of by the present generation of Banjoists) "Lucy Long," "Jenny get your oat [sic] cake done," etc., so impressed Mackney, that night after night he was to be found a rapt listener.... all of whom were enchanted with his playing, very few knowing the name of the instrument he played.
>
> Mr. Mackney could not keep away from the Theatre, he had got all Sweeney's tunes off by heart, he felt that if only he could get a Banjo he would soon be Sweeney's equal,—this was the trouble; in those days the Banjo was quite unknown, but by stratagem Mackney had a look at Sweeney's "jo" and so soon as he reached home made a rough sketch of it, this sketch he handed to a carpenter who soon knocked up something like a Banjo; of course made of wood.
>
> So soon as Mackney got strings on it he sailed right ahead and succeeded in earning for it a place on the stage; having a good knowledge of the Spanish Guitar he managed to play in both American and English style.[64]

During the same period that Mackney and Cave were admiring Joe Sweeney's banjo playing, the American blackface performer Edward R. "Ned" Harper, credited with creating "Jim Along Josey" (see Chapter Eleven), was on tour in Great Britain (see Chapter Two). Not much is known of Harper's background. Around the same age as Joel Sweeney, Edward Harper is first acknowledged as a member of Nathan A. Howe's and Richard Sands' American Circus during their winter show of 1835.[65] Ned Harper's first documented tour of the British Isles was in 1839, and since that time, he had been a perennial favorite in Great Britain. Although there are some tantalizing references to Harper's possible on stage use of the banjo before Joe Sweeney's arrival in the British Isles, it appears that Ned's employment of the banjo was as little more than a prop. With Sweeney now featuring the banjo, Harper claimed to play as well, alternately billing himself "on his own Josiana Banjo"[66] and "on his Old Louisiana Banjo."[67] Ned Harper's touring with the banjo continued throughout Sweeney's residency in Great Britain.[68]

By the time Sweeney had left London, or possibly because of it, Joseph Cave was ready to test his skills in public. He approached the manager of the Marylebone Theatre, a John Douglass,[69] for whom Cave had previously appeared:

> I stated the object of my visit, which was to get a start as negro impersonator and banjo player. He replied by saying he had every confidence in me, and arranged to hear me before he announced me to appear with so novel an entertainment. On the following day I turned up, banjo and all, and in the green room sang a couple of songs to him, who at once said, "All right, Cave, that'll do. You go into the bill on Whit-Monday"—near date. My first attempt was a great success.[70]

Joseph Cave was still performing on his banjo at the Marylebone as late as March 2, 1844.[71] Some of E.W. Mackney's earliest performances date to 1845, when he appeared at the concert hall of Doughty's Tavern, on Broad Street in Bristol.[72]

Other Brits took to the banjo as did Cave and Mackney. As Sweeney's British sojourn continued, other performers followed Joe Sweeney's example, playing his songs accompanied on the banjo. Mr. Nathan introduced the audience at the Albert Saloon, Hoxton, to "his never-to-be-forgotten nigger melodies, Jim Along Josey, Sich a getting Upstairs & Miss Lucy Long accompanying himself on a real American banjo" in the fall of 1843.[73] Another British Ethiopian was a Mr. T. "Yankee" Mellor (the American nickname presumably indicating the authenticity of his performances), first documented during a December 1843 Liverpool run immediately preceding Sweeney's as a part of "a host of rival nigger singers."[74] Banjoist William H. Bateman presented a veritable kitchen sink of blackface material. In 1844 at Glasgow's Adelphi Theatre, Bateman sang "Lucy Long" and "De Light Banjo" accompanied on the instrument, lectured on phrenology, and ended his appearance with T.D. Rice's Jim Crow drama, "The Flight to America."[75]

John Van Brammer, Sweeney's old partner, teamed up with Mr. F. Phillips, the "Unrivalled [sic] Banjo Player." Phillips is known to have sung a "Negro Chant" at the Theatre Royal in Dumfries on November 13, 1843,[76] and joined with Van Brammer (as "Van Brehmer") from the end of 1844 into the first part of 1845.[77] Phillips was back on his own by August 1845, when he appeared at Cork's Theatre Royal singing pieces of Sweeney's like "Old Virginia Breakdown" and "Come Along Dumbo Sound Your Horn," next to Dan Emmett's "Dandy Jim from Caroline" and "It Will Never Do to Give It Up So."[78]

"American" Palmer (again, "American" referred to the style of music being presented, not to the birthplace of the performer) first appeared at London's Strand Theatre in early 1844. Billed as "the Kentucky Banjo Player," and "the only Real Player of that Instrument in London," he presented "a variety of new and genuine Kentucky melodies, accompanied entirely by himself on the Banjo."[79] One reviewer called Palmer:

> a second Sweeney—his banjo playing is quite equal to the great original. The audience were evidently delighted with his humour, for they (as Mr. American Palmer himself elegantly expressed it) almost "wore the nigger out," by encoring him no less than four times.... The house was well attended.[80]

That May, Palmer was in Liverpool, where he was praised by the *Liverpool Journal* as "an excellent representative of the coloured songsters, has a very sweet voice, and is a perfect master of the [banjo]. His Transatlantic readings from Shakspeare [sic] told well." In a surprising move, he also advertised banjo lessons, "terms may be known on application."[81] "American" Palmer was back in London four years later, appearing "after the tragedy" at the Olympic Theatre.[82]

Even after Joe Sweeney's departure for the United States, British banjo fever continued unabated and new musicians took to the instrument. John W. Sharp (or Sharpe; 1817–1856), who coincidentally shared his initials with Joe Sweeney, was a featured comic singer at London area resorts and taverns and songbook author before taking up the banjo. Sharp was also music director for the Vauxhall Gardens from 1846 to 1853. John Sharp was well enough known that Thackeray saw fit to caricature the singer.[83] Another English banjoist was Alfred Eugene Cooke (born circa 1821)[84], an equestrian with Cooke's Circus and son of the owner.[85] Cooke was singing minstrel songs like "Jim Along Josey" by the end of 1845.[86] During November 1848, Alfred is listed as an equestrian artist and "banjo minstrel."[87] Perhaps Cooke studied one of the Americans like Dan Emmett who had appeared with his father's company. John Gray, "The Great Virginian Banjo Melodist, And only correct delineator of a Life of Slavery in North America," was a singer and dancer who appeared with his son or brother on bones in the north of England during the summer of 1846, in towns such as Hartlepool and Stockton. Again, Gray "borrowed" from Sweeney and the Virginia Minstrels, using "Dan Tucker," the "Ole Virginny Breakdown" and a locomotive imitation alongside "the Vicissitudes of the Mississippi Raftsman, the Wild Chanting of the Negro Crossing the Alleghany Mountains; together with the Fascinating and Fantastic Evolutions in the Lousiana Cane Breaks."[88]

None of these British banjoists were playing in public before Sweeney's arrival in 1842, and it wasn't until after Joe's London performances in the first part of 1843 that any are advertised in newspapers and broadsides.

Sweeney's Influence Abroad and at Home

The mash that created a sensation, though, was one that developed in a New York Bowery theatre, one night, when a young woman elegantly attired jumped out of a private box, and embracing a performer who was just finishing a banjo solo, shouted in a voice that was clear and loud, "You're the sort of a man I like!" The audience cheered lustily and the young woman accepted the applause with a courtesy, while the banjoist staggered into the wings, too much amazed to be flattered. A young man from whose side the lady had made her leap upon the stage, succeeded with some difficulty in coaxing her back into the box and the show went on. The pair had been dining and wining together, and the young gentleman had not been as attentive to his companion as she thought proper. So she had chosen the original method of at once rebuking and shaming him. She succeeded. He did not dare to look at another woman on or off the stage again until the curtain fell.[89]

Joe Sweeney's efforts, combined with a wealth of imitators, moved the banjo from an African American folk instrument into the musical theater of the United States. Solo banjo performers on variety bills in the circus and on the stage gave way to full ensembles commanding a whole evening's entertainment. As the music of minstrelsy changed from the rough and tumble songs of the frontier and dance hall to the sophisticated nostalgia of Stephen Foster, so changed the nature of the banjo.

The upshot of groups like the Ethiopian Serenaders and Buckley's New Orleans Serenaders was the introduction of a new repertoire and sensibility to the minstrel stage. These were the second generation of performers, brought up within the milieu and trained by other minstrels. No longer would composers be seeking African American material. Instead, the songs and bits would come from the minds of Anglo Americans. The blackface mask would be retained to present parodies of highbrow culture and sentimental renderings of southern life, far removed from the slave experience.

These bands at the same time reflected and also led this change, both in Great Britain and in the United States. Of course, only rarely does change occur suddenly and unequivocally. Single performers and duos continued to present the older repertoire and styles, and the elder statesmen of minstrelsy were still very much in the public eye. As the years progressed, English, Irish and Scottish Ethiopians would add some unique British touches to the procedures borrowed from the Americans. But, that is outside the reach of this investigation.

The playing style of the banjo changed as well. When those first white banjoists of Joe Sweeney's generation took up the instrument, they also adopted the down-stroking style of playing used by the African American performers. This style involved striking the strings with the nails of the "picking" hand, with the thumb plucking the short, drone string and the other four noted strings. As the music played in minstrelsy evolved and gained more European influences, so too did the playing method. A notier, more complex technique emerged. By the 1860s, alongside the sentimental songs of the time, minstrel banjoists were performing European waltzes, mazurkas and polkas. This new repertoire edged out the older minstrel compositions, and affected a change from the original down-stroking style to an up-picking style borrowed from the guitar, which increasingly became the dominant playing method. In the last three decades of the century, compositions written specifically for the banjo, as well as music borrowed from other instruments and the light classical music of the time joined to form a new banjo repertoire.

Banjoists were also making their move out of the minstrel show. Efforts to legitimize the instrument led to the return of the solo banjoist. However, instead of wearing cork and the ragged clothes associated with southern blacks, musicians appeared in "white" face and evening dress in salon and concert situations. The late nineteenth century also heralded the rise of the banjo orchestra, ensembles or clubs often, but not exclusively, made up of banjo family instruments. Banjos of varying sizes and pitches were utilized to cover the various parts in the music, much as the members of the violin family—violin, viola, cello and bass—perform in different frequency ranges. These groups were frequently affiliated with secondary schools, colleges and universities, with their membership drawn from these institutions. The 1880s and 1890s were the time of the banjo performer, teacher and manufacturer, who also led the burgeoning orchestras of banjo players.

Not surprisingly, the banjo also played a key part in the developing rural country music from which it had come. While retaining some of the repertoire and playing style of the minstrel show, musicians outside of the mainstream developed their own mix of popular and folk styles to produce a brand new musical form. Of course, southern musicians had kept playing the European violin and African banjo since Joe Sweeney had brought them to New York City. Minstrel bands as well featured the violin and banjo when they toured rural America. Although there is anecdotal evidence for the joining of the fiddle and banjo in the South during the early nineteenth century, the postwar period saw these two instruments become the basis for the first southern string bands. Accompanied by the banjo, the ballads of the British Isles and the compositions of published songwriters joined the early minstrel repertoire in the rural musician's song bag. Recent studies have shown that rural America of the late nineteenth century and the south in particular had access to the national popular culture, with bits and pieces of music infiltrating the barriers of distance and seclusion. While musicians in the cities of the nation kept up with current musical trends, rural players were content to mix and match half-remembered old world ballads and melodies with those from song sheets and traveling players.

By the end of the nineteenth century, the banjo was among the most popular instruments in America. As a result of Sweeney's efforts and those of musicians he influenced, the banjo became ensconced in American society. By the time of his death in 1860, this musical icon of the minstrel show had moved into the mass culture, where it continues to exert its hold on American music throughout the present time.

However, Joe Sweeney's influence reached far beyond the world of the banjo, as Sweeney also served as a broker between the black and white races. The banjoist learned the African American music of south side Virginia and carried it out of his area and into theater and circus stages, venues closed to the black musicians of his time.

Even within the United States, African and Anglo American cultures had been interacting since the first slaves arrived in America. This interchange was most obvious within our musical culture. Musicians in particular seemed to possess the ability to ignore race and class barriers erected by society to prevent just such interchanges. Music makers on both sides of the color divide have always searched out the best instrumentalist and the most brilliant singer performing the greatest song, regardless of their color or ethnic group. Consequently, African Americans took up the European fiddle and dance tunes, and Anglo Americans were attracted to the banjo and African rhythms. Granted, the impetus on African Americans to learn the music of white society has always been enforced from the outside, first by slave masters eager for entertainment and later by the economics of the music business. Nonetheless, the bottom line is that it's the mixture of African and Anglo roots that make our music interesting, and that this is recognized by both sides of the black/white divide.

Sadly, when those with white, European heritage control society, other ethnic groups are often denied a voice within that society. Therefore, Anglo American musicians, with access to the stages and media of the United States, haven taken those lessons learned from African American players and singers to an audience far removed from African American musicians. In the case of Sweeney and his successors, such as Jimmy Rodgers, Bill Monroe, Hank Williams and Elvis Presley to name just a few, white entertainers gained recognition for the achievements of black teachers. The distressing part of the inequity lies with the lack of credit and financial rewards reaped by the African American side of the equation. Regardless, it is from the interaction of white Americans such as Joe Sweeney and African Americans that our great and unique American music is derived.

Joe Sweeney died just as the Civil War was about to break out. But his legacy of banjo playing—and his song repertory—would survive both in Great Britain and at home as the next generation of Sweeney imitators hit the stages. But it was primarily on the banjo itself— and an explosion of interest in its manufacture and performance—that Sweeney's legacy rests.

FOURTEEN

Sam Sweeney: War Years
with J.E.B. Stuart

With all the actor's grace and quick light charm
That makes the women adore him—a wild cavalier
Who worships as sober a God as Stonewall Jackson
A Rupert who seldom drinks, very often prays
Loves his children, singing, fighting, spurs and wife
Sweeney, his banjo player, follows him.[1]

* * *

Every time J.E.B. Stuart comes around, with Sweeny and his banjo, he makes all my division
want to "jine" the cavalry.[2]

The spring after the death of his brother Dick, Sam Sweeney joined Orton & Older's Great Southern Circus's affiliate, the Sable Harmonists minstrel group. The Harmonists had allied themselves with the Wisconsin-based show[3] as early as June 25, 1857, the same year other circus companies began separating blackface performers from their main companies in side or after shows.[4] Orton & Older, with the Sable Minstrels after show, began their 1859 tour in February, heading north out of Georgia, through the middle of North Carolina and over to coastal Virginia.[5] Sam Sweeney is first mentioned as a group member for the Tuesday, May 10, engagement in Alexandria, Virginia.[6] The circus spent the next few months heading south, playing small towns and larger cities in Virginia, Tennessee, Alabama, Mississippi, Arkansas, and finishing the year with a two-and-a-half month sojourn in Texas. They then went east in early 1860, reaching Mississippi again in February, and then a month later played engagements in Alabama and Tennessee en route to Kentucky, Indiana, and Illinois. Although the Harmonists stayed with Orton through the remainder of the tour, Sam could have left anytime after June 9, when his name disappears from newspaper accounts.[7]

By the end of August, Sam Sweeney was back in Appomattox County. Unfolding events around the nation that eventually led the country into the Civil War were inspiring southerners to return home. In late August, reacting to John Brown's raid at Harpers Ferry, "The Military of Appomattox" (the local militia unit) had reformed and encamped behind the Clover Hill Tavern.[8] They marched about the courthouse streets to music supplied on "drum, fife, banjo and violin" by Sam and his cousin Robert Sweeney (see below). The Lynchburg paper praised Bob and Sam's musical skills, while repeating the folklore of Joe having appeared before the English monarch:

> efforts on the violin and banjo stand unequalled, except by the world-renowned Joe Sweeney,
> who threw around the banjo the first halo of attraction and importance—demonstrating the

fact that genius needs no royal instrument to excite the wonder and admiration of the world; for with the simple banjo, talented Joe secured the attention and presence of her Majesty, Queen Victoria. The Sweeneys are indeed a wonder! A mere scientific in competition with them would be as little observed and respected as the chirping grass-hopper amidst the booming cannon.[9]

Changing events within the country drew attention away from the personal triumphs and foibles of the Sweeney family. Tensions between the slave holding south and the slave-free north, building for decades, finally came to a head in early 1861. The southern states seceded from the United States and the remainder declared war in order to bring the south back into the fold.

When the Civil War broke out, Sam Sweeney was out on tour (An "S.S. Sweeney" is mentioned at a meeting of Virginians in Nashville, where he pledged to return home and sign up to protect the South. Sam was back in Appomattox by the end of 1861, assumed to be a part of the "Sweeneys" that played for a Christmas dance).[10] Meanwhile, Sam's neighbors at home in Appomattox County were rallying to the war cause. On May 24, 1861, Company H of the Second Regular Virginia Cavalry (the "Appomattox Rangers")[11] was formed,[12] with Captain Joel W. Flood, Jr. (born 1838), a long-time

Pomeroy · 1890 · 920 Main Street, Kansas City, Mo.

Joe Sweeney's younger brother Sam Sweeney, portrait done probably in the 1850s and copied in 1890. Sam Sweeney achieved his greatest fame as banjoist to General J.E.B. Stuart during the War Between the States.

acquaintance of the Sweeney family, commanding his friends and neighbors. Sam Sweeney's brother-in-law Allen Conner (circa 1825–1885) was an original member of Company H, as was his cousin Robert Miller Sweeney. Company H eventually included another member of Sam's extended family, Robert's brother, Private Charles H. Sweeney (November 5, 1837–May 19, 1909). Sam Sweeney enlisted in Company H as a private at their winter encampment twenty-two miles to the southwest of Washington, D.C., sometime between January 1 and February 1, 1862.[13]

> Sweeney is traditionally the patron-saint of the banjo in Virginia, the man whose thimbling and thumbing echo through the pages of Confederate history. Did not JEB Stuart make him of his headquarters troops, so that Sweeney's banjo might bump wherever Stuart's long sabre rattled against the flank of his horse? Did not Stuart take Sweeney to Lee's encampment and have him play until the feet of all the young staff-officers began to shuffle, and the general himself had in his eyes a light akin to that which must have shone there in happier days, when he and Smith and Charles Carter and all their kin galloped up to Arlington to dance? Did not Sweeney go down with Stuart to Jackson's sober headquarters at "Moss Neck" on the

Rappahannock in 1863, and did not Jackson listen to the banjo and the songs, till even he relaxed and laughed and was almost ready to join in Stuart's roaring chorus?[14]

Sam's talents and value as an entertainer soon came to the attention of James Ewell Brown Stuart, the fun-loving and heroic cavalry general of the Confederacy. Stuart, after all, was only twenty-nine-years old when Sampson joined his command, close to Sweeney in age. Both men were Virginians, Stuart hailing from Patrick County, in the mountains southwest of Lynchburg,[15] and Sweeney from Appomattox County, just to the east. J.E.B. had the well-earned reputation for enjoying song and frivolity, which was shared by his headquarters staff. Their lightheartedness was not unusual, due to the mood of the Confederacy in the early years of the Civil War, which, after all, was winning the dispute, and to the age of Stuart and his compatriots. And so, when the fun-loving general came upon Sweeney, unusual in that he had been a professional entertainer before the war, Stuart recognized Sam as a highly prized commodity.

Stuart already had his own string band drawn from members of his staff and was looking for other musicians to add to the ensemble. As William Willis Blackford (March 23, 1831–1905), a member of Stuart's headquarters company through January 1864 wrote, in the autumn of 1861, "Bob, the General's mulatto servant, worked the bones, and then there was a violin player and a guitar player and quite a number of singers among the staff and couriers."[16] By the end of August 1862, Sam Sweeney was a member of J.E.B. Stuart's band and Headquarters Company.

Sam Sweeney served several musical functions while with Stuart's command. He accompanied the general as his personal balladeer, performed for small gatherings of officers and staff, entertained visiting dignitaries, as well as played in J.E.B.'s string band for local dances.

1
Child-hoods days now pass before me
Forms and scenes of long a-go
Like a dream they ho-ver o'er me
Calm and bright as ev'ning's glow
Days that knew no shade of sor-row
When my young heart pure and free
Joyful hailed each com-ing mor-row
In the cot-tage by the sea
2
Fan-cy sees the rose-trees twi-ning
'Round the old and rus-tic door
And be-low the white beach shi-ning
Where I gathered shells of yore

Hears my mother's gen-tle war-ning
As she took me on her knee
And I feel a-gain life's mor-ning
In the cot-tage by the sea
3
What though years have rolled a-bove me
Though mid fair-er scenes I roam
Yet I ne'er shall cease to love thee
Child-hoods dear and hap-py home
And when life's long day is clo-sing
Oh! How pleasant would it be
On some faith-ful breast re-po-sing
In the cot-tage by the sea.

The songs performed by Sam Sweeney while he was serving with Stuart reflect the changes that minstrelsy had undergone since the heyday of Sam's famous brother. Blackface pieces like "Stephen" and Joe Sweeney's "Jonny Boker" sat alongside sentimental compositions of the day such as "Sweet Evelina" and "Faded Flowers." The latter had words by J.H. Brown and music by James Power of the Harmoneons (see Chapter Nine), and had been published in 1851. The program from one concert showed Sam Sweeney favoring a cross section of period hits, including "Cottage by the Sea" by J.R. Thomas (see lyrics above), "Lilly, Dear," probably "Farewell My Lilly Dear" the Stephen Foster composition from 1851," "Going Down to Town," the minstrel stalwart "Lynchburg Town," "Ever of Thee," published in 1860,[17] and the blackface song "I Ain't Got No Time To Tarry."[18] Another of Stuart's officers, Major Heros Von Borcke, adds that "Sweeny's banjo was attuned also to hymns: on

Sundays. Cavalry headquarters had its music, but it was sacred music—'Rock of Ages' for 'Alabama Gals, Won't You Come Out Tonight?' and 'I Will Not Live Alway(s)' for 'Old Joe Hooker, Won't You Come Out o' the Wilderness.'"[19]

"Old Joe Hooker," also known as "The Old Grey Hoss" (aka: "The Old Grey Mare"), and as "Jine the Cavalry," is perhaps the song most closely associated with General Stuart.[20] It served as J.E.B.'s theme song and was possibly composed by him. The lyrics include: "Old Joe Hooker, will you come out of the Wilderness ... /Bully boys, ho," with the chorus: "If you want to have a good time jine the cavalry.... /Bully boys, ho." Joe Ayers, a modern-day musician who specializes in performing nineteenth century compositions, mentions the similarity between "Jine the Cavalry" and "Down in Alabama." The latter piece was published in 1858 as a part of *Phil Rice's Correct Method for the Banjo: With or Without a Master* by the Boston music concern of Oliver Ditson & Company.[21]

The Bower

The mansion was brilliantly lighted up, many fair ones had already assembled, and the whole company awaited, with impatience and anxiety, the arrival of their distinguished guests and the promised music. Sweeney lost no time in his orchestral arrangements. In a very few minutes the banjo vibrated under his master hand, the two fiddles shrieked in unison, and Bob's bones clattered their most hideous din; and in the animated beat of the music, and the lively measures of the dance, was soon forgot the little *desagremens* of our journey.... It was quite delightful to see our foreign friend winding through the mazes of many bounding quadrilles and Virginia reels with an evident enjoyment of the same. After several hours of mirth and dancing, we accepted the kind offer of our host to lend us one of his own waggons [sic] for our return to headquarters, where we arrived a short time before daybreak, little thinking how soon we should be aroused by the notes of a very different music from that of Sweeney's orchestra.[22]

During October 1862, General Stuart and his soldiers encamped at the Bower, located eight miles from Martinsburg and ten miles from Charleston. The Bower was the long-time residence of the Dandridge family, described by William Blackford as:

A large, old-fashioned Virginia mansion, cresting a hill around which wound the silvery waters of the Opequan.... Our headquarters encampment, consisting of about one hundred persons including staff officers, couriers and servants and about two hundred horses, was pitched in the edge of the beautiful park a few hundred yards from the house.[23]

Stuart's order of the day seems to have been to dance and carry on, and the Dandridges were in agreement with the General's wishes. John Thomason, Major Von Borcke, and Henry Kyd Douglas, a member of Stonewall Jackson's command, all write how music and dancing was used in entertaining Stuart's troops as well as the crowds of young ladies left behind by their enlisting men folk.[24] Von Borcke provides us with the most detailed description of the frivolity. Not surprisingly, Stuart had quite the reputation as a ladies man, and always seemed to be in the midst of any carryings on. "Regularly every night" wrote Von Borcke "we proceeded with our band to the house, where dancing was kept up till a late hour."[25]

To further enliven the proceedings, Fitzgerald Ross, an English soldier of fortune, Francis Lawley, a member of the British Parliament and correspondent for the *London Times*, and Frank Vizetelly (1830–1883), an English war correspondent and artist for *Illustrated London News*, arrived in mid–October. Ross wrote:

Engraving, "Night Amusements In The Confederate Camp," depicting Sam Sweeney playing the banjo for J.E.B. Stuart's troops. The dancer is probably Stuart's manservant "Bob." *Illustrated London News*, **January 10, 1863, 40.**

> Every evening, when we cluster around our pine-log fires, the "darkies" press in amongst us and listen to the yarns their masters spin. In our camp we are fortunate enough to possess the most famous banjo-player in the Southern States, and when Sweeny strikes up one of his quaint old Virginian breakdowns, some nigger is sure to "wade" in and put his legs through a series of marvellous gyrations, to the delight of the sympathetic lookers-on, who beat time for him. Although the enemy is within cannon-shot, no one experiences the least uneasiness, and the universal refrain is, "We'll sing to-night and fight to-morrow—bullyboys, oh!"

And to make Ross' observations more graphic, Vizetelly recorded the scene on his sketch-pad. The original drawing, titled "Night Amusements in the Confederate Camp,"[26] was made into an engraving and published in January 1863.[27]

> When weary of work or talk, [J.E. B. Stuart] would mount one of his horses ... and set off to serenade some lady—taking Sweeny along, with his banjo.[28]

At the end of November 1862, the various divisions of the Army of Northern Virginia settled into their winter camps. Stuart's troops settled five miles south of Fredericksburg on Telegraph Road.[29] J.E.B., with his usual wit, named the new headquarters "Camp No-Camp." "The days and nights were full of song and laughter," wrote staff member John Esten Cooke. "Stuart's delight was to have his banjo-player, Sweeney, in his tent; and even while busily engaged in his official correspondence, he loved to hear the gay rattle of the instrument, and the voice of Sweeney singing.... As frequently he would join in the song, or volunteer one of his own."[30] As the winter progressed, music continued to help to pass the time. Sweeney played a Christmas concert in the general's tent, a "Fandango with Sweeney's songs and banjo-playing to negro dances...," and, in early January 1863, a theatre was erected for a performance by Negro minstrels.[31]

> Stuart carries around with him a banjo player and a special correspondant [sic]. This claptrap is noticed and lauded as a peculiarity of genius, when, in fact, it is nothing but the act of a buffoon to get attention.[32]

By the end of 1863, Sam Sweeney had obtained musical reinforcements. His cousin and former musical accompanist, fiddler Robert M. Sweeney (see above), after being discharged in early 1862 for being overage, had been conscripted and reassigned in August 1863.

In the ten years before, Bob Sweeney had been actively playing for community functions around Appomattox. One of his companions was the locally renowned dance violinist Charles G. Johnson, who was reported as playing for area gatherings in an 1845 issue of the Lynchburg newspaper. About seventy or eighty Clover hill residents attended a "Country Ball" in February of that year, at which Johnson fiddled and "blind Billy" played the flute.[33] Besides community dances, another local establishment that required music was the healing springs in what was then Amherst County. Buffalo Springs was just one of a string of regional resorts popular with nineteenth and early twentieth century folk. One could take advantage of the fresh air and mineral waters that were either bathed in or swallowed for their medicinal qualities. This establishment featured a ballroom ideal for "off season" (i.e.: winter) festivals, and Charles Johnson's band was often called upon to provide the music. During Christmastime 1853, a weeklong Masonic Ball was held where John Morriss and Robert Sweeney joined Johnson. Several months later, Charles Johnson, "the best Ball Room Fiddler in the Union," headed a band that probably included some of the Sweeneys.[34] Indeed, the extended Sweeney family was certain to have played a number of area house and public dances during the 1850s.

Stuart quickly recognized Bob's musicianship and he was recruited from Company H for J.E.B.'s headquarters band. Officially, Bob joined Stuart the first day of January 1864, although members of the staff remember him from an earlier date. Several others were instrumentalists as well. Flutist Pvt. William M. Pegram was a member of the 4th Virginia Cavalry's Company H and was attached to Stuart's headquarters as a clerk for Major H.B. McClellan, and McClellan himself played the guitar.

Theodore Garnett (1844–1915), Stuart's clerk from October 1863 until the General's death in 1864, wrote about how music making would help to pass the time between fighting. Garnett told that:

> At night we would often get together our Amateur Glee-Club with old Sam Sweeney as leader of the band, Bob [Sweeney], his cousin, the left-handed violinist, [Willie] Pegram with his flute, and occasionally Major Mc.Cl. [H.B. McClellan] with his fine guitar, and your humble servant with the triangle and all assembling in the General's tent, go through with a mixed program of songs, jokes, back-stepping and fun-making generally until the general, tiring of our performances, would rise up on his buffalo-robe and say, "Well, Good evening to you all, gentlemen."[35]

> On Xmas night, 1863, a serenading party left camp to go into the [Orange] Court House, and give the ladies some music. How well I remember Sam Sweeney's banjo that night!— almost the last time he ever played it, poor fellow,—for in less than two weeks from that night he was in his grave. Von Borcke in his "Memoirs of the Confederate War" has, unintentionally I am sure, done Sam an injustice,—or in other words he has mistaken *Sam* for his cousin *Bob*.... They were both with us that night serenading;—stopping at one house to awake, as we

thought, the fair sleepers with our dulcet strains, we found that they had not retired, and as soon as they discovered who we were, the door was thrown open and all hands invited to enter. We accepted, and found in the parlor an egg-nogg party going on. It was at once proposed to clear the floor for a dance, and in a few minutes our partners were selected, the music struck up, and we chased the golden hours with flying feet until the dawn of the day reminded us of our camp behind the hills, towards which with unwilling steps we wound our way, first having escorted our ladies to their respective homes, thus realizing the sentiment of the old Sailor's song—"We'll dance all night, till broad day light/And go home with the girls in the morning."[36]

As Garnett mentions, Sam Sweeney did not survive the War. On January 13, 1864, the last extant Sweeney brother died of smallpox in the hospital at Orange Court House, Virginia, and was buried in an unmarked grave.[37] J.E.B. Stuart, who was to fall in battle a scant four months later, wrote to his wife, Flora, "I suppose you heard the sad tidings of poor Sweeny's death.... His loss is deeply felt." Stuart's scribe, John Esten Cooke, eloquently wrote, "Poor Sweeney is dead—a great (loss)! ... He was a gentleman in character and manner—had the *savoir faire* which makes a man graceful in the (hut or), the palace, and war ever (modest), obliging, respectful."

[The rebel soldiers] were great lovers of music, and many of them told me that they had never heard much music in their lives, except banjo music.

—Ezra Hoyt Ripple[38]

Sampson Sweeney was the most famous banjoist on either side of the War for Southern Independence. This was due in no small part to his association with the flamboyant J.E.B. Stuart, although, being an acclaimed minstrel performer certainly added to his reputation. However, the youngest musical brother of early Anglo American banjoist Joel Walker Sweeney was not singular in his musical pursuits. Noted Civil War historian James I. Robertson, Jr., in his *Soldiers Blue and Gray* mentions that, "Next to letter writing, music was the most popular diversion found in the armies of the 1860's.... Many ... soldiers were proficient with the ... banjo."[39] Photographs and illustrations made during the war depict an array of banjoists, and a number of instruments survive with a Civil War provenance attached.

Numerous writers describe players on the southern side of the struggle. Frank Converse, in his "Banjo Reminiscences, IX," recalls his student Charles S. Mattison, who later served with the Confederate forces, carrying his banjo and violin with him.[40] Alexander Hunter, looking back on wartime experiences in Winchester, Virginia, recalled "Bob Rogers [born in Orange County on January 9, 1833, who] would outpick [sic] the celebrated Joe Sweeney on the banjo."[41] Samuel Moorman Gregory was born in Petersburg in 1833, enlisting in the 2nd Company E of the 41st Virginia, a part of Lee's Army of Northern Virginia. Gregory served part of his service as "musician" and was noted to play the banjo. As B.J. Rogers wrote in the Petersburg newspaper:

Gregory is famed in war annals of the South as "the banjoist of Gen. R.E. Lee's army," who drove care from camp fires and cheered anxious soldiers on the eve of battle. "Old Joe Hooker, Come Out the Wilderness," caroled Gregory in the camps of Lee's Infantry.
Often he was called to play at General Lee's headquarters. He ended his military career almost on the spot that he learned to pick the banjo strings.
Even now, when he picks his beloved banjo in his quarters and bursts into the war songs that stirred his hearers in the wilderness or in the trenches around Petersburg, the "Rebel yell" can be heard as of old.[42]

There were other confederate banjoists as well. Private Wiley Burnett (b. circa 1840) was a North Carolinian from Franklin County captured and confined in the Point Lookout,

Maryland, prison camp. Burnett possibly performed in camp minstrel shows, one of which was depicted in a painting by fellow prisoner John Omenhausser.[43] Finally, Andy Cahan, in "Manly Reece and the Dawn of North Carolina Banjo," quotes a remarkable collection of family letters to document Reece's (1830–March, 1864) Civil War service. Cahan tells how:

> A Provost Guard in Pickett's division, Manly is said to have been given special treatment on account of his musical talents.... Family information ... asserts that Manly had also been recognized by Lee and Stuart, who personally invited him to entertain the troops on several occasions.... Kahle [Brewer, a Reece descendant] recollects a letter within the collection which mentioned Lee and Stuart's intentions of introducing Manly to one of the Sweeney boys. The meeting, however, was destined never to take place."[44]

Unfortunately, we know little to nothing of the important details from these musicians' instruction, style and repertoire.

Three compatriots of Sweeney's in the Southern Army for whom we are left significant biographies are James Dearing, Thomas Booker and James "Polk" Miller. All were Virginians, and all hailed from the same section of the state as the Sweeney family. Interestingly, all three differed from Sam Sweeney in that they came from prominent Southside families (Tom Booker's father was a lawyer and Polk Miller's father served in the state Legislature; all were planters). That Booker, Miller and the Sweeneys' shared similar backgrounds helps to further illuminate Sam and Joe Sweeney's own roots and experiences. It also shows the prevalence of the banjo within white Southside Virginia communities by the decade preceding the Civil War.

> General James Dearing, a young cadet at the U[nited] S[tates] M[ilitary] A[cademy], destined later to become a general, CSA, used to entertain his fellow students to the accompaniment of a strange instrument called the "banjo...." It was [Joe Sweeney's] own instrument that Jim Dearing had at West Point and memories of his playing are to be found in the published stories of his classmates.[45]

James Griffin Dearing, Jr., was born on his grandfather's tobacco plantation, "Otterburne," April 15, 1840. James Jr., was appointed to West Point, entering the Academy on July 1, 1858. Morris Schaff, in *The Spirit of Old West Point*, wrote that Dearing's banjo earned him many friends, and that he introduced "Dixie" to the school.[46] It is unclear if James Dearing owned one of the instruments originally belonging to Joe Sweeney, who, after all, lived just east of Dearing's home place, or, if the above writer for the *Lynchburg News* just meant "a banjo" by "Joe Sweeney's own instrument."

When the war broke out, James Dearing resigned from the United States Military Academy, within weeks joining a Confederate Artillery unit, distinguishing himself in service and quickly rising through the ranks. "When he was unable to promote other types of diversions," writes William L. Parker,

> Dearing could be counted on to stroll through the camp, stumming [sic] his banjo and serenading officers and men with his rich bass voice. Very likely, this form of entertainment was encouraged by Jeb Stuart, the famed cavalryman, and (Sam) Sweeney, the popular banjoist who enlivened many a night with his musical selections [Dearing and Sweeney met at least once, on November 12, 1862]. The officers and men reacted so enthusiastically to Dearing's one-man concerts that the lieutenant organized a band of wandering minstrels. Soon the troubadours were performing nightly before appreciative audiences.[47]

Wounded in battle just before Lee and Grant's famous meeting, General James Dearing died April 23, 1865, two weeks after the surrender at Appomattox.[48]

"I've heard 'em al" said an ancient fiddler of Prince Edward at a Confederate reunion in Farmville, "and I want to say that, in my judgement, Tom Booker can outplay any of 'em—even
Sweeney."[49]

Thomas Hobson Booker was born at Cedar Grove in Amelia County September 7,
1844.[50] Fiddling and dancing were widespread around the Amelia County of Booker's youth.
Although Tom's banjo influences are unknown,[51] it appears that a relative on his mother's
side, Thomas M. Hobson (born ca. 1843[52]), also played the instrument and carried it during the war. This may have reflected the commonness of the banjo in Booker's area, or indicated the presence of music in the Hobson/Booker family. Sadly, Tom Hobson, a member
of Company E, 23rd Virginia Volunteers that served under J.E.B. Stuart, was killed at Payne's
Farm on December 27, 1863.[53]

Along with his brother William O. Booker, Tom Booker enlisted as a private at Amelia
Courthouse on September 3, 1862. He served with Captain James N. Lamkin's Battery of
Colonel J.C. Haskell's Artillery Battalion.[54]

Published local histories abound with post–War stories of Booker's music. Hadfield
and McConnaughey, in their *Historical Notes on Amelia County, Virginia*, write that:

> "Osmore," Mr. Hooker's plantation, and "Bird Grove," the home of "Marse Tom," known also
> as "Banjo Tom" Booker, had large pavilions in the yards for dancing. Illumination was pro-
> vided by hanging Japanese lanterns and the entertainment was likely to be furnished by those
> renowned banjo players and "delineators of the Old South" Polk Miller and Tom Booker.
> Miss Mattie Booker, the spinster daughter of "Marse Tom," took it upon herself to teach all
> the young people in the neighborhood to dance.[55]

In another account, at Amelia Springs off the present day Route 642, Tom Booker on banjo
and Dr. Junius Seay on violin "helped the Miller boys [probably meaning Polk and his
brother Tony, see below] make music for balls" during the "Tournament of Knights," an
interesting community event centered around the restaging for medieval contests of skill.[56]

Booker also appeared at the numerous reunions of the Southern troops with Polk
Miller and "Captain" Anthony W. (probably Webster) "Tony" Miller. Tony, the older Miller
sibling, played the violin, and was a dancer to boot. "Colonel" Booker (both Captain and
Colonel were honorary titles bestowed on veterans after the War, no matter what their rank
had been) was playing his banjo, which he named "Old Betsy," as late as a 1925 soldiers'
meeting. H.C. Bradshaw comments that Tom Booker:

> delighted many an annual reunion of Prince Edward veterans. Booker was a capitol enter-
> tainer; even as an old man he had a fine, clear voice; he played his banjo with a charming
> vivacity; and he sang the old songs which the veterans had known and loved through the
> years.[57]

Tom Booker was dead of "cancer of rectum" on Sunday, April 8, 1928. Booker was buried
the next day in Jetersville cemetery.[58]

> Polk Miller never failed to attract a crowd or to delight it. His entertainment was one of the
> premier attractions of his day. Mark Twain said that when Prince Henry of Germany missed
> Polk Miller's concert at Carnegie Hall, New York, he missed about the only thing originally
> and utterly American.[59]

> We rode with Stuart, Hampton
> With Fitz Lee, Duke and Morgan
> With Forrest and Joe Wheeler
> They were good enough for me
> Chorus: We are old-time Confederates
> They're good enough for me[60]

Jane Anthony Webster Miller gave birth to her fifth son on August 2, 1844.[61] Although his given name was James Agnew Miller, the boy acquired the nickname of "Polk" in the year of his birth. As the story goes, when James Polk was elected to the presidency of the United States, Miller's father Giles offered that President Polk "will bring the country no good," a declamation overheard by the family's mammy. When the young Miller gave her particular trouble the next morning, she scolded him, "Hush yo'mouf. Yo' is as bad as ole Poke." And the name stuck.[62]

The Millers lived on a plantation at Grape Lawn near Burkeville in Prince Edward County. Giles A. Miller, who served several terms as a member of the state legislature, owned 200 slaves.[63] In an 1892 Richmond newspaper article, Polk Miller commented that his banjo playing was learned from these African Americans.[64]

Polk Miller moved to Richmond in February 1860 and found employment at the drug store of Meade and Baker on the corner of Fifth and Marshall Streets. During June 1864, Miller joined the 2nd Company, Richmond Howitzers, First Virginia Artillery, with whom he served as a private.[65] After the War, Miller farmed in Amelia County. He again worked at Meade and Baker's, and then at Powhatan Dupuy on Broad Street in Richmond before entering into the partnership of Miller and Pierce. In 1871, the associates opened their own drug company in the basement of the Haniwinkel Building. Polk showed his great love for his hunting dog, Sargeant, by developing and naming a line of animal preparations after him.[66]

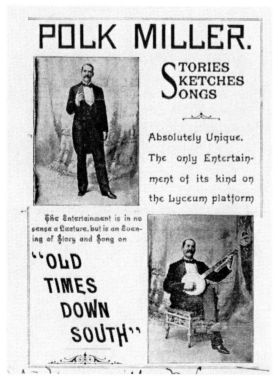

Program and detail of undated photograph, "Polk Miller. Stories Sketches Songs. Absolutely Unique. The only Entertainment of its kind on the Lyceum platform. The Entertainment is in no sense a lecture, but is an Evening of Story and Song on 'Old Times Down South.'"

Polk Miller began in the sideline of Negro delineation around 1892 as an active and popular entertainer at area Confederate reunions and monument dedications.[67] The following year, Miller began performing for pay after presenting a paper on an old time Christmas in the South before the local chapter of the Chautauqua Literary and Scientific Circle. Before he realized it, Miller had been persuaded to repeat his presentation, titled "Old Times Down South," for several churches. Soon, the demands on Miller's time became so numerous that it interfered with his business, and he concluded that the only way to stop the requests was to charge for the entertainment. When he received a letter from Norfolk asking him how much he would require for delivering the lecture there, Miller wrote "a hundred dollars and hotel and railroad expenses." The next morning he received a telegram: "We accept your terms." From that day onward, Miller appeared throughout the country, on occasion sharing the platform with the author Mark Twain and the poet James Whitcomb Riley.[68] By 1906, he had given nearly two thousand five hundred performances from Maine to Texas.[69] One of the honors Polk received was the gift of a banjo. In June 1895, manufacturer H.C. Dobson and the Richmond Music Company saluted Miller with a custom made instrument.[70] Polk Miller died October 20, 1913, and is buried at the Hollywood Cemetery in Richmond.[71]

A number of the early banjoists chronicled in this chapter lived into the age of recording. If only they would have given us a better sense of their repertoire and the way their music sounded by leaving behind a documentary of their playing. One performer had the celebrity to be asked to make records, and that was Polk Miller. Fourteen years before his death, Miller entered the studios of the Edison Company to make cylinder transcriptions of his music. Only for "The Bonnie Blue Flag," published in New Orleans in 1861 and well known during the Southern conflict, does Miller strum a simple banjo accompaniment. Unfortunately, no other hard evidence survives of Polk Miller's playing or repertoire.[72]

In the 1830s, when Joe Sweeney became interested in the African American banjo, the instrument was a novelty within white southern society. By the time of the Civil War, the banjo had moved into Anglo American culture in Sweeney's section of Virginia. Even the progeny of the wealthy classes had adopted the instrument. The scant descriptions left behind mostly tell of southside banjoists accompanying their own singing. However, by the end of the nineteenth century at least one musician, Tom Booker (sometimes in association with Tony and Polk Miller), was using his banjo in conjunction with a fiddler to play for white dances. This conjoining served as the basis for the white string band sound that eventually led to the creation of bluegrass music in the later part of the twentieth century.

Appendix: A Sweeney Performance Chronology

11/12/1836—Rocky Mount Falls, NC, possibly with Barnum
11/19–23/1836—Raleigh, NC, as above
11/24–26/1836—Fayetteville, NC, as above
12/00/1836—or thereabouts, Camden, SC, as above
12/02–09+18/1836—Richmond, VA
02/12–23/1839—Charleston, SC, with Menagerie and Circus United
04/16–18/1839—New York, NY, National Theatre
05/04/1839—New York, NY, Franklin Theatre
11/25–12/04/1839—New York, NY, Bowery Amphitheatre, June, Titus, Angevine and Co.
12/09/1839–04/08/1840—New York, NY, Broadway Circus, Welch & Bartlett
01/09–10/1840—New York, NY, Bowery Theatre
04/09–11/1840—Brooklyn, NY, Welch & Bartlett
04/13/1840—departure by steamboat for Providence, RI
04/15–17/1840—Providence, RI, Welch & Bartlett
04/18/1840—Pawtucket, RI, Welch & Bartlett
04/20/1840—Fall River, MA, Welch & Bartlett
04/00/1840—New Bedford and various MA, Welch & Bartlett
04/27/1840—Taunton, MA, Welch & Bartlett
04/00/1840—Plymouth and various MA, Welch & Bartlett
05/01/1840—Hingham, MA, Welch & Bartlett
05/02/1840—or thereabouts, Hanover, MA, Welch & Bartlett
05/04/1840—or thereabouts, Milton Mills, MA, Welch & Bartlett
05/05–06/06/1840—Boston, MA, Welch & Bartlett
05/15/1840—Tremont Theatre, Boston, MA
06/00–10/23/1840—various MA and NY, Welch & Bartlett

06/00/1840—Watertown, MA Welch & Bartlett
06/00/1840—Waltham, MA Welch & Bartlett
06/00/1840—Bolton, MA Welch & Bartlett
06/00/1840—Lancaster, MA Welch & Bartlett
06/00/1840—Concord, MA Welch & Bartlett
06/00/1840—Fitchburg, MA Welch & Bartlett
06/00/1840—Leominster, MA Welch & Bartlett
06/00/1840—Deerfield, MA Welch & Bartlett
06/00/1840—Peru, MA Welch & Bartlett
06/00/1840—Hinsdale, MA Welch & Bartlett
06/26/1840—Pittsfield, MA, Welch & Bartlett
06/00/1840—Lebanon Springs, NY, Welch & Bartlett
06/00/1840—Sand Lake, NY, Welch & Bartlett
07/01–04/1840—Albany, NY, Welch & Bartlett
07/06–07/1840—Troy, NY, Welch & Bartlett
07/00/1840—Waterford, NY, Welch & Bartlett
07/00/1840—Mechanicsville, NY, Welch & Bartlett
07/00/1840—Schuylerville, NY, Welch & Bartlett
07/00/1840—Cambridge, NY, Welch & Bartlett
07/00/1840—Fort Edward, NY, Welch & Bartlett
07/00/1840—Whitehall, NY, Welch & Bartlett
07/00/1840—Glens Falls, NY, Welch & Bartlett
07/00/1840—Sandy Hill, NY, Welch & Bartlett
07/20–25/1840—Saratoga Springs, NY, Welch & Bartlett
07/27/1840—or thereabouts, Ballston Springs, NY, Welch & Bartlett
07/28–29/1840—Schenectady, NY, Welch & Bartlett

07/00/1840—Amsterdam, NY, Welch & Bartlett

07/00/1840—Fonda, NY, Welch & Bartlett

08/00/1840—Fort Plain, NY, Welch & Bartlett

08/00/1840—Cooperstown, NY, Welch & Bartlett

08/00/1840—Cherry Valley, NY, Welch & Bartlett

08/00/1840—Berlin, NY, Welch & Bartlett

08/00/1840—New Berlin, NY, Welch & Bartlett

08/00/1840—Sharon, NY, Welch & Bartlett

08/00/1840—Hamilton, NY, Welch & Bartlett

08/00/1840—Waterville, NY, Welch & Bartlett

08/00/1840—Vernon, NY, Welch & Bartlett

08/11–13/1840—Utica, NY, Welch & Bartlett

08/14/1840—Rome, NY, Welch & Bartlett

08/00/1840—Canastota, NY, Welch & Bartlett

08/00/1840—Cazenovia, NY, Welch & Bartlett

08/00/1840—Manlius, NY, Welch & Bartlett

08/00/1840—Syracuse, NY, Welch & Bartlett

08/18/1840—Chittenango, NY, Welch & Bartlett

08/25–26/1840—Auburn, NY, Welch & Bartlett

08/00/1840—Port Byron, NY, Welch & Bartlett

08/00/1840—Clyde, NY, Welch & Bartlett

08/00/1840—Lyons, NY, Welch & Bartlett

08/00/1840—Newark, NY, Welch & Bartlett

09/01/1840—Palmyra, NY, Welch & Bartlett

09/02/1840—or thereabouts, Pittsford, NY, Welch & Bartlett

09/03–05/1840—Rochester, NY, Welch & Bartlett

09/07/1840—or thereabouts, Churchville, NY, Welch & Bartlett

09/08/1840—or thereabouts, Honey Falls, NY, Welch & Bartlett

09/09/1840—or thereabouts, Mud Hollow, NY, Welch & Bartlett

09/10/1840—Canandaigua, NY, Welch & Bartlett

09/00/1840—Penn Yan, NY, Welch & Bartlett

09/00/1840—Dundee, NY, Welch & Bartlett

09/00/1840—Havana, NY, Welch & Bartlett

09/00/1840—Union, NY, Welch & Bartlett

09/18–19/1840—Ithaca, NY, Welch & Bartlett

09/00/1840—Oswego, NY, Welch & Bartlett

09/00/1840—Uniontown, NY, Welch & Bartlett

09/00/1840—Binghamton, NY, Welch & Bartlett

09/00/1840—Harpersville, NY, Welch & Bartlett

09/00/1840—Bainbridge, NY, Welch & Bartlett

09/00/1840—Unadilla, NY, Welch & Bartlett

09/00/1840—Franklin, NY, Welch & Bartlett

09/00/1840—Walton, NY, Welch & Bartlett

09/00/1840—Delhi, NY, Welch & Bartlett

09/00/1840—Stamford, NY, Welch & Bartlett

09/00/1840—Osborneville, NY, Welch & Bartlett

09/00/1840—Prattsville, NY, Welch & Bartlett

09/00/1840—Cairo, NY, Welch & Bartlett

09/25/1840—New York, NY, Bowery Theatre

10/00/1840—Catskill, NY, Welch & Bartlett

10/00/1840—Coxsackie, NY, Welch & Bartlett

10/10–13/1840—Albany, NY, Welch & Bartlett

10/15–17/1840—Troy, NY, Welch & Bartlett

10/00/1840—Hudson, NY, Welch & Bartlett

10/00/1840—Claremont, NY, Welch & Bartlett

10/00/1840—Rhinebeck, NY, Welch & Bartlett

10/23/1840—Poughkeepsie, NY, Welch & Bartlett

10/00/1840—Newburgh, NY, Welch & Bartlett

10/00/1840—Peekskill, NY, Welch & Bartlett

10/00/1840—Sing Sing, NY, Welch & Bartlett

11/02–07/1840—New York, NY, Chatham Theatre

11/23–12/04/1840—Boston, MA, Tremont Theatre

12/07–25/1840—Boston, MA, Harrington's Museum

01/22–25/1841— Washington, DC, National Theatre

01/30/1841—Richmond, VA

02/13/1841—or thereabouts, Petersburg, VA

03/03–06/1841—Baltimore, MD, American Theatre

03/18–24+04/05/1841—Bowery Theatre, NY Circus

05/03–06/05/1841—Baltimore, MD, American Theatre, Bartlett and Delavan, NY Circus

06/07/1841—or thereabouts, Washington, DC, Bartlett and Delavan, NY Circus

06/00/1841—Georgetown, VA, NY Circus

06/00/1841—Fredericksburg, VA, NY Circus

06/00/1841—Port Royal, VA, NY Circus

06/00/1841—Bowling Green, VA, NY Circus

06/28–07/03+05/1841—Richmond, VA, Bartlett and Delavan, NY Circus

07/05–08/05/1841—various VA, MD, PA, Welch, Mann and Delavan

07/00/1841—Petersburg, VA, Welch and Mann

07/13–17/1841—Norfolk, VA, Welch and Mann

07/00/1841—Portsmouth, VA, Welch and Mann

07/19–24/1841—Baltimore, MD, Welch and Mann

07/26/1841—or thereabouts, York, PA, Welch and Mann

08/02–03/1841—Harrisburg, PA, New York Circus, Bartlett and Delavan

08/06–07/1841—Lancaster, PA, Welch, Mann and Delavan

08/08–10/23/1841—Various PA and NY, Welch, Mann and Delavan

08/00/1841—Reading, PA, Welch and Mann

08/00/1841—Hamburg, PA, Welch and Mann

08/00/1841—Pottsville, PA, Welch and Mann

08/00/1841—Danville, PA, Welch and Mann

08/18/1841—Muncy, PA, Welch and Mann

08/00/1841—Williamsport, PA, Welch and Mann

08/00/1841—Iron Run, PA, Welch and Mann

08/00/1841—Blossburg, PA, Welch and Mann

08/00/1841—Lawrence[ville], PA, Welch and Mann

08/00/1841—Painted Post, NY, Welch and Mann

08/00/1841—Corning, NY, Welch and Mann

08/00/1841—Elmira, NY, Welch and Mann

08/00/1841—Mecklenburg, NY, Welch and Mann

08/27–28/1841—Ithaca, NY, Welch and Mann

08/31/1841—or thereabouts, Geneva, NY, Welch and Mann

09/01–02/1841—Canandaigua, NY, Welch and Mann

09/06–07/1841—Batavia, NY, Welch and Mann

09/08/1841—or thereabouts, Clarence Hollow, NY, Welch and Mann

09/09–11/1841—Buffalo, NY, Welch and Mann

09/21–22/1841—Rochester, NY, Welch and Mann

09/00/1841—Leroy, NY, Welch and Mann

09/00/1841—Angelica, NY, Welch and Mann

09/00/1841—Pikeville, NY, Welch and Mann

09/00/1841—Ellicottville, NY, Welch and Mann

10/00/1841—Havana, NY, Welch and Mann

10/00/1841—Dundee, NY, Welch and Mann

10/00/1841—Penn Yan, NY, Welch and Mann

10/00/1841—Rushville, NY, Welch and Mann

10/00/1841—Waterloo, NY, Welch and Mann

10/00/1841—Seneca Falls, NY, Welch and Mann

10/00/1841—Auburn, NY, Welch and Mann

10/08/1841—Chittenango, NY, Welch and Mann

10/00/1841—Syracuse, NY, Welch and Mann

10/00/1841—Cazanovia, NY, Welch and Mann

10/00/1841—Rome, NY, Welch and Mann

10/13–14/1841—Utica, NY, Welch and Mann

10/00/1841—Herkimer, NY, Welch and Mann

10/00/1841—Little Falls, NY, Welch and Mann

10/00/1841—Fort Plain, NY, Welch and Mann

10/00/1841—Fonda, NY, Welch and Mann

10/00/1841—American, NY, Welch and Mann

10/00/1841—Schenectady, NY, Welch and Mann

10/00/1841—Albany, NY, Welch and Mann

10/22–23/1841—Troy, NY, Welch and Mann

11/22–12/11/1841—Boston, MA, Harrington's Museum

12/20–30/1841—Boston, MA, Tremont Circus

01/17–29/1842—New York, NY, Bowery Amphitheatre

01/31–02/09/1842—Philadelphia, PA, American Theatre, Philadelphia Circus

02/11–12/1842—New York, NY, Bowery Amphitheatre

02/13–03/18/1842—or thereabouts, en route to England

03/28–04/23/1842—Liverpool, England, Royal Amphitheatre, Sands American Circus

04/25/1842—St Helen's, England, Sands American Circus

05/02–07/1842—Manchester, England, Sands American Circus

05/11/1842—Rochdale, England, Sands American Circus

05/13–14/1842—Halifax, England, Sands American Circus

05/16–19/1842—Leeds, England, Sands American Circus

05/23–31/1842—Sheffield, England, Sands American Circus

01/16–04/08/1843—London, England, Theatre Royal, Lyceum, English Opera—House, Van Amburgh

04/10–15/1843—London, England, Sadler's Wells Theatre

04/17–05/27/1843—London, England, Davidge's Royal Surrey

05/18/1843—London, England, Lyceum, English Opera House

07/13–24+29/1843—Edinburgh, Scotland, Adelphia Theatre

08/02–09/1843—Perth, Scotland Cooke's Circus

09/25–10/04/1843—Birmingham, England, Theatre Royal

10/28/1843—and thereabouts, Leicester, London, England, Batty's Amphitheatre

02/10–25/1844—Liverpool, England, Theatre Royal

03/04–30/1844—Liverpool, England, Van Amburgh and Sands Royal Amphitheatre

04/24–05/07/1844—or thereabouts, Dublin, Ireland, Theatre Royal

05/08–11/1844—or thereabouts, Cork, Ireland

05/13–18/1844—Belfast, Ireland, Theatre Royal

05/20–06/03/1844—Glasgow, Scotland, Theatre Royal Adelphia

06/05–08/1844—Edinburgh, Scotland, Waterloo Rooms

06/15–22/1844—Glasgow, Scotland, City Hall

07/22–08/14/1844—Liverpool, England, Amphitheatre

08/26–28/1844—Liverpool, England, Liver Theatre

10/11–12/1844—Nottingham, England, Assembly Rooms

12/20/1844—Nottingham, England, Van Amburgh's Circus

01/20–02/08/1845—Liverpool, England, Theatre Royal and Modern Arena of Arts

02/22/1845—Sheffield, England, Van Amburgh

03/31–04/07/1845—Birmingham, England, Theatre Royal

05/29–31/1845—New York, NY, New Bowery Theatre

06/02–10/04/1845—various NJ, NY and Canada, Welch and Mann

06/02–03/1845—Newark, NJ, Welch and Mann

06/09–10/1845—Albany, NY, Welch and Mann

06/11–12/1845—Schenectady, NY, Welch and Mann

06/13/1845—West Troy, NY, Welch and Mann

06/14/1845—Lansingburgh, NY, Welch and Mann

07/03–04/1845—Utica, NY, Welch and Mann

07/06/1845—Rome, NY, Welch and Mann

07/10/1845—Turin, NY, Welch and Mann

07/11/1845—Lowville, NY, Welch and Mann

08/11/1845—Brockville, ONT, Welch and Mann

08/12/1845—Ogdensburgh, NY, Welch and Mann

09/06/1845—Norwich, NY, Welch and Mann

09/10/1845—Binghampton, NY, Welch and Mann

09/11/18145—Harpersville, NY, Welch and Mann

09/12/1845—North Bainbridge, NY, Welch and Mann

09/15–18/1845—Utica, NY, Welch and Mann

09/30–10/01/1845—Troy, NY, Welch and Mann

10/02–04/1845—Albany, NY, Welch and Mann

12/01–04/1845—Richmond, VA

12/11/1845—Lynchburg, VA

05/23/1846—or thereabouts, touring Virginia including Halifax and Charlotte Counties

09/09–10/1846—Petersburg, VA

07/04/1848—Lynchburg, VA

09/18–20/1848—Petersburg, VA, Mechanics Hall

09/22–23/1848—Richmond, VA, Odd Fellows' Hall

10/12/1848—Lynchburg, VA, Masonic Hall

11/01–02/1848—Raleigh, NC

11/21–25/1848—Charleston, SC, Temperance Hall

01/29–31/1849—Petersburg, VA, Old Fellows Hall

03/12/1849—Lynchburg, VA, Masonic Hall

07/12/1849—Lynchburg, VA, Universalist Church

11/12–14/1849—Knoxville, TN

12/17–19/1849—Nashville, TN, Masonic Hall

01/20–02/18/1851—Richmond, VA

12/28–29/1852—Baton Rouge, LA, Harney House Saloon

08/17–18/1854—Washington, DC

08/24–26/1854—Baltimore, MD, Carroll Hall

08/28/1854—or thereabouts, Petersburg, VA

11/22/1855—Lynchburg, VA, Dudley Hall

03/09–10/1857—Edgefield, SC, Masonic Hall

04/15–16/1857—Charlotte, NC

04/22/1857—Salisbury, NC, Murphy's Hall

05/22–26/1857—Lynchburg, VA, Dudley Hall

05/27–06/02/1857—Richmond, VA, Metropolitan Hall

11/05–07/1857—Lynchburg, VA, Dudley Hall

12/16–18/1857—Atlanta, GA, Hayden's Hall

12/21–25/1857—Atlanta, GA, Athenaeum

12/31/1857–01/02/1858—Columbus, GA, Temperance Hall

11/20/1858—Fredericksburg, VA, Citizens' Hall

11/22–27/1858—Washington, DC, Melodeon Hall

12/20–24/1858—Norfolk, VA, Mechanics Hall

12/28/1858–01/01/1859—Petersburg, VA, Mechanics Hall

01/11–15/1859—Baltimore, MD, Museum

01/17–27+02/15/1859—Washington, DC, Melodeon Hall

11/05/1859—or thereabouts, Petersburg, VA, Phoenix Hall

Chapter Notes

Acknowledgments

1. Lowell Schreyer, "Joel Sweeney," *Figa News* (March/April, 1997), 12–15.1.

Preface

1. Robert B. Winans, "The Folk, the Stage, and the Five-String Banjo in the Nineteenth Century," *Journal of American Folklore 89* (October-December, 1976), 417–418.
2. Robert Cantwell, *Bluegrass Breakdown: The Making of the Old Southern Sound* (Urbana: University of Illinois Press, 1984), 257.
3. They are: Eric Lott, *Love and Theft: Blackface Minstrelsy and the American Working Class* (1993); Ken Emerson, *Doo-Dah! Stephen Foster and the Rise of American Popular Culture* (1997); Dale Cockrell, *Demons of Disorder: Early Blackface Minstrels and Their World* (1997); W.T. Lhamon, Jr., *Raising Cain: Blackface Performance from Jim Crow to Hip Hop* (1998); and William J. Mahar, *Behind the Burnt Cork Mask: Early Blackface Minstrelsy and Antebellum American Popular Culture* (1999).
4. Hans Nathan, *Dan Emmett and the Rise of Early Negro Minstrelsy* (1962), and Robert Toll, *Blacking Up: The Minstrel Show in Nineteenth-Century America* (1974).
5. R.B. Pore to G.W. Inge (July 25, 1890), Louisiana County Museum typescript; Ruth I. Mahood to Robert Van Eps (January 29, 1955), collection of James Bollman.

Chapter 1

1. G.W. Inge to J.E. Henning (1890), quoted in Frank B. Converse, "Banjo Reminiscences 7," *The Cadenza* (December, 1901), 11; "He Invented the Banjo," *Chattanooga Republican* (November 2, 1890).
2. *Virginia Gazette* (February 18, 1775).
3. Thomas Jefferson, *Notes on the State of Virginia; Written in the Year 1781, some what corrected and enlarged in the Winter of 1782* (Paris: 1782), 257, reprinted (Chapel Hill, NC: UNC Press, 1982), 288.
4. Thomas Fairfax, *Journey from Virginia to Salem Massachusetts;* quoted in Robert B. Winans, *The Banjo in Virginia* (Ferrum, VA: 2000), 3.
5. P.C. Sutphin, "Who Invented the Banjo," Glasgow, Kentucky *Times,* reprinted in *Lynchburg News* (February 7, 1895), 4.
6. James Grant Wilson and John Fiske, *Appleton's Cyclo-*pedia of American Biography (New York: D. Appleton, 1887–9), quoted on famousamericans.net.
7. *Letters from the South, by a Northern Man* (New York: Harper and Brothers, 1835: I), 96–97, quoted in Epstein, *The Folk Banjo,* 355.
8. John P. Kennedy, *Swallow Barn, or A Sojourn in the Old Dominion* (Philadelphia: Carey and Lea, 1832), reprinted (New York: Hafner, 1962).
9. Kennedy, 101–103.
10. perseus.tufts.edu.
11. "Old Titus—The Original Banjo-Man," *Richmond Dispatch* (April 21, 1852), 2.
12. The instrument was used by blacks in this regard and mentioned in William B. Smith, "The Persimmon Tree and Beer Dance," *Farmer's Register, VI* (April 1838), 59–60, reprinted in Bruce Jackson, *The Negro and His Folklore in Nineteenth-Century Periodicals* (Austin: University of Texas Press, 1967); John Smyth, *A Tour in the United States of America-Volume 1* (London: Printed for G. Robinson, 1784); Kennedy; Bessie M. Henry, "A Yankee schoolmistress Discovers Virginia," *Essex Institute Historical Collections.*
13. "On an Old Virginia Plantation in the Peaceful Days Before the Civil War," *The Baltimore Sun* (June 14, 1908).
14. Charles L. Perdue, Jr., Thomas E. Barden and Robert K. Phillips, *Weevils in the Wheat* (Charlottesville: University Press of Virginia, 1976), 49–50.
15. Perdue, 141.
16. Perdue, 225–226.
17. Perdue, 231.
18. Perdue, 326.
19. Joe Wilson, "The Wood Banjo," *Masters of the Banjo,* 9–10; Joe Wilson, "The Luthier's Art," Dixie Frets (Chattanooga, TN: Hunter Museum of Art, 1994).
20. See the writings of George Gibson.
21. 1850 census.
22. George Collins, "The American Banjo, Part II," *Fretts* (Feb-March, 1959), reprinted *Figa* (March-April, 1979).African
23. R.B. Pore to G.W. Inge (July 25, 1890), Louisiana County Museum typescript; Ruth I. Mahood to Robert Van Eps (January 29, 1955), collection of James Bollman.
24. Sutphin, 4.
25. For example, Robert Williamson, mentioned in Chapter One, who was playing in the period of 1828–1831. Noah Smithwick, *Evolution of a State* (Austin: University of Texas Press, 1983), 49, quoted in Jodella K. Dyreson, "Sporting Activities in the American-Mexican Colonies of Texas, 1832 to 1835," *Journal of Sport History 24/3* (Fall 1997), 273.

Chapter 2

1. Richard Moody, *American Takes the Stage: Romanticism in American Drama and Theatre, 1750-1900* (Bloomington: Indiana University, 1955), 33–34.

2. *Cincinnati Commercial Advertiser* (January 28, 1830), Cowell, 36, quoted by Cockrell, 63; *Louisville Public Advertiser* (November 30, 1830.)

3. *Cincinnati Independent Press* (July 17, 1823), quoted in Lawrence Barrett, *Life of Forrest*, quoted in *Curiosities of the American Stage*, 94–111; Richard Moody, *Edwin Forrest* (New York: Alfred A. Knopf, 1960), 28–29.

4. Charles Dibdin, Jr., "The Bonja Song."

5. Russell Sanjek, *American Popular Music and Its Business* 1 (New York: Oxford University, 1988), 313.

6. Sanjek, 310.

7. Song Sheet, Harvard Theater Collection.

8. George Odell, *Annals of the New York Stage* 2 (New York: Columbia University, 1927–49), 247.

9. *Odell III*, 315.

10. Ritchey, 93, via Cockrell.

11. Sanjek, 98.

12. Issac John Greenwood, *The Circus, Its Origins and Growth* (New York: William Abbatt, 1898/1909), 123; Hall, 1920, via Cockrell; W.W. Clapp, Jr., *History of the Boston Stage*, quoted in Laurence Hutton, *Curiosities of the American Stage* (New York: Harper, 1891), 94–111.

13. For example *The New York Journal or General Advertiser* (April 9, 1767); *Odell II*, 146–7.

14. *New York Herald* (November 1–2, 1853), 5; H.P. Phelps, *Players of a Century* (Joseph McDonough: 1880), 227–282.

15. Sol Smith, *Theatrical Management in the West And South for Thirty Years*, quoted in Hutton, 94–111; Phelps, 165, 227–282.

16. Greenwood, 118–119; Clapp, 93–94.

17. Vera Brodsky Lawrence, 1978, quoted in Sanjek, 161–2.

18. Thomas Devoe, *The Market Book* (New York, 1868), 344–345, quoted in Peter G. Buckley, "The Place to Make an Artist Work: Micah Hawkins and William Sidney Mount in New York City," *Catching the Tune: Music and William Sidney Mount* (Stony Brook: The Museums at Stony Brook, 1984), 26–27.

19. Buckley, 27.

20. Lyric reproduced in W.T. Lhamon, Jr., *Jump Jim Crow* (Cambridge, MA: Harvard University, 2003), 94–95.

21. Greenwood, 124; Charity Hospital Admission Books, 1861–1862, 92, quoted in Dale Cockrell, *Demons of Disorder: Early Blackface Minstrels and Their World* (New York: Cambridge University, 1997), 96 and note #9, 189.

22. Stuart Thayer, *Annals of the American Circus* I (Seattle: Thayer, 1976), 126.

23. *Odell III*, 354.

24. *Odell III*, 413.

25. *Odell III*, 472.

26. *Advertiser* (January 1, 1830).

27. cemetery.state.tx.us.

28. Noah Smithwick, *Evolution of a State* (Austin: University of Texas, 1983), 49, quoted in Jodella K. Dyreson, "Sporting Activities in the American-Mexican Colonies of Texas, 1832-1835," *Journal of Sport History* 24/3 (Fall 1997), 273.

29. *New York Clipper Annual* (1884), 6; Wilson 561, 566, via Cockrell; *Odell IV*, 39; *New York Herald* (January 5–6, 1839).

30. levysheetmusic.mse.jhu.edu.

31. *Patriot* (December 11, 1833); *Intelligencer* (November 7, 1833); *May's Encyclopedia*, Maryland Historical Society.

32. *May's*.

33. levysheetmusic.mse.jhu.edu; ahpcs.org/library/cilist.htm.

34. Lyric reproduced in *Jump Jim Crow*, 95–102.

35. Moody, 34; Phelps, 165–167.

36. Joseph N. Ireland, *Records of the New York Stage* 2 (New York: Bert Franklin, 1866–7/1968), 55–6; *Odell III*, 354.

37. Adams, 23, 55, via Cockrell; *Cincinnati Daily Gazette* (July 16, August 12 and November 2, 1829), quoted in Geraldine C. Harris, "Chapter IV: Negro Minstrelsy," *The History of the Theatre in Ohio 1815-1850* (Ohio State Thesis, 1937), 68; *Louisville Public Advertiser* (July 4, 1829–December 27, 1830).

38. *Louisville Public Advertiser* (May 21, 1830), quoted in *Jump Jim Crow*, 36.

39. Robert P. Nevin, *Atlantic Monthly*, November, 1867, quoted in *Players of a Century*, 165–167.

40. Edmon [Edwin?] Conner, *New York Times*, June 5, 1981, quoted in *Curiosities of the Am Stage*, 115–119.

41. This discussion of the "Jim Crow" song is based on the writings of W.T. Lhamon, Jr., in his book cited above.

42. *May's*, Box V, Folder 1, Reel 5, Jacket 29; *Washington Intelligencer* (October 30-November 5, 1832).

43. *New York Courier & Enquirer* (November 28, 1832).

44. *Boston Semi-Weekly Courier* (November 2, 1837).

45. *Spirit of the Times* (October 22, 1836).

46. *Spirit of the Times* (July 16, 1836).

47. *New York Herald* (September 25, 27, October 4, 20, 1837); *Odell 4*, 239.

48. *Boston Semi-Weekly Courier* (May 25, 1837).

49. *New York Sun* (February 6 and March 23, 1835); *New York Transcript* (February 6–7, 1835); *Odell IV*, 39, 43.

50. *Spirit of the Times* (October 28, 1837).

51. William J. Mahar, *Behind the Burnt Cork Mask* (Urbana and Chicago: University of Illinois, 1994), 171.

52. *American Beacon* (March 19, 1836), quoted in Stuart Thayer, "The Circus Roots of Negro Minstrelsy," *Bandwagon*, 45.

53. Thayer, *Traveling Showmen*, 102; Thayer 2 (1986), 160–161.

54. Thayer.

55. *United States Telegraph* (July 3, 1830), quoted in Thayer 2, 94, 164.

56. Stuart Thayer, *Annals of the American Circus 1793-1860* (Seattle: Dauven & Thayer, 2000), 224.

57. *New Orleans Mercantile Advertiser* (March 7, 1831), quoted in Thayer 2, 10, 160.

58. Thayer research notes; *New York Clipper* (December 14, 1867), quoted in Thayer 2, 10, 159–160.

59. *New York Sun* (January 18, 1834).

60. *Richmond Whig* (July 4, 1834), quoted in Albert Stoutamire, *Music of the Old South: Colony to Confederacy* (Cranbury, NJ: Associated University Presses, Inc, 1972) 148; Thayer; *Richmond Enquirer* (July 1–8, 1834).

61. Gavin Weightman, *Bright Lights, Big City* (London: Collins & Brown, 1992), 64.

62. Toll, 87, quoted in Michael Pickering, "White Skin, Black Masks: Nigger Minstrelsy in Victorian England," *Music Hall Performance and Style* (Philadelphia: Open University, 1986), 72–73, 82; Sam Dennison, *Scandalize My Name: Black Imagery in American Popular Music* (New York: Garland, 1982); Anne Jackson Mathews, *The Memoirs of Charles Mathews, Comedian* (London: R. Bentley, 1838–39).

63. Sanjek, 156–157; Nathan, 46.

64. Derek Scott, *The Singing Bourgeois*, 82.

65. Nathan, 46.

66. James Kirke Paulding, *Letters from the South, written during an excursion in the summer of 1816* (New York: James Eastburn & Co., 1817), quoted in Nathan, 48.

67. *Spirit of the Times* (June 11, 1836); "Letter from T.D. Rice," *New York Herald* (August 30, 1837); Cave, 66–67; Barry Anthony, "Early Nigger Minstrel Acts in Britain," *Music Hall* 12 (London, April, 1980), 118; Broadsides, 313, volume two, British Library; *Spirit of the Times* (August 27 and September 10, 1836).

68. Broadside (August 15, 1836), 313, volume two, British Library.

69. *Figaro in London* (September 17, 24, 1836, October 15, 22 and November 5, 1836) quoted in *Spirit of the Times* (November 12, 1836); Broadsides (September 12–November 2, 1836), 313, volume two, British Library; Broadside (November 10–12, 18, 1836), Bill Box G2 A23, Folger; "Letter from T.D. Rice," *New York Herald* (August 30, 1837).

70. Broadsides (December 7–13, 19, 1836), 313, volume two, British Library.

71. *London Satirist*, quoted in *Spirit of the Times* (March 18, 1837).

72. *Spirit of the Times* (January 14 and February 4, 1837).

73. Broadsides (February 22, 24, 27 and March 4 and April 3–8, 1837), Bill Box G2A23, Folger; Broadsides (March 21, 1837), 313, volume two, British Library; *Sunday Times* (April 16, 1837), quoted in *Spirit of the Times* (May 27, 1837); *Spirit of the Times* (June 17, 1837).

74. *Spirit of the Times* (June 17, 1837).

75. *The Age* (May 7, 1837), quoted in *Spirit of the Times* (June 17, 1837).

76. *Cork Herald*; *Spirit of the Times* (May 13, 1837).

77. "Letter from Jim Crow," *Spirit of the Times* (August 26, 1837).

78. *New York Herald* (December 29, 1836 and July 29 and September 12, 1837).

79. *New York Express*, quoted in *Spirit of the Times* (February 25, 1837).

80. *Star*, quoted in *Spirit of the Times* (August 26, 1837); Moody, 37.

81. *Spirit of the Times* (November 26, 1836).

82. *London Satirist*, quoted in *Spirit of the Times* (February 4, 1837).

83. *Spirit of the Times* (August 27 and October 1, 1836 and June 10, 1837).

84. *Spirit of the Times* (February 2, 19 and March 30 and April 13, 1839); *Morning Post* (December 17, 1838); Anthony, 118; *New York Herald*, February 20, 1839; *London Age* (February 3, 1839), quoted in *Spirit of the Times* (March 9,1839); Broadsides (January 7–26 and February 2, 4–9 and March 4–19, 21, 1839), G2A23, Folger; Adelphi (December 31, 1838), Vol. III, 431/443,British Library.

85. Cockrell, 20–21.

86. *Spirit of the Times* (November 2, 9, 1839); Broadside (September 30, 1839–October 12, 16, 1839), G2A23, Folger.

87. *Spirit of the Times* (December 7, 1839 and January 11, 1840); Broadsides, Minstrels "R" folder, Harvard.

88. Broadside (December 18–23, 1839), G2A23, Folger.

89. *Spirit of the Times* (February 1, 1839), (April 25, 1840), 2; *London Age*, quoted in *Spirit of the Times* (February 29 and March 14, 21, 1840).

90. Broadsides (November 2–7, 1840), 389, volume one, British Library.

91. Glenroy, 28–29.

92. Broadsides (November 2–December 22, 1840), 389, volume one, British Library.

93. *Bristol Standard* (March 4, 1841).

94. Broadsides (November 2–7, 25, 1840), 389 volume one, British Library.

95. *Monarchs*, 24.

96. *Sunday Morning Atlas* (February 23, 1840), quoted on Broadsides (November 9–14, 1840), 389 volume one, British Library.

97. Broadsides (November 9–14, 23–28, 1840), 389 volume one, British Library.

Chapter 3

1. "Letter from Appomattox to the Editor," *The Richmond Dispatch*, reprinted in *the Cadenza* 1/3 (January 2, 1895), 5.

2. Letter, Mrs. Vicki Jamerson to Mrs. Mary W. Stanley (June 16, 1978), National Park Service.

3. John Hammond Moore, *Appomattox Court House: Community, Village and Families 1845-1870* (Appomattox Court House: National Park Service), 217.

4. VA State Vital Statistics.

5. *Appomattox Death Records* (1860), 155, original Jones Library; *Petition* (December 17, 1831), 15.

6. Stuart McDearmon Farrar, *Historical Notes of Appomattox County, Virginia* (Appomattox: privately published, nd), 209.

7. *Historical Base Map* (Appomattox Courthouse: National Park Service, 1962).

8. Harriett A. Chilton, *Appomattox County, Virginia Tax Lists* (February, 1975), 10; Moore, 217.

9. 1850 census; Moore, 217.

10. 1860 census; gravesite.

11. Pore to Henning, *Cadenza* (November-December, 1898).

12. Converse, 4, 10.

13. T. N. French, *The Cadenza* (September, 1919).

14. "Oh! Hush!," reprinted in Lhamon, *Jump Jim Crow*, 148.

15. *Richmond Whig* (December 2, 1836), 2.

16. "S.S. Sanford Interview," *Wash Republican*, reprinted in "Joe Sweeney," *Lynchburg News* (September 15, 1874) 3.

17. *Richmond Whig* (February 17, 21, 1837), 3.

18. Letter to *Lynchburg News* (April 5, 1905).

19. Thayer 2, 205–206, 230–231; *Lynchburg Virginian* (August 23, 27, 30, 1838), 2, (September 6, 1838), 3; *Staunton Spectator* (September 13, 1838), 2; *Richmond Enquirer* (October 23, 26, 30, 1838), 4; *American Constellation* (October 30, 1838), 2, WPA LibVA index; *Western Carolinian* (November 15, 29, 1838), 3; *Charlotte Journal* (December 7, 1838), 1; *Edgefield Advertiser* (December 13, 20, 24, 1838), 3; *Daily Georgian* (December 20, 22, 25, 29, 1838 and January 1, 4, 1839), 3; *Charleston Courier* (January 24-February 12, 1839), 3. [0]

20. *Charleston Courier* (February 13, 16, 18–19, 1839), 3.

21. *New York Herald* (April 16–18, 1839), 3; Odell, 300.

22. William B. Wood, *Personal Recollections of the Stage* (Philadelphia: Henry Carey, 1855).

23. Philip B. Kunhardt, Jr., Philip B. Kunhardt III, Peter W. Kunhardt, *P.T. Barnum: America's Greatest Showman* (New York: Alfred A. Knopf, 1995), 26–27.

24. *New York Clipper Almanac* (1892), 13.

25. *New York Herald* (April 17, 1839), 2, (April 16–18, 1839), 3; Odell, 300; *New York Post* (April 16–18, 1839), 3; Broadsides (April 16–18, 1839), Harvard.

26. T. Allston Brown, "The Theatre In America 1," (1888), 65.

27. *New York Clipper Annual* (1884), 6.

28. Odell IV, 511, quoting *New York Herald* (November 30, 1840).

29. Rice, 24.

30. *New York Herald* (November 25, 1839), 5; Thayer 2, 239.

31. *New York Tattler* (November 25–27, 1839), 3.

32. *Evening Tattler* (November 29–30, 1839).

33. *Odell IV*, 315; *New York Herald* (June 18–19, 1839).
34. *Evening Tattler* (December 14, 1839), 2, 3.
35. *New York Herald* (December 17–20, 1839), 3.
36. *New York Post* (December 23, 1839), 3.
37. *New York Morning Courier* (December 30–31, 1839), 2.
38. *Evening Tattler* (December 17, 1839), 2; *New York Post* (December 17–19, 1839), 3.
39. Rice, 42.
40. P.T. Barnum, 106.
41. *New York Morning Herald* (January 18, 1840).
42. *New York Post* (January 21, 1840), 2.
43. *New York Post* (January 23–25, 1840), 3; *New York Herald* (January 23–25, 1840), 3.
44. *New York Post* (January 25, 1840), 2.
45. *Odell IV*, 422; *New York Post* (February 7–8, 1840), 3.
46. *New York Post* (January 10, 1840), 3.
47. *New York Morning Courier* (March 9, 1840), 2.
48. *New York Herald* (March 4, 1840).
49. *New York Herald* (March 23, 1840), 2.
50. *New York Herald* (April 3, 1840), 2, 3.
51. *New York Herald* (April 8, 1840).
52. *New York Herald* (March 31–April 2, 1840), 2, 3.
53. *Boston Transcript* (December 9, 1840), 2.
54. *Daily Argus* (June 22-July 4, 1840), 3; *Albany Microscope* (June 27 and July 7, 1840), 3.
55. Thayer 2, 266; *Glenroy*, 29; *Providence Journal*, (April 14–17, 1840), 3.
56. Thayer 2, 247; *Spirit of the Times* (April 25, 1840), 96.
57. Thayer 2, 266; *Glenroy*, 29; *Providence Journal* (April 14–17, 1840), 3; *Fall River Patriot* (April 16, 1840), 3; *Taunton Whig* (April 22, 1840), 3.
58. *Boston Post* (May 4–5, 16, 1840), 2; *Boston Transcript* (May 5, 1840), 2.
59. *Glenroy*, 29.
60. *Boston Post* (May 4, 1840), 2.
61. *Boston Transcript* (May 6, 1840), 2.
62. *Boston Transcript* (May 7, 8, 1840), 2.
63. *Boston Courier* (May 14, 1840), 2.
64. Playbill, Harvard Theatre Collection.
65. Wood, 401–2.
66. *New York Clipper Annual* (1884), 6; *Evening Tattler* (January 27 and February 10, 1840), 3; *New York Post* (February 11, 1840), 3; Brown 1, 117; *New York Morning Courier* (February 10, 1840), 2.
67. *Boston Atlas* (May 11, 1840), 2; *Boston Post* (May 18, 1840), 2.
68. *Boston Transcript* (May 7, 8, 1840), 2.
69. *Boston Bulletin*, quoted in *Utica Observer* (August 4, 11, 1840), 3.
70. *Boston Post* (May 30 and May–June, 1840), 2; *Boston Atlas* (May 30 and May–June, 1840), 3; *Boston Transcript* (May 30 and June 1–4, 1840), 3; *American Traveller* (June 2, 4, 1840), 3.
71. Thayer 2, 266; *Glenroy*, 30–32; *Pittsfield* (June 18, 25, 1840), 3.
72. *Odell IV*, 390.
73. *Boston Morning Post* (June 18, 1840), 2.
74. levysheetmusic.mse.jhu.edu; memory.loc.gov.
75. *Daily Argus* (June 22–July 4, 1840), 3; *Albany Microscope* (June 27 and July 7, 1840), 3, (July 4, 1840), 2.
76. Annals; *Ontario Repository* (August 26 and September 2, 1840), 3.
77. *Auburn Journal and Advertiser* (August 12, 17, 1840), 3.
78. *Rochester Advertiser* (August 31–September 5, 1840), 3.
79. *Rochester Advertiser* (September 5, 1840), 2.
80. *Troy Northern Budget* (July 6 and October 2–17,
81. Glenroy, 32; *Poughkeepsie Journal* (September 30–October 21, 1840), 3.

1840), 3; *Troy Daily Whig* (June 29–July 3, 6–7 and October 7, 10–16, 1840), 2.
81. Glenroy, 32; *Poughkeepsie Journal* (September 30–October 21, 1840), 3.
82. *Poughkeepsie Journal* (September 30–October 21, 1840), 3.
83. Playbills 389, 1, British Library.
84. Glenroy, 32.
85. Thayer 2, 266; Glenroy, 34; *Spirit of the Times* (September 26, 1840), 360.
86. *New York Herald* (November 2–7, 1840), 2, 3.
87. Broadside (November 23, 1840), Harvard; *Broadway Down East* (Trustees of the Public Library of the City of Boston, 1978), 16, 156.
88. Broadsides (November 24, 25 and December 2, 1840), Harvard.
89. Broadside (December 4, 1840), Harvard; *Boston Post* and *Boston Courier* (December 2, 1840), 3.
90. *Boston Courier* (December 4, 1840), 2.
91. *Boston Post* (November 26, 1840), 2, 3; Broadside (November 27, 30 and December 1, 1840), Harvard.
92. *Boston Post* (December 4, 1840), 2.
93. *Boston Post* (December 4, 1840), 3; *Boston Courier* (December 4, 1840), 2; *Boston Transcript* (December 4, 1840), 2.
94. Andrea Stulman Dennett, *Weird and Wonderful* (New York: NYU Press, 1997), 86.
95. *Boston Post* (November 24–25, 1840), 2.
96. *Boston Post* (May 18–20, 1840), 2; *Boston Transcript* (May 18–20, 1840), 3; *Boston Atlas* (May 18–23, 1840), 3; *Boston American Traveller* (May 19, 1840), 3.
97. *Boston Post* (December 7–9, 1840), 3; *American Traveller* (December 8, 11, 1840), 3.
98. William W. Clapp, Jr., *A Record of the Boston Stage* (New York: Benjamin Blom, 1853/1868), 342–3; Donald C. King, *A History of Boston's Theatres* (Boston: Bostonian Soc manuscript, 1987), 11–12.
99. *American Traveller* (May 5, 1840), 3; *Boston Transcript* (May 21–23, 1840), 3; Donald C. King, 11–12.
100. *American Traveller* (December 11, 1840), 2; *Boston Post* (December 15, 26, 1840), 2; *Boston Transcript* (December 16, 24, 1840), 2.
101. *Boston Post* (December 7–9, 1840), 3; *American Traveller* (December 8, 11, 1840), 3.
102. *Boston Post* (December 9, 1840), 2.
103. *Boston Transcript* (December 9, 1840), 2.
104. *Boston Post* (December 21, 1840), 2.
105. *American Traveller* (December 25, 1840), 3.
106. Broadsides (January 28 and February 19, 1841), Rare Books, Boston Public Library.
107. Glenroy, 36–37; Thayer 2, 277.
108. *National Intelligencer* (January 22, 23, 25, 1841), 3.
109. *Spirit of the Times* (February 13, 1841), 600; Letter from Mrs. Ralph Catterall, Valentine Museum to Colonel Collins (December 20, 1953).
110. *Baltimore Sun* (March 3–6, 1841), 3.
111. *Baltimore American* (March 6, 1841), 3.
112. *New York Herald*, via Cockrell.
113. *New York American/Courier* (March 18–24, 1841), 2; *New York Post*, 3; *New York Herald* (March 24, 1841), 2; *Odell*, 476.
114. Dingess, 144; *New York Clipper Annual* (1884), 8.
115. *New York Post* (March 19, 1841), 2.
116. *New York Herald* (March 18, 19, 1841), 3.
117. Broadside, Bowery Theatre (March 18, 1841), American Antiquarian Society, BDSDS.1841-F, quoted in Cockrell, 148.
118. *New York Post* (March 23, 24, 1841), 3, 2.
119. *New York Herald* (March 24, 1841), 2.

120. *Baltimore American* (May 26, 1841), 3.
121. *Baltimore Sun* (May 5, 1841), 2.
122. *Baltimore American* (May 6 and June 5, 1841), 2, 3.
123. *Baltimore Sun* (May 5–6, 1841), 2, 3.
124. *Baltimore American* (May 27–28 and June 1–2, 4, 1841), 3.
125. *Baltimore American* (May 26, 1841), 2.
126. *Baltimore Sun* (May 25–26, 1841), 2.
127. Thayer 2, 1April and 267, 277; Glenroy, 37.
128. Glenroy, 37.
129. *Baltimore Sun* (July 20, 22, 1841), 2.
130. *American and Commercial Advertiser* (July 22, 1841), 3.
131. Glenroy.
132. *Troy Northern Budget* (October 13–22, 1841), 3; *Daily Whig* (October 15, 23, 1841), 2.
133. Glenroy, 38.
134. *New York Tribune* (October 23–November 10, 17, 1841); *New York Eve Post* (October 25, 29–30 and November 4, 9, 13, 15, 20, 1841).
135. Unaccredited newspaper clipping, Box 1, Collins Papers, LibVA.
136. *Boston Post* (November 22, 1841), 2, (November 22–25, 27, 1841), 3; *Boston Transcript* (November 22, 1841), 2, (November 22–24, 26–27, 1841), 3.
137. *American Traveller* (November 23, 1841), 2.
138. *Boston Transcript* and *Boston Post* (December 11, 1841), 3; *Boston Post* (December 11, 1841), 2.
139. King, 12; *Boston Post* (November 22–December 31, 1841), 3, (January 1–15, 1842).
140. *Boston Post* (December 13, 20, 23, 1841), 2, (December 28–30, 1841), 3.
141. *Boston Post* (December 20, 1841), 3.
142. *Boston Post* (December 28–30, 1841), 3.

Chapter 4

1. Joseph Arnold Cave, *A Jubilee of Dramatic Life and Incident Of* (London: Thomas Vernon, 1894), 69–73.
2. *New York Herald* (January 16–19, 1842), 3.
3. *New York Evening Post* (November 15, 1841).
4. *New York Post* (January 17–19, 1842), 3.
5. *New York Herald* (January 12–19, 28–29, 1842), 2, 3.
6. *Philadelphia Inquirer* (February 4, 1842), 3.
7. John A. Dingess, ms., 103–104, Hertzberg; also C.G. Sturdivant, *Who's Who in American Circus 2*, ms., 3A88, 375, Hertzberg.
8. *New York Herald* (January 26, 1842), 4; Broadside, June, Titus & Angevine (January 21, 1842), William Bailey Collection, Somers Circus Museum.
9. *Philadelphia Public Ledger* (February 2, 1842), 3.
10. *New York Herald* (January 25, 1842), 3; *New York Post* (January 25, 1842), 2.
11. *Philadelphia Inquirer* (January 31, 1842), 3; *Philadelphia Public Ledger* (January 31, 1842), 3; *Amphitheatres and Circuses*, 33.
12. *Philadelphia Inquirer* (January 28–29, 1842), 3.
13. *New York Post* (January 24, 1842), 2.
14. *New York Herald* (February 12, 1842), 2, 3; *New York Post* (February 12, 1840), 2.
15. Thayer 2, 134.
16. Dingess, 103–104; Sturdivant, 375.
17. *The Albion* (March 21, 1842); *The Liverpool Chronicle* (April 23, 1842).
18. *The Albion* (April 11, 1842).
19. *The Liverpool Chronicle* (March 26, 1842).

20. *Liverpool Courier and Commercial Advertiser* (March 30, 1842).
21. *Liverpool Mail* (April 5, 1842).
22. *Liverpool Journal* (April 9, 1842), 8.
23. *The Albion* (April 18, 1842).
24. *Mercury* (April 22, 1842), 1; *The Liverpool Chronicle* (April 23, 1842); *Manchester Guardian* (April 30, 1842), 1.
25. *New York Herald* (November 18, 1842).
26. *Atlas* (February 4, 1843), 78.
27. *New York Herald* (November 18, 1842), 2; Adelphi Theatre website.
28. *Theatrical Observer* (December 7, 1842), 1.
29. Broadside, Vol., G2A23 (December 26, 1842), Folger; *Theatrical Observer* (December 19, 1842), 1; *The Dramatic and Musical Review* (December 31, 1842), 488.
30. (January 28, 1843).
31. *Theatrical Journal* (January 21, 1843), 23.
32. (February 4, 1843), 78.
33. *The Theatrical Journal* (March 25, 1843), 93, (December 14, 1844), 395.
34. *John Bull* (January 21, 1843), 44.
35. *Bell's Life* (January 22, 1843), quoted in *Spirit of the Times* (March 4, 1843).
36. *Spirit of the Times* (February 25, 1843).
37. Cooke, *Reminiscences*; Thayer 2, 29; mail-archive.com/lamoreaux-l@rootsweb.com/msg0February43.html.
38. Dingess, 244.
39. Thayer 2, 29.
40. *Theatrical Observer* (December 8, 1842), 1; *The Dramatic and Musical Review* (December 10, 1842), 452.
41. *London Observer* (January 22, 23, 1843), 4; Broadside, London Theatre Museum; *Theatrical Journal* (January 21, 1843), 20.
42. *John Bull* (January 21, 1843), 44.
43. *London Times* (November 21, 1912), 9 and *The Stage*, 27, quoted in George B. Bryan, *Stage Deaths-1850-1990, Volume One* (Westport, CT: Greenwood, 1991), 225.
44. Cave, 66–67, 69–73.
45. *London Observer* (January 22, 23, 1843), 4; *Illustrated London News* (January 21, 1843), 44.
46. *John Bull* (January 21, 1843), 44.
47. *Theatrical Journal* (March 11, 1843), 75–6.
48. Broadside (March 15–17, 1843), G2E58, #350, Folger.
49. *London Times* (March 20–25, 1843), 5; *London Observer* (March 19, 1843), 1; *Atlas* (March 25, 1843), 185.
50. Robert Wood, *Victorian Delights* (London: Evans Brothers, 1967), 61; *Theatrical Journal* (May 29, 1843), 159; *Journal of Henry Steel Thrilway*, quoted by Frank Dean, *Circus Report*; *Age & Argus* (November 25, 1843), 12.
51. Broadsides (March 20 and April 6–8, 1843), G2E58, #351, 255, Folger.
52. *The Dramatic and Musical Review* (April 15, 1843), 182; *Morning Chronicle* (May 25, 1843), 2.
53. *London Times* (April 18, 1843), 5.
54. *Theatrical Journal* (April 22, 1843), 125–6.
55. *The Dramatic and Musical Review* (May 6, 1843), 219.
56. Charles Humphries, and William C. Smith, *Music Publishing in the British Isles* (London: Cassell, 1954).
57. *Atlas* (May 13, 1843), 304.
58. Broadsides (May 15–20, 1843), 389 volume two, British Library; *Morning Chronicle* (May 25, 1843), 2.
59. *Morning Chronicle* (May 25, 1843), 2.
60. Broadside (June 27, 28, 1843), Playbill, G4A231, Folger.
61. Broadside (July 13, 1843), Harvard.
62. *Edinburgh Evening Courant* (July 15, 1843), 3.
63. Letter by Richard Ward Pelham to *Hague's Minstrel and Dramatic Journal*, Liverpool, quoted in *New York Clip-*

per (August 8, 1874), 148; Playbill, Cooke's Circus, (August 9, [1843]), Circus World Museum and Library.

64. Broadsides (July 29 and August 21, 1843), Playbill, G4A23, 231, Folger.

65. *New York Herald* (August 31, 1843), quoted in *Theatrical Journal* (September 23, 1843), 303.

66. Broadside (February 6, 1844), Theatre Royal.

67. Thayer says John Aymar was killed in England, but gives his dates as 1826–1859. *New York Clipper Almanac* (1875), 42; *The Dramatic and Musical Review* (August 26, 1843), 417; Thayer, 157, 310.

68. *Aris's Birmingham Gazette* (September 25, 1843).

69. Broadside (September 25–October 4, 1843), Minstrel, SK-SW, Harvard; Broadside, (October 2–3, 1843), Folger.

70. *Boston Evening Transcript* (October 10, 1843), quoted in the *New York Herald* (October 12, 1843).

71. *Liverpool Chronicle* (February 24, 1844).

72. Broadside (October 28, 1843), Harvard.

73. *Theatrical Journal* (October 28, 1843), 343?

74. *Liverpool Chronicle* (February 10, 1844), 1.

75. *Liverpool Mail* (February 17, 1844), 2.

76. *The Era* (February 25, 1844).

77. *Liverpool Chronicle* (March 9, 1844), 4.

78. *Liverpool Journal* (March 9, 1844), 1, 5.

79. Broadside (March 25, 1844), Harvard.

80. Broadside (March 29, 1844).

81. Broadside (July 22, 1844), Playbill, G3L75ra, Folger.

82. *Liverpool Standard* (August 13, 1844).

83. *Liverpool Mail and Liverpool Journal* (July 20, 1844).

84. *Liverpool Courier* (July 31, 1844).

85. *The Albion* (August 5, 1844), 8.

86. *Liverpool Standard* (August 13, 1844).

87. *The Albion* (August 26, 1844); Broadside (August 28, 1844), Playbill, G3L75lt, Folger; *Liverpool Chronicle* (August 24, 1844).

88. Moreau, vol. 2; Sturdivant, 361; *New York Clipper* (August 8, 1874), 148.

89. *Nottingham Journal* (October 11, 1844).

90. *Theatrical Journal* (November 2, 1844), 351.

91. *Nottingham Journal* (December 20, 1844).

92. *Liverpool Chronicle* (January 11, 1845).

93. *The Albion* (January 13, 1845).

94. *Mercury* (January 17, 1845), 1; *Liverpool Journal* (January 18, 20, 1845), 5; *Liverpool Courier* (January 18, 1845).

95. *Liverpool Journal* (January 11–25, 1845); *Liverpool Courier* (January 22, 1845); *The Albion* (January 27, 1845); *The Era* (February 2, 1845).

96. *Liverpool Journal* (January 25, 1845), 5.

97. *Liverpool Journal* (January 25, 1845); *The Albion* (January 27, 1845).

98. Broadside (February 7, 1845), reprinted in Rice, 185; *Mercury* (February 7, 1845), 1.

99. Broadside (February 8, 1845), 3C40, Hertzberg.

100. Playbill, KB/UB.

101. Dianne Robinson to the author.

102. Broadsides (October 25–December 14, 1841 and May 22 and July 10, 1843 and February 19–20, 1845), Playbill, G3B53tr, Folger.

103. *Birmingham Advertiser* (April 5, 1845).

104. *New York Herald* (May 29–31 and June 1, 1845), 3; Odell, 112.

105. Leslie Banner Cottingham and Carol Lowe Timblin, *The Bard of Ottaray: The Life, Letters and Documents of Shepherd Monroe Dugger* (Banner Elk, NC: Puddingstone Press, 1979), 121–124.

106. Burke Davis, "The Swinging Sweeneys," *The Iron Worker* (XXXIII/4, autumn, 1969), 2–12.

107. Cole.

108. George Rowell, *Queen Victoria Goes to the Theatre* (London: Paul Elk, 1978), 24, 28; Wallett, 67; Pamela Clark, Deputy Registrar, Royal Archives, Windsor Castle, to Carlin (April 3, 2000).

109. Davis, 2–12.

Chapter 5

1. "First Man to Play the Bones."

2. Thayer, 309; Broadside (February 11, 1845), Free Library of Philadelphia.

3. *New York Herald* (May 29–June 1, 1845), 3; Odell, 112.

4. *Newark Daily Advertiser* (May 30–June 2, 1845), 3.

5. *Albany Eve Journal* (June 9, 1845), 2.

6. *Albany Argus* (June 10–12, 1845), 3.

7. *Republican Advocate* (June 17, 24, 1845), 4; Glenroy, 55–56.

8. *Chenango Telegraph* (August 27 and September 3, 1845), 3; *Albany Eve Atlas* (June 3–10, 1845), 3; *Albany Eve Journal* (June 3–10, 1845), 3.

9. Thayer; *Utica Daily Gazette* (July 1–4, 1845), 3, *Northern Journal* (July 3, 10, 1845), 3, *Saint Lawrence Republican* (July 22–August 5, 1845), 3.

10. *Albany Argus* (September 23–October 4, 1845), 3; *Albany Eve Journal* (September 23–October 4, 1845), 3; *Spirit of the Times* (June 10–October 30, 1845).

11. *Richmond Whig and Richmond Enquirer* (December 1–3, 1845), 2/3, quoted in Stoutamire, 152; *New York Herald* (November 11 and December 3, 1845); *Richmond Whig* (December 4, 1845), 3; *Spirit of the Times* (December 6, 1845), 488.

12. *Lynchburg Virginian* (December 11, 1845), quoted in Farrar, 39.

13. *Milton Chronicle*, quoted in *Lynchburg Virginian* (May 23, 1846), 2.

14. *Milton Chronicle*, quoted in *Lynchburg Virginian* (May 23, 1846), 2.

15. *The Rep* (September 9, 1846), 2, WPA LibVA index.

16. *Lynchburg Virginian* (July 3, 1848), 3, quoted in Farrar, 64.

17. *Nashville Republican Banner* (December 1–2, 1870), quoted in Jill L. Garrett, *Obituaries from Tennessee Newspapers* (Easley, SC: Southern Historical Press, 1980), 284.

18. "When Barnum Blacked Up"; *Lynchburg Virginian* (April 8, 1847), 3.

19. *Richmond Whig* (September 22, 1848), 2.

20. *Charleston Courier* (November 20, 1848), 2.

21. *Petersburg Republican* (September 18, 1848), 2, (September 20, 1848), 3, WPA LibVa index.

22. *Richmond Whig* (September 22, 1848), 2.

23. Circushistory.org/Cork/BurntCork3.htm, 67, quoting T. Allston Brown.

24. *Lynchburg Virginian* (October 12, 1848), 3; *Raleigh Register* (November 1, 1848), 3.

25. *Petersburg Republican* (January 26, 29, 31, 1849), 3, WPA LibVa index.

26. *Raleigh Register* (November 1, 1848), 3.

27. Dr. Kemp P. Battle, *History of the University of North Carolina*, 1 (Raleigh: Edwards and Broughton Printing Company, 1907), 596; loc.gov.

28. *Charleston Courier* (November 20–24, 1848), 2, 3; *Charleston Mercury* (November 25, 1848), 3, (November 20, 1848), 2.

29. Ludlow, *Dramatic Life as I Found It*, 645–6.

30. *Charleston Mercury* (November 23, 1848), 2.

31. *Petersburg Republican* (January 26, 29, 31, 1849), 2, 3, WPA LibVa index.
32. *Lynchburg Virginian* (March 5 and July 12, 1849), 3.
33. *Nashville Daily Gazette* (December 16, 1849), 2; *Brownlow's Knoxville Whig and Independent Journal* (November 10, 1849), 3, quoted in Emma Katherine Crews, "Early Musical Activities in Knoxville, Tennessee, 1791–1861," *The East Tennessee Historical Society's Publications* (Knoxville: ETHS, No. 32, 1960), 15–16.
34. *Nashville Daily Gazette* (December 16, 1849), 2.
35. *Brownlow's Knoxville Whig and Independent Journal* (November 10, 1849), 3, quoted in Crews, 15–16; *Knoxville Register* (November 14, 1849), 2.
36. *Nashville Daily Union* (December 18, 1849), 2.
37. *Brownlow's Knoxville Whig and Independent Journal* (November 10, 1849), 3, quoted in Crews, 15–16.
38. *Nashville Daily Gazette* (December 16, 1849), 2.
39. *Lynchburg Virginian* (May 26, 1857), 2, 3.
40. Farrar.
41. Census, 1850
42. *Richmond Whig* (February 14, 18, 1851), 3; Broadside (February 17, 18, 1851), Valentine Museum.
43. Broadside (January 20 and February 14, 1851), Valentine Museum; Brown (April 27, 1912).
44. Harry Wooding, *Danville History*, mss, (1926–7).
45. *Daily Comet* (December 28–29, 1852), 2, quoted in Varnado, 17.
46. *Lynchburg Daily Virginian* (January 14, 1853), 3.
47. *Evening Star* (August 16–18, 1854), 2.
48. *Baltimore Sun* (August 24–26, 1854), 3, quoted in May.
49. *Daily Southside Democrat* (August 19, 1854), 2, WPA LibVA index.
50. *Lynchburg Virginian* (November 9–11, 13–15, 17, 19–22, 1855), 2.
51. *Lynchburg Virginian* (January 20–February 14, 16, 18, 20 and March 20–31 and April 1 and June 14–17, 19–20, 1854), 2; *Daily Southside Democrat* (April 8 and June 3 and September 4, 8 and October 18, 1854), 2, WPA LibVA index.
52. *Western Democrat, NC Whig* (April 12, 1857), 3.
53. Rice, 94.
54. *Edgefield Advertiser* (March 11, 1857), 2.
55. *Carolina Watchman* (April 21, 1857), 3.
56. *Lynchburg Virginian* (May 20–22, 26, 1857), 2, 3.
57. *Richmond Enquirer* (May 23–June 6, 1857), 3; *Richmond Dispatch* (May 23–June 6, 1857), 1, 2.
58. *Richmond Dispatch* (June 1, 1857), 1–2.
59. *Richmond Enquirer* (June 2, 1857), 2, 3.
60. Circushistory.org/Cork/BurntCork4.htm, quoting Brown, T. Allson.
61. Rice, 68; *Lynchburg Tri-Weekly Virginian* (November 4, 1857), 2
62. *Richmond Whig* (October 9, 1857), 3; *Daily Express* (October 9, 1857), 3; *Daily Southside Democrat* (October 10, 1857), 2, WPA LibVa index.
63. *Lynchburg Tri-Weekly Virginian* (November 4, 6, 1857), 2.
64. *Daily Atlanta Intelligencer* (December 16, 1857), quoted in Peg Gough, "On Stage in Atlanta, 1860–1870," *Atlanta Historical Bulletin* (XXI, 2, Summer, 1977), 49.
65. *Daily Sun* (December 29, 1857–January 1, 1858), 3, quoted in Langley, 203.
66. Letter to *Richmond Dispatch* (February 17, 1895), 1.
67. *Pennsylvania Daily Telegraph* (February 27, 1862), quoted in Baines, 293.
68. *North American and Unites States Gazette* (March 8, 1860), quoted in Baines, 292.
69. *Fredericksburg Weekly Advertiser* (November 20, 1858).

70. *Southern Argus* (December 22–24, 1858), 2/3.
71. *Washington Evening Star* (November 20–24, 27, 1858), 2; *New York Clipper* (December 11, 1858), 270.
72. *National Intelligencer* (November 27, 1858), 3.
73. *Southern Argus* (December 20–24, 1858), 2, 3.
74. *The Press* (December 28–31, 1858), 1, 2, WPA LibVa index.
75. *Baltimore Sun* (January 11–15, 1859), 2, 3.
76. *Washington Evening Star* (January 18–22, 24–27, 1859), 1–3; *National Intelligencer* (January 26, 1859); Collins.
77. George Wunderlich to the author (November 8, 2003).
78. Appomattox Co Death Records, 141, line 3.
79. *Evening Star* (February 14, 1859), 2.
80. Dr. George W. Bagby, "Fishing In The Appomattox," *Selections from the Miscellaneous Writings*, 1 (Richmond, VA: Whittet & Shepperson, 1884), 250, 257, 259.
81. *Daily Express* (November 5, 1859), 1, WPA LibVa index.
82. Bagby, 250, 257, 259.
83. Death Records, Appomattox Co, #131, Jones Lib.
84. Census.
85. George Wunderlich to author (November 10, 2003).
86. Appomattox Death Records, 1860, original Jones Library, quoted by Department of Health, Commonwealth of Virginia, Bureau of Vital Records and Health Statistics, Richmond, 155, Line 132.

Chapter 6

1. *Baltimore American* (May 26, 1841), 3.
2. *New York Courier*, quoted in Broadside, Harvard/Minstrel/Playbills/Virginia Minstrels (March 22, 1843).
3. Unidentified clipping, Harry Ransom Center, University of Texas.
4. Longsworth, *New York City Directory* (1835); Edw. LeRoy Rice, *Monarchs of Minstrelsy: From Daddy Rice to the Present* (New York: Kenny, 1911), 12.
5. *New York Clipper* (December 13, 1878), 21 and (January 17, 1912).
6. *New York Morning Herald* (January 18, 1840).
7. *New York Herald* (April 7, 8, 1840); *Providence Journal* (April 16–18, 20, 1840), 3; *Spirit of the Times* (April 18, 1840), 84.
8. *Providence Journal* (April 18, 20, 1840), 3; *Spirit of the Times* (April 18, 1840), 84.
9. *New York Herald* (May 9, 25–30, 1840); Broadside (June 22, 1840), McAllister Scrapbooks, Playbills, Vol. 24, 34, Library Company of Philadelphia; *Boston Post* (June 3–6, 10, 1840); *Boston Semi-Weekly Courier*; Odell IV, 396.
10. *Boston Post* (June 4, 1840); *Boston Semi-Weekly Courier* (June 8, 1840).
11. National Theatre, Boston, playbill (June 5, 1840), Harvard, Diamond file, quoted in Nathan, 115; Broadside, Harvard, Playbills, Warren Theatre (1840–43), Boston Theatres.
12. Odell IV, 391.
13. Saxon, 81.
14. *Philadelphia Inquirer* (October 9, 1880).
15. *New York Herald* (September 12–23, 1840), 1, 3.
16. *New York Herald* (November 29–December 11, 1841 and January 20–21, 25–26–30–31 and February 1–4, 1842), 2–4; *New York Sun* (January 24, 1842); *New York Post* (January 24–25, 1842), 2, (January 24, 26, 29, 1842), 3; "Negro Minstrelsy.... Charley White's Recollections," clipping, Harvard.

17. *Odell IV*, 584; *New York Herald* (May 22–June 4, 1842).

18. *New York Herald* (June 4, 1842).

19. Dingess, 104.

20. *New York Morning Courier* (January 11, 1840), 2; *New York Herald* (January 11, 1840), 3.

21. Brown, "Early History of Negro Minstrelsy," (February 24, 1912).

22. *Tattler* (February 13–14, 1840).

23. Unidentified clipping, HRC-UT; Rice, 23.

24. Unidentified clipping, HRC-UT; Dingess, 99–100.

25. Broadside, Philadelphia; *Spirit of the Times* (April 27–May 2, 1840), 3, (May 4–7, 1840), 2.

26. *Southwest Virginian* (August 1, 1840), 3.

27. "Letter from C.J. Rodgers, Philadelphia, *New York Clipper* (June 20, 1874), 95, quoted in Nathan, 111.

28. John Edmund Stealey III, "Slavery and the Western Virginia Salt Industry," *The Journal of Negro History* 59 (April, 1974), 105–131.

29. *Lexington Observer* (September 19, 1840), 1.

30. Nathan, 111.

31. *Louisville Journal* (September 10–29 and October 1–16, 1840), 2, 3.

32. *Louisville Public Advertiser* (October 10, 1840), 3; *Louisville Journal* (October 10, 1840), 2.

33. Broadside (October 12, 1840); *Louisville Journal* (October 12, 1840), 2.

34. Thayer.

35. *New York Clipper* (June 20, 1874).

36. *Cincinnati Enquirer* (April 10–May 15, 1841).

37. Broadside, Harvard Theatre Collection; *Cincinnati Times* (April 22–23, 1841), 3; *Cincinnati Enquirer* (April 22–May 1, 1841), 3.

38. Broadside, Harvard Theatre Collection.

39. Nathan, 111.

40. Nathan, 359–60.

41. Nathan, 104.

42. N.N. Hill, *History of Knox County* (Mount Vernon: 1881), 806, quoted in Nathan, 98–99.

43. Nathan, 104–108.

44. White, "Old Time Minstrels"; Moreau, "Negro Minstrelsy," quoted in Nathan, 109.

45. McClane, "Daniel Decatur Emmett," quoted in Howard L. and Judith Rose Sacks, *Way Up North in Dixie* (Washington and London: Smithsonian Institution Press, 1993), 168.

46. Nathan, 111.

47. Broadside (July 7–10, 1841).

48. Thayer 2.

49. Broadside (July 7–10, 1841).

50. Broadside (October 12, 1840).

51. Broadside (October 12, 1840).

52. *Daily Georgian* (October 16, 18–23, 25, 1841), 3; *Savannah Republican* (January 12–18, 1841), 3; Thayer 2, 276.

53. *Charleston Courier* (January 17–18, 24–25, 28–February 1, 1842), 3, (January 19, 1842).

54. Thayer 2, 244.

55. *Philadelphia Chronicle* (October 10–November 5, 8–11, 14–19, 1842), 3; *Pennsylvania Inquirer and National Gazette* (October 10–13 and November 3–11, 1842), 3; *Philadelphia Public Ledger* (October 12–November 2, 1842), 3.

56. *New York Herald* (November 28–December 5, 1842), 3; "Negro Minstrelsy," (August 30, 1885), Minstrel clippings, Harvard.

57. *New York Herald* (December 18, 1842–January 10, 1843), 2, 3; *New York Clipper* (November 10, 1877), quoted in *Annals of the American Circus*, 281; *Evening Post* (January-

ary 13, 1843), *Evening Post and New York Herald* (December, 1842), quoted in Nathan, 114.

58. *New York Herald* (December 21, 1842), quoted in Cockrell, 149.

59. *New York Herald* (January 13, 1843), 3; *Evening Post* (January 13, 1843), quoted in Nathan, 114.

60. *New York Herald* (January 14, 16, 19–20, 27, 1843), 3; Ireland, Harvard Theatre Collection; *New York Sporting Whip* (January 28, 1843).

61. (Boston: C.H. Keith, 1843).

62. Broadside (January 31, 1843), quoted in Frank Dumont, "The Golden Days of Minstrelsy. The Musings of An Old Timer," *The New York Clipper* (December, 1914); *New York Clipper* (April 13, 1878); *Odell IV*, 674.

63. *New York Herald* (February 1, 1843).

64. *New York Sporting Whip* (February 4, 1843).

65. *New York Herald* (February 6–11, 1843); Broadside (February 6–11, 1843), quoted by Dumont; Nathan, 118.

66. Brown 1, 413; *New York Herald* (February 16, 1843); *New York Sporting Whip* (February 18, 1843).

67. *New York Herald* (February 17–March 1, 1843).

68. *New York Herald* (February 23, 26, 1843); *New York Sporting Whip* (March 4, 1843).

69. *New York Herald* (March 1, 1843), quoted in Nathan, 108–9.

70. *New York Sporting Whip* (March 4, 1843).

71. *New York Courier*, quoted in Broadside (March 20–22, 1843), Harvard, Minstrel, Playbills, Virginia Minstrels.

72. Rice, 19, 43; *Buffalo Morning Express* (January 15, 1846), quoted in Nathan, 144; "The Origin of the Christy's Minstrels," *The Theatre* (March 1, 1882), 129–134; *New York Evening Post* (November 20, 1841), 3; Thayer 2, 278, 281.

73. Vertical File, Welch, Rufus, Hertzberg; *New York Herald* (January 25–February 23, 1843); *New York Sun* (February 4, 1843); Ireland, Harvard.

74. *New York Sporting Whip* (February 25 and March 4, 1843).

75. *New York Herald* (February 27–March 17, 1843).

76. Ireland 2, 9, Harvard.

77. *Odell IV*, 643; *New York Herald* (March 10–11, 1843).

78. *New York Herald* (March 17, 1843).

79. *Boston Post* (March 14, 1843); playbills and *Evening Transcript*, both quoted in Nathan, 121.

80. Broadsides (March 25, 27, 28–April 1, 1843), Minstrel Playbills, Kentucky Minstrels, Warren Theater, Harvard.

81. Broadside (March 17, 28–April 1, 1843), Playbills, Warren Theater, Harvard.

82. *Lowell Courier* (April 8–15, 1843); Broadside (April 28, 1843), Playbills, Warren Theater, Harvard; *Boston Post* (May 2, 1843).

83. *Emmit's Celebrated Negro Melodies* (London: D'Almaine & Co, nd).

84. *Boston Post* (March 14, 1843).

85. *Boston Semi-Weekly Courier* (March 16, 1843).

86. Broadside (March 20–22, 1843) Minstrel, Playbills, Virginia Minstrels, Harvard.

87. *Lowell Courier* (March 30, 1843).

88. Quoted in *Lowell Courier* (April 1, 1843).

89. Broadside (March 20–22, 1843), Minstrel, Playbills, Virginia Minstrels, Harvard.

90. *New York Clipper* (May 19, 1877), quoted in Nathan, 119.

91. *Boston Post* (March 14, 1843); Thayer 2, 281, 311.

92. Broadside (March 23–29, 1843), playbills, Minstrel Playbills, Virginia Minstrels, Harvard, quoted in Nathan, 121.

93. Broadsides (March 29 and April 3–5, 1843); *Evening Transcript*, both quoted in Nathan, 121.

94. (Boston: C.H. Keith, 1843).
95. *New York Clipper* (November 4, 1876 and May 19, 1877), quoted in Nathan, 122; Odell IV, 618; Day, 7; Letter from Richard Ward Pelham, *Hague's Minstrel and Dramatic Journal*, quoted in *New York Clipper* (August 8, 1874), 148.
96. Reynolds, 83; *New York Clipper* (August 8, 1874), 148.
97. *Liverpool Courier* (May 24, 1843), 1; *Mercury* (May 26, 1843), 8.
98. *Liverpool Mail* (May 27, 1843).
99. *The Era* (June 4, 1843); *Liverpool Chronicle* (June 3, 1843); *Liverpool Mail* (May 27, 1843); *Mercury* (May 26 and June 2, 1843), 1, 8.
100. *Manchester Times* (June 10, 1843), 4; *Manchester Guardian* (June 3, 1843), 1; *New York Clipper*, (August 8, 1874), 148.
101. *Manchester Guardian* (June 3, 1843), 1.
102. *Manchester Times* (June 10, 1843), 4.
103. *Manchester and Salford Advertiser and Chronicle* (June 10, 1843), 4.
104. *Manchester Times* (June 10, 1843), 4.
105. Knowlson; *New York Clipper* (August 8, 1874), 148; Brown (February 24, 1912).
106. Broadside, reprinted possibly *New York Clipper*, partial inserted in S.S. Sandford autobiography, October, UT, quoted in Brown (February 24, 1912).
107. *Theatrical Journal* (April 15, 1843), 120; Adelphi Theatre Website; Westervelt Scrapbook, Barnum, Vol. IV, item 5, New York Historical Society; *New York Clipper* (August 8, 1874), 148.
108. *The Dramatic and Musical Review* (June 24, 1843), 306; *Age* (July 2, 1843), 7.
109. *London Times* (June 24–30, 1843), 4, (July 1–14, 1843), 5; *Morning Chronicle* (June 30, 1843); *Morning Post* (June 27, 1843); *London Observer* (June 25 and July 9, 12, 1843), 1; *Atlas* (June 24, 1843), 408, (July 1, 1843), 428, (January 14–May 27 and June 10–July 15 and October 21–November 4, 1843 and April 6–27, 1844); *John Bull* (June 24 and July 2, 8, 1843), 1; *Age* (July 2, 12, 1843), 1.
110. *Theatrical Journal* (July 1, 1843), 204; *Era* (June 25, 1843), quoted in Reynolds, 84.
111. *Atlas* (June 24, 1843), 400.
112. *The Dramatic and Musical Review* (June 24, 1843), 306.
113. Clipping, uncredited, "Adelphi" ("June, 1843") handwritten, London Theatre Museum; *London Examiner* (July 1, 1843).
114. June 19, 1843, Broadside, reprinted possibly *New York Clipper*, partial inserted in S.S. Sandford autobiography, October, UT, quoted by Brown (February 24, 1912).
115. *New York Clipper* (May 19, 1877); *London Times* (June 17–23, 1843), 5; *Morning Chronicle* (June 19, 23, 1843), 4; *Atlas* (June 17, 1843), 392; *London Observer* (June 18, 1843), 1; *The Era* (June 18, 1843).
116. *New York Herald* (September 14–15, 1843); Brown 1, 173; *Odell V*.
117. *Odell V*, 29–30.
118. Broadside (August 28–September 2, 1843), Harvard.
119. Broadsides (September 11–13, 15–16, 1843), Playbills, 389, British Library.
120. *New York Clipper* (August 8, 1874), 148.
121. Broadside (October 17 and November 6–11, 1843), Harvard.
122. *Theatrical Journal* (November 18, 1843), 365.
123. Broadside (November 13, 1843), Finsbury Library.
124. Broadside (October 17, 1843), Harvard.
125. Broadside (November 13, 1843), Finsbury Library.
126. *Theatrical Journal* (November 11, 1843), 356.

127. (Boston: C.H. Keith, 1843).
128. *New York Clipper* (August 8, 1874 and May 19, 1877), quoted in Nathan, 140.
129. *The Era* (August 20, 1843).
130. Broadside, author's collection; Broadside (October 21–23, 1843), playbill, Virginia Minstrels, Harvard, quoted in Nathan, 139.
131. *Freeman's Journal* (April 25, 1844), 2.
132. Broadside (May 7, 1844), G6D85tr, Folger; *Freeman's Journal* (May 7, 1844), 1.
133. Letter, Dave Moran to the author, May 5, 2005; sheet music published by Cramer, Beale and Co., London, author's collection.
134. *New York Clipper*, quoted by Collins in *Fretts*.
135. *Northern Whig* (May 6, 1844).
136. *Freeman's Journal* (April 24, 1844), 1; Broadside, Harvard.
137. *Northern Whig* (May 16, 1844).
138. *Belfast News Letter* (May 16, 1844).
139. *Northern Whig* (May 16, 1844).
140. For example, Broadside (May 20, 29, 1844), playbill, Mitchell Lib; Broadside (May 31, 1844), reprinted in *New York Clipper* (December 13, 1873), 293, inserted in S.S. Sanford, quoted in Nathan.
141. Broadside (May 31, 1844), reprinted in *New York Clipper* (December 13, 1873), 293, inserted in S. S. Sanford, quoted in Nathan.
142. Nathan, 301–303; *Edinburgh Evening Post* (June 12, 1844).
143. *Edinburgh Evening Post* (June 8, 12, 1844).
144. *Glasgow Argus* (June 20, 1844), 2, 3.
145. Broadside (June 15, 1844), reprinted in *New York Clipper* (January 10, 1874), 325; Broadside (October 23, 1844), *New York Clipper* (May 19, 1877), quoted in Nathan, 291–2.
146. *Glasgow Argus* (June 20, 1844), 2, 3.
147. *Northern Whig* (May 18, 1844).
148. *Odell V*, 229.
149. *Newcastle Journal* (November 2–6, 1844).
150. Brown, *Volume One*, 361–2; *Monarchs*, 35.
151. *Monarchs*, 60.
152. Broadside (September 23, 1850 and November 7, 1852), Harvard, minstrel, Playbills, Charley White/Serenaders; *Odell, V and VI*.
153. *New York Herald*, quoted in Odell, V; *Odell, VI*.
154. *Odell, V*.
155. *Monarchs*, 38.
156. *Monarchs*, 39.
157. *Monarchs*, 43.
158. *Monarchs*, 39.
159. *Monarchs*, 19; *Odell, V*; *New York Daily Tribune* (January 17, 1848), 3.
160. *Monarchs*, 19.
161. *Raleigh Register* (January 21, 1857), 3.
162. Brown, *Volume One*, 174; *New York Herald* (April 13, 1850), quoted in Odell, V.
163. Brown, *Volume One*, 468.
164. Broadside (March 4, 8, 1852), Harvard, minstrel, playbills, Wood's; *Odell, VI*.
165. *Odell, VI*.
166. *Monarchs*, 20.
167. Moody, 45.
168. Brown, *Volume One*, 410, 468.
169. Howard L. and Judith Rose Sacks, *Way Up North in Dixie* (Washington, D.C.: Smithsonian Institution, 1993), 3; Nathan; *Odell, VI*; Brown, *Volume One*, 365.
170. Jimmy Dalton Baines, *Samuel S. Sanford and Negro Minstrelsy* (PhD Dissertation, Tulane University, 1967), 151, 215; *Monarchs*, 34.

171. Baines, 139–144.
172. *Philadelphia Public Ledger* (November 15, 1855 and September 12, 1859), quoted in Baines; *New York Clipper* (February 26, 1859), 359.
173. Baines, 163.
174. *Philadelphia Public Ledger* (February 21–27, 1859), quoted in Baines, 199–200.
175. *Philadelphia Public Ledger* (January 25, 1859), quoted in Baines, 198.
176. *Philadelphia Public Ledger* (November 1, 1855 and March 17, 1856), quoted in
Baines, 152–3, 163, 167.

Chapter 7

1. "Comic Song, Sung By Christian Jones, written by J. Frazer, music arranged by Louis Emanuel (London: T.E. Purday), nd, Mander-Mitcheson.
2. Playbill (June 3–8, 1844), Strand Theatre, London Theatre Museum.
3. *Lincoln Standard* (February 7, 1844).
4. *The Era* (January 5, 1845); *The Theatrical Journal* (January 11, 1845), 12.
5. Michael Pickering, "White Skin, Black Masks: Nigger Minstrelsy in Victorian England," *Music Hall Performance and Style* (Milton Keynes and Philadelphia: Open University Press, 1986), 72–3, quoted in J. S. Bratton, "English Ethiopians," *Yearbook of English Studies* (Leeds: W.S. Maney and Son, vol. 11, 1981).
6. Mayhew, *Volume III*, 190–4.
7. Playbills (November 17–22, 1845), G2G81, Folger.
8. *Monarchs*, 48.
9. *Monarchs*, 31.
10. *Monarchs*, 26.
11. *Monarchs*, 24.
12. *Monarchs*, 24.
13. *New York Post* (September 25, 1840).
14. *Odell IV*, 646.
15. *Richmond Whig* (November 2, 1843), quoted in *Music of the Old South*, 149.
16. *Richmond Whig* (March 26, 1844), quoted in *Music of the Old South*, 149.
17. *Odell V*; Brown, Volume One, 339.
18. *Odell V*.
19. (September 9, 1843).
20. *Odell V*.
21. *New York Herald* (September 4–9, 1843).
22. *Spirit of the Times* (circa November 16, 1847), quoted in *Odell V*.
23. *Liverpool Chronicle* (October 3, 10, 1846); Sarah Meer, "The Serenaders and Ethnic Exhibition," *Liberating Sojourn* (Athens: University of Georgia, 1999), 146.
24. "Early Nigger Minstrel Acts in Britain," 121–2.
25. *Brighton Herald* (August 8, 15, 1846); *Liverpool Chronicle* (October 3, 10, 1846); *Liverpool Chronicle* (October 10, 1846); Broadside (November10, 1846), NLI, Microfilm #P4041, 39; *Brighton Herald* (December 5, 1846); R. J. Broadbent, *Annals of the Liverpool Stage* (New York/London: Benjamin Blom, August 19, 1969), 214; *The Old Marylebone Theatre*; *Odell V*.
26. Scott, Derek, 87.
27. Robert B. Winans and Elias J. Kaufman, "Minstrel and Classic Banjo: American and English Connections," *American Music* (12, no 1, spring, 1994), 6.
28. *The Old Marylebone Theatre*, 21.
29. *Liverpool Chronicle* (June 27 and July 4, 1846).
30. *Brighton Herald* (May16, 23, 30, 1846).

31. Playbills (August 25–28, 1847) 360, British Library.
32. *Liverpool Chronicle* (June 27 and July 4, 1846); *Liverpool Mail* (July 4,1846).
33. *Liverpool Courier* (July 1, 1846).
34. Playbills (August 4–5, 1846), 334, British Library; Broadside, 48, 49, NLI, Microfilm #P4041.
35. *Bristol Mercury* (circa July12–13, 1847).
36. *Nottingham Mercury* (November 6, 1846).
37. Playbill (January 4–5, 1847), G3N87tr, Folger.
38. Broadside (November 9 and December 7–19, 1847), NLI, Microfilm #P4041, 46.
39. *The Old Marylebone Theatre*, 21.
40. Playbills (May 11, 13, 21, 1847), 327, volume two, British Library.
41. Playbill (May14, 1847), G2A23, #52, 53, Folger; Playbills (July19, 21, 1847), 327, volume two, British Library.
42. http://www.ukbanjo.com/bjop2.htm.
43. *Monarchs*, 58.
44. *Monarchs*, 51.
45. Broadside (February 16–17 and March 14, 1849), NLI, Microfilm #P4041, 52.
46. (July 23–August 11, 1849), Al Fostell Collection, Paul Melzer Rare Books, eBay, May 6, 2002.
47. Brown, (February 2, 1912).
48. Broadside (July 25, 1849), NLI, Microfilm #P4041, 58.
49. Broadside (September 1, 1849), Szego collection.
50. *Monarchs*, 46; *Alta California* (October 25, 1854), also *The Wild West*, October 29, 1854, CA State Lib.
51. Unidentified clipping, HRC-UT; Brown (February 2, 1912).
52. *Odell V*; Brown, Volume One, 423.
53. *Odell V*.
54. *New York Herald* (February 12, 1842), 2, 3.
55. *American Notes*, 138–9.
56. Playbill (August 3, 1842), republished in the *New York Clipper* (June 13, 1874), quoted in Nathan, 67.
57. *New York Sporting Whip* (January 28, 1843).
58. *Odell V*; Brown, Volume One, 236.
59. Brown, Volume One, 361–2.
60. *Monarchs*, 34.
61. Sanford, 31, quoted in Baines, 31.
62. Sanford, 36, quoted in Baines, 33.
63. Sanford, quoted in Baines, 34–37, 40.
64. Baines, 37–8.
65. Sanford, 43, 44, 46, quoted in Baines, 43, 44.
66. Broadside (March 11, 1845, 1847), NLI, Microfilm #P4041, 27, 46.
67. Broadside (July 16, 1847), *Victorian Delights*, plate 148, 120.
68. *The Globe* (March 8, 1847), quoted in Baines, 51.
69. Brown, Volume One, 124; fmi, see Baines, 31–63, mostly quoting Sanford.
70. (Boston: C. H. Keith, 1843).
71. Mayhew, Henry, *London Labour and the London Poor, Volume I* (New York: Dover, 1968), 221.
72. Mayhew, *Volume III*, 51.
73. Mayhew, *Volume III*, 119.
74. Mayhew, *Volume III*, 191–4.
75. Mayhew, *Volume III*, 191–4.

Chapter 8

1. Katharine Brisbane, editor, *Entertaining Australia* (Sydney: Currency, 1991), 12.
2. Buffalo Gals, sheet music (New York: William Hall & Son, 1848), loc.gov.

3. nugrape.net/banjo.htm.

4. *Sydney Morning Herald* (October 7, 1850); *Bell's Life in Sydney* (March 30, April 6, 1850).

5. *Sydney Morning Herald* (January 27, 1851), 1.

6. *Melbourne Daily News* (July 12, 13, 1850), 3; *Melbourne Daily News* (July 16, 1850), 3; *Geelong Advertiser* (July 20, 1850), 3; *Melbourne Daily News* (August 6, 1850), 3; *Melbourne Daily News* (August 12, 1850), 3; *Sidney Morning Herald* (October 9, 1850), 1; *Sydney Morning Herald* (January 27, 1851), 1, quoted in John Whiteoak, *Playing Ad Lib: Improvisatory Music in Australia 1836-1970* (Sydney: Currency, 1999), 105.

7. (July 17, 1850), 2, quoted in *Playing Ad Lib*, 104.

8. *Launceston Examiner* (July 27, 1850), 474.

9. levysheetmusic.mse.jhu.edu.

10. Nathan, 324, 461.

11. levysheetmusic.mse.jhu.edu

12. levysheetmusic.mse.jhu.edu

13. levysheetmusic.mse.jhu.edu

14. (July 10, 1850), 2, quoted in *Playing Ad Lib*, 104.

15. *Melbourne Daily News* (August 12, 1850), 3; *Melbourne Daily News* (August 15, 1850), 3.

16. levysheetmusic.mse.jhu.edu.

17. levysheetmusic.mse.jhu.edu.

18. levysheetmusic.mse.jhu.edu.

19. *Cornwall Chronicle* (September 18, 1850), 614, (September 21, 1850), 623, (October 3, 1850), 654, (October 17, 1850), (October 22, 1850), 723, (November 5, 1850), 772; *Launceston Examiner* (September 21, 1850), 611, (September 11, 1850), 582, (September 14, 1850), 586, (September 21, 1850), 611, (October 23, 1850), 678, (November 9, 1850), 726.

20. *Launceston Examiner* (September 28, 1850), 627, (October 23, 1850), 678.

21. *Sydney Morning Herald* (December 9, 17, 1851), 1.

22. *Playing Ad Lib*, 105.

23. *Sydney Morning Herald* (February 17, March 19, 1851), 1.

24. loc.gov.

25. *Sydney Morning Herald* (June 21, July 11, 14, 23, 25, 1851), 1.

26. levysheetmusic.mse.jhu.edu; Helene Wickham Koon, *Gold Rush Performers* (Jefferson: McFarland, 1994), 176; *Bell's Life in Sydney* (June 28, 1851), 36; E. Daniel and Annette Potts, *Young America And Australian Gold* (St. Lucia: University of Queensland, 1974), 152; *Sydney Morning Herald* (September 26, October 1, 8, 10, 15, 17, 22, 1851), 1; *Bell's Life in Sydney* (November 26, 1853), 3.

27. nla.gov.au.

29. *Sydney Morning Herald* (June 21, 1853), quoted in E. Daniel and Annette Potts, 152; *Melbourne Argus* (November 1, December 4, 6, 8, 16, 1852); Melbourne Bell, 48–9; Wittke, *Tambo And Bones*, 103; *Entertaining Australia*, 47.

30. *Playing Ad Lib*, 106.

31. *Monarchs*, 30–31; *Sydney Morning Herald* (February 23, 26, 1851, February 26, March 1, 4, 8, 1852), 1.

32. *Playing Ad Lib*, 106.

33. *Bell's Life in Victoria* (December 29, 1866, January 5, 1867); *Clipper* (June 8, 1912).

34. *Monarchs*, 73–4.

35. *Sydney Morning Herald* (December 30, 1863, January 4, 1864), 1.

36. *Monarchs*, 122.

37. *Richard Waterhouse, from Minstrel Show to Vaudeville* (New South Wales University Press, 1990), 23.

38. *Emerson's Age* (August 4, 1873), 2.

39. *Sydney Morning Herald* (December 16, 1876–January 6, 1877), 2; *Evening News* (December 28, 1876), 2.

40. *New York Clipper* (January 6, 13,1877), *Sydney Morning Herald* (December 28, 1876), *Illustrated Sydney News* (January 6, 1877), *Australasian* (January 24, April 14, 1877), quoted in Waterhouse, 64.

41. *The Argus* (July 9, 10, 1877), 8.

42. *Sydney Morning Herald* (December 21, 1877), 2.

43. Death certificate.

44. *L'entre'acte'* (January 15, 19, April 24, 27, 1878), 1; *Sydney Morning Herald* (December 21, 24, 1877), 2, 5; *The Argus* (November 24, 1877); *The Lorgnette* (September 11, 1877), 2.

45. *The Lorgnette* (August 7, 18, 1882), 2.

46. *L'entr'arte* (February 15, 1887), 20, 39.

47. *Lorgnette* (February, 1889), 1; Waterhouse, 88, 93.

48. Garry Shearston, "Bessy Campbell, Australia's Queen Of Banjo," *In Tradition* 3, 3, (October 1966), 3, quoted in *Playing Ad Lib*, 108.

49. Obituary, *Sydney Mail* (July 1, 1899); John Whiteoak, "Banjo," *Currency Companion to Music and Dance in Australia* (Strawberry Hills, New South Wales: Currency House, 2003), 82.

50. Tivoli Theatre Program (April 12, 1904), quoted in *Playing Ad Lib*, 108, and reproduced, along with a catalogue containing the reference to "Dreams Of Darkie Land," in Mike Tucker, 7.

51. "Banjo," *Currency Companion to Music And Dance in Australia*, 82–83.

Chapter 9

1. J.B. Howe, *A Cosmopolitan Actor* (London: Bedford, 1888), 92–93.

2. *New York Clipper* (February 12, 1859), quoted in *Tambo and Bones*, 59–60.

3. Rice, 19, 43; *Buffalo Morning Express* (January 15, 1846), quoted in Nathan, 144; "The Origin of the Christy's Minstrels," *The Theatre* (March 1, 1882), 129–134; *New York Eve Post* (November 20, 1841), 3; Thayer 2, 278, 281.

4. Nick Tosches, *Where Dead Voices Gather* (Boston: Little, Brown, 2001), 17–18.

5. *New York Herald* (December 3, 1843).

6. *New York Herald* (November 30, 1843); Playbill (December 16, 1843), New York Historical Society; Nathan, 143.

7. Bailey, 323–4; Toulmin, 429.

8. *Monarchs*, 20.

9. Wyoline Hester, *The Savannah Stage* (Thesis, 1930, Auburn U, Aub-the-H5885); Arnold.

10. *Monarchs*, 39.

11. *Monarchs*, 39.

12. Varnado, 18; *Sentinel*, quoted in Oran Teague, *Professional Theatre in Rural Louisiana* (Thesis, LSU, 378.76-L930–1952).

13. *Daily Southside Democrat* (January 24, 1856, January 9, 1857), 2; *Daily Express* (January 25, 1856, January October, 1857), 3.

14. *Monarchs*, 43.

15. *Vicksburg Daily Whig* (September 23, 1856), quoted in Keeton, 158.

16. Toulmin, 664.

17. *Mississippi Daily Free Trader* (February 23, 1859), quoted in Keeton, 158; *Petersburg Daily Express* (March 15, 1859), 2.

18. Broadside (June 17, 1843), Minstrel Playbills, Minstrels G, Harvard.

19. *Odell V*.

20. *Daily True Delta* (November 21, 1849); Ferguson, 18; Keeton, 258; *Tri-Weekly Sentinel* (January 17, 1850), 2.

21. *Savannah Republican* (October 20–21, 25, 27, 1847), 2, 3.

22. *Petersburg Republican* (January 26, 29, 31, 1849), 2, 3.

23. *New Orleans Picayune* (December 13, 1848–January 13, 1849), 2, 3; *Crescent* (December 18, 1848–January 13, 1849), 3, 4.

24. *Matt Peel's Banjo* (New York City, 1858); *New York Clipper Annual* (1884), 8.

25. *Matt Peel's Banjo*, 7.

26. *Monarchs*, 42.

27. *Monarchs*, 52.

28. *Matt Peel's Banjo*, 8; *Monarchs*, 75.

29. Brown, *Volume One*, 365; *Monarchs*, 59.

30. Charles C. Moreau, Scrapbook *Negro Minstrelsy in New York, Volume I*, Harvard.

31. *Monarchs*, 58–9; *Odell V*.

32. Mahar, 159, Playbills, Harvard; email (April 15, 1999).

33. *New York Clipper Almanac* (1875), 42.

34. *Savannah Stage*; William Osler Langley, *Theatre in Columbus, GA, 1828–1878* (Thesis, AL Polytechnic [now Auburn], 1937), 203; Arnold; Katherine Hines Mahan, *Showboats to Soft Shoes* (Columbus, GA, 1968); *Baton Rouge Gazette* (January 10, 1852), quoted in Varnado, 16; *Tri-Weekly Sentinel* (January 24, 1852), quoted in Keeton, 157.

35. *Enquirer* (December 13, 1853), quoted in Langley, 203, 56.

36. *Savannah Stage*; *Mississippi Free Trader* (December 9, 1855), quoted in Keeton, 157–8.

37. *Monarchs*, 59.

38. *Chronicle and Sentinel* (December 14–16, 1857), 3; Garvin, as previous; Toulmin, 675–6; *Savannah Stage*; Langley, 203; *Daily South Carolinian* (November 18, 1857), 3; *Natchez Daily Democrat* (November 11, 1859), quoted in Ben E. Bailey, "The Minstrel Show in Mississippi" (*The Journal of Mississippi History*, LVII, 2, Summer, 1995), 146.

39. *One Man in His Time*, 115.

40. *Comet* (December 26, 1852), 2.

41. *Richmond Daily Dispatch* (January 2, 1854) and *Philadelphia Public Ledger* (January 4, 1854), quoted in Baines, 128; *Richmond Daily Dispatch* (February 6, 1854), quoted in Baines, 129.

42. *Lynchburg Virginian* (January 4–14, 16, 20–22, 24–26, 28, 31, February 2–4, 1854), 2.

43. *New York Clipper Annual* (1884), 8.

44. *Monarchs*, 50.

45. *Monarchs*, 52; *Richmond Daily Dispatch* (February 6, 1854), quoted in Baines, December6.

46. Arnold; *Richmond Whig* (December 18, 22, 1857), 3.

47. Rice, 39.

48. *Richmond Whig* (September 9, 1853), 2.

49. *Spirit of the Times* (September 9, 1854), 360.

50. *National Intelligencer* (August 21, 1854), 3; *Daily Union* (August 29, September 2, 7, 1854), 3; *Evening Star* (August 24, September 1, 1854), 2; *Spirit of the Times* (September 9, 1854), 360; *Richmond Whig* (September 5, 8, 1854), 2, (September 12, 1854), 3; *Richmond Dispatch* (August 28, September 4, 8, 9–10, 1854); *Lynchburg Virginian* (September 19–23, 25–27, 1854), 2; *Daily Southside Democrat* (April 24, 1855), 2.

51. *Daily Southside Democrat* (September 18, 20, 25, October 2, 1854, November 26, 28, 1855), 2, 3.

52. *Monarchs*, 55.

53. *Lynchburg Virginian* (November 15, 17–18, 1856), 2.

54. *Petersburg Express* and *Southside Democrat*, quoted in *Lynchburg Virginian*, (November 15, 17, 1856), 3; *Southside Democrat*, quoted in *Lynchburg Virginian*, (November 17, 1856), 3; *Southside Democrat*, quoted in *Lynchburg Virginian* (November 18, 1856), 3.

55. *Lynchburg Virginian* (November 15, 17–21, 1856), 2; *Lynchburg Virginian* (November 21, 1856), 2.

56. *New York Clipper 4* (November 22, 1856), 246, quoted in Richard W. Flint, "The Evolution of the Circus in Nineteenth-Century America" (*American Popular Entertainment*, Westport, CT: Greenwood, 1979), 188–9.

57. Thayer 2, 263, 308.

58. Thayer 2, 330–1; *Lynchburg Virginian* (August 7, 1848, July 30, 1849), 3.

59. *New York Clipper* (November 27, 1875), quoted in Thayer 2, 248.

60. Toulmin, 320, 404–405.

61. *Spirit of the Times* (February 11, 1843).

62. Thayer 3, 14, 109, 139, 145; *Lynchburg Virginian* (August 7, 1848), 3.

63. Thayer.

64. *Savannah Stage*.

65. Thayer.

66. Stoutamire, 149; *Richmond Whig* (February 3, 5, 1845), 3.

67. Words by M.S. Pike, Arranged by L.V.H. Crosby (Boston: C. Bradlee, 1846), Levysheetmusic.mse.jhu.edu.

68. Account book (January 1, 1847), used with permission of Roddy Moore, Blue Ridge Institute, Ferrum College.

69. Rice, 28.

70. Rice, 50.

71. chicagohs.org/fire/oleary/pic0033.html.

72. Rice, 51.

73. Odell 5; *New York Herald* (August 9–21, 1843).

74. Lester Levy collection.

75. Levy collection.

76. Account book, 1.

77. *Norfolk-Portsmouth Beacon* (January 19, 1847), 1.

78. *Richmond Whig* (December 4, 1846), 2.

79. *Richmond Enquirer* (December 7, 1846), 3.

80. *Richmond Enquirer* (December 9, 1846), 3; *Richmond Times and Compiler* (January 2, 1847), 4.

81. *Richmond Enquirer* (December 16, 1846), 2.

82. *Richmond Enquirer* (December 21–24, 1846), 2, 3; *Richmond Whig* (December 22, 25, 1846), 3.

83. Account book, 1.

84. *Richmond Times and Compiler* (January 7, 1847), 3.

85. *Richmond Whig* (January 5, 1847), 2; *Richmond Times-Compiler* (January 7, 9, 1847), 3.

86. *Richmond Times-Compiler* (January 7, 9, 1847), 3.

87. Account book, 2–4.

88. *Petersburg Republican* (January 11–15, 1847), 2, 3.

89. Account book, 5–6.

90. *Norfolk-Portsmouth Beacon* (January 21, 23, 26, 28, 1847), 1, 2.

91. Account book, 6–9.

92. *Petersburg Republican* (February 1, 1847), 2.

93. *Richmond Whig* (February 2, 1847), 2.

94. Account book, 10.

95. *Petersburg Republican* (February 5, 1847), 2, 3.

96. *Richmond Times-Compiler, Whig* (February 6–12, 1847).

97. Account book, 12–14.

98. *DC Union* (February 15, 1847), 1; *Intelligencer* (February 16–19, 1847), 1, 3.

99. Account book, 16–17.

100. *DC Union* (February 23–25, 1847), 3; *Intelligencer* (February 24–26, 1847), 3.

101. *Intelligencer* (February 24–March 1, 1847), 1.
102. Account book, 20.
103. *Intelligencer* (February 24, March 8, 1847), 3, 4; *DC Union* (March 16, 1847), 2.
104. *DC Union* (March 10, 12, 1847), 2, 3; Account book, 2.
105. Account book, 20–22.
106. *Baltimore Sun* (March 11–13, 1847), 2–4.
107. Account book, 23–24.
108. Account book, 24–5.
109. Words by J.S. Davis, music by L.V.H. Crosby (Boston: C. Bradlee, 1845), Levysheetmusic.mse.jhu.edu.
110. Quoted in David S. Reynolds, "I Hear America Singing: Whitman and Music of His Time," 3, american-composers.org.
111. Rice, 28, 50.
112. W. L. Montague, memory.loc.gov; Lester Levy.

Chapter 10

1. *Triweekly Whig* (June 23, 1859), 2.
2. Worcester newspaper? (July 26, 1828), via Cockrell.
3. M.R. Werner, *Barnum* (Garden City, NY: Garden City Publishing, 1923), 3–8, 14.
4. Kunhardt, 9.
5. *Annals 1*, 7.
6. Philip B. Kunhardt, Jr., Philip B. Kunhardt III and Peter W. Kunhardt, *P. T. Barnum: America's Greatest Showman* (New York: Alfred A. Knopf, 1995), 24–25.
7. Stuart Thayer, *Traveling Showmen*, 102, *Annals American Circus*, 220–221; *Annals 1793-1860*, 165; *Raleigh Star* (November 17, 1836), 3, quoted in *Annals American Circus*.
8. Greenwood, *The Circus*, 131.
9. Kunhardt, 24–25.
10. *Virginia Herald* (October 1, 5, August, 1836).
11. *Annals Am Circus*.
12. Kunhardt claims $600.00.
13. P.T. Barnum, *Struggle And Triumphs: or, Forty Years' Recollections* (Hartford: J.B. Burr, 1870), 88–90.
14. *Monarchs*, 23, 24.
15. Henry Dickinson Stone, *Personal Recollections of the Drama* (Albany: C. Van Benthuysen & Sons, 1873), 181.
16. *Raleigh Register* (November 11, 15, 1836), 2.
17. "When Barnum Blacked Up," unidentified clipping, University of Texas-Harry Ransom Center; Saxon, *P.T. Barnum* (New York: Columbia University, 1989), 78–80.
18. Joel Benton, *Life of the Honorable PT Barnum* (Philadelphia, PA: Edgewood Pub Co, 1891), 85.
19. *Richmond Whig* (December 2, 1836), 2.
20. Barnum, 88–90.
21. Barnum, 92.
22. Joseph Csida, and June Bundy, *American Entertainment* (New York: Watson-Guptill, 1978), 59; Barnum, 100.
23. Kunhardt, 24–25; Barnum, 101.
24. *Monarchs*, 42.
25. Barnum, 106.
26. *Odell IV*, 312; *New York Herald* (April 1–2, 1839); *New York Morning Herald* (April 20, 1839); Brown, *Volume One*, 251–2; Brown, "Early History of Negro Minstrelsy" (February 24, 1912); Broadside (October 18, 1839), Harvard, Misc. Minstrel, PL.C03.June.20. Boston.
27. *New York Morning Herald* (January 18, 1840).

28. *New York Herald* (February 24–28, 1840), 3.
29. *New York Herald* (March 25, 1840), 2.
30. *New York Morning Courier* (March 26–28, 1840), 2; *New York Herald* (March 31, 1840), 2, 3; *New York Herald* (April 7, 8, 1840); *Providence Journal* (April 16–18, 20, 1840), 3; *Spirit of the Times* (April 18, 1840), 84.
31. *Odell IV*, 434; *New York Herald* (July 18, 1840), quoted in Nathan, 62; Brown, "Early History of Negro Minstrelsy" (February 24, 1912).
32. Barnum, 106; Saxon, 81.
33. Barnum, 107.
34. *New Orleans Picayune* (January 16, 1841), 3.
35. Sol. Smith to E. Woolf, New Orleans (February 7, 1841), quoted in Smith, 155.
36. Brown, "Early History of Negro Minstrelsy" (February 24, 1912), Museum of the City of New York; Smither 173, 178; *Daily Picayune* (January 26, 1841); *Spirit of the Times* (January 30, 1841), 576.
37. Broadside, Mobile (February 24, 1841), copied in Nathan (1962), 61; *Spirit of the Times* (March 13, 1841).
38. Barnum, 107; Letter, Barnum to Smith and Ludlow (February 27, 1841), Missouri Historical Society; *Selected Letters of P.T. Barnum*, October 12.
39. Barnum, 108–9.
40. *Baltimore Sun* (May 15, 1841), 3.
41. Barnum, 109–110.
42. *New York Herald* (June16, 19, August 16, 1841).
43. *Monarchs*, 44.
44. Brown, Volume One, 236.
45. Brown, "Early History of Negro Minstrelsy" (February 24, 1912).
46. *New York Herald* (August 23–September 23, 1841).
47. *New York Herald* (August 25, 1841).
48. *New York Herald* (August 26, 1841).
49. *New York Herald* (September 1, 1841); *Sunday Mercury* (September 6, 1841).
50. *New York Herald* (September 3, 1841).
51. *New York Herald* (September 4, 6, 8, October–11, 1841); *New York Mercury* (September 8, 1841).
52. *New York Herald* (September 17, 23, 1841).
53. Obituary, MCNY, Volume 45; *Annals 2*, 11; letter, Thayer to Carlin (March 7, 2003).
54. Letter, Smith to Ludlow, MHS; *Annals 2*, 250.
55. Letter (October 18, 1840), Sol Smith, New Orleans, to Noah Ludlow, St. Louis, Ludlow, Field and Maury Collection, MHS; Sol. Smith to E. Woolf, New Orleans (February 7, 1841), quoted Sol Smith, 154–5; *Annals 2*, 88, 250.
56. *Annals 2*, 88, 250.
57. *Annals 2*, 89; Letter, Smith to Ludlow, MHS.
58. Sol. Smith to E. Woolf, New Orleans (February 7, 1841); quoted in Sol Smith, 154–5.
59. *Annals 2*, 89, quoting Sol Smith account book, MHS; Letter (April 22, 1841), Smith to Ludlow, MHS.
60. Letter, Smith to Ludlow, MHS.
61. *Annals 2*, 89.
62. *Annals*, 182.
63. Letter (April 29, 1841), Smith to Ludlow, MHS.
64. Letter (May 3, 1841), Smith to Ludlow, MHS.
65. Searched *Republican* (May 1–June 16, 1841); scanned *Republican* (August, 1841); searched *St Louis Daily Pennant* (May 29–October19, 1841).
66. *Missouri Republican* (May 29–June 14, 1841), 2; *Missouri Argus* (June 10, 1841).
67. *Missouri Republican* (June 11, 1841), 2; *St Louis Pennant* (June 11, 1841), 2.
68. *Daily Republican Banner* (September 15, 1841), quoted in *Annals 2*, 273–4.

69. *New Orleans Daily Picayune* (October 23, 1841), quoted in *Annals*, 250.

70. *New Orleans Bee* (October 25–26, 1841), 2; *New Orleans Picayune* (October 23–24, 26, 1841), 3.

71. Smither 188.

72. *Boston Post* (November 27, 1841), 2; *The True Flash* (December 4, 1841).

73. *New York Herald* (November 29–30, 1841).

74. Smither, 316–317, 183–184, 201–2; Bailey, 293.

75. Sol Smith to E. Woolf, Natchez, MS (January 2, 1842), quoted in Sol Smith, 161.

76. *New York Sporting Whip* (January 28, 1843).

77. *New York Herald* (February 22–March 3, 1842).

78. *New York Herald* (March 5, 1842).

79. *New York Herald* (March 28–April 2, 1842); Brown, "Early History of Negro Minstrelsy" (February 17, 1912).

80. *New York Herald* (April 6–7, 1842).

81. "Negro Minstrelsy," minstrel clippings, Harvard; "Charley White's Recollections."

82. Wilson, 264, 686, 705.

83. *New York Herald* (May 14, 1842).

84. *New York Herald* (May 14, 1842).

85. *Odell IV*, 584; *New York Herald* (May 22–June 4, 1842).

86. *New York Herald* (June 7–September 24, 1842); *Tattler* (June 9, 1842); *Odell IV*, 557; Playbill (June 28, 1842), Folger.

87. Ireland II, 9, Harvard; *New York Herald* (November 2–4, 1842).

88. *Odell IV*, 670–1; *Flash* (November 12, 1842); *New York Herald* (November 1–18, 1842).

Chapter 11

1. Mrs. Robert Rosa Faulkner Yancey, *Lynchburg and Its Neighbors* (Richmond: J.W. Fergusson and Sons, 1935), 217–221.

2. E. Newman Eubank, quoted in Yancey, 217–221.

3. *Historical Notes*, 210.

4. *Historical Notes*, 6.

5. *Historical Notes*, 110.

6. Yancey, 217–221.

7. Historic Marker K-150, Department of Historical Resources, north side of Route 426 between Concord and Lynchburg.

8. Yancey, 217–221.

9. *Historical Notes*, 73.

10. Yancey, 217–221.

11. Collins, box 3, folder 11.

12. Bedford City/County Museum, VA, letter from Ellen A Wandrei to author (July 3, 2000).

13. Mary Louise Gills, *It Happened at Appomattox* (Richmond: Dietz, 1948), 8.

14. William J. Mahar, *Behind the Burnt Cork Mask: Early Blackface Minstrelsy and Antebellum American Popular Culture* (Urbana and Chicago: University of Illinois), 20, 257–8.

15. *Boston Transcript* (December 15, 1840), 2.

16. *Baltimore American* (March 3, 6, 1841), 3; *New York Herald* (January 25, 1842), 3; *New York Post* (January 25, 1842), 2.

17. Broadside (April 6–8, 1843), G2E58, #355, Folger.

18. Ditson, Tuckahoe Music, republication 1992 from Brown University.

19. Dingess, 103; *New York Clipper* (November 30, 1872), quoted in *Annals 2*, 258.

20. *New York Herald* (February 11–May 2, 1839).

21. Broadsides (November 2–7, 1840), 389, volume one, British Library.

22. *Sunday Morning Atlas* (February 23, 1840), quoted on Broadsides (November 9–14, 1840), 389 volume one, British Library.

23. Gumbo Chaff [Elias Howe], *The Complete Preceptor for the Banjo* (Boston: Oliver Ditson, 1851), 8.

24. *New York Post* (December 9–14, 1839), 3.

25. *New York Herald* (March 4, 1840).

26. *Boston Post* (November 20, 1841), 4; *Boston Transcript* (November 20, 1841), 1.

27. levysheetmusic.mse.jhu.edu.

28. Mahar, 231.

29. Slave narrative, printed in Julius Lester, *To Be A Slave* (New York: Dell, 1970), quoted in Mahar, 13–14.

30. memory.loc.gov.

31. *Tattler* (February 13–14,1840).

32. *Boston Post* (May 11–12, 1840), 2; *Boston Courier*, *Boston Atlas* (May 11–12, 1840), 3.

33. *Baltimore American* (March 6, 1841), 3.

34. *National Intelligencer* (January 22, 23, 25, 1841), 3.

35. *Boston Post* (November 20, 1841), 4; *Boston Transcript* (November 20, 1841), 1.

36. Cave, 66–67, 69–73; William Temlett, *The Banjo: Its Origins* (London: Willcocks, 1888); Playbill, (August 9, [1843]), Circus World Museum and Library; Broadside (October 2, 1843), BCL; Playbill, Local History Dept, Birmingham Central Library; Broadside (October 4, 1843), Minstrel Broadsides SK-SW, Harvard; Broadside (October 3, 1843), Folger.

37. Broadsides (May 15–20, 23, 1843), 389 volume two, British Library; Broadsides (May 22–27, 1843), Harvard.

38. Broadside (April 6–8, 1843), G2E58, #355, Folger; Broadsides (May 15–20, 23, 1843), 389 volume two, British Library; Broadsides (May 22–27, 1843), Harvard.

39. *National Intelligencer* (January 22, 23, 25, 1841), 3; *Baltimore American* (March 6, 1841), 3; Playbill (August 9, [1843], Circus World Museum and Library; Broadside (December 4, 1840), Harvard.

40. Letter to *Richmond Dispatch* (February 17, 1895), 1.

41. *Auburn Journal and Advertiser* (August 12, 17, 1840), 3.

42. Broadside (December 4, 1840), Harvard; *Boston Post*, *Boston Courier* (December 2, 1840), 3.

43. Mahar, 230–233.

44. *Baltimore American* (March 6, 1841), 3.

45. *New York Post* (January 17–19, 1842), 3; *New York Herald* (January 22–25, 1842), 3, 4.

46. *Leeds Intelligencer*, *Leeds Mercury* (May 14, 1842), 1, 4.

47. Playbill (August 9, [1843], Circus World Museum and Library; Broadside (October 2, 1843), BCL; Playbill, Local History Department, Birmingham Central Library; Broadside (October 4, 1843), Minstrel Broadsides SK-SW, Harvard; Broadside (October 3, 1843), Folger; Broadside (June 15, 1844), reprinted in *New York Clipper* (January 10, 1874), 325; Broadside (October 23, 1844); *New York Clipper* (May 19, 1877), quoted in Nathan, 291–2.

48. Mahar, 19, 31, 398.

49. Broadside (December 4, 1840), Harvard.

50. Playbill (August 9, [1843], Circus World Museum and Library.

51. Mahar, 307–316.

52. Thayer, "The Circus Roots of Negro Minstrelsy," *Bandwagon* (November–December, 1996), 44.

53. Whitlock, unpublished autobiography, quoted in Nathan, 130.

54. Broadside (October 12, 1840); *Louisville Journal* (October 12, 1840), 2; *Annals 2*, 225.

55. *New York Post* (January 17–19, 1842), 3.

56. *New York Herald* (January 12–19, 28–29, 1842), 2, 3.

57. *New York Post* (January 20–22, 27–28, 1842), 3; *New York Herald* (January 22–26, 1842), 3, 4; Broadside (January 21, 1842), William Bailey Collection, Somers Circus Museum.

58. *Leeds Intelligencer, Leeds Mercury* (May 14, 1842), 1, 4; Cave, 66–67, 69–73; Temlett; Playbill (August 9, [1843], Circus World Museum and Library; Broadside (October 2, 1843), BCL; Playbill, Local History Department, Birmingham Central Library; Broadside (October 4, 1843), Minstrel Broadsides SK-SW, Harvard; Broadside (October 3, 1843), Folger; Nathan, 301–303; *Edinburgh Evening Post* (June 12, 1844).

59. Broadsides (May 15–20, 23, 1843), 389 volume two, British Library; Broadsides (May 22–27, 1843), Harvard.

60. Nathan, 301–303; *Edinburgh Evening Post* (June 12, 1844).

61. Mahar, 20, 257–8, 320–322.

62. *Leeds Intelligencer, Leeds Mercury* (May 14, 1842), 1, 4.

63. Cave, 66–67, 69–73.

64. *Baltimore American* (March 6, 1841), 3.

65. *New York Herald* (May 4, 1839), 3.

66. Broadside (January 20, February 14, 1851), Valentine Museum; Brown (April 27, 1912).

67. Nathan, 301–303; *Edinburgh Evening Post* (June 12, 1844).

68. Broadside (June 15, 1844), reprinted in *New York Clipper* (January 10, 1874), 325; Broadside (October 23, 1844), *New York Clipper* (May 19, 1877), quoted in Nathan, 291–2.

69. *Boston Post* (November 20, 1841), 4; *Boston Transcript* (November 20, 1841), 1.

70. For example, he places Sam Sweeney on banjo in 1842, when Joe's brother was only ten. And the elder Sweeney wasn't even in the United States, let alone the South, for the majority of this year.

71. "The Banjo's Origin," *Richmond Dispatch* (February 17, 1895).

Chapter 12

1. Mrs. Robert [Rosa Faulkner] Yancey, *Lynchburg and Its Neighbors* (Richmond: J.W. Fergusson and Sons, 1935), 217–221.

2. William Marvel, *A Place Called Appomattox* (Chapel Hill and London: University of North Carolina, 2000), 303; *Pension Application*, Chas Sweeney.

3. R.B. Pore to G.W. Inge (July 25, 1890), L.A. County Museum typescript; Ruth I. Mahood to Robert Van Eps (January 29, 1955), collection of James Bollman.

4. *Richmond Dispatch* (February 17, 1895), 1.

5. Frank B. Converse, "De History ob de Banjo," *Frank Converse's "Old Cremona" Songster* (New York: Dick & Fitzgerald, 1863), 53.

6. Ulf Jagfors and Daniel Jatta.

7. Conversation by author with Malian griot Cheick Hamala Diabate (April 14, 2006).

8. The Valentine Museum, Richmond History Center, reproduced in *The Birth of the Banjo*, 20.

9. Unknown artist, possibly South Carolina, c.1790–1800, Abby Aldrich Rockefeller Folk Art Museum, Colonial Williamsburg Foundation, Williamsburg, VA, reproduced in *The Birth of the Banjo* (Katonah, NY: 2003), 4.

10. Musical Instrument Museum, Brussels, Belgium.

11. Quoted in Robert B. Winans, *The Banjo in Virginia* (Ferrum, VA: 2000), 3.

12. *Richmond Dispatch* (February 17, 1895), 1.

13. Sutphin, 4.

14. G.W. Inge to J.E. Henning (1890), quoted in Frank B. Converse, "Banjo Reminiscences 7," *The Cadenza* (December, 1901), 11; "He Invented the Banjo," *Chattanooga Republican* (November 2, 1890).

15. Sutphin, 4.

16. Mrs. J.O. Cole, "Joe Sweeney, Banjo Virtuoso of Appomattox," *Lynchburg News* (April 29, 1940), 8.

17. *Richmond Whig* (February 17, 1837), 3.

18. *New York Clipper* (April 13, 1878), 21.

19. Frank Converse, *The Cadenza* (12, 1901); letter from Inge to Henning (1890); Collins, box 3, folder November; quoted in W.M. Brewer, "The Banjo in American," *B.M.G.* (March, 1953), 150.

20. Converse, 11.

21. Cave, 66–67, 69–73.

22. James Bollman and Phillip Gura, *America's Instrument: The Banjo in the Nineteenth Century* (Chapel Hill: University of North Carolina, 1999), 42.

23. Bollman and Gura, 55; Ross, 38–44.

24. George Wunderlich, phone with author (January 11, 2006).

25. Jayson Dobney, "Transitions in American Snare Drums," abstract of paper given to GS/AMIS Conference On Musical Instruments, music.ed.ac.uk/euchmi/galpin/gxka.html.

26. Lloyd P. Farrar, "Under the Crown & Eagle," *Namis* (XVI/3, October 1989), 9.

27. Scott C. Steward, "William Boucher and His Descendants" (2006).

28. Lloyd P. Farrar, "Under the Crown & Eagle," *Namis* (XV/2, June, 1986), 4.

29. *Annual Report of the Board of Managers of the Maryland Institute for the Promotion of the Mechanic Arts* (Baltimore: Mills, 1851), 47, 68, 74; *The Book of the Exhibition: Ninth Annual Exhibition of the Maryland Institute for the Promotion of the Mechanic Arts* (Baltimore: Mills, 1856) 85, 185; *Twelfth Annual Report of the Board of Managers and Treasurer of the Maryland Institute for the Promotion of the Mechanic Arts* (Baltimore: Mills, 1860), 29, 183–84; *Official Catalogue*, 95; all quoted in Gura and Bollman, 47–48.

30. Email, Dobney to Author (January 11, 2006). Baltimore directories, Libin typescript; Farrar (XVI/3), 9; 1850 Federal Census.

31. Lloyd P. Farrar, "Under the Crown & Eagle," *Namis* (XVI/3, October 1989), 8.

32. 1840 Federal Census, M704_159, 274, quoted in "William Boucher and His Descendants," Scott C. Steward (2006).

33. Lloyd P. Farrar, "Under the Crown & Eagle," *Namis* (XVI/3, October 1989), 9, (XV/2, June, 1986), 4.

34. Industrial Notes Scrapbooks, "Musical Instruments" folder, MS 481, Box 2, Maryland Historical Society.

35. *Maryland Gazette* (February 25, 1772), Industrial Notes Scrapbooks, "Musical Instruments" folder, MS 481, Box 2, Maryland Historical Society; *Maryland Journal* (October 21, 1788), Industrial Notes Scrapbooks, "Musical Instruments" folder, MS 481, Box 2, Maryland Historical Society.

36. Gura and Bollman, 64–5; Dobney, Thesis, 114.

37. Lloyd P. Farrar, "Under the Crown & Eagle," *Namis* (XVI/3, October 1989), 8.

38. Scott Steward to Laurence Libin, (July 13, 1980).

39. *Matchett's Baltimore Director, for 1847-8* (1847), 42, quoted in "William Boucher and His Descendants," Scott C. Steward (2006).

40. 1850 Federal Census, M432_282, 41, quoted in "William Boucher and His Descendants," Scott C. Steward (2006).

41. Libin to Burch; Laurence Libin, curator, Department of Musical Instruments, Metropolitan Museum of Art, letter to William Boucher III (November 14, 1979), copy from Farrar; Boyd's directory for 1858, Libin, typescript; 1860 Federal Census, quoted in "William Boucher and His Descendants," Scott C. Steward (2006).

42. Lloyd P. Farrar, "Under the Crown & Eagle," Namis (XVI/3, October 1989), 9.

43. Lloyd P. Farrar, "Under the Crown & Eagle," Namis (XVI/3, October 1989), 8.

44. Lloyd P. Farrar, "Under the Crown & Eagle," Namis (XVI/3, October 1989), 9.

45. Letter, Lloyd P. Farrar to Peter Szego (April 8, 1988 [1998?]).

46. Lloyd P. Farrar and author, phone conversation (January 2006); Letter, Lloyd P. Farrar to Peter Szego (April 8, 1988 [1998?]).

47. Libin, American Musical Instruments in the Metropolitan Museum of Art (New York: W.W. Norton, 1985), 170.

48. Maryland Historical Society, sheet music collection, box 40.

49. library.upenn.edu/collections/rbm/keffer/willig. html.

50. Maryland Historical Society, sheet music collection, box 53; also memory.loc.gov; Scott C. Steward, "William Boucher and His Descendants" (2006).

51. Maryland Historical Society, sheet music collection, box 35, 729B; Scott C. Steward, "William Boucher and His Descendants" (2006).

52. Groce, 32, 82, 99, 134, 88; Transactions of the American Institute of the City of New-York, for the Year 1851 (Albany: Van Benthuysen, 1852), 642; Official Catalogue of the New-York Exhibition of the Industry of All Nations (New York: George P. Putnam, 1853), 95; Transactions of the American Institute of the City of New-York, for the Years, 1859-60 (Albany: Van Benthuysen, 1860), 76; Kaufman, 262, 265, 267; all quoted in Gura, 43.

53. Catalogue of Books, Stationery, Music and Musical Instruments and Fancy Goods for Sale by J. W. Randolph (121 Main Street, Richmond, VA, 1850), 11, 103.

54. P. H. Taylor's Music Store ad featuring banjos for sale, No 188 Main Street, Richmond, Jeffersonian Republican (November 11, 1858), 3.

55. Nigger Melodies: Being the Only Entire and Complete Work of Ethiopian Songs Extant (Cornish, Lamport & Co., 1850).

56. Republished by Tuckahoe Music.

57. William Ferguson Goldie, [pseud.], Sunshine and Shadow of Slave Life: Reminiscences as Told to Isaac C. Williams to "Tege" (East Saginaw, Michigan: Evening News Printing and Binding House, 1885; reprinted in New York: AMS, 1975), 62.

58. Virginia Biography, Volume 5 (Chicago: The American Historical Society, 1924), 134–136; Grace Davidson, Record of the Diuguid Family (Manuscript, 1965?); D.P. Diuguid, "Death Notice," Lynchburg Daily Virginian (July 5, 1864); Diuguid Family file, Jones Library; Diuguid's Furniture Company: 1820-1830, company account book, Jones Library; W. Asbury Christian, Lynchburg and Its People (Lynchburg: J.P. Bell, c. 1900); Lynchburg Historical Society; Peter Szego.

59. Cadenza (XV/1, July 1908), 15, quoting New York Herald (May 28, 1908).

60. Converse, 10–12.

Chapter 13

1. New York Herald (February 8–March 1, 1841).

2. Phil. Rice's Correct Method for the Banjo: With Or Without A Master (Boston: Oliver Ditson, 1858, reprint by Bremo Bluff, VA: Tuckahoe Music, 1998), 32–33.

3. Thayer 2, 197–198; Daily Georgian (January 6–7, 1837), 2, (January 9–20, 1837), 3; New York Clipper (April 13, 1878), 21.

4. Thayer 2, 197–8; Lynchburg Virginian (May 11–June 1, 1837), 4; Milledgeville Federal Union (April 4, 1837), 3; Macon Georgia Telegraph (March 29–30, 1837), 3; GA Messenger (March 29–30, 1837), 3; Daily Georgian (January 6–7, 1837), 2, (January 9–20, 1837), 3.

5. Richmond Enquirer (June 9–30, 1837), 3; Richmond Whig (June 9–July 4, 1837), 3; Thayer.

6. Unidentified clipping, Harry Ransom Center, University of Texas.

7. New York Clipper (April 13, 1878), 21. Whitlock's biography has been reprinted in every important work on minstrelsy, from W.M. Brewer's "The Banjo in America" to Robert C. Toll's Blacking Up: The Minstrel Show in Nineteenth-Century America (New York: Oxford University, 1974) and Hans Nathan's Dan Emmett and the Rise of Early Negro Minstrelsy (Norman, Oklahoma: University of Oklahoma, 1962/1977).

8. New York Clipper (April 13, 1878), 21.

9. New York Herald (March 25, 1840), 2.

10. John Glenroy, Ins and Outs of Circus Life or Forty-Two Years Travel (Boston: M.M. Wing, 1885), 28–29.

11. For example, New York Clipper (April 13, 1878).

12. New York Morning Herald (January 18, 1840).

13. "Letter from C.J. Rodgers, Philadelphia, New York Clipper (June 20, 1874), 95, quoted in Nathan, 111.

14. Rice, 30.

15. T. Allston Brown, "Early History of Negro Minstrelsy," New York Clipper (February 17, 1912); T. Allston Brown, "Origins of Minstrelsy," Fun in Black (New York: Robert M. DeWitt, 1874), 5.

16. Converse, 5.

17. Rice, 30.

18. Phil Rice's Method for the Banjo (Boston: Oliver Ditson, 1858).

19. New York Herald (October 15–19, 1857), 7.

20. Letter from Charles Morrell, "The First Banjo Tournament in America," S.S. Stewart's Banjo and Guitar Journal 7/2 (Philadelphia, PA: June and July, 1890), 1–2.

21. Unaccredited newspaper clipping, Box 1, Collins Papers, LibVA.

22. Rice, 16.

23. Jimmy Dalton Baines, Samuel S. Sanford and Negro Minstrelsy (Dissertation, Tulane University, 1987), 11.

24. Rice, 15–16.

25. For example, American Traveller (November 30, 1841), 2.

26. For example, Collins, Fretts (November/December, 1955), 5–7.

27. Tri-Weekly Memphis Enquirer (May 14, 1846), quoted in Baines, 23–24.

28. Brown, "Early History of Negro Minstrelsy," New York Clipper (March 9, 1912), quoted in Baines, 11.

29. New York Herald (June 8, 1845), 2.

30. Sanford, quoted in Baines, 17–18.

31. Richmond Whig (August 4, 1845), quoted in Schreyer; Lynchburg Virginian (August 11, 1845), 3; Lynchburg News (August 11, 1845).

32. Nashville Republican Banner? (September 14, 1846), quoted by Baines, 25–26.

33. Joe Ross, "Banjos at the Smithsonian," Bluegrass

Unlimited (November, 1992), 38–44; Typescript copy of a letter to J.E. Henning/Elite Banjoist from "An Old Timer," Cold Spring Harbor, Suffolk Company, N.Y. (November 28, 1890) Louisiana County Museum to Van Eps, as elsewhere; Letter, Fred Mather, "Gatcomb's Banjo and Guitar Gazetter," 2/2 (November and December, 1888), 2; Arthur Woodward, "Joel Walker Sweeney and the First Banjo," *Los Angles County Museum Quarterly*, 7 (1949), 9; Winans, "The Folk, the Stage"; Burke Davis.

34. *Brooklyn Eagle* (November 7, 1857), 2.

35. For example, *New York Herald* (May 2, 1842); *Rochester Daily Democrat* (September 16 and 20 and 27, 1842), 2.

36. Rice, 46; *Alta California* (October 25, 1854); *The Wild West* (October 29, 1854).

37. Broadside (October 18, 1839), Harvard, Misc Minstrel, PL.Co3.June.20. Boston.

38. Broadsides (January 28 and February 19, 1841), Rare Books, Boston Public Library.

39. Rice, 43.

40. Rice, 31

41. Rice, 26

42. Rice, 36.

43. Rice, 47.

44. Donald Mullin, *Victorian Actors and Actresses in Review* (Westport, CT: Greenwood, 1983), 64 and 76.

45. Stanley Kimmel, *The Mad Booths of Maryland* (New York: Bobbs-Merrill, c. 1940), 71, quoted in Andy Alexis Thesis, *Theater in Nevada City* (Stanford University).

46. Helene Wickham Koon, *Gold Rush Performers* (Jefferson, NC: McFarland, 1994), 25.

47. John Adam Ellsler, *The Stage Memories of John A. Ellsler* (Cleveland: Rowfant Club, 1950), 148–9.

48. Kimmel, 73.

49. Kimmel, 72.

50. Koon, 25.

51. Kimmel, 98 and 100.

52. Ellsler, 148–9.

53. Levy collection.

54. Koon, 25.

55. Ireland, *Volume II*, 578–8.

56. Ireland, *Volume II*, 592.

57. Richard Moody, *Edwin Forrest: First Star of the American Stage* (New York: Alfred A. Knopf, 1960), 203.

58. Ireland, *Volume II*, 389.

59. *Atlas* (April 29, 1848), 288.

60. Review, clipping, Strand Theatre file, London Theatre Museum.

61. Thayer 2 and 120.

62. Cave, 66–67 and 69–73.

63. Rice, 47; email from Eli Kaufman to the author.

64. William Temlett, *The Banjo: Its Origins* (London: Willcocks & Co., 1888).

65. *Annals 2*, 201 and 174; *New York Transcript* (March 31–April 11, 1835).

66. Playbill (February 6 and 7, 1843), Local History Dept, Birmingham Central Library, also Folger; *Aris's Birmingham Gazette* (February 6, 1843); Playbill (February 3, 1843), G3B53tr, Folger.

67. Broadside (February 15, 1843), BCL, also at Folger.

68. For example, *The Era* (February 16, 1845), 6.

69. *Age & Argus* (February 24, 1844), 1.

70. Joseph Arnold Cave, *A Jubilee of Dramatic Life and Incident Of*, edited by Robert Soutar (London: Thomas Vernon, 1894), 66–67 and 69–73; originally published in *The Stage* and quoted in "The Early Banjo," *Dallas' Musical Monthly and Advertiser* (January, 1909), 43; *The Old Marylebone Theatre*, 17; "Early Nigger Minstrel Acts in Britain," 120.

71. *Age & Argus* (February 24, 1844), 1.

72. Kathleen Barker, "Early Music Hall in Bristol" (Bristol Historical Association, 1979), quoted in Geoff Woolfe (October 15, 2001); *Greenwich Industrial History* (vol. 3, issue 1, January, 2000), gihs.gold.ac.uk/gihsNovember.html.

73. Playbill (October 18, 1843), collection of the author.

74. *The Era* (December 31, 1843 and January 28, 1844).

75. Broadside (April 2, 1844), Mitchell Lib.

76. Playbill, G5D89tr, Folger.

77. *Bristol Standard?* (December 7, 1844); *Brighton Herald* (March 8, 1845).

78. Broadside (August 5 and 11, 1845), Playbill, G6C81tr, Folger.

79. *London Times* (January 8 and 11, 1844), 4; *Morning Chronicle* (February 12, 1844), 2.

80. *The Dramatic and Musical Review* (January 20, 1844), 33.

81. *Liverpool Journal* (May 4, 1844), 5.

82. Broadside (April 26–27, 1848), Large Portfolio, Playbills, Lyceum-Olympic, Westminster.

83. Laurence Senelick, *Tavern Singing in Early Victorian London* (London: Society For Theatre Research, 1997), 17.

84. greatallied.fsnet.co.uk/docs/cen1851.htm.

85. nottingham.ac.uk/film/journal/filmrev/silent-shakespeare.htm.

86. Playbills (December 1, 1845), 171, PB mic-c13137, British Library.

87. Dianne Robinson to the author.

88. Wood, 38 and 117.

89. John J. Jennings, *Theatrical and Circus Life* (Cincinnati: W.E. Dibble), 1886.

Chapter 14

1. Stephen Vincent Benet, "John Brown's Body," quoted in Davis, 2–12.

2. A.P. Hill, quoted in John W. Thomason, Jr., *J.E.B. Stuart* (New York/London: Charles Scribner's Sons, 1930), 5.

3. Thayer, *Traveling Showmen*, 115.

4. *Fayetteville Observer* (June 25, 1857), quoted in Stuart Thayer, "The History of the Concert or After-Show," *The Bandwagon* (9–10,1997).

5. Thayer 3, 249.

6. *Alexandria Gazette* (May 4–10, 1859), 1.

7. *Republican* (May 31, June 7, 1860), 2; *Annals 3*, 249.

8. Marvel, 83.

9. Justitia, *Lynchburg Virginian* (September 4, 1860), 3, quoted in Farrar, 158.

10. Lynchburg newspaper (May 4, 1861), quoted in Marvel, 82 and Farrar, 163; Letter from Evelyn Dupuy Gilliam to fiancé John Basta Moseley (December 30, 1861), quoted in Moore, 43–44.

11. Confederate Records.

12. Moore, 50.

13. Henderson, *41st VA Infantry*, 12; Confederate Records 8, 68–70, 189, 193; Davis, 2–12; Graveyard; Pension Records; Moore, 247.

14. "Tom Booker and the Banjo," *Richmond News Leader* (April 9, 1928), 8.

15. Tom Perry, "Going Home with the Beau Sabreur," *The Maryland Line*, 3, from J.E.B. Stuart Birthplace Preservation Trust, Inc.

16. Lt. Colonel William W. Blackford, *War Years with J.E.B. Stuart* (New York: Charles Scribner's Sons, 1945), 50.

17. Levy Collection.

18. Davis, 2–12.

19. Maj Heros Von Borcke, *My Memoirs of the Confederate War for Independence* (New York: Peter Smith, 1938).

20. John Esten Cooke, *Surry of Eagle's Nest* (1866), 84–85.

21. Caroline Moseley, "'Those Songs Which So Much Remind Me of You': The Musical Taste of General J.E. B. Stuart," *American Music* 9, (1991), 384–404.

22. Von Borcke 2, 88–93.

23. Blackford, 154; Robert J. Trout, *They Followed the Plume* (Stackpole Books, Mechanicsburg, PA, 1993), 44–45; Blackford Family Papers, SHC, Manuscript Dept, Wilson Library, UNC-CH.

24. Henry Kyd Douglas, *I Rode with Stonewall* (Mockingbird Books, 1983), 188.

25. Von Borcke 1, 270–271, 292–295.

26. PFMS AM 1585, Houghton Library, Harvard University.

27. *Illustrated London News* (January 10, 1863), 40–1.

28. *Surry of Eagle's Nest*, 376.

29. Von Borcke 2, 70, 72–3, 80–85, quoted in Emory M. Thomas, *Bold Dragon—The Life of J.E.B. Stuart* (New York: Vintage Books, Random House, 1986, 1988), 191–192; Thomason, 316; J.E.B. Stuart to Flora Stuart (November 25, 1862), Virginia Historical Society, Richmond, VA.

30. John Esten Cooke, *General Stuart in Camp and Field*, quoted in Moseley, "Musical Taste," 387; *Annals of the War Written by Leading Participants North* (Philadelphia, Times, 1879), 674.

31. Von Borcke 2, 165, 173–4.

32. General Lafayette McLaws to General Richard Ewell (February 1863), quoted in Percy Gatling Hamlin, *"Old Bald Head" General R.S. Ewell: The Portrait of a Soldier* (Strasburg, VA: Shenandoah, 1940), 133.

33. *Lynchburg Virginian* (March 10, 1845), quoted in Farrar, 32.

34. *Lynchburg Virginian* (November 23 24, December 25, 1853, January 30, February 6, 1854).

35. Theodore Stanford Garnett, *Riding With Stuart* (Shippensburg, PA: White Mane, 1994), 30.

36. Garnett, 30–31.

37. Official Records; Kenneth M. Clark, Orange County Historical Society.

38. Ezra Hoyt Ripple, *Dancing Along the Deadline* (Presidio Press, Novato, CA, 1996), 107.

39. (Columbia: University of South Carolina, 1988), 83–4, 87.

40. 19, 24.

41. "13th Virginia Infantry Humor," *Confederate Veteran Magazine* (XVI, no. 7, 1908), 340; David F. Riggs, *13th Virginia Infantry* (Lynchburg: H.E. Howard, 1988).

42. Official Records, quoted in William D. Henderson, *41st Virginia Infantry* (Lynchburg, VA: H.E. Howard, 1986), 109; B.J. Rogers, "Banjoist of Army of Northern Virginia," *Petersburg Index-Appeal*, reprinted in *Confederate Veteran* (circa 3/1912), 112.

43. North Carolina Troops: 1861–1865; MDHS, reproduced in *Tenting Tonight*, 143.

44. Andy Cahan, "Manly Reece and the Dawn of North Carolina Banjo," *The North Carolina Banjo Collection* (Cambridge, MA: Rounder Records, 1998).

45. *Lynchburg News* (October 11, 1936), Collins folder 11, Lib of VA.

46. Morris Schaff, *The Spirit of Old West Point* (Boston: Houghton Mifflin Co, 1907), 236–7.

47. William Miller Owen, *In Camp and Battle with the Washington Artillery* (Boston: Tickmor, 1895), quoted in William L. Parker, *General James Dearing CSA* (Lynchburg: H.E. Howard, 1990), 21.

48. Parker, 91.

49. "Tom Booker and the Banjo."

50. Family Bible, quoted in *Historical Notes on Amelia County, Virginia*, 283.

51. Hadfield, 71.

52. 1850 Census.

53. Ebay, cgi.ebay.com, item 6602863721 (February 5, 2006).

54. W. Cullen Sherwood, *The Nelson Artillery: Lamkin and Rives Batteries* (Lynchburg: H.E. Howard, 1991), 48; Pension Application, Service Records; pay slip.

55. *Historical Notes on Amelia County, Virginia*, 168.

56. Mary Armstrong Jefferson, *Old Homes and Buildings of Amelia County, Volume I* (Self-published, 1964), 90.

57. Herbert Clarence Bradshaw, *History of Prince Edward County, VA* (Richmond: Dietz Press, 1955).

58. "Colonel 'Marse Tom' Booker Obituary," *Richmond Times-Dispatch* (April 9, 1928), 10; "'Marse Tom' Dies in Bird Grove Home," *Richmond News-Leader* (April 9, 1928), 18, (May 9, 1928); Widow of Confederate Soldier pension.

59. *Farmville Herald* (May 30, 1902), quoted in Bradshaw, 663; Delle Walton Scrapbook, owned by Mrs. Herbert L. Bradshaw, quoted in Bradshaw, 662–663.

60. "Composed by Capt. W.H. Harrison, of Atlanta, Georgia, and sung, for the first time, by Polk Miller, at the Confederate Reunion at Louisville in 1900." Collection of the Valentine Museum.

61. Lyon G. Tyler, *Men of Mark in Virginia* (Men of Mark: Washington, D.C., 1907), 263.

62. Neil November, "I Remember When...," undated newspaper article; Geo. W. Rogers, "Polk Miller Wrote Colorful Chapter in Drug History," undated newspaper article.

63. *Richmond Times Dispatch* (October 13, 1935), 6, quoted among others in Doug Seroff, "Polk Miller and the Old South Quartette," *78 Quarterly* (January 3, 1988), 33.

64. Richmond newspaper (August, 1892), quoted in Seroff, 28.

65. *Confederate Military History* (Confederate, Atlanta, GA, 1899), 1041, quoted in Lee A. Wallace, Jr., *Richmond Howitzers* (Lynchburg: H.E. Howard, 1993), 144.

66. Polk Miller, 265.

67. *Richmond Dispatch* (June 30, 1896), 19–21; *Richmond Times* (December 24, 1893); Academy of Music program (December 6, 1892); *Richmond Dispatch* (December 7, 1892); *Richmond Times* (December 7, 1892); *Richmond Times* (March 9, 1893); *Richmond Dispatch* (May 27, 1892); *Richmond Times* (May 28, 1892); *Petersburg Daily Index-Appeal* (October 5, 1892); "Mozart Academy," Program (December 22, 1893); Scrapbook; quoted in *At the Falls*, 209.

68. *Chautauqua Assembly Herald* (August 16, 1895), scrapbook.

69. Polk Miller, 264.

70. "Banjo for Polk Miller," *Richmond Dispatch*; "Polk Miller Given a Banjo," *Richmond Times* (June 9, 1895), scrapbook.

71. "Polk Miller," *Confederate Veteran* (Volume 21, 1913) 598–599.

72. Caroline Moseley, "Irrepressible Conflict: Differences Between Northern and Southern Songs of the Civil War," *Journal of Popular Culture* (25:2, fall, 1991), 53; *Edison Phonograph Monthly* (January 1910), 5, 18, 19, republished by Wendell Moore; *The Early Negro Vocal Quartets, Volume 1*, Document DLP 583 (Vienna, Austria, 1990).

Selected Bibliography

Album Notes

Cahan, Andy. "Manly Reece and the Dawn of North Carolina Banjo." *The North Carolina Banjo Collection*, Cambridge, MA: Rounder Records, 1998.

Moore, Wendell. *The Early Negro Vocal Quartets, Volume 1.* Document DLP 583, Vienna, Austria, 1990.

Public Records

Appomattox County Death Records, #131 and #141, line 3, Jones Library.

Appomattox Death Records (1860), #155, original Jones Library, quoted by Department of Health, Commonwealth of Virginia, Bureau of Vital Records and Health Statistics, Richmond, 155, Line 132.

Census, 1850 and 1860.

Confederate Records.

Pension Application, Charles Sweeney.

Petition (December 17, 1831).

Widow of Confederate Soldier Pension Records.

Magazine and Journal Articles

Anthony, Barry. "Early Nigger Minstrel Acts in Britain." *Music Hall* 12. London, April 1980, 118.

Bailey, Ben E. "The Minstrel Show in Mississippi." *The Journal of Mississippi History*, (LVII, 2, Summer, 1995), 146.

Brewer, W. M. "The Banjo in American." *B.M.G.* (March, 1953), 150.

Cadenza (XV/1, July 1908), 15.

Collins, George. "The American Banjo, Part II." *Fretts* (February-March, 1959).

Converse, Frank B. "Banjo Reminiscences 7." *The Cadenza* (December 1901), 11.

Crews, Emma Katherine. "Early Musical Activities in Knoxville, Tennessee, 1791–1861," *The East Ten-*nessee *Historical Society's Publications*. Knoxville: ETHS, No. 32, 1960.

Davis, Burke. "The Swinging Sweeneys." *The Iron Worker*. (XXXIII/4, autumn, 1969), 2–12.

Dyreson, Jodella K. "Sporting Activities in the American-Mexican Colonies of Texas, 1832–1835," *Journal of Sport History* 24/3 (Fall 1997), 273.

"The Early Banjo." *Dallas' Musical Monthly and Advertiser*. January 1909, 43.

Epstein, Dena J. "The Folk Banjo: A Documentary History." *Ethnomusicology* (19, no. 3, September 1975), 347–37.

Farrar, Lloyd P. "Under the Crown & Eagle." *Namis* (XV/2+3June, 1986, XVI/3, October 1989), 9.

Figa (March-April, 1979).

French, T. N. *The Cadenza* (September 1919).

Gough, Peg. "On Stage in Atlanta, 1860–1870." *Atlanta Historical Bulletin* (XXI, 2, Summer, 1977), 49.

Henry, Bessie M. "A Yankee Schoolmistress Discovers Virginia." *Essex Institute Historical Collections*.

Letter from Charles Morrell. "The First Banjo Tournament in America." *S.S. Stewart's Banjo and Guitar Journal* 7/2 (Philadelphia, PA: June and July 1890), 1–2.

Letter, Fred Mather, "Gatcomb's Banjo and Guitar Gazetter," 2/2 (November and December 1888), 2.

Letter, Pore to Henning, *Cadenza* (November-December, 1898).

Moseley, Caroline. "Irrepressible Conflict: Differences Between Northern and Southern Songs of the Civil War." *Journal of Popular Culture* (25:2, fall, 1991), 53.

_____. "'Those Songs Which So Much Remind Me of You': The Musical Taste of General J.E.B. Stuart." *American Music* 9, (1991), 384–404.

"Polk Miller." *Confederate Veteran Magazine* (Volume 21, 1913), 598–599.

Rogers, B. J. "Banjoist of Army of Northern Virginia." *Petersburg Index-Appeal*, reprinted in *Confederate Veteran* (circa 3/1912), 112.

Ross, Joe. "Banjos at the Smithsonian." *Bluegrass Unlimited* (November 1992), 38–44.

Schreyer, Lowell. "Joel Sweeney." *Figa News* (March/April 1997), 12–15.

Seroff, Doug. "Polk Miller and the Old South Quartette." *78 Quarterly* (January 3, 1988), 33.

Shearston, Garry. "Bessy Campbell, Australia's Queen of Banjo." *In Tradition* 3, (October 1966), 3.

Stealey, John Edmund III. "Slavery and the Western Virginia Salt Industry." *The Journal of Negro History* 59 (April 1974), 105–131.

Thayer, Stuart. "The Circus Roots of Negro Minstrelsy," *Bandwagon* (November-December, 1996), 44+45.

_____. "The History of the Concert or After-Show," *The Bandwagon* (9–10, 1997).

"13th Virginia Infantry Humor." *Confederate Veteran Magazine* (XVI, no. 7, 1908), 340.

Winans, Robert B., and Kaufman, Elias J. "Minstrel and Classic Banjo: American and English Connections." *American Music* (12, no 1, spring, 1994), 6.

Winans, Robert B. *The Banjo in Virginia*. Ferrum, VA: 2000, 3.

_____. "The Folk, The Stage, and the Five-String Banjo in the Nineteenth Century." *Journal of American Folklore* 89 (October-December, 1976).

Woodward, Arthur. "Joel Walker Sweeney and the First Banjo." *Los Angles County Museum Quarterly*, 7 (1949), 9.

Theses

Alexis, Andy. Thesis, *Theater in Nevada City* (Stanford University).

Baines, Jimmy Dalton. *Samuel S. Sanford and Negro Minstrelsy* (Ph.D. dissertation, Tulane University, 1967).

Dobney, Jayson. *Innovations in American Snare Drums 1850–1920* (master's thesis, University of South Dakota, 2001).

Harris, Geraldine C., "Chapter IV: Negro Minstrelsy," *The History of the Theatre in Ohio 1815–1850* (Ohio State thesis, 1937).

Hester, Wyoline. *The Savannah Stage* (thesis, 1930, Auburn U, Aub-the-H5885).

Langley, William Osler. *Theatre in Columbus, GA, 1828–1878* (thesis, AL Polytechnic [now Auburn], 1937).

Teague, Oran. *Professional Theatre in Rural Louisiana* (thesis, LSU, 378.76-L930–1952).

Manuscripts

"Negro Minstrelsy," minstrel clippings, Harvard.

Account book (January 1, 1847), used with permission of Roddy Moore, Blue Ridge Institute, Ferrum College.

Blackford Family Papers, SHC, Manuscript Dept, Wilson Library, UNC-CH.

Chilton, Harriett A. *Appomattox County, Virginia Tax Lists* (February 1975).

Davidson, Grace. *Record of the Diuguid Family* (Manuscript, 1965?).

Duiguid's Furniture Company: 1820-1830. Company account book, Jones Library.

Industrial Notes Scrapbooks, "Musical Instruments" folder, MS 481, Box 2, Maryland Historical Society.

J.E.B. Stuart to Flora Stuart (November 25, 1862), Virginia Historical Society, Richmond, VA.

John A. Dingess, ms, 103–104, Hertzberg.

King, Donald C. *A History of Boston's Theatres* (Boston: Bostonian Society manuscript, 1987).

Letter (October 18, 1840, May 3, 1841, April 22, 1841, April 29, 1841,), Sol Smith, New Orleans, to Noah Ludlow, St. Louis, Ludlow, Field and Maury Collection, Missouri Historical Society.

Letter from Mrs. Ralph Catterall, Valentine Museum to Colonel Collins (December 20, 1953).

Letter, Barnum to Smith and Ludlow (February 27, 1841), Missouri Historical Society.

Letter, Laurence Libin, curator, Department of Musical Instruments, Metropolitan Museum of Art to William Boucher III (November 14, 1979).

Letter, Mrs. Vicki Jamerson to Mrs. Mary W. Stanley (June 16, 1978), National Park Service.

Letter, R.B. Pore to G.W. Inge (July 25, 1890), Louisiana County Museum typescript.

Letter, Ruth I. Mahood to Robert Van Eps (January 29, 1955), collection of James Bollman.

Letter, Scott Steward to Laurence Libin, (July 13, 1980).

Letter, Sol. Smith to E. Woolf, New Orleans (February 7, 1841), Field and Maury Collection, Missouri Historical Society.

May's Encyclopedia, Maryland Historical Society.

McAllister Scrapbooks, Playbills, Vol 24, 34, Library Company of Philadelphia.

Moreau, Charles C., Scrapbook *Negro Minstrelsy in New York, Volume 1*, Harvard.

Review, clipping, Strand Theatre file, London Theatre Museum.

Sol Smith account book, Missouri Historical Society.

Steward, Scott C. "William Boucher and His Descendants" (2006).

Sturdivant, C. G. *Who's Who in American Circus 2*, ms, 3A88, 375, Hertzberg.

Typescript copy of a letter to J.E. Henning/Elite Banjoist from "An Old Timer," Cold Spring Harbor, Suffolk County, NY (November 28, 1890) Louisiana County Museum.

Westervelt Scrapbook, Barnum, Vol IV, item 5, New York Historical Society.

Wooding, Harry, *Danville History*, mss, (1926-7).

Books

Bagby, Dr. George W. "Fishing in the Appomattox," *Selections from the Miscellaneous Writings* 1. Richmond, VA: Whittet & Shepperson, 1884.

Barnum, P.T. *Struggle and Triumphs: or, Forty Years' Recollections.* Hartford: J.B. Burr, 1870.

Battle, Dr. Kemp P. *History of the University of North Carolina,* 1. Raleigh: Edwards and Broughton, 1907.

Benton, Joel. *Life of the Honorable P.T. Barnum.* Philadelphia: Edgewood, 1891.

The Birth of the Banjo. Katonah, NY: Katonah Museum of Art, 2003.

Blackford, Lt. Colonel William W. *War Years with J.E.B. Stuart.* New York: Charles Scribner's Sons, 1945.

Bollman, James, and Philip Gura. *America's Instrument: The Banjo in the Nineteenth Century.* Chapel Hill, NC: UNC Press, 1999.

Borcke, Maj. Heros Von. *My Memoirs of the Confederate War for Independence.* New York: Peter Smith, 1938.

Bradshaw, Herbert Clarence. *History of Prince Edward County, VA.* Richmond: Dietz Press, 1955.

Bratton, J.S. "English Ethiopians," *Yearbook of English Studies.* Leeds: W. S. Maney and Son Ltd, vol 11, 1981.

Brisbane, Katharine, ed. *Entertaining Australia.* Sydney: Currency Press, 1991.

Broadbent, R. J. *Annals of the Liverpool Stage.* New York/London: Benjamin Blom, August 19, 1969.

Broadway Down East. Trustees of the Public Library of the City of Boston, 1978.

Brown, T. Allston. *Amphitheatres and Circuses: A History from Their Earliest Date to 1861.* Reprinted; San Bernardino: The Borgo Press, 1994.

Brown, T. Allston. "Origins of Minstrelsy," in *Fun in Black.* New York: Robert M. DeWitt, 1874.

_____. "The Theatre in America 1." (1888).

Bryan, George B. *Stage Deaths: 1850–1990, Volume One.* Westport, CT: Greenwood, 1991.

Buckley, Peter G. "The Place to Make an Artist Work: Micah Hawkins and William Sidney Mount in New York City," *Catching the Tune: Music and William Sidney Mount.* Stony Brook, NY: The Museums at Stony Brook, 1984.

Cantwell, Robert. *Bluegrass Breakdown: The Making of the Old Southern Sound.* Urbana: University of Illinois, 1984.

Catalogue of Books, Stationery, Music and Musical Instruments and Fancy Goods for Sale by J.W. Randolph. 121 Main Street, Richmond, VA, 1850.

Cave, Joseph Arnold. *A Jubilee of Dramatic Life and Incident Of.* London: Thomas Vernon, 1894.

Chaff, Gumbo [Elias Howe]. *The Complete Preceptor for the Banjo.* Boston: Oliver Ditson & Co., 1851.

Christian, W. Asbury. *Lynchburg and Its People.* Lynchburg, VA: J.P. Bell, c. 1900.

Clapp, W.W., Jr. *A Record of the Boston Stage.* New York: Benjamin Blom, 1853/1868.

Cockrell, Dale. *Demons of Disorder: Early Blackface Minstrels and Their World.* New York: Cambridge University, 1997.

Confederate Military History. Confederate, Atlanta, GA, 1899.

Converse, Frank B. "De History ob de Banjo," in *Frank Converse's "Old Cremona" Songster.* New York: Dick & Fitzgerald, 1863.

Cooke, John Esten. *General Stuart in Camp and Field, Annals of the War Written by Leading Participants.* Philadelphia Times, 1879.

_____. *Surry of Eagle's Nest.* New York: C. Chauncey Burr, 1866.

Cottingham, Leslie Banner, and Carol Lowe Timblin. *The Bard of Ottaray: The Life, Letters and Documents of Shepherd Monroe Dugger.* Banner Elk, NC: Puddingstone, 1979.

Csida, Joseph, and June Bundy. *American Entertainment.* New York: Watson-Guptill, 1978.

Dennett, Andrea Stulman. *Weird and Wonderful.* New York: NYU Press, 1997.

Dennison, Sam. *Scandalize My Name: Black Imagery in American Popular Music.* New York: Garland, 1982.

Douglas, Henry Kyd. *I Rode with Stonewall.* Aptos Village, CA: Mockingbird Books, 1983.

Ellsler, John Adam. *The Stage Memories of John A. Ellsler.* Cleveland: Rowfant Club, 1950.

Farrar, Stuart McDearmon. *Historical Notes of Appomattox County, Virginia.* Appomattox: privately published, nd.

Flint, Richard W. "The Evolution of the Circus in Nineteenth-Century America" in *American Popular Entertainment.* Westport, CT: Greenwood, 1979.

Garnett, Theodore Stanford. *Riding with Stuart.* Shippensburg, PA: White Mane, 1994.

Garrett, Jill L. *Obituaries from Tennessee Newspapers.* Easley, SC: Southern Historical Press, 1980.

Gills, Mary Louise. *It Happened at Appomattox.* Richmond: Dietz, 1948.

Glenroy, John. *Ins and Outs of Circus Life or Forty-Two Years Travel.* Boston: M.M. Wing, 1885.

Goldie, William Ferguson [pseud.]. *Sunshine and Shadow of Slave Life: Reminiscences as Told to Isaac C. Williams to "Tege."* East Saginaw, Michigan: Evening News, 1885; reprinted in New York: AMS Press, 1975.

Greenwood, Issac John. *The Circus, Its Origins and Growth.* New York: William Abbatt, 1898/1909.

Gura, Philip F. *C.F. Martin and His Guitars: 1796–1873.* Chapel Hill, NC: University of North Carolina Press, 2003.

Hadfield, Kathleen. *Historical Notes on Amelia County, Virginia.* Amelia: Amelia County Historical Society, n.d.

Hamlin, Percy Gatling. *"Old Bald Head" General R.S. Ewell: The Portrait of a Soldier.* Strasburg, VA: Shenandoah, 1940.

Henderson, William D. *41st Virginia Infantry.* Lynchburg, VA: H.E. Howard, Inc, 1986.

Henry, Mayhew. *London Labour and the London Poor, Volume I and III.* New York: Dover Publications, 1968.

Hill, N. N. *History of Knox County.* Mount Vernon: 1881.

Historical Base Map. Appomattox Courthouse: National Park Service, 1962.

Howe, J.B. *A Cosmopolitan Actor.* London: Bedford, 1888.

Humphries, Charles, and William C. Smith. *Music Publishing in the British Isles.* London: Cassell, 1954.

Hutton, Laurence. *Curiosities of the American Stage.* New York: Harper & Bros, 1891.

Ireland, Joseph N. *Records of the New York Stage 1 and 2.* New York: Bert Franklin, 1866–7/1968.

Jackson, Bruce. *The Negro and His Folklore in Nineteenth-Century Periodicals.* Austin: University of Texas Press, 1967.

Jefferson, Mary Armstrong. *Old Homes and Buildings of Amelia County, Volume I.* Self published, 1964.

Jefferson, Thomas. *Notes on the State of Virginia; Written in the Year 1781, some what corrected and enlarged in the Winter of 1782.* Paris: 1782, reprinted Chapel Hill: UNC Press, 1982.

Jennings, John J. *Theatrical and Circus Life.* Cincinnati: W.E. Dibble, 1886.

Kennedy, John P. *Swallow Barn, or A Sojourn in the Old Dominion.* Philadelphia: Carey and Lea, 1832, reprinted New York: Hafner, 1962.

Kimmel, Stanley. *The Mad Booths of Maryland.* New York: Bobbs-Merrill, c. 1940.

Koon, Helene Wickham. *Gold Rush Performers.* Jefferson, NC: McFarland, 1994.

Kunhardt, Philip B., Jr., Philip B. III and Peter W. *P.T. Barnum: America's Greatest Showman.* New York: Alfred A. Knopf, 1995.

Lester, Julius. *To Be a Slave.* New York: Dell, 1970.

Lhamon, W. T., Jr. *Jump Jim Crow.* Cambridge, MA: Harvard University Press, 2003.

Libin, Lawrence. *American Musical Instruments in the Metropolitan Museum of Art.* New York: W.W. Norton, 1985.

Longsworth. *New York City Directory.* 1835.

Ludlow, Noah. *Dramatic Life As I Found It.* Bronx, NY: Benjamin Blom, 1966.

Mahan, Katherine Hines. *Showboats to Soft Shoes.* Columbus, GA, 1968.

Mahar, William J. *Behind the Burnt Cork Mask: Early Blackface Minstrelsy and Antebellum American Popular Culture.* Urbana and Chicago: University of Illinois Press, 1999.

Marvel, William. *A Place Called Appomattox.* Chapel Hill, NC and London: University of North Carolina, 2000.

Mathews, Anne Jackson. *The Memoirs of Charles Mathews, Comedian.* London: R. Bentley, 1838–39.

Matt Peel's Banjo. New York City, 1858.

Meer, Sarah. "The Serenaders and Ethnic Exhibition," in *Liberating Sojourn.* Athens: University of Georgia, 1999.

Moody, Richard. *American Takes the Stage: Romanticism in American Drama and Theatre, 1750–1900.* Bloomington: Indiana University, 1955.

_____. *Edwin Forrest: First Star of the American Stage.* New York: Alfred A. Knopf, 1960.

Moore, John Hammond. *Appomattox Court House: Community, Village and Families 1845–1870.* Appomattox Court House: National Park Service.

Mullin, Donald. *Victorian Actors and Actresses in Review.* Westport, CT: Greenwood, 1983.

Nathan, Hans. *Dan Emmett and the Rise of Early Negro Minstrelsy.* Norman, Oklahoma: University of Oklahoma, 1962/1977.

Nigger Melodies: Being the Only Entire and Complete Work of Ethiopian Songs Extant. Cornish, Lamport, 1850.

Odell, George. *Annals of the New York Stage.* New York: Columbia University, 1927–49.

Owen, William Miller. *In Camp and Battle with the Washington Artillery.* Boston: Tickmor, 1895.

Parker, William L. *General James Dearing CSA.* Lynchburg: H. E. Howard, 1990.

Paulding, James Kirke. *Letters from the South, by a Northern Man.* New York: Harper and Brothers, 1835.

_____. *Letters from the South, Written During an Excursion in the Summer of 1816.* New York: James Eastburn, 1817.

Perdue, Charles L., Jr., Thomas E. Barden and Robert K. Phillips. *Weevils in the Wheat.* Charlottesville: University Press of Virginia, 1976.

Phelps, H.P. *Players of a Century.* Joseph McDonough: 1880.

Phil. Rice's Correct Method for the Banjo: With or Without a Master. Boston: Oliver Ditson, 1858, reprint by Bremo Bluff, VA: Tuckahoe Music, 1998.

Pickering, Michael. "White Skin, Black Masks: Nigger Minstrelsy in Victorian England," in *Music Hall Performance and Style.* Milton Keynes and Philadelphia: Open University, 1986.

Potts, E. Daniel, and Annette. *Young America and Australian Gold.* St. Lucia: University of Queensland, 1974.

Rice, Edw. LeRoy. *Monarchs of Minstrelsy: From Daddy Rice to the Present.* New York: Kenny, 1911.

Riggs, David F. *13th Virginia Infantry.* Lynchburg: H. E. Howard, 1988.

Ripple, Ezra Hoyt. *Dancing Along the Deadline.* Presidio Press, Novato, CA, 1996.

Rowell, George. *Queen Victoria Goes to the Theatre.* London: Paul Elk, 1978.

Sacks, Howard L., and Judith Rose. *Way Up North in Dixie.* Washington and London: Smithsonian Institution Press, 1993.

Sanjek, Russell. *American Popular Music and Its Business 1.* New York: Oxford University, 1988.

Saxon, Arthur. *P.T. Barnum.* New York: Columbia University, 1989.

_____. *Selected Letters of P.T. Barnum.* New York: Columbia University, 1983.

Scott, Derek. *The Singing Bourgeois: Songs of the Victorian Drawing Room and Parlour.* Aldershot, 2001.

Senelick, Laurence. *Tavern Singing in Early Victorian*

London. London: Society for Theatre Research, 1997.

Sherwood, W. Cullen. *The Nelson Artillery: Lamkin and Rives Batteries*. Lynchburg: H.E. Howard, 1991.

Smith, Sol. *Theatrical Management in the West and South for Thirty Years*. New York: Harper, 1868.

Smithwick, Noah. *Evolution of a State*. Austin: University of Texas, 1983.

Smyth, John. *A Tour in the United States of America-Volume 1*. London: Printed for G. Robinson, 1784.

Stone, Henry Dickinson. *Personal Recollections of the Drama*. Albany: C. Van Benthuysen & Sons, 1873.

Stoutamire, Albert. *Music of the Old South: Colony to Confederacy*. Cranbury, NJ: Associated University Presses, 1972.

Temlett, William. *The Banjo: Its Origins*. London: Willcocks, 1888.

Thayer, Stuart. *Annals of the American Circus 1793–1860*. Seattle: Dauven & Thayer, 2000.

_____. *Traveling Showmen*. Seattle: Astley & Ricketts, 1997.

Thomas, Emory M. *Bold Dragon: The Life of J E.B. Stuart*. New York: Vintage Books, Random House, 1986, 1988.

Thomason, John W., Jr. *J.E.B. Stuart*. New York/London: Charles Scribner's Sons, 1930.

Toll, Robert C. *Blacking Up: The Minstrel Show in Nineteenth-Century America*. New York: Oxford University, 1974.

Tosches, Nick. *Where Dead Voices Gather*. Boston: Little, Brown and Company, 2001).

Trout, Robert J. *They Followed the Plume*. Stackpole Books, Mechanicsburg, PA, 1993.

Tyler, Lyon G. *Men of Mark in Virginia*. Washington, D.C.: Men of Mark: 1907.

Tyler-McGraw, Marie. *At the Falls: Richmond, Virginia, and Its People*. Chapel Hill, NC: University of North Carolina, 1994.

Virginia Biography, Volume 5. Chicago: American Historical Society, 1924.

Wallace, Lee A., Jr. *Richmond Howitzers*. Lynchburg: H.E. Howard, 1993.

Waterhouse, Richard. *From Minstrel Show to Vaudeville*. Sydney, Australia: New South Wales University, 1990.

Weightman, Gavin. *Bright Lights, Big City*. London: Collins & Brown, 1992.

Werner, M. R. *Barnum*. Garden City, NY: Garden City, 1923.

Whiteoak, John. "Banjo," in *Currency Companion to Music and Dance in Australia*. Strawberry Hills, NSW: Currency House, 2003.

Whiteoak, John. *Playing Ad Lib: Improvisatory Music in Australia 1836–1970*. Sydney: Currency Press, 1999.

Wilson, Joe. "The Luthier's Art," in *Dixie Frets*. Chattanooga, TN: Hunter Museum of Art, 1994.

_____. "The Wood Banjo," in *Masters of the Banjo*. Arhoolie, 1994.

Wittke, Carl. *Tambo and Bones*. Durham, NC: Duke University, 1930.

Wood, Robert. *Victorian Delights*. London: Evans Brothers, 1967.

Wood, William B. *Personal Recollections of the Stage*. Philadelphia: Henry Carey, 1855.

Yancey, Mrs. Robert Rosa Faulkner. *Lynchburg and Its Neighbors*. Richmond: J.W. Fergusson and Sons, 1935.

Websites

Adelphi Theatre, emich.edu/public/english/adelphi_calendar/acpmain.htm.

Ahpcs.org/library/cilist.htm.

Barker, Kathleen, "Early Music Hall in Bristol" (Bristol Historical Association, 1979), quoted in Geoff Woolfe (October 15, 2001); *Greenwich industrial history* (vol 3, issue 1, January, 2000), gihs. gold.ac.uk/gihsNovember.html.

Cemetery.state.tx.us.

Chicagohs.org/fire/oleary/pic0033.html.

Circushistory.org/Cork/.

Dobney, Jayson, "Transitions in American Snare Drums," abstract of paper given to GS/AMIS Conference on Musical Instruments, music.ed. ac.uk/euchmi/galpin/gxka.html.

Famousamericans.net.

Greatallied.fsnet.co.uk/docs/cen1851.htm.

Levysheetmusic.mse.jhu.edu.

Library.upenn.edu/collections/rbm/keffer/willig. html.

Loc.gov.

Mail-archive.com/lamoreaux-1@rootsweb.com/msg0February43.html.

Nla.gov.au.

Nottingham.ac.uk/film/journal/filmrev/silent-shakespeare.htm.

Nugrape.net/banjo.htm.

Persetus.tufts.edu.

Reynolds, David S., "I Hear America Singing: Whitman and Music of His Time," 3, americancomposers.org.

Ukbanjo.com/bjop2.htm.

Newspaper Articles

"Banjo for Polk Miller," *Richmond Dispatch*, Polk Miller Scrapbook.

"The Banjo's Origin," *Richmond Dispatch*, February 17, 1895.

Brown, T. Allston. "Early History of Negro Minstrelsy," *New York Clipper*, February 2, 17 and 24, March 9, April 27, 1912.

Cole, Mrs. J. O. "Joe Sweeney, Banjo Virtuoso of Appomattox," *Lynchburg News*, April 29, 1940, 8.

"Colonel 'Marse Tom' Booker Obituary," *Richmond Times-Dispatch*, April 9, 1928, 10.

Death Notice. D.P. Diuguid, *Lynchburg Daily Virginian*, July 5, 1864.

Dumont, Frank. "The Golden Days of Minstrelsy. The Musings of an Old Timer," *The New York Clipper*, December 1914.

Eubank, E. Newman. Letter to *Lynchburg News*, April 5, 1905.

"He Invented the Banjo," *Chattanooga Republican*, November 2, 1890.

Justitia. *Lynchburg Virginian*, September 4, 1860, 3.

"Letter from Appomattox to the Editor," *The Richmond Dispatch*, reprinted in *The Cadenza* 1/3, January 2, 1895, 5.

"Letter from C.J. Rodgers, Philadelphia, *New York Clipper*, June 20, 1874, 95.

"Letter from Jim Crow," *Spirit of the Times*, August 26, 1837.

Letter by Richard Ward Pelham to *Hague's Minstrel and Dramatic Journal*, Liverpool, quoted in *New York Clipper*, August 8, 1874, 148.

Letter from T. D. Rice, *New York Herald*, August 30, 1837.

"'Marse Tom' Dies in Bird Grove Home," *Richmond News-Leader*, April 9, 1928, 18.

"Negro Minstrelsy.... Charley White's Recollections," clipping, Harvard.

New York Clipper Almanac, 1892.

New York Clipper Annual, 1884, 8.

November, Neil. "I Remember When...," undated newspaper article, Polk Miller Scrapbook.

Obituary, Hosea Easton, *Sydney Mail*, July 1, 1899.

"Old Titus—The Original Banjo-Man," *Richmond Dispatch*, April 21, 1852, 2.

"On an Old Virginia Plantation in the Peaceful Days Before the Civil War," *The Baltimore Sun*, June 14, 1908.

P.H. Taylor's Music Store ad featuring banjos for sale, No. 188 Main Street, Richmond, *Jeffersonian Republican*, November 11, 1858, 3.

"Polk Miller Given a Banjo," *Richmond Times*, Polk Miller Scrapbook, June 9, 1895.

"The Origin of the Christy's Minstrels," *The Theatre*, March 1, 1882, 129–134.

Perry, Tom. "Going Home with the Beau Sabreur," *The Maryland Line*, from J.E.B. Stuart Birthplace Preservation Trust, Inc.

Rogers, Geo. W. "Polk Miller Wrote Colorful Chapter in Drug History," undated newspaper article, Polk Miller Scrapbook.

"S.S. Sanford Interview," *Wash Republican*, reprinted in "Joe Sweeney," *Lynchburg News*, September 15, 1874, 3.

Sutphin, P. C. "Who Invented the Banjo," Glasgow, Kentucky, *Times*, reprinted in *Lynchburg News*, February 7, 1895, 4.

"Tom Booker and the Banjo," *Richmond News Leader*, April 9, 1928, 8.

"When Barnum Blacked Up," unidentified clipping, University of Texas-Harry Ransom Center.

Index

Numbers in *bold italic* indicate photographs